SO-AGE-269

CHILDREN'S DAILY PRAYER

for the School Year 2020–2021

Karla Hardersen

LTP
LITURGY
TRAINING
PUBLICATIONS

Nihil Obstat
Rev. Mr. Daniel G. Welter, JD
Chancellor
Archdiocese of Chicago
November 21, 2019

Imprimatur
Most Rev. Ronald A. Hicks
Vicar General
Archdiocese of Chicago
November 21, 2019

The *Nihil Obstat* and *Imprimatur* are official declarations that the material is free from doctrinal or moral error, and thus is granted permission to publish in accordance with c. 827. No legal responsibility is assumed by the grant of this permission. No implication is contained herein that those who have granted the *Nihil Obstat* and *Imprimatur* agree with the content, opinions, or statements expressed.

The Scripture quotations are from the *New Revised Standard Version Bible: Catholic Edition* copyright © 1989, National Council of the Churches of Christ in the United States of America. Used by permission. All rights reserved.

Excerpts from the English translation of *The Liturgy of the Hours* © 1973, 1974, 1975, International Commission on English in the Liturgy (ICEL); excerpts from the English translation of *The Roman Missal* © 2010, ICEL. All rights reserved.

Blessing prayer for birthdays adapted from *Book of Blessings*, additional blessings for use in the United States, © 1968, United States Conference of Catholic Bishops, Washington, DC. Used with permission.

Many of the concepts and guidelines, as well as various prayer services offered in this book, were originally conceived and developed by Dr. Sofia Cavalletti, Ms. Gianna Gobbi, and their collaborators. Theological underpinnings and many elements of these prayer services were first documented in Cavalletti's foundational books including, *The Religious Potential of the Child* and *The Religious Potential of the Child, 6 to 12 Years Old*.

Liturgy Training Publications acknowledges the significant contribution made by Elizabeth McMahon Jeep to the development of *Children's Daily Prayer*. For more than fifteen years, Ms. Jeep worked tirelessly to cultivate this book into the essential prayer resource it is today for children and their parents, as well for teachers and catechists. We are indebted to her for her authorship and guidance.

CHILDREN'S DAILY PRAYER 2020-2021 © 2020 Archdiocese of Chicago: Liturgy Training Publications, 3949 South Racine Avenue, Chicago, IL 60609; 800-933-1800; fax: 800-933-7094; email: orders@ltp.org; website: www.LTP.org. All rights reserved.

This book was edited by Michaela I. Tudela. Christian Rocha was the production editor. Juan Alberto Castillo directed the cover art and revised the original design by Mary Bowers. Luis Leal was the production artist.

Cover art by Mikela Smith. Interior art by Paula Wiggins © LTP. Paperclip image by Babich Alexander/Shutterstock.com

Printed in the United States of America

ISBN: 978-1-61671-538-0

CDP21

CONTENTS

CONTENTS

The editors appreciate your feedback.
Email: cdp@ltp.org.

INTRODUCTION

UNDERSTANDING THE ORDER OF PRAYER

Children's Daily Prayer is a form of the Liturgy of the Hours, adapted for children. It is based on the Church's tradition of Morning Prayer. A selected psalm is prayed for several weeks at a time. The readings for the daily prayers have been chosen to help children become familiar with significant themes and major stories in Scripture. The Sunday reading is always the Gospel of the day. Reflection questions for silent meditation or group conversation follow the reading.

For schools and homeschooling families, this book provides an order of prayer for each day of the school year (Prayer for the Day). For religious education settings, it provides prayer services for once a week (Prayer for the Week). Not every prayer element in the order of prayer will be useful in every situation. From the elements listed below, you can choose the ones that will be most effective for your group, setting, and time available.

OPENING

This gives the context for the Scripture reading and, when space allows, introduces the saint to be remembered that day. It also indicates when a particular theme or focus will be followed for the week. Sometimes difficult words or concepts in the reading are explained.

SIGN OF THE CROSS

An essential ritual action Catholics use to begin and end prayer. By making the Sign of the Cross, we place ourselves in the presence of the Father, the Son, and the Holy Spirit. Young children may need to practice making the Sign of the Cross.

PSALM

Praying the psalm is central to Morning Prayer. You may use the short version on the prayer page or the longer version on the Reproducible Psalms pages.

READING OR GOSPEL

Daily Scripture texts have been carefully selected to help children "walk through the Bible" and become familiar with the great stories and themes of Salvation History. By following a story or exploring a theme for several days, the children experience how God has spoken to us through the words of Scripture and also through particular people and events in history. They begin to see how people have cooperated with God in bringing about God's Kingdom on earth and to realize their role in this great work. The Prayer for the Week always uses the Sunday Gospel.

FOR SILENT REFLECTION

This is designed to be a time of silence so the children can ponder the Scripture they have heard and experience the value of silence in prayer. You might prefer to use this question at another time when discussing the reading or for journal writing. You may want to substitute your own instruction and questions. Regardless, some silence should be kept after proclaiming the Scripture.

CLOSING PRAYER

This prayer element begins with intercessions and ends with a brief prayer related to the liturgical season. In preparing for daily prayer, children can write the intercessions for the day and include relevant events to school and classroom life, as well as the world. They can also be encouraged to offer their own intentions spontaneously. You may choose to end with the Our Father.

PRAYER SERVICES

Children need to learn that the Church's prayer forms are rich and varied. We have the celebration of the Eucharist and traditional prayers such as the Rosary. We also have a long tradition of other forms of prayer, such as the Liturgy of the Hours, which emphasizes the psalms, or the Liturgy of the Word, which focuses on Holy Scripture. Additional prayer services are offered in this book for specific liturgical times, memorials, feasts, or solemnities. (Check the table of contents.) You may prefer to use one of these instead of the Prayer for the Day. Consider using these prayer services when the whole school gathers to celebrate a season. You might add an entrance procession and children and adults can do the ministerial roles.

GRACE BEFORE MEALS AND PRAYER AT DAY'S END

In order to instill in children the habit of prayer, use these prayers before lunch or at the end of the day.

PSALMS AND CANTICLES

Additional psalms and canticles (liturgical songs from the Bible: e.g., the Magnificat) are provided at the end of the book, and you will find many more in your Bible. Substitute these for any of the psalm excerpts in the prayer services or pray these with the children at any time a different choice is better for what is happening in your classroom community.

HOME PRAYERS

Children enjoy connecting their classroom and home lives. The Home Prayers offer a wonderful catechetical tool and resource for family prayer. You may photocopy these pages to send home.

CREATING A SACRED SPACE AND TIME FOR PRAYER

Children and adults benefit from having a consistent time for prayer. Where possible, it is helpful to the formation of prayer life to have a "sacred space"—that is, a designated place or table with religious objects such as the Bible, a cross, a beautiful cloth that reflects the color of the liturgical season. The introductions to each liturgical season will offer specific ideas on how to do the following:

1. Use the language in the introduction to help the children understand the character of the time.

2. Look for practical suggestions for how to celebrate the liturgical time in a classroom setting:

- how to arrange a sacred space within the classroom
- what colors and objects to use in the sacred space
- what songs to sing in each liturgical time
- suggestions for special prayers for that liturgical time and how best to introduce them to children
- help with adapting ideas from this book to special circumstances, especially for catechists who meet with students once a week

HOW CHILDREN PRAY

THE YOUNGEST CHILDREN

Children are natural liturgists and theologians. Young children (up until age 6) will pray simple but profound acclamations when they are given a real opportunity to hear the Word of God or to experience the language of signs found in our liturgy. Their spontaneous prayers most often reflect their understanding of the Word of God, their thanks-giving for God's goodness, and the joy they receive in their relationship with Christ. Here are some examples of prayers collected by catechists: "Thank you, Lord, for the light!" (a 3-year-old); "Thank you

TIPS FOR GIVING CHILDREN A GREATER ROLE IN PRAYER

This book is intended to be used by children. It will help them become comfortable as leaders of prayer and will form them in the habit of daily prayer.

1. Ideally daily prayer takes place at the beginning of the day in individual classrooms. Consider inviting the children to work in groups to prepare and lead the prayer in your classroom. The group can take on the roles of leader, psalmist, lector, and perhaps music leader for the *Alleluia*. An intercessor might compose and lead a few petitions and then invite the class to add individual ones.

2. If it is necessary to begin the prayer over the public address system, consider doing only the opening and Sign of the Cross over the loud speaker. Then invite the individual classrooms to continue the prayer in their own setting.

3. If you wish to lead the whole prayer over the public address system, consider inviting children from the various grades to do the roles listed in the first paragraph.

4. To help the younger children learn to lead prayer consider inviting older children to lead in the lower grade classrooms as mentioned in item one.

5. Invite your older students to help orient the younger ones to the prayer service. The older ones can help the younger ones practice the readings and compose intercessions so that eventually the younger ones can lead prayer in their own classrooms.

for everything!" (a 4-year-old); "I love you!" (a 3-year-old); and "I want to take a bath in your light" (a 4-year-old). These prayers point to the young child's ability to appreciate the greatest of realities: life in relationship with God.

When praying with these "little ones," it is best to proclaim the Scripture (explaining difficult words in advance to help their understanding) and then to ask one or two open-ended questions to help them to reflect on what the passage is saying to them. If you then invite them to say something to Jesus about what they've heard, you may be surprised at what comes out of the mouths of those budding little theologians!

PRAYING WITH OLDER CHILDREN

Older children (ages 6–12) begin to appreciate the gift of prayer language. We should go slowly and use a light touch, though. When they're younger, give them one beautiful phrase ("Our Father, who art in heaven") that they can begin to appreciate and love. As they grow you can add a second phrase, then a third. But make sure that they understand the words they are using, and encourage them to pray slowly.

Older children also enjoy leading prayer and composing their own prayers. If you give them each a small prayer journal and give them time to write in it, they will produce meaningful prayers and little theological drawings (particularly if you give them time to write and draw right after reading Scripture together).

PSALMS

The psalms offer a treasure trove of prayer language. Consider praying with one or two verses at a time. You could write one or two verses onto an unlined index card and display it up on your prayer table. You can invite older children to copy them into their prayer journals. But remember to go over each word with the class, asking them to reflect on what the prayer wants to say to God. Children need time to explore the rich implications in their prayer. Also, psalms may be sung or chanted (after all, they were written as songs). Perhaps a parish cantor or choir member would lead a sung version of the psalm once in a while. At least the refrain might be sung on one note.

MUSIC IN PRAYER

It is a fact that the songs we sing in church are all prayers, so include singing in your classroom prayer life. What a wonderful difference it makes! Don't be shy, and don't worry about how well you sing. Even if you don't think you have a good voice, children will happily sing with you. So go ahead and make a joyful noise! Children enjoy the chance to lift their voices to God. You may even have a few gifted singers in the class who can help you lead the singing.

The best music to use in the classroom is what your parish sings during the Sunday liturgy. You might incorporate the Penitential Act ("Lord Have Mercy, Christ Have Mercy, Lord Have Mercy") in Lent, the refrain of the Gloria in Easter, the Gospel Acclamation (Alleluia), even a chanted Our Father. But any songs, hymns, or chants that your parish sings would be a good choice. Your parish music director or diocesan director of music can be good resources.

Also, in the introductions to each liturgical time, you will find a wealth of music suggestions.

ART AS PRAYER

Once in a while suggest the children draw a picture after having heard the Scripture reading. Their drawings often reveal their joy and love in ways that language can't always express. Some children are more visual than verbal. Drawing allows them to lengthen and deepen their enjoyment of prayer time.

Don't give the children assignments or themes for these "prayer" drawings, and don't offer a lot of fancy art supplies or media. The best, most reverent drawings come from children who are simply invited to draw something that has to do with what they have just heard in the Scripture reading, something to do with the Mass, or anything to do with God. These open-ended suggestions allow the Holy Spirit room to enter into the children's work.

PRAYER CANNOT BE EVALUATED

This book is most often used in school or religious education programs. In these settings, teachers are often required to give children a grade in religion. However, prayer is not class work and teachers and catechists who have any choice in the matter should make certain **not to give the children a grade for prayer!** Prayer expresses an inner, mysterious reality, for which teachers can provide the environment. Prayer is a person's conversation with God. Consider Jesus' teaching on prayer (Matthew 6:5–13) or take a close look at his parable of the Pharisee and the tax collector (Luke 18:9–14). We don't want the children to pray for the benefit of a grade or praise from the teacher; rather, we want them to pray from their feeling of relationship with a listening God.

JOY

In all you do with the children, feel free to communicate your joy to them, especially your joy in praying. Joy is a great sign of the presence of Christ. If you take pleasure in your students' company, they will understand that they are precious children of God. If you take pleasure in your work, they will understand that work is a beautiful gift. If you listen to them and take their words seriously, you will be incarnating Christ, who so valued children.

Perhaps you will be the initial prayer leader and model that role. Something to model is a relaxed attitude when things go wrong (e.g., someone begins the Scripture too early). Try to give simple, clear directions ahead of time and then correct the situation as gently as possible. While you must keep order in your classrooms and an atmosphere of dignity in prayer, don't be afraid of a little silliness at times. Both laughter and tears are signs of the presence of the Holy Spirit.

ABOUT THE AUTHOR

Karla Hardersen is a wife and mother of three teenagers. She has studied religion and theology at the undergraduate and graduate levels and was a Bernardin Scholar at the Catholic Theological Union, Chicago. She is an active member of a Catholic faith community, where she has also been an assistant catechist for the Catechesis of the Good Shepherd program.

ABOUT THE ARTISTS AND THE ART

The cover art is by illustrator Mikela Prevost, who received her BA in painting from the University of Redlands, California, and her MFA from California State Fullerton. Her artistic rendering of children leading prayer and praying together in the classroom captures the spirit and intent of this annual resource.

The interior art is by Paula Wiggins, who lives and works in Cincinnati. At the top of the page for each day's prayer, you will find a little picture that reflects on the liturgical time. During Ordinary Time in the autumn, a sturdy mustard tree with tiny seeds blowing from it reminds us of the parable of the mustard seed. For Advent we find the familiar Advent wreath. During the short season of Christmas Time, there is a manger scene with sheep and a dove. As we begin counting Ordinary Time, we find an oyster shell

with pearls—an image for the parable of the pearl of great price. During Lent, bare branches remind us of this time of living simply, without decoration and distraction, so that we can feel God's presence. During Easter Time, we find the empty tomb in the early dawn of the first Easter. And as we return to Ordinary Time after Pentecost, a beautiful grape vine reminds us of Jesus' parable of the vine and the branches.

At the beginning of each new liturgical time, special art accompanies the Grace before Meals and Prayer at Day's End, and you will find appropriate scenes for the various prayer services throughout the year. Finally, notice the harps accompanying the psalms, reminding us that these prayers were originally sung. The incense on the pages of canticles pictures the way we want our prayers to rise to God.

A NOTE ABOUT COPIES

As a purchaser of this book, you have permission to duplicate only the Reproducible Psalms pages, the Grace before Meals and Prayer at Day's End pages, the Prayer Services, and the Home Prayer pages; these copies may be used only with your class or group. The Home Prayer pages may be used only in the students' households. You may not duplicate the psalms or prayers unless you are using them with this book. Other parts of this book may not be duplicated without the permission of Liturgy Training Publications or the copyright holders listed on the acknowledgments page.

INSTRUCTIONS FOR PRAYER FOR THE DAY AND WEEK

FOR THE WHOLE GROUP

All of us participate in the prayer each day by lifting our hearts and voices to God. When the leader begins a Scripture passage by saying, "A reading from the holy Gospel according to . . . ," we respond "Glory to you, O Lord." At the conclusion of the Gospel, we say, "Praise to you, Lord Jesus Christ." At the conclusion of other Scripture readings, we say, "Thanks be to God." We offer our prayers and our intentions to God. When we conclude a prayer we say, "Amen."

Amen means: "Yes! I believe it is true!" Let your "Amen" be heard by all.

FOR THE LEADER

1. Find the correct page and read it silently. Parts in bold black type are for everyone. All others are for you alone.

2. Practice reading your part aloud, and pronounce every syllable clearly. The parts marked with ◆ and ✛ are instructions for what to do. Follow the instructions but do not read them or the headings aloud. If you stumble over a word, repeat it until you can say it smoothly.

3. Pause after "A reading from the holy Gospel according to . . . " so the class can respond. Pause again after "The Gospel of the Lord." Remember to allow for silence when the instructions call for it, especially after the Gospel and after reading the questions "For Silent Reflection."

4. Pause after "Let us bring our hopes and needs to God . . . " so that individuals may offer their prayers aloud or in silence. After each petition, the group responds, "Lord, hear our prayer."

5. When you make the Sign of the Cross, use your right hand and do it slowly and reverently, first touching your forehead ("In the name of the Father"), next just below your chest ("and of the Son"), then your left shoulder ("and of the Holy Spirit"), and finally your right shoulder ("Amen").

6. At prayer time, stand in the front of the class straight and tall. Ask the students to use their reproducible sheet of psalms for reading their part. Read slowly and clearly.

IF THERE ARE TWO LEADERS

One leader reads the Reading or Gospel while the other reads all of the other parts. Practice reading your part(s). Both leaders should stand in front of the class during the entire prayer.

Remember to read very slowly, with a loud, clear voice.

ORDINARY TIME, AUTUMN

Psalm for Sunday, August 16—Friday, October 2

Psalm 66:1–3a, 5, 8, 16–17

LEADER: Make a joyful noise to God, all the earth.

ALL: **Make a joyful noise to God, all the earth.**

LEADER: Make a joyful noise to God, all the earth;
sing the glory of his name;
give to him glorious praise.
Say to God, "How awesome are
your deeds!"

ALL: **Make a joyful noise to God, all the earth.**

Short version: use above only; Long version: use above and below.

SIDE A: Come and see what God has done:
he is awesome in his deeds
among mortals.
Bless our God, O peoples,
let the sound of his praise be heard.

SIDE B: Come and hear, all you who fear God,
and I will tell you what
he has done for me.
I cried aloud to him,
and he was extolled with my tongue.

ALL: **Make a joyful noise to God, all the earth.**

ORDINARY TIME, AUTUMN

Psalm for Sunday, October 4—Friday, October 30

Psalm 145:2–3, 4–5, 10–11

LEADER: I will praise your name for ever, Lord.

ALL: **I will praise your name for ever, Lord.**

LEADER: Every day I will bless you,
and praise your name forever and ever.
Great is the Lord, and greatly
to be praised;
his greatness is unsearchable.

ALL: **I will praise your name for ever, Lord.**

Short version: use above only; Long version: use above and below.

SIDE A: One generation shall laud your works
to another, and shall declare your
mighty acts.
On the glorious splendor of your majesty,
and on your wondrous works,
I will meditate.

SIDE B: All your works shall give thanks to you,
O Lord, and all your faithful shall
bless you.
They shall speak of the glory of your
kingdom, and tell of your power.

ALL: **I will praise your name for ever, Lord.**

CHILDREN'S DAILY PRAYER 2020–2021 © 2020 Archdiocese of Chicago: Liturgy Training Publications, 3949 South Racine Avenue, Chicago, IL 60609. All rights reserved. Orders: 800-933-1800 or www.LTP.org. Scripture excerpts are taken from *The New Revised Standard Version Bible: Catholic Edition*, © 1989, Division of Christian Education of the National Council of the Churches of Christ in the United States of America. Used with permission. All rights reserved.

ORDINARY TIME, AUTUMN

Psalm for Sunday, November 1—Wednesday, November 25

Psalm 98:1, 2–3, 3–4

LEADER: The LORD has made known his victory.

ALL: **The LORD has made known his victory.**

LEADER: O sing to the LORD a new song,
for he has done marvelous things.
His right hand and his holy arm have
gotten him victory.

ALL: **The LORD has made known his victory.**

Short version: use above only; Long version: use above and below.

SIDE A: The LORD has made known his victory;
he has revealed his vindication in the
sight of the nations.
He has remembered his steadfast love
and faithfulness to the house of Israel.

SIDE B: All the ends of the earth have seen the
victory of our God.
Make a joyful noise to the LORD,
all the earth; break forth into joyous
song and sing praises.

ALL: **The LORD has made known his victory.**

ADVENT

Psalm for Sunday, November 29—Thursday, December 24

Psalm 85:4a, 8, 10–11, 12–13

LEADER: Restore us again,
O God of our salvation!

ALL: **Restore us again,
O God of our salvation!**

LEADER: Let me hear what God the LORD
will speak,
for he will speak peace to his people,
to his faithful, to those who turn to
him in their hearts.

ALL: **Restore us again, O God of our
salvation!**

Short version: use above only; Long version: use above and below.

SIDE A: Steadfast love and faithfulness will meet;
righteousness and peace will kiss
each other.
Faithfulness will spring up from
the ground,
and righteousness will look down
from the sky.

SIDE B: The LORD will give what is good,
and our land will yield its increase.
Righteousness will go before him,
and will make a path for his steps.

ALL: **Restore us again,
O God of our salvation!**

CHILDREN'S DAILY PRAYER 2020–2021 © 2020 Archdiocese of Chicago: Liturgy Training Publications, 3949 South Racine Avenue, Chicago, IL 60609. All rights reserved. Orders: 800-933-1800 or www.LTP.org. Scripture excerpts
are taken from The New Revised Standard Version Bible: Catholic Edition, © 1989, Division of Christian Education of the National Council of the Churches of Christ in the United States of America. Used with permission. All rights reserved.

CHRISTMAS TIME

Psalm for Sunday, January 3—Sunday, January 10

Psalm 96:1–2a, 2b–3, 5b–6, 11a

LEADER: Let the heavens be glad and the
earth rejoice!

ALL: **Let the heavens be glad and the
earth rejoice!**

LEADER: O sing to the LORD a new song;
sing to the LORD, all the earth.
Sing to the LORD; bless his name.

ALL: **Let the heavens be glad and the
earth rejoice!**

Short version: use above only; Long version: use above and below.

SIDE A: Tell of his salvation from day to day.

Declare his glory among the nations,
his marvelous works among all
the peoples.

SIDE B: The LORD made the heavens.
Honor and majesty are before him;
strength and beauty are in his sanctuary.

ALL: **Let the heavens be glad and the
earth rejoice!**

ORDINARY TIME, WINTER

Psalm for Monday, January 11—Tuesday, February 16

Psalm 23:1–3a, 3b–4, 5, 6

LEADER: I shall dwell in the house of the LORD my
whole life long.

ALL: **I shall dwell in the house of the LORD my
whole life long.**

LEADER: The LORD is my shepherd,
I shall not want.
He makes me lie down in
green pastures;
he leads me beside still waters;
he restores my soul.

ALL: **I shall dwell in the house of the LORD my
whole life long.**

Short version: use above only; Long version: use above and below.

SIDE A: He leads me in right paths
for his name's sake.
Even though I walk through the
darkest valley,
I fear no evil; for you are with me;
your rod and your staff—
they comfort me.

SIDE B: You prepare a table before me
in the presence of my enemies;
you anoint my head with oil;
my cup overflows.

ALL: **I shall dwell in the house of the LORD my
whole life long.**

CHILDREN'S DAILY PRAYER 2020–2021 © 2020 Archdiocese of Chicago: Liturgy Training Publications, 3949 South Racine Avenue, Chicago, IL 60609. All rights reserved. Orders: 800-933-1800 or www.LTP.org. Scripture excerpts are taken from *The New Revised Standard Version Bible: Catholic Edition*, © 1989, Division of Christian Education of the National Council of the Churches of Christ in the United States of America. Used with permission. All rights reserved.

LENT

Psalm for Wednesday, February 17—Wednesday, March 31

Psalm 34:4–5, 6–7, 16–17, 18–19

LEADER: The LORD saves the crushed in spirit.

ALL: **The LORD saves the crushed in spirit.**

LEADER: I sought the LORD, and he answered me,
and delivered me from all my fears.
Look to him, and be radiant;
so your faces shall never be ashamed.

ALL: **The LORD saves the crushed in spirit.**

Short version: use above only; Long version: use above and below.

SIDE A: This poor soul cried, and was heard by
the LORD,
and was saved from every trouble.
The angel of the LORD encamps
around those who fear him, and
delivers them.

SIDE B: The face of the LORD is against evildoers,
to cut off the remembrance of them
from the earth.
When the righteous cry for help,
the LORD hears,
and rescues them from all
their troubles.

ALL: **The LORD saves the crushed in spirit.**

LEADER: The LORD is near to the brokenhearted,
and saves the crushed in spirit.
Many are the afflictions of the righteous,
but the LORD rescues them from
them all.

ALL: **The LORD saves the crushed in spirit.**

EASTER TIME

Psalm for Sunday, April 4—Friday, April 30

Psalm 105:1–2, 3–4, 6–7

LEADER: Let the hearts of those who seek the
LORD rejoice.

ALL: **Let the hearts of those who seek the
LORD rejoice.**

LEADER: O give thanks to the LORD, call on
his name,
make known his deeds among
the peoples.
Sing to him, sing praises to him;
tell of all his wonderful works.

ALL: **Let the hearts of those who seek
the LORD rejoice.**

Short version: use above only; Long version: use above and below.

SIDE A: Glory in his holy name;
let the hearts of those who seek the
LORD rejoice.
Seek the LORD and his strength;
seek his presence continually.

SIDE B: O offspring of his servant Abraham,
children of Jacob, his chosen ones.
He is the LORD our God;
his judgments are in all the earth.

ALL: **Let the hearts of those who seek
the LORD rejoice.**

CHILDREN'S DAILY PRAYER 2020–2021 © 2020 Archdiocese of Chicago: Liturgy Training Publications, 3949 South Racine Avenue, Chicago, IL 60609. All rights reserved. Orders: 800-933-1800 or www.LTP.org. Scripture excerpts are taken from *The New Revised Standard Version Bible: Catholic Edition*, ©1989, Division of Christian Education of the National Council of the Churches of Christ in the United States of America. Used with permission. All rights reserved.

EASTER TIME

Psalm for Sunday, May 2—Sunday, May 23

Psalm 118:1–2, 4, 22–24, 25–27a

LEADER: The stone that the builders rejected
has become the chief cornerstone.

ALL: **The stone that the builders rejected
has become the chief cornerstone.**

LEADER: O give thanks to the Lord, for he is good;
his steadfast love endures forever!
Let Israel say,
"His steadfast love endures forever."
Let those who fear the Lord say,
"His steadfast love endures forever."

ALL: **The stone that the builders rejected
has become the chief cornerstone.**

Short version: use above only; Long version: use above and below.

SIDE A: The stone that the builders rejected
has become the chief cornerstone.
This is the Lord's doing;
it is marvelous in our eyes.
This is the day that the Lord has made;
let us rejoice and be glad in it.

SIDE B: Save us, we beseech you, O Lord!
O Lord, we beseech you,
give us success!
Blessed is the one who comes in the name
of the Lord.
We bless you from the house
of the Lord.
The Lord is God,
and he has given us light.

ALL: **The stone that the builders rejected
has become the chief cornerstone.**

ORDINARY TIME, SUMMER

Psalm for Monday, May 24—Friday, June 25

Psalm 85:8–9, 10–11, 12–13

LEADER: The Lord speaks of peace to his people.

ALL: **The Lord speaks of peace to his people.**

LEADER: Let me hear what God the Lord
will speak,
for he will speak peace to his people,
to his faithful, to those who turn to
him in their hearts.
Surely his salvation is at hand for those
who fear him,
that his glory may dwell in our land.

ALL: **The Lord speaks of peace to his people.**

Short version: use above only; Long version: use above and below.

SIDE A: Steadfast love and faithfulness will meet;
righteousness and peace will kiss
each other.
Faithfulness will spring up from
the ground,
and righteousness will look down
from the sky.

SIDE B: The Lord will give what is good,
and our land will yield its increase.
Righteousness will go before him,
and will make a path for his steps.

ALL: **The Lord speaks of peace to his people.**

CHILDREN'S DAILY PRAYER 2020–2021 © 2020 Archdiocese of Chicago: Liturgy Training Publications, 3949 South Racine Avenue, Chicago, IL 60609. All rights reserved. Orders: 800-933-1800 or www.LTP.org. Scripture excerpts are taken from *The New Revised Standard Version Bible: Catholic Edition*, ©1989, Division of Christian Education of the National Council of the Churches of Christ in the United States of America. Used with permission. All rights reserved.

ORDINARY TIME
AUTUMN

SUNDAY, AUGUST 16 — WEDNESDAY, NOVEMBER 25

AUTUMN ORDINARY TIME

THE MEANING OF ORDINARY TIME

Times and seasons on our liturgical calendar, in contrast to the secular calendar, are valued in a different, altogether new way. Our Christian calendar even has a different shape! Instead of a rectangle, we draw all the days of a year in a circle. Instead of marking off times according to the weather, we celebrate those great moments when God reveals a great love for us in marvelous and mysterious ways.

Our liturgical calendar has four primary seasons. Advent (the four weeks before Christmas); Christmas; Lent (the six weeks before Easter); Easter (which extends for fifty days after Easter through Pentecost) but, the longest part of the calendar is called Ordinary Time.

Ordinary Time is thirty-three or thirty-four weeks a year. It is called "Ordinary Time" because the weeks are numbered. The Latin word *ordinalis*, which refers to numbers in a series and stems from the Latin word *ordo*, from which we get the English word *order*. Ordinary time is therefore "ordered time." Calling it "Ordered Time" reminds us of God's great plan for creation. There was a specific time for the creation of light, planets, water, earth, plants, animals, and humankind. Ordinary Time begins after Christmas, continues until Ash Wednesday when it stops for Lent and Easter, then picks up again after Pentecost Sunday and runs through the summer and autumn until the beginning of Advent. Each Sunday in Ordinary Time has a number and the numbers increase each week.

During autumn Ordinary Time, there are weekly themes for the Scripture readings. Some of the themes help us to understand qualities of our faith: importance of community, friendship, keeping the Sabbath holy, prayer, service and the great commandment to love God and love one another. In these weeks, the readings cover a historical spectrum of Scripture.

From the New Testament, we will read parables or stories that Jesus told. With moral parables in week twenty-one, like the sower, the wicked tenants, and the barren fig tree, Jesus teaches us about the consequences of our behavior.

From the Old Testament we will read beautiful passages about Wisdom in the Book of Sirach. We will read from the Book of Genesis and wonder at the marvelous story of Creation. We will spend three weeks on the story of Moses who was one of the greatest heroes in the Old Testament. God chose Moses to lead the Hebrew people out of slavery in Egypt. During their escape and on their long journey through the deserts, the people met many challenges: the Egyptian army, lack of food and water, hostile tribes. But God was always with them and taking care of them. One of the greatest gifts God gave to the Hebrew people and to people of all time is the Gift of the Law: the Ten Commandments, which give clear instructions on how people can live together in peace.

As we come to the end of Ordinary Time and prepare for Advent in the thirty-third and thirty fourth weeks, the theme is, "Who is Jesus?" Jesus is Messiah, Savior of Israel, Son of Man, Lord of the Sabbath, Teacher and Healer, Good Shepherd, and Christ the King!

PREPARING TO CELEBRATE ORDINARY TIME IN THE CLASSROOM

SACRED SPACE

You want the prayer table or space to be in a place where the children will see it often and perhaps go to it in their free moments. If you can have a separate prayer table it should not be too small, perhaps a coffee-table size. You may wish to buy one or two inexpensive cushions to place before your prayer table so that children will feel invited to sit or kneel there. The essential things for the prayer table are a cross or crucifix (unless one is on the wall), a Bible, a substantial candle and a cloth of liturgical color. Cover the prayer table with a plain green cloth or one that mixes green with other Autumn colors. Large table napkins or placemats work, or remnants from a sewing store. Green, the color of hope and life, is the color of Ordinary Time. If you can, set the Bible on a bookstand. Point out the candle beside the Bible, and remind them that Jesus said, "I am the Light of the world" (John 8:12). You might light the candle, open the Bible, and read that verse to the class. Other objects you might want to include are a simple statue of Mary (September 8), images of angels (Archangels, September 29 and Guardian, October 2), an image of St. Francis or the children's pets (October 4), a rosary (October 7). Use natural objects, too, such as flowers, dried leaves or small gourds. If there is the space, pictures of loved ones who have died would be appropriate in November.

MOVEMENT AND GESTURE

Consider reverencing the Word of God in the Bible by carrying it in procession. Place a candle ahead of it and perhaps carry wind chimes as it moves through the room. At the prayer space the processors turn and the Bible is raised. The class reverences with a profound bow (a bow from the waist) then the Bible and candle are placed, and the chimes' are silenced. Also consider reverencing the crucifix or the cross near September 14, the Exaltation of the Holy Cross. Take the crucifix from the wall (or use another one) and carry it in procession at the beginning of prayer in a similar manner or take the cross to each child and let them kiss it or hold it or make a head bow before it.

FESTIVITY IN SCHOOL AND HOME

For Ordinary Time in autumn, *Children's Daily Prayer* provides several special prayer services to use in the classroom—or with larger groups such as the whole school—to celebrate the beginning of the school year, to pray for peace (on September 11), and to honor Our Lady of the Rosary (October 7). The Home Prayer pages can be duplicated for the students to take home and share with their families: Morning Prayer for Families Departing for the Day; Home Prayer for Remembering the Dead; and a Meal Prayer for Thanksgiving.

SACRED MUSIC

One of the best ways to help the children enter into the special qualities of this or any liturgical time is by teaching them the Sunday music of their parish. Teach the children (or invite the school music teacher, parish music director or a choir member/ cantor to do it) how your church sings her "Alleluia!" See what songs and hymns the children know and love. For example, in Ordinary Time, consider "For the Beauty of the Earth" and "Make Me a Channel of Your Peace." Learn and sing just a good refrain. Singing is an integral part of how we pray.

PRAYERS FOR ORDINARY TIME

During this season, take some time to discuss the meaning of the various intercessions of the Our Father with the children in your class. In particular, discuss the Kingdom of God—that time of peace and justice proclaimed by and fulfilled in Jesus. Ask what it means for God's Kingdom to come. Go through the prayer one intercession at a time asking what each means. Explore with them what Jesus is teaching us about how we should pray: We ask for God's name to be treated as blessed and holy, for the coming of the Kingdom of God, for God's will to be accomplished on earth, for our "daily bread," for forgiveness, and for strength in the face of temptation.

A NOTE TO CATECHISTS

Because you meet with your students once a week, you may wish to use the Prayer for the Week pages. These weekly prayer pages contain an excerpt from the Sunday Gospel and will help to prepare the children for Mass. Sometimes, though, you may wish to substitute the Prayer for the Day if it falls on an important solemnity, feast, or memorial of the Church (Our Lady of the Rosary, October 7, for example). In this introduction, you will see the suggestions for your prayer space. You may have to set up a prayer space each time you meet with your group. Think in advance about where to place it, have all your materials in one box, and always set it up in the same place.

GRACE BEFORE MEALS
FOR ORDINARY TIME • AUTUMN

LEADER:
Lord, you gift us with your love in so many ways.

ALL: We praise you and thank you!

✛ All make the Sign of the Cross.

In the name of the Father, and of the Son, and of the Holy Spirit. Amen.

LEADER:
Father, Son, and Spirit,
you bring us joy
through your abundant grace.
As we gather to share this meal,
may we be grateful for the
loving people who prepared it
every step of the way.
We thank all those in lands far from us
and those nearby who
helped grow, nurture, package,
transport, store, and cook our food.
We bless these brothers and sisters
as we bless each other here,
for you created all of us in
your image of goodness and love.
May this meal nourish our bodies
to give you glory and to build your Kingdom.
We ask this through Jesus Christ, our Lord.

ALL: Amen.

✛ All make the Sign of the Cross.

In the name of the Father, and of the Son, and of the Holy Spirit. Amen.

PRAYER AT DAY'S END

FOR ORDINARY TIME • AUTUMN

LEADER:

God of all wisdom,
we offer back to you
all that we have done today
through the gift of your gentle Spirit.

ALL: For your love is in our hearts!

✚ All make the Sign of the Cross.

> **In the name of the Father, and of the Son, and of the Holy Spirit. Amen.**

LEADER:

We are grateful for
the signs and wonders of this day,
for the ordinary events and its surprises,
big and small.
We thank you for the
loving people who surround us.
May we continue to reflect your goodness
to others in your name.
We ask this through your beloved Son, Jesus.

ALL: Amen.

✚ All make the Sign of the Cross.

> **In the name of the Father, and of the Son, and of the Holy Spirit. Amen.**

PRAYER SERVICE
BEGINNING OF THE YEAR FOR SCHOOL STAFF

Seek volunteers to lead this prayer service. You may involve up to seven leaders (as marked below). The fourth leader will need a Bible for the Scripture passage. Choose hymns for the beginning and ending if you wish.

FIRST LEADER:
We gather in Christ's name
to celebrate all of God's children.
Let us ask the Holy Spirit for guidance
as we begin our journey again with them.

◆ Gesture for all to stand.

Together we enter this time of prayer as we make the Sign of the Cross.

✠ All make the Sign of the Cross.

In the name of the Father, and of the Son, and of the Holy Spirit. Amen.

SECOND LEADER:
Spirit of God,
enlighten our minds
as we begin another school year, for
these children are gifts of new life.
Draw us closer to all
that is good and true
so that through us
all that they see
is you.
We ask this through Christ our Lord.

Amen.

THIRD LEADER:
Spirit of your Son Jesus,
grant us your wisdom and
integrity each and every day,
for you are the breath of all
that is holy.

CHILDREN'S DAILY PRAYER 2020–2021, © 2020 Archdiocese of Chicago: Liturgy Training Publications. All rights reserved. Orders: 800-933-1800 or www.LTP.org.

Refresh us with ideas that
inspire our youth with your energy
and enthusiasm.
We ask this in Christ's name.

Amen.

- ◆ Gesture for all to sit.

FOURTH LEADER: Romans 8:31b–35, 37–39
A reading from the Letter of Paul to Romans.

- ◆ Read the Scripture passage from the Bible.

The Word of the Lord.

- ◆ All observe silence.

FIFTH LEADER:

- ◆ Gesture for all to stand.

Let us bring our hopes and needs to God as we
pray from the Opening Prayer of our Church
leadership as they embarked on the Second
Vatican Council. Our response will be: **Guide
us with your love.**

For light and strength to know your will,
to make it our own,
and to live it in our lives,
we pray to the Lord.

ALL: Guide us with your love.

For justice for all;
enable us to uphold the rights of others;
do not allow us to be misled by ignorance
or corrupted by fear or favor,
we pray to the Lord.

ALL: Guide us with your love.

Unite us to yourself in the bond of love
and keep us faithful to all that is true,
we pray to the Lord.

ALL: Guide us with your love.

May we temper justice with love,
so that all our discussions and reflections
may be pleasing to you, and earn the reward
promised to good and faithful servants,
we pray to the Lord.

ALL: Guide us with your love.

SIXTH LEADER:
Let us pray as Jesus taught us:
Our Father . . . Amen.

- ◆ Pause and then say:

Let us offer one another the sign of
Christ's peace.

- ◆ All offer one another a sign of peace.

SEVENTH LEADER:
Let us pray:
God, our Creator,
your presence through the
Holy Spirit strengthens us
for the days ahead.
Guide us with your patience
and compassion as we
mentor our future leaders in Christ.

Amen.

- ✛ All make the Sign of the Cross.

**In the name of the Father, and of the
Son, and of the Holy Spirit. Amen.**

PRAYER SERVICE
BEGINNING OF THE YEAR FOR STUDENTS

This prayer service may be led by the eighth grade students or by older students. The third and fifth leaders will need a Bible for the passages from Matthew and Luke. Take time to help the third and fifth leaders practice the readings. You may wish to sing "This Little Light of Mine" as the opening and closing songs. If the group will sing, prepare someone to lead the songs.

FIRST LEADER:

We are embarking on a journey together
in this brand new school year.
As we look ahead at all that this year
might reveal,
let us remember Jesus,
who will walk beside us every step of the way.

SONG LEADER:

Let us begin by singing the first few verses of
our song.

◆ Gesture for all to stand, and lead the first few
verses of the song.

SECOND LEADER:

✚ All make the Sign of the Cross.

**In the name of the Father, and of the
Son, and of the Holy Spirit. Amen.**

Let us pray:
God our Creator,
we were made in
your image and likeness.
Help us to be gentle with
ourselves and each other
as we mature this year with your grace.

CHILDREN'S DAILY PRAYER 2020–2021, © 2020 Archdiocese of Chicago: Liturgy Training Publications. All rights reserved. Orders: 800-933-1800 or www.LTP.org.

Guide us in our studies and help us develop
with knowledge and maturity.
We ask this through Christ our Lord.

Amen.

◆ Remain standing and sing Alleluia.

THIRD LEADER: Matthew 5:14–16
A reading from the holy Gospel according
to Matthew.

◆ Read the Gospel passage from the Bible.

The Gospel of the Lord.

◆ All sit and observe silence.

FOURTH LEADER:

◆ Gesture for all to stand.

Let us bring our hopes and needs to God as we
pray, Let your light shine through us.

ALL: Let your light shine through us.

Help us to show honor and respect
to all those who teach and coach us,
we pray to the Lord.

ALL: Let your light shine through us.

Guide us with your counsel, Lord,
when we are frustrated with our studies,
we pray to the Lord.

ALL: Let your light shine through us.

Help us to take care of our
minds and bodies
so that we give you glory in
everything we do,
we pray to the Lord.

ALL: Let your light shine through us.

Help us to remember all that we learn
so that we can apply it to our lives
in the months and years ahead,
we pray to the Lord.

ALL: Let your light shine through us.

FIFTH LEADER: Luke 6:31–36
Let us listen to what Jesus teaches
to his disciples:

A reading from the holy Gospel according
to Luke.

◆ Read the Gospel passage from the Bible.

The Gospel of the Lord.

SIXTH LEADER:
Let us pray:
O God,
we know you are with us on this journey.
Help us to love one another
as you love us.
Guide us with your light of mercy and justice.
May we be considerate with our friends
and respectful of all who lead us.
Help us to learn and grow in your
wisdom throughout this year.
We ask this through Christ our Lord.

Amen.

✞ All make the Sign of the Cross.

**In the name of the Father, and of the
Son, and of the Holy Spirit. Amen.**

SONG LEADER:
Please join in singing the final verses of our
closing song.

HOME PRAYER
MORNING PRAYER FOR FAMILIES DEPARTING FOR THE DAY

The Catechism of the Catholic Church *calls the family the "domestic church" where children are first introduced to the faith (CCC, 2204 and 2225). A blessing is a prayer that acknowledges and thanks God for the good things in our lives and asks God to be with us. When the household gathers in the morning, perhaps at breakfast, a parent, grandparent, or other adult may lead this blessing.*

The longer prayer can be used on one of the first days of school and other special occasions. At other times, you may just want to bless the child with the Sign of the Cross on the forehead and a "God bless you" as he or she leaves for school.

✝ All make the Sign of the Cross.

In the name of the Father, and of the Son, and of the Holy Spirit. Amen.

LEADER:

We each have important things
to do today, and so we ask God's blessing.
We go to school and to work.
We learn and play.
We praise and thank God for each other
and for the love we share.
We ask God to be with those
who are lonely or sick
or without basic needs.
We ask this in Jesus' name.

All: Amen.

LEADER:

Holy God,
giver of all good gifts,
walk with us today,
guide our words and our actions,
and keep us on the path of truth.
Bring us back together in peace
at the end of this day.
We ask this through Christ our Lord.

✝ The leader makes the Sign of the Cross on one person's forehead saying:

"God bless you and keep you today."

ALL: Amen.

10 CHILDREN'S DAILY PRAYER 2020–2021 © 2020 Archdiocese of Chicago: Liturgy Training Publications, 3949 South Racine Avenue, Chicago, IL 60609. All rights reserved. Orders: 800-933-1800 or www.LTP.org. Scripture excerpts are taken from *The New Revised Standard Version Bible: Catholic Edition*, copyright © 1989, Division of Christian Education of the National Council of the Churches of Christ in the United States of America. Used with permission. All rights reserved.

PRAYER FOR THE WEEK

WITH A READING FROM THE GOSPEL FOR **SUNDAY, AUGUST 16, 2020**

OPENING

In today's Gospel, a Canaanite woman asks Jesus to heal her daughter. At first, both the disciples and Jesus seem to dismiss her pleas harshly, but the woman persists. Jesus listens to the woman, witnesses her steadfast devotion and faith, and heals her daughter.

✚ All make the Sign of the Cross.

In the name of the Father, and of the Son, and of the Holy Spirit. Amen.

PSALM

(For a longer psalm, see page xi.)
Psalm 66:1–3a

Make a joyful noise to God, all the earth.

Make a joyful noise to God, all the earth.

Make a joyful noise to God, all the earth;
  sing the glory of his name;
  give to him glorious praise.
Say to God, "How awesome are your deeds!"

Make a joyful noise to God, all the earth.

◆ All stand and sing **Alleluia.**

GOSPEL

Matthew 15:21–28

A reading from the holy Gospel according to Matthew.

Jesus went to the district of Tyre and Sidon. Just then a Canaanite woman from that region came out and started shouting, "Have mercy on me, Lord, Son of David; my daughter is tormented by a demon." But he did not answer her at all. And his disciples came and urged him, saying, "Send her away, for she keeps shouting after us." He answered, "I was sent only to the lost sheep of the house of Israel."

But she came and knelt before him, saying, "Lord, help me." He answered, "It is not fair to take the children's food and throw it to the dogs." She said, "Yes, Lord, yet even the dogs eat the crumbs that fall from their masters' table." Then Jesus answered her, "Woman, great is your faith! Let it be done for you as you wish." And her daughter was healed instantly.

The Gospel of the Lord.

◆ All sit and observe silence.

FOR SILENT REFLECTION

Think about this silently in your heart. Jesus told the woman that she had great faith. How might we have such faith?

CLOSING PRAYER

Let us pray to God for our needs and the needs of others: our family, neighborhood, and the world. For each need we say, "Lord, hear our prayer."

◆ All may add their own prayers here.

Let us pray: **Our Father . . . Amen.**

O loving God,
we thank you for knowing our hearts
and hearing our prayers.
Give us courage and strength and persistence
to always follow you in faith,
We ask this through Christ our Lord.

Amen.

✚ All make the Sign of the Cross.

OPENING

In today's reading, we learn about prayer. Solomon was king of Israel more than nine hundred years before Jesus' birth. Solomon prayed and praised God in front of all Israel. The Lord responded to his prayer and appeared to Solomon, telling him how to pray so that God will hear in heaven.

✦ All make the Sign of the Cross.

In the name of the Father, and of the Son, and of the Holy Spirit. Amen.

PSALM

(For a longer psalm, see page xi.)
Psalm 66:1–3a

Make a joyful noise to God, all the earth.

Make a joyful noise to God, all the earth.

Make a joyful noise to God, all the earth;
  sing the glory of his name;
  give to him glorious praise.
Say to God, "How awesome are your deeds!"

Make a joyful noise to God, all the earth.

READING

2 Chronicles 6:12, 13fg–14b; 7:12ab, 14

A reading from the Second Book of Chronicles.

Then Solomon stood before the altar of the LORD in the presence of the whole assembly of Israel, and spread out his hands. Then he knelt on his knees in the presence of the whole assembly of Israel, and spread out his hands toward heaven. He said, "O LORD, God of Israel, there is no God like you, in heaven or on earth." Then the LORD appeared to Solomon in the night and said to him: "I have heard your prayer. If my people who are called by my name humble themselves, pray, seek my face, and turn from their wicked ways, then I will hear from heaven, and will forgive their sin and heal their land."

The Word of the Lord.

◆ All observe silence.

FOR SILENT REFLECTION

Think about this silently in your heart. God tells us to humble ourselves in prayer. What does it mean to humble ourselves?

CLOSING PRAYER

Let us pray to God for our needs and the needs of others: our family, neighborhood, and the world. For each need we say, "Lord, hear our prayer."

◆ All may add their own prayers here.

Let us pray: **Our Father . . . Amen.**

Heavenly God,
we praise your name!
Hear our prayers
and open our hearts to your Word.
Help us to seek your presence
and remain faithful to your guidance.
Through Christ our Lord.

Amen.

✦ All make the Sign of the Cross.

OPENING

A prophet is someone who brought, inter- preted, and proclaimed the word of God. Today's reading is from the prophet Isaiah [ī-ZAY-uh]. Isaiah lived around seven hundred years before the birth of Jesus. Isaiah says that God wants us to live justly, do what is right, and keep the sabbath. The sabbath is the Jewish holy day that occurs each week. Catholic Christians celebrate this day on Sundays, when we are called to celebrate together at Mass.

✚ All make the Sign of the Cross.

In the name of the Father, and of the Son, and of the Holy Spirit. Amen.

PSALM

(For a longer psalm, see page xi.)
Psalm 66:1–3a

Make a joyful noise to God, all the earth.

Make a joyful noise to God, all the earth.

Make a joyful noise to God, all the earth;
  sing the glory of his name;
  give to him glorious praise.
Say to God, "How awesome are your deeds!"

Make a joyful noise to God, all the earth.

READING

Isaiah 56:1–2ace, 6eg, 7–8

A reading from the Book of the prophet Isaiah.

Thus says the LORD: Maintain justice, and do what is right, for soon my salvation will come, and my deliverance be revealed. Happy is the mortal who does this, who keeps the sabbath, and refrains from doing any evil. All who keep the sabbath, and do not profane it, and hold fast my covenant—these I will bring to my holy mountain, and make them joyful in my house of prayer; their burnt offerings and their sacri- fices will be accepted on my altar; for my house shall be called a house of prayer for all peoples. Thus says the Lord GOD, who gathers the out- casts of Israel, I will gather others to them besides those already gathered.

The Word of the Lord.

◆ All observe silence.

FOR SILENT REFLECTION

Think about this silently in your heart. How might we be joyful in church?

CLOSING PRAYER

Let us pray to God for our needs and the needs of others: our family, neighborhood, and the world. For each need we say, "Lord, hear our prayer."

◆ All may add their own prayers here.

Let us pray: **Our Father . . . Amen.**

Just and loving God,
may we gather together in your name
with great joy.
May we be faithful in keeping your day
a holy one.
May we not put other gods before you.
We pray in Christ's name.

Amen.

✚ All make the Sign of the Cross.

PRAYER FOR
WEDNESDAY, AUGUST 19, 2020

OPENING

Today is the feast of St. John Eudes. St. John believed that a spiritual life has Christ at its center. He gave his life to God by serving others, including those who were rejected or abandoned by society, and by preaching as a traveling missionary. In today's Gospel, Jesus also traveled from town to town preaching and teaching.

✛ All make the Sign of the Cross.

In the name of the Father, and of the Son, and of the Holy Spirit. Amen.

PSALM

(For a longer psalm, see page xi.)
Psalm 66:1–3a

Make a joyful noise to God, all the earth.

Make a joyful noise to God, all the earth.

Make a joyful noise to God, all the earth;
   sing the glory of his name;
   give to him glorious praise.
Say to God, "How awesome are your deeds!"

Make a joyful noise to God, all the earth.

◆ All stand and sing **Alleluia.**

GOSPEL

Mark 1:21–22, 35–39

A reading from the holy Gospel according to Mark.

Jesus and the disciples went to Capernaum; and when the sabbath came, Jesus entered the synagogue and taught. They were astounded at his teaching, for he taught them as one having authority, and not as the scribes. In the morning, while it was still very dark, he got up and went out to a deserted place, and there he prayed. And Simon and his companions hunted for him. When they found him, they said to him, "Everyone is searching for you." He answered, "Let us go on to the neighboring towns, so that I may proclaim the message there also; for that is what I came out to do." And he went throughout Galilee, proclaiming the message in their synagogues and casting out demons.

The Gospel of the Lord.

◆ All sit and observe silence.

FOR SILENT REFLECTION

Think about this silently in your heart. Jesus often went to a quiet place to pray. Where do you pray?

CLOSING PRAYER

Let us pray to God for our needs and the needs of others: our family, neighborhood, and the world. For each need we say, "Lord, hear our prayer."

◆ All may add their own prayers here.

Let us pray: **Our Father . . . Amen.**

Lord God,
your son Jesus taught us how to pray.
Help us, too, to seek your
loving presence in our day,
to find the quiet and listen to your voice,
and to share your name with all we meet.
Through Christ our Lord.
Amen.

✛ All make the Sign of the Cross.

OPENING

Today is the feast day of St. Bernard of Clairvaux (1090–1153). St. Bernard was a monk who is remembered for his good advice, his ability to settle arguments, and his inspirational preaching. He was often called the "honey-tongued teacher." In today's Gospel, Jesus gives us the words to pray to God, the Our Father.

✦ All make the Sign of the Cross.

In the name of the Father, and of the Son, and of the Holy Spirit. Amen.

PSALM

(For a longer psalm, see page xi.)
Psalm 66:1–3a

Make a joyful noise to God, all the earth.

Make a joyful noise to God, all the earth.

Make a joyful noise to God, all the earth;
   sing the glory of his name;
   give to him glorious praise.
Say to God, "How awesome are your deeds!"

Make a joyful noise to God, all the earth.

✦ All stand and sing **Alleluia.**

GOSPEL

Matthew 5:2; 6:9–14

A reading from the holy Gospel according to Matthew.

Jesus spoke to his disciples and taught them, saying: "Pray then in this way: Our Father in heaven, hallowed be your name. Your kingdom come. Your will be done, on earth as it is in heaven. Give us this day our daily bread. And forgive us our debts, as we also have forgiven our debtors. And do not bring us to the time of trial, but rescue us from the evil one.

For if you forgive others their trespasses, your heavenly Father will also forgive you."

The Gospel of the Lord.

◆ All sit and observe silence.

FOR SILENT REFLECTION

Think about this silently in your heart. Why do you think Jesus gave us these words to pray?

CLOSING PRAYER

Let us pray to God for our needs and the needs of others: our family, neighborhood, and the world. For each need we say, "Lord, hear our prayer."

◆ All may add their own prayers here.

Let us pray: **Our Father . . . Amen.**

Heavenly Father,
may we help bring your Kingdom
to earth
and help bring your word to the world.
May we forgive others as we ask to
be forgiven.
We pray in the name of your Son,
Jesus Christ our Lord.

Amen.

✦ All make the Sign of the Cross.

PRAYER FOR
FRIDAY, AUGUST 21, 2020

OPENING

Today is the feast of St. Pius X (1835–1914), who is best known for encouraging children to receive Holy Communion. Having been poor his whole life, Pope Pius X tirelessly devoted his life to social justice and charity. He believed that only through them could peace be achieved. In today's reading, Paul reminds us to always do good to one another.

✦ All make the Sign of the Cross.

In the name of the Father, and of the Son, and of the Holy Spirit. Amen.

PSALM

(For a longer psalm, see page xi.)
Psalm 66:1–3a

Make a joyful noise to God, all the earth.

Make a joyful noise to God, all the earth.

Make a joyful noise to God, all the earth;
   sing the glory of his name;
   give to him glorious praise.
Say to God, "How awesome are your deeds!"

Make a joyful noise to God, all the earth.

READING

1 Thessalonians 5:12a, 13b–18, 23–25

A reading from the First Letter of Paul to the Thessalonians.

But we appeal to you, brothers and sisters, be at peace among yourselves. And we urge you, beloved, to admonish the idlers, encourage the fainthearted, help the weak, be patient with all of them. See that none of you repays evil for evil, but always seek to do good to one another and to all. Rejoice always, pray without ceasing, give thanks in all circumstances; for this is the will of God in Christ Jesus for you. May the God of peace himself sanctify you entirely; and may your spirit and soul and body be kept sound and blameless at the coming of our Lord Jesus Christ. The one who calls you is faithful, and he will do this. Beloved, pray for us.

The Word of the Lord.

◆ All observe silence.

FOR SILENT REFLECTION

Think about this silently in your heart. Paul encourages us to "rejoice always, pray without ceasing, give thanks in all circumstances." How can we remember to do these things?

CLOSING PRAYER

Let us pray to God for our needs and the needs of others: our family, neighborhood, and the world. For each need we say, "Lord, hear our prayer."

◆ All may add their own prayers here.

Let us pray: **Our Father . . . Amen.**

God Most High,
we praise you and thank you
for your loving mercy and kindness.
May we remember to seek you
always in prayer
and serve one another with love and humility,
as St. Pius did.
We pray in Christ's name.

Amen.

✦ All make the Sign of the Cross.

PRAYER FOR THE WEEK

OPENING

Many people in Jesus' day did not know who he was and were unsure what to call him. Only Peter recognized that Jesus was the Messiah, the Son of God. Jesus praises and blesses Peter.

✛ All make the Sign of the Cross.

In the name of the Father, and of the Son, and of the Holy Spirit. Amen.

PSALM

(For a longer psalm, see page xi.)
Psalm 66:1–3a

Make a joyful noise to God, all the earth.

Make a joyful noise to God, all the earth.

Make a joyful noise to God, all the earth;
    sing the glory of his name;
    give to him glorious praise.
Say to God, "How awesome are your deeds!"

Make a joyful noise to God, all the earth.

◆ All stand and sing **Alleluia.**

GOSPEL

Matthew 16:13b–17b, 17c–19

A reading from the holy Gospel according to Matthew.

Jesus asked his disciples, "Who do people say that the Son of Man is?" And they said, "Some say John the Baptist, but others Elijah, and still others Jeremiah or one of the prophets." He said to them, "But who do you say that I am?" Simon Peter answered, "You are the Messiah, the Son of the living God." And Jesus answered him, "Blessed are you, Simon! For flesh and blood has not revealed this to you, but my Father in heaven. And I tell you, you are Peter, and on this rock I will build my church, and the gates of Hades will not prevail against it. I will give you the keys of the kingdom of heaven, and whatever you bind on earth will be bound in heaven, and whatever you loose on earth will be loosed in heaven."

The Gospel of the Lord.

◆ All sit and observe silence.

FOR SILENT REFLECTION

Think about this silently in your heart. When Jesus says, "whatever you bind on earth will be bound on heaven," he is talking about forgiveness. Why do you think forgiveness is so important to Jesus?

CLOSING PRAYER

Let us pray to God for our needs and the needs of others: our family, neighborhood, and the world. For each need we say, "Lord, hear our prayer."

◆ All may add their own prayers here.

Let us pray: **Our Father . . . Amen.**

Loving and merciful God,
we give thanks for your Son Jesus
and for the gift of forgiveness.
Help us to forgive others
and ask for forgiveness ourselves,
as you forgive us.
Through Christ our Lord.

Amen.

✛ All make the Sign of the Cross.

OPENING

Today is the feast of St. Bartholomew. He was one of the Twelve Apostles and a faithful follower of Jesus. Today's Gospel is one of several parables for the week. A parable is a story that teaches us about God and the Kingdom of heaven. Parables often use commonly known images. Today, Jesus tells us the parable of the mustard seed. We learn how something small can grow so mighty.

✛ All make the Sign of the Cross.

In the name of the Father, and of the Son, and of the Holy Spirit. Amen.

PSALM

(For a longer psalm, see page xi.)
Psalm 66:1–3a

Make a joyful noise to God, all the earth.

Make a joyful noise to God, all the earth.

Make a joyful noise to God, all the earth;
  sing the glory of his name;
  give to him glorious praise.
Say to God, "How awesome are your deeds!"

Make a joyful noise to God, all the earth.

◆ All stand and sing **Alleluia.**

GOSPEL

Matthew 13:31–32, 34–35

A reading from the holy Gospel according to Matthew.

Jesus put before them a parable: "The kingdom of heaven is like a mustard seed that someone took and sowed in his field; it is the smallest of all the seeds, but when it has grown it is the greatest of shrubs and becomes a tree, so that the birds of the air come and make nests in its branches." Jesus told the crowds all these things in parables; without a parable he told them nothing. This was to fulfill what had been spoken through the prophet: "I will open my mouth to speak in parables; I will proclaim what has been hidden from the foundation of the world."

The Gospel of the Lord.

◆ All sit and observe silence.

FOR SILENT REFLECTION

Think about this silently in your heart. Why do you think Jesus uses the image of a small mustard seed to teach about the Kingdom of God?

CLOSING PRAYER

Let us pray to God for our needs and the needs of others: our family, neighborhood, and the world. For each need we say, "Lord, hear our prayer."

◆ All may add their own prayers here.

Let us pray: **Our Father . . . Amen.**

Jesus,
help us to see that, even when we feel small or unimportant,
we can do great things when we have faith.
Who live in reign with God the Father,
in the unity of the Holy Spirit,
one God, for ever and ever.

Amen.

✛ All make the Sign of the Cross.

OPENING

Today is the feast of Sts. Louis of France and Joseph Calasanz (1556–1648). St. Louis was a powerful king, but he cared a great deal about the people he ruled. His reign was marked by compassion and honesty. St. Joseph grew up in a wealthy family in Spain, but throughout his life, he worked tirelessly to serve poor children. He opened schools that provided free education to the underprivileged. Today's Gospel gives us new images to help us understand the Kingdom of God.

✦ All make the Sign of the Cross.

In the name of the Father, and of the Son, and of the Holy Spirit. Amen.

PSALM

(For a longer psalm, see page xi.)
Psalm 66:1–3a

Make a joyful noise to God, all the earth.

Make a joyful noise to God, all the earth.

Make a joyful noise to God, all the earth;
   sing the glory of his name;
   give to him glorious praise.
Say to God, "How awesome are your deeds!"

Make a joyful noise to God, all the earth.

✦ All stand and sing **Alleluia.**

GOSPEL

Matthew 13:33, 44–46

A reading from the holy Gospel according to Matthew.

Jesus told them another parable: "The kingdom of heaven is like yeast that a woman took and mixed in with three measures of flour until all of it was leavened. The kingdom of heaven is like treasure hidden in a field, which some-one found and hid; then in his joy he goes and sells all that he has and buys that field. Again, the kingdom of heaven is like a merchant in search of fine pearls; on finding one pearl of great value, he went and sold all that he had and bought it."

The Gospel of the Lord.

✦ All sit and observe silence.

FOR SILENT REFLECTION

Think about this silently in your heart. What do yeasted flour, a treasure in a field, and a merchant in search of pearls tell us about the Kingdom of God?

CLOSING PRAYER

Let us pray to God for our needs and the needs of others: our family, neighborhood, and the world. For each need we say, "Lord, hear our prayer."

✦ All may add their own prayers here.

Let us pray: **Our Father . . . Amen.**

Creator God,
may we see that all of us are your children,
and may we serve and protect all those
in need.
Help us to open our hearts and minds
to the teaching of your Son Jesus.
We pray in Christ's name.

Amen.

✦ All make the Sign of the Cross.

PRAYER FOR
WEDNESDAY, AUGUST 26, 2020

OPENING

Jesus often uses parables of gardening or farming. In today's Gospel, Jesus likens the Kingdom of God to seeds sprouting, growing, and being harvested. The gardener might not know how the seed sprouts and grows, only that it does. Only God understands the wonders of creation.

✝ All make the Sign of the Cross.

In the name of the Father, and of the Son, and of the Holy Spirit. Amen.

PSALM
(For a longer psalm, see page xi.)
Psalm 66:1–3a

Make a joyful noise to God, all the earth.

Make a joyful noise to God, all the earth.

Make a joyful noise to God, all the earth;
  sing the glory of his name;
  give to him glorious praise.
Say to God, "How awesome are your deeds!"

Make a joyful noise to God, all the earth.

◆ All stand and sing **Alleluia.**

GOSPEL
Mark 4:26–29, 33–34

A reading from the holy Gospel according to Mark.

Jesus also said, "The kingdom of God is as if someone would scatter seed on the ground, and would sleep and rise night and day, and the seed would sprout and grow, he does not know how. The earth produces of itself, first the stalk, then the head, then the full grain in the head. But when the grain is ripe, at once he goes in with his sickle, because the harvest has come." With many such parables he spoke the word to the crowds, as they were able to hear it; he did not speak to them except in parables, but he explained everything in private to his disciples.

The Gospel of the Lord.

◆ All sit and observe silence.

FOR SILENT REFLECTION

Think about this silently in your heart. Why do you think Jesus spoke in parables?

CLOSING PRAYER

Let us pray to God for our needs and the needs of others: our family, neighborhood, and the world. For each need we say, "Lord, hear our prayer."

◆ All may add their own prayers here.

Let us pray: **Our Father . . . Amen.**

Creator God,
we thank you for seeds to plant,
the earth to grow in,
water to nourish,
and the sun for warmth.
Help us to open our hearts and minds
to the teachings of your Son Jesus.
Help us to grow in his name
and bear good fruit.

Amen.

✝ All make the Sign of the Cross.

OPENING

Today's Gospel compares the Kingdom of God to a wedding banquet. In this parable, the king prepares a celebration for his son's wedding, but those he invited did not come. He then invites everyone in the streets to the celebration. The slaves we will hear about refer to servants of the king. Also, today we remember St. Monica, the mother of St. Augustine. She is the patron saint of mothers, wives, and conversion.

✛ All make the Sign of the Cross.

In the name of the Father, and of the Son, and of the Holy Spirit. Amen.

PSALM

(For a longer psalm, see page xi.)
Psalm 66:1–3a

Make a joyful noise to God, all the earth.

Make a joyful noise to God, all the earth.

Make a joyful noise to God, all the earth;
    sing the glory of his name;
    give to him glorious praise.
Say to God, "How awesome are your deeds!"

Make a joyful noise to God, all the earth.

◆ All stand and sing **Alleluia.**

GOSPEL

Matthew 22:2–4b, 4d–5, 8–10

A reading from the holy Gospel according to Matthew.

Jesus said: "The kingdom of heaven may be compared to a king who gave a wedding banquet for his son. He sent his slaves to call those who had been invited to the wedding banquet, but they would not come. Again he sent other slaves, saying, 'Tell those who have been invited: my oxen and my fat calves have been slaughtered, and everything is ready; come to the wedding banquet.' But they made light of it and went away, one to his farm, another to his business. Then the king said to his slaves, 'The wedding is ready, but those invited were not worthy. Go therefore into the streets, and invite everyone you find to the wedding banquet.' Those slaves went out into the streets and gathered all whom they found, both good and bad; so the wedding hall was filled with guests."

The Gospel of the Lord.

◆ All sit and observe silence.

FOR SILENT REFLECTION

Think about this silently in your heart. Why do you think the king invited everyone to the celebration? What does that say about the Kingdom of God?

CLOSING PRAYER

Let us pray to God for our needs and the needs of others: our family, neighborhood, and the world. For each need we say, "Lord, hear our prayer."

◆ All may add their own prayers here.

Let us pray: **Our Father . . . Amen.**

O God,
we thank you for welcoming us into
your Kingdom.
May we help it grow on earth
as it is in heaven.

Amen.

✛ All make the Sign of the Cross.

PRAYER FOR
FRIDAY, AUGUST 28, 2020

OPENING

Today is the feast of St. Augustine of Hippo (354–430). The son of St. Monica, he is known as a Doctor of the Church because of his many writings, many of which are used and studied today. Today's parable is about ten bridesmaids. Some of them were wise and prepared for the wedding banquet, and some were foolish and not ready.

✝ All make the Sign of the Cross.

In the name of the Father, and of the Son, and of the Holy Spirit. Amen.

PSALM
(For a longer psalm, see page xi.)
Psalm 66:1–3a

Make a joyful noise to God, all the earth.

Make a joyful noise to God, all the earth.

Make a joyful noise to God, all the earth;
  sing the glory of his name;
  give to him glorious praise.
Say to God, "How awesome are your deeds!"

Make a joyful noise to God, all the earth.

◆ All stand and sing **Alleluia.**

GOSPEL
Matthew 25:1–6, 8–10

A reading from the holy Gospel according to Matthew.

Jesus said, "Then the kingdom of heaven will be like this. Ten bridesmaids took their lamps and went to meet the bridegroom. Five of them were foolish, and five were wise. When the foolish took their lamps, they took no oil with them; but the wise took flasks of oil with their lamps. As the bridegroom was delayed, all of them became drowsy and slept. But at mid-night there was a shout, 'Look! Here is the bridegroom! Come out to meet him.' The foolish said to the wise, 'Give us some of your oil, for our lamps are going out.' But the wise replied, 'No! there will not be enough for you and for us; you had better go to the dealers and buy some for yourselves.' And while they went to buy it, the bridegroom came, and those who were ready went with him into the wedding banquet; and the door was shut."

The Gospel of the Lord.

◆ All sit and observe silence.

FOR SILENT REFLECTION

Think about this silently in your heart. How can we prepare and ready ourselves for God's presence?

CLOSING PRAYER

Let us pray to God for our needs and the needs of others: our family, neighborhood, and the world. For each need we say, "Lord, hear our prayer."

◆ All may add their own prayers here.

Let us pray: **Our Father . . . Amen.**

Dearest God,
help us await your presence
with open eyes, ears, and hearts.
May our lights always shine brightly.
We ask this through Christ our Lord.

Amen.

✝ All make the Sign of the Cross.

PRAYER FOR THE WEEK

OPENING

In today's Gospel, Jesus began to prepare his disciples for the difficulties and suffering ahead for him and his followers. Following Jesus is not an easy path—for his disciples or for us.

✚ All make the Sign of the Cross.

In the name of the Father, and of the Son, and of the Holy Spirit. Amen.

PSALM

(For a longer psalm, see page xi.)
Psalm 66:1–3a

Make a joyful noise to God, all the earth.

Make a joyful noise to God, all the earth.

Make a joyful noise to God, all the earth;
  sing the glory of his name;
  give to him glorious praise.
Say to God, "How awesome are your deeds!"

Make a joyful noise to God, all the earth.

◆ All stand and sing **Alleluia.**

GOSPEL

Matthew 16:21b–d, 22–23, 24b–25

A reading from the holy Gospel according to Matthew.

Jesus began to show his disciples that he must go to Jerusalem and undergo great suffering at the hands of the elders and chief priests and scribes, and be killed, and on the third day be raised. And Peter took him aside and began to rebuke him, saying, "God forbid it, Lord! This must never happen to you." But he turned and said to Peter, "Get behind me, Satan! You are a stumbling block to me; for you are setting your mind not on divine things but on human things. If any want to become my followers, let them deny themselves and take up their cross and follow me. For those who want to save their life will lose it, and those who lose their life for my sake will find it."

The Gospel of the Lord.

◆ All sit and observe silence.

FOR SILENT REFLECTION

Think about this silently in your heart. Sometimes it is hard to make a right decision. Has it ever been difficult to do what you know is right?

CLOSING PRAYER

Let us pray to God for our needs and the needs of others: our family, neighborhood, and the world. For each need we say, "Lord, hear our prayer."

◆ All may add their own prayers here.

Let us pray: **Our Father . . . Amen.**

Heavenly God,
thank you for your son Jesus.
Help us to choose
what is good and just
so that we may follow
in your Son's path.
May the Holy Spirit inspire us
when we have to make difficult choices in life.
For this we pray
through Christ our Lord.

Amen.

✚ All make the Sign of the Cross.

OPENING

Moses was a great prophet to the Israelites in the Old Testament. Moses received the Ten Commandments from God on Mount Sinai [SĬ-nī]. The words *statutes* and *ordinances* mean "laws" and are another way to express *commandment*. In today's reading, Moses shares the greatest commandment with the people of Israel.

✚ All make the Sign of the Cross.

In the name of the Father, and of the Son, and of the Holy Spirit. Amen.

PSALM

(For a longer psalm, see page xi.)
Psalm 66:1–3a

Make a joyful noise to God, all the earth.

Make a joyful noise to God, all the earth.

Make a joyful noise to God, all the earth;
   sing the glory of his name;
   give to him glorious praise.
Say to God, "How awesome are your deeds!"

Make a joyful noise to God, all the earth.

READING

Deuteronomy 5:1a; 6:1, 3b, 5–9

A reading from the Book of Deuteronomy.

Moses convened all Israel, and said to them: Now this is the commandment—the statutes and the ordinances—that the LORD your God charged me to teach you to observe in the land that you are about to cross into and occupy, so that it may go well with you, and so that you may multiply greatly in a land flowing with milk and honey. You shall love the LORD your God with all your heart, and with all your soul, and with all your might. Keep these words that I am commanding you today in your heart. Recite them to your children and talk about them when you are at home and when you are away, when you lie down and when you rise. Bind them as a sign on your hand, fix them as an emblem on your forehead, and write them on the doorposts of your house and on your gates.

The Word of the Lord.

◆ All observe silence.

FOR SILENT REFLECTION

Think about this silently in your heart. How can we show God our great love?

CLOSING PRAYER

Let us pray to God for our needs and the needs of others: our family, neighborhood, and the world. For each need we say, "Lord, hear our prayer."

◆ All may add their own prayers here.

Let us pray: **Our Father . . . Amen.**

Dear God,
we love you with
all our heart,
with all our soul,
and with all our might.
Help us to love others
as you have loved us.
We pray in Christ Jesus' name.

Amen.

✚ All make the Sign of the Cross.

PRAYER SERVICE
FOR THE CARE OF CREATION ON SEPTEMBER 1

In 2015 Pope Francis declared September 1 to be a world-wide day of prayer for the care of creation. His encyclical Laudato Si' (Praised Be) *is subtitled* On Care for Our Common Home. *Using the words of St. Francis, he compares the earth, our common home, to a "sister with whom we share our life and a beautiful mother who opens to embrace us." For this prayer service, divide the class into two groups. This could be girls and boys or another simple division of voices to pray the Canticle of St. Francis. Song suggestions are "All Creatures of Our God and King," "Joyful, Joyful, We Adore Thee," or another hymn which honors creation.*

ALL

O Most High, all-powerful, good Lord God,
to you belong praise, glory,
honor and all blessing.

GROUP I

Be praised, my Lord, for all your creation
and especially for our Brother Sun,
who brings us the day and the light;
he is strong and shines magnificently.
O Lord, we think of you when we look
at him.

GROUP II

Be praised, my Lord, for Sister Moon,
and for the stars
which you have set shining and lovely
in the heavens.

GROUP I

Be praised, my Lord,
for our Brothers Wind and Air
and every kind of weather
by which you, Lord,
uphold life in all your creatures.

GROUP II

Be praised, my Lord, for Sister Water,
who is very useful to us,
and humble and precious and pure.

GROUP I

Be praised, my Lord, for Brother Fire,
through whom you give us light in the
darkness:
he is bright and lively and strong.

GROUP II

Be praised, my Lord,
for Sister Earth, our Mother,
who nourishes us and sustains us,
bringing forth
fruits and vegetables of many kinds
and flowers of many colors.

GROUP I

Be praised, my Lord,
for those who forgive for love of you;
and for those
who bear sickness and weakness
in peace and patience
you will grant them a crown.

GROUP II

Be praised, my Lord, for our Sister Death,
whom we must all face.
I praise and bless you, Lord,
and I give thanks to you,
and I will serve you in all humility.

ALL

O Most High, all-powerful, good Lord God,
to you belong praise, glory, honor and all
blessing. Amen.

OPENING

As Moses did in yesterday's reading, today Jesus shares the greatest commandment. Jesus adds that the second greatest commandment is to love your neighbor as yourself. The Pharisees [FAYR-uh-seez] and Sadducees [SAD-yoo-seez] were priests and religious leaders of Jesus' day.

✝ All make the Sign of the Cross.

In the name of the Father, and of the Son, and of the Holy Spirit. Amen.

PSALM

(For a longer psalm, see page xi.)

Psalm 66:1–3a

Make a joyful noise to God, all the earth.

Make a joyful noise to God, all the earth.

Make a joyful noise to God, all the earth;
   sing the glory of his name;
   give to him glorious praise.
Say to God, "How awesome are your deeds!"

Make a joyful noise to God, all the earth.

◆ All stand and sing **Alleluia.**

GOSPEL

Matthew 22:34–40

A reading from the holy Gospel according to Matthew.

When the Pharisees [FAYR-uh-seez] heard that Jesus had silenced the Sadducees, they gathered together, and one of them, a lawyer, asked him a question to test him. "Teacher, which commandment in the law is the greatest?" Jesus said to him, "'You shall love the Lord your God with all your heart, and with all your soul, and with all your mind.' This is the greatest and first commandment. And a second is like it: 'You shall love your neighbor as yourself.' On these two commandments hang all the law and the prophets."

The Gospel of the Lord.

◆ All sit and observe silence.

FOR SILENT REFLECTION

Think about this silently in your heart. Who is our neighbor? How can we love our neighbor as ourselves?

CLOSING PRAYER

Let us pray to God for our needs and the needs of others: our family, neighborhood, and the world. For each need we say, "Lord, hear our prayer."

◆ All may add their own prayers here.

Let us pray: **Our Father . . . Amen.**

Loving God,
help us to follow your commandments,
and show our love for you
through kindness and compassion
for others.
Help us to see you
in everyone we meet.
We ask this through Christ our Lord.

Amen.

✝ All make the Sign of the Cross.

OPENING

We will learn the story of the Good Samaritan today and tomorrow. Samaritans were not friendly with the Jews. In fact, they were often considered enemies. Priests and Levites were some of the religious leaders of the day. Jesus uses this story to teach us who our neighbor is.

✛ All make the Sign of the Cross.

In the name of the Father, and of the Son, and of the Holy Spirit. Amen.

PSALM
(For a longer psalm, see page xi.)
Psalm 66:1–3a

Make a joyful noise to God, all the earth.

Make a joyful noise to God, all the earth.

Make a joyful noise to God, all the earth;
   sing the glory of his name;
   give to him glorious praise.
Say to God, "How awesome are your deeds!"

Make a joyful noise to God, all the earth.

◆ All stand and sing **Alleluia.**

GOSPEL
Luke 10:25–26b, 27, 29–32

A reading from the holy Gospel according to Luke.

A lawyer stood up to test Jesus. "Teacher," he said, "what must I do to inherit eternal life?" Jesus said to him, "What is written in the law?" The lawyer answered, "You shall love the Lord your God with all your heart, and with all your soul, and with all your strength, and with all your mind; and your neighbor as yourself." But wanting to justify himself, he asked Jesus, "And who is my neighbor?" Jesus replied, "A man was going down from Jerusalem to Jericho, and fell into the hands of robbers, who stripped him, beat him, and went away, leaving him half dead. Now by chance a priest was going down that road; and when he saw him, he passed by on the other side. So likewise a Levite, when he came to the place and saw him, passed by on the other side."

The Gospel of the Lord.

◆ All sit and observe silence.

FOR SILENT REFLECTION

Think about this silently in your heart. Why would the priest and Levite pass by the hurt man without helping? Why would Jesus tell us this parable?

CLOSING PRAYER

Let us pray to God for our needs and the needs of others: our family, neighborhood, and the world. For each need we say, "Lord, hear our prayer."

◆ All may add their own prayers here.

Let us pray: **Our Father . . . Amen.**

Kind and loving God,
you call us to love
and serve others.
Help us to love all
those that we meet,
especially in their time of need.
We pray in Christ's name.

Amen.

✛ All make the Sign of the Cross.

OPENING

Today we continue the parable of the Good Samaritan. Remember, Samaritans and Jews were not friendly with one another. We heard yesterday that the priest and Levite passed the injured man on the road. Listen for who stops and helps him. We remember St. Gregory the Great, who cared for persecuted Jews and victims of famine and plague. He is one of the four Fathers who are Doctors of the Church.

✝ All make the Sign of the Cross.

In the name of the Father, and of the Son, and of the Holy Spirit. Amen.

PSALM

(For a longer psalm, see page xi.)
Psalm 66:1–3a

Make a joyful noise to God, all the earth.

Make a joyful noise to God, all the earth.

Make a joyful noise to God, all the earth;
sing the glory of his name;
give to him glorious praise.
Say to God, "How awesome are your deeds!"

Make a joyful noise to God, all the earth.

◆ All stand and sing **Alleluia.**

GOSPEL

Luke 10:33–37

A reading from the holy Gospel according to Luke.

"But a Samaritan while traveling came near him; and when he saw him, he was moved with pity. He went to him and bandaged his wounds, having poured oil and wine on them. Then he put him on his own animal, brought him to an inn, and took care of him. The next day he took out two denarii, gave them to the inn-keeper, and said, 'Take care of him; and when I come back, I will repay you whatever more you spend.' Which of these three, do you think, was a neighbor to the man who fell into the hands of the robbers?" The lawyer said to Jesus, "The one who showed him mercy." Jesus said to him, "Go and do likewise."

The Gospel of the Lord.

◆ All sit and observe silence.

FOR SILENT REFLECTION

Think about this silently in your heart. After hearing the parable, what do you think Jesus means when he says to love your neighbor?

CLOSING PRAYER

Let us pray to God for our needs and the needs of others: our family, neighborhood, and the world. For each need we say, "Lord, hear our prayer."

◆ All may add their own prayers here.

Let us pray: **Our Father . . . Amen.**

Christ Jesus,
thank you for teaching us
to love our neighbors.
Help us to show kindness and love
to all we meet.
Who live and reign with God the Father,
in the unity of the Holy Spirit,
one God, for ever and ever.

Amen.

✝ All make the Sign of the Cross.

OPENING

St. Paul writes a letter to the Ephesians to encourage them to get along with one another and describes how to live a holy life in Christ. He tells them to speak the truth, use their words to uplift each other, and be kind and forgiving to one another.

✜ All make the Sign of the Cross.

In the name of the Father, and of the Son, and of the Holy Spirit. Amen.

PSALM

(For a longer psalm, see page xi.)
Psalm 66:1–3a

Make a joyful noise to God, all the earth.

Make a joyful noise to God, all the earth.

Make a joyful noise to God, all the earth;
　sing the glory of his name;
　give to him glorious praise.
Say to God, "How awesome are your deeds!"

Make a joyful noise to God, all the earth.

READING

Ephesians 4:25, 29, 31–32; 5:1–2

A reading from the Letter of Paul
to the Ephesians.

Putting away falsehood, let all of us speak the truth to our neighbors, for we are members of one another. Let no evil talk come out of your mouths, but only what is useful for building up, as there is need, so that your words may give grace to those who hear. Put away from you all bitterness and wrath and anger and wrangling and slander, together with all malice, and be kind to one another, tenderhearted, forgiving one another, as God in Christ has forgiven you. Therefore be imitators of God, as beloved children, and live in love, as Christ loved us and gave himself up for us, a fragrant offering and sacrifice to God.

The Word of the Lord.

◆ All observe silence.

FOR SILENT REFLECTION

Think about this silently in your heart. How can we use our words to help build each other up?

CLOSING PRAYER

Let us pray to God for our needs and the needs of others: our family, neighborhood, and the world. For each need we say, "Lord, hear our prayer."

◆ All may add their own prayers here.

Let us pray: **Our Father . . . Amen.**

O Lord,
may our voices be used
to spread love, compassion,
and kindness.
May we lift up one another
and bear each other's burdens.
Let us reflect your love
wherever we go.
We ask this through Christ our Lord.

Amen.

✜ All make the Sign of the Cross.

OPENING

In today's Gospel, Jesus gives us very clear instructions on how to settle disagreements with one another. Jesus tells us that he is with us when we seek reconciliation and when we pray as a community.

✛ All make the Sign of the Cross.

In the name of the Father, and of the Son, and of the Holy Spirit. Amen.

PSALM

(For a longer psalm, see page xi.)
Psalm 66:1–3a

Make a joyful noise to God, all the earth.

Make a joyful noise to God, all the earth.

Make a joyful noise to God, all the earth;
  sing the glory of his name;
  give to him glorious praise.
Say to God, "How awesome are your deeds!"

Make a joyful noise to God, all the earth.

◆ All stand and sing **Alleluia.**

GOSPEL

Matthew 18:15–17, 19–20

A reading from the holy Gospel according to Matthew.

Jesus said to his disciples, "If your brother sins against you, go and point out the fault when the two of you are alone. If he listens to you, you have regained that one. But if you are not listened to, take one or two others along with you, so that every word may be confirmed by the evidence of two or three witnesses. If he refuses to listen to them, tell it to the church; and if he refuses to listen even to the church, then treat him as you would a Gentile and a tax collector. Truly I tell you, if two of you agree on earth about anything you ask, it will be done for you by my Father in heaven. For where two or three are gathered in my name, I am there among them."

The Gospel of the Lord.

◆ All sit and observe silence.

FOR SILENT REFLECTION

Think about this silently in your heart. How can we use Jesus' words to help us through an argument or misunderstanding with friends?

CLOSING PRAYER

Let us pray to God for our needs and the needs of others: our family, neighborhood, and the world. For each need we say, "Lord, hear our prayer."

◆ All may add their own prayers here.

Let us pray: **Our Father . . . Amen.**

O Lord,
give us courage,
right judgment, compassion,
and forgiveness,
so that we can lead others
along the path of reconciliation.
May we take Jesus' name to heart
whenever we need guidance.
We ask this in his name.

Amen.

✛ All make the Sign of the Cross

OPENING

Today is the feast of the Nativity of the Blessed Virgin Mary, the mother of Jesus. We honor her life of great love and faith in God. In today's reading, James reminds us that in addition to listening to God's Word, we are all called to live out God's word through action.

✚ All make the Sign of the Cross.

In the name of the Father, and of the Son, and of the Holy Spirit. Amen.

PSALM

(For a longer psalm, see page xi.)
Psalm 66:1–3a

Make a joyful noise to God, all the earth.

Make a joyful noise to God, all the earth.

Make a joyful noise to God, all the earth;
   sing the glory of his name;
   give to him glorious praise.
Say to God, "How awesome are your deeds!"

Make a joyful noise to God, all the earth.

READING

James 1:19–20, 22–25

A reading from the Letter of James.

You must understand this, my beloved: let everyone be quick to listen, slow to speak, slow to anger; for your anger does not produce God's righteousness. Be doers of the word, and not merely hearers who deceive themselves. For if any are hearers of the word and not doers, they are like those who look at themselves in a mirror; for they look at themselves and, on going away, immediately forget what they were like. But those who look into the perfect law, the law of liberty, and persevere, being not hearers who forget but doers who act—they will be blessed in their doing.

The Word of the Lord.

◆ All observe silence.

FOR SILENT REFLECTION

Think about this silently in your heart. How can we be "doers" of the word of God?

CLOSING PRAYER

Let us pray to God for our needs and the needs of others: our family, neighborhood, and the world. For each need we say, "Lord, hear our prayer."

◆ All may add their own prayers here.

Let us pray: **Our Father . . . Amen.**

Loving God,
may our actions
reflect your Word,
so that we may be
the hands, feet, and voice of Christ
in the world.
May we look to the Blessed Virgin Mary,
whose birth we celebrate today.
She is our role model of faith and trust.
She shows us how to say yes to doing
your will.
We pray in Christ Jesus' name.

Amen.

✚ All make the Sign of the Cross.

OPENING

Today is the feast of St. Peter Claver (1580–1654). Though born in Spain, St. Peter lived in South America, traveling in the center of the slave trade. He worked to ease the suffering of the slaves by providing for their physical and spiritual needs. In today's reading, Paul instructs the Romans that they are not to obey the laws but to go out in the world and live them.

✛ All make the Sign of the Cross.

In the name of the Father, and of the Son, and of the Holy Spirit. Amen.

PSALM

(For a longer psalm, see page xi.)
Psalm 66:1–3a

Make a joyful noise to God, all the earth.

Make a joyful noise to God, all the earth.

Make a joyful noise to God, all the earth;
    sing the glory of his name;
    give to him glorious praise.
Say to God, "How awesome are your deeds!"

Make a joyful noise to God, all the earth.

READING

Romans 2:13–16

A reading from the Letter of Paul to the Romans.

For it is not the hearers of the law who are righteous in God's sight, but the doers of the law who will be justified. When Gentiles, who do not possess the law, do instinctively what the law requires, these, though not having the law, are a law to themselves. They show that what the law requires is written on their hearts, to which their own conscience also bears witness; and their conflicting thoughts will accuse or perhaps excuse them on the day when, according to my gospel, God, through Jesus Christ, will judge the secret thoughts of all.

The Word of the Lord.

◆ All observe silence.

FOR SILENT REFLECTION

Think about this silently in your heart. How can we not just listen to the word of God but practice it throughout our daily lives?

CLOSING PRAYER

Let us pray to God for our needs and the needs of others: our family, neighborhood, and the world. For each need we say, "Lord, hear our prayer."

◆ All may add their own prayers here.

Let us pray: **Our Father . . . Amen.**

Loving God,
help us to be both
listeners and doers
of your word,
and be your most faithful followers.
We look to your Son Jesus as our guide.
In his name we pray.

Amen.

✛ All make the Sign of the Cross.

OPENING

Today's reading is from the Book of Sirach [SEER-ak], often called Ecclesiasticus. Sirach is a book that teaches us ways to live our lives. We learn today that what we say is important. We are advised to choose our words carefully to not cause any harm.

✚ All make the Sign of the Cross.

In the name of the Father, and of the Son, and of the Holy Spirit. Amen.

PSALM

(For a longer psalm, see page xi.)

Psalm 66:1–3a

Make a joyful noise to God, all the earth.

Make a joyful noise to God, all the earth.

Make a joyful noise to God, all the earth;
    sing the glory of his name;
    give to him glorious praise.
Say to God, "How awesome are your deeds!"

Make a joyful noise to God, all the earth.

READING

Sirach 5:10–15a

A reading from the Book of Sirach.

Stand firm for what you know, and let your speech be consistent. Be quick to hear, but deliberate in answering. If you know what to say, answer your neighbor; but if not, put your hand over your mouth. Honor and dishonor come from speaking, and the tongue of mortals may be their downfall. Do not be called double-tongued and do not lay traps with your tongue; for shame comes to the thief, and severe condemnation to the double-tongued. In great and small matters cause no harm.

The Word of the Lord.

◆ All observe silence.

FOR SILENT REFLECTION

Think about this silently in your heart. How can our words honor God? How can they dishonor God?

CLOSING PRAYER

Let us pray to God for our needs and the needs of others: our family, neighborhood, and the world. For each need we say, "Lord, hear our prayer."

◆ All may add their own prayers here.

Let us pray: **Our Father . . . Amen.**

Heavenly God,
may we honor you
through our voices,
and sing your praises
with our words.
We pray in the name of Jesus Christ,
your Son,
who lives and reigns with you in the unity
of the Holy Spirit,
one God, for ever and ever.

Amen.

✚ All make the Sign of the Cross.

OPENING

Today is a National Day of Service and Remembrance for all those who died in the terrorist attacks on September 11, 2001. All Americans are asked to do an act of service in remembrance of those who died that day. In today's Gospel, Jesus reminds us that an act of service for another who is hungry, sick, or in need is also an act of serving God.

✚ All make the Sign of the Cross.

In the name of the Father, and of the Son, and of the Holy Spirit. Amen.

PSALM

(For a longer psalm, see page xi.)

Psalm 66:1–3a

Make a joyful noise to God, all the earth.

Make a joyful noise to God, all the earth.

Make a joyful noise to God, all the earth;
    sing the glory of his name;
    give to him glorious praise.
Say to God, "How awesome are your deeds!"

Make a joyful noise to God, all the earth.

◆ All stand and sing **Alleluia.**

GOSPEL

Matthew 25:34–37, 40

A reading from the holy Gospel according to Matthew.

The king will say to those at his right hand, "Come, you that are blessed by my Father, inherit the kingdom prepared for you from the foundation of the world; for I was hungry and you gave me food, I was thirsty and you gave me something to drink, I was a stranger and you welcomed me, I was naked and you gave me clothing, I was sick and you took care of me, I was in prison and you visited me." Then the righteous will answer him, "Lord, when was it that we saw you hungry and gave you food, or thirsty and gave you something to drink?" And the king will answer them, "Truly I tell you, just as you did it to one of the least of these who are members of my family, you did it to me."

The Gospel of the Lord.

◆ All sit and observe silence.

FOR SILENT REFLECTION

Think about this silently in your heart. What act of service might you do today?

CLOSING PRAYER

Let us pray to God for our needs and the needs of others: our family, neighborhood, and the world. For each need we say, "Lord, hear our prayer."

◆ All may add their own prayers here.

Let us pray: **Our Father . . . Amen.**

O God Most High,
be with us when we are in need or hurting.
Fill us with strength and courage when we
need it the most.
We remember those who lost their lives nineteen years ago.
Keep them in your loving care.
Through Christ our Lord.

Amen.

✚ All make the Sign of the Cross.

PRAYER SERVICE
NATIONAL DAY OF SERVICE AND REMEMBRANCE ON SEPTEMBER 11

Prepare six leaders for this service. The second leader will need a Bible for the Scripture and may need help practicing for the reading. You may begin by singing "Healer of Our Every Ill," "Song of the Body of Christ," or "This Is My Song," or perhaps begin in silence with a simple tolling of a hand bell.

FIRST LEADER:
May the grace and peace of our Lord Jesus Christ be with us, now and for ever.

Amen.

Let us pray:
Lord Jesus Christ,
we remember all those who died
on that September day in 2001,
people of different faiths and
backgrounds and ways of life.
We turn to you now, Lord of all,
to give us the courage to be peacemakers
and servants to all people in the world.

Amen.

◆ All stand and sing **Alleluia.**

SECOND LEADER: Luke 6:36–37
A reading from the holy Gospel according
to Luke.

◆ Read the Gospel passage from the Bible.

The Gospel of the Lord.

THIRD LEADER:
Let us pause and pray in silence for all those who have died in wars and other conflicts around the world.

◆ Allow a minute of silence.

FOURTH LEADER:
We recall the beautiful prayer of peace of
St. Francis of Assisi:

Lord, make me an instrument of your peace;
where there is hatred, let me sow love;
where there is injury, pardon;
where there is doubt, faith;
where there is despair, hope;
where there is darkness, light;
and where there is sadness, joy.
Grant that I may not so much seek
to be consoled as to console;
to be understood as to understand;
to be loved as to love;
for it is in giving that we receive,
it is in pardoning that we are pardoned,
and it is in dying that we are born to
eternal life.

Amen.

FIFTH LEADER:
Now let us offer to one another a sign of
Christ's peace:

◆ All offer one another a sign of peace.

SIXTH LEADER:
And may the Lord bless us,

✚ All make the Sign of the Cross.

protect us from all evil,
and bring us to everlasting life.

Amen.

PRAYER FOR THE WEEK
WITH A READING FROM THE GOSPEL FOR **SUNDAY, SEPTEMBER 13, 2020**

OPENING

In today's Gospel, Jesus tells a story about forgiveness. Jesus wants us to forgive others, just as God will always forgive us. True forgiveness is without resentment or judgment and frees us from grudges or hurt feelings. The king completely forgives and erases the debt of the man in this parable, even though he didn't have to.

✦ All make the Sign of the Cross.

> **In the name of the Father, and of the Son, and of the Holy Spirit. Amen.**

PSALM

(For a longer psalm, see page xi.)
Psalm 66:1–3a

Make a joyful noise to God, all the earth.

Make a joyful noise to God, all the earth.

Make a joyful noise to God, all the earth;
    sing the glory of his name;
    give to him glorious praise.
Say to God, "How awesome are your deeds!"

Make a joyful noise to God, all the earth.

◆ All stand and sing **Alleluia.**

GOSPEL

Matthew 18:21acd, 22–24b, 25–27

A reading from the holy Gospel according to Matthew.

Then Peter came and said to Jesus, "Lord, how often should I forgive? As many as seven times?" Jesus said to him, "Not seven times, but, I tell you, seventy-seven times. For this reason the kingdom of heaven may be compared to a king who wished to settle accounts with his slaves. One who owed him ten thousand talents was brought to him; and, as he could not pay, his lord ordered him to be sold, together with his wife and children and all his possessions, and payment to be made. So the slave fell on his knees before him, saying, 'Have patience with me, and I will pay you everything.' And out of pity for him, the lord of that slave released him and forgave him the debt."

The Gospel of the Lord.

◆ All sit and observe silence.

FOR SILENT REFLECTION

Think about this silently in your heart. Why do you think Jesus wants us to forgive so many times? Do you think it's easy to forgive?

CLOSING PRAYER

Let us pray to God for our needs and the needs of others: our family, neighborhood, and the world. For each need we say, "Lord, hear our prayer."

◆ All may add their own prayers here.

Let us pray: **Our Father . . . Amen.**

Merciful God,
we thank you for the gift of forgiveness.
Help us to forgive others,
and to treat others with love and compassion.
We ask this in Christ's name.

Amen.

✦ All make the Sign of the Cross.

OPENING

Today is the feast of the Exaltation of the Holy Cross. The cross is a sign of Jesus' great suffering and death. It is also a sign of triumph and love. Through the cross, we remember that our entire being belongs to God—our hands, minds, souls, and hearts. In today's Gospel, we hear that only seeds that are planted in good soil can bear much fruit.

✚ All make the Sign of the Cross.

In the name of the Father, and of the Son, and of the Holy Spirit. Amen.

PSALM

(For a longer psalm, see page xi.)
Psalm 66:1–3a

Make a joyful noise to God, all the earth.

Make a joyful noise to God, all the earth.

Make a joyful noise to God, all the earth;
    sing the glory of his name;
    give to him glorious praise.
Say to God, "How awesome are your deeds!"

Make a joyful noise to God, all the earth.

◆ All stand and sing **Alleluia.**

GOSPEL

Matthew 13:2–8

A reading from the holy Gospel according to Matthew.

Such great crowds gathered around him that Jesus got into a boat and sat there, while the whole crowd stood on the beach. And he told them many things in parables, saying: "Listen! A sower went out to sow. And as he sowed, some seeds fell on the path, and the birds came and ate them up. Other seeds fell on rocky ground, where they did not have much soil, and they sprang up quickly, since they had no depth of soil. But when the sun rose, they were scorched; and since they had no root, they withered away. Other seeds fell among thorns, and the thorns grew up and choked them. Other seeds fell on good soil and brought forth grain, some a hundredfold, some sixty, some thirty. Let anyone with ears, listen!"

The Gospel of the Lord.

◆ All sit and observe silence.

FOR SILENT REFLECTION

Think about this silently in your heart. What do the seeds represent in today's parable? What do you think the soil means?

CLOSING PRAYER

Let us pray to God for our needs and the needs of others: our family, neighborhood, and the world. For each need we say, "Lord, hear our prayer."

◆ All may add their own prayers here.

Let us pray: **Our Father . . . Amen.**

Dear Jesus,
may we remember your great sacrifice
out of love for humankind.
Help us welcome your presence in our hearts,
so seeds of love, kindness, and mercy
may grow in our hearts forever.
In your name we pray.

Amen.

✚ All make the Sign of the Cross.

PRAYER FOR
TUESDAY, SEPTEMBER 15, 2020

OPENING

Today is the memorial of Our Lady of Sorrows. Because of her deep love for her son Jesus, Mary shared in his suffering. Today we remember and pray for all mothers who have suffered, have lost a child, or felt alone in their motherhood. In today's Gospel, we hear how generous our God is.

✚ All make the Sign of the Cross.

In the name of the Father, and of the Son, and of the Holy Spirit. Amen.

PSALM
(For a longer psalm, see page xi.)
Psalm 66:1–3a

Make a joyful noise to God, all the earth.

Make a joyful noise to God, all the earth.

Make a joyful noise to God, all the earth;
  sing the glory of his name;
  give to him glorious praise.
Say to God, "How awesome are your deeds!"

Make a joyful noise to God, all the earth.

◆ All stand and sing **Alleluia.**

GOSPEL
Matthew 20:1–2, 6a, 7c–8, 10, 11b–13, 15b

A reading from the holy Gospel according to Matthew.

"The kingdom of heaven is like a landowner who went out early in the morning to hire laborers for his vineyard. After agreeing with the laborers for the usual daily wage, he sent them into his vineyard. About five o'clock he went out and found others standing around; 'You also go into the vineyard.' When evening came, the owner of the vineyard said to his manager, 'Call the laborers and give them their pay, beginning with the last and then going to the first.' Now when the first came, they thought they would receive more; but each of them also received the usual daily wage. They grumbled against the landowner, saying, 'These last worked only one hour, and you have made them equal to us who have borne the burden of the day and the scorching heat.' But he replied to one of them, 'Friend, I am doing you no wrong; did you not agree with me for the usual daily wage? Are you envious because I am generous?'"

The Gospel of the Lord.

◆ All sit and observe silence.

FOR SILENT REFLECTION

Think about this silently in your heart. How has God been generous to you? How can you respond to that generosity?

CLOSING PRAYER

Let us pray to God for our needs and the needs of others: our family, neighborhood, and the world. For each need we say, "Lord, hear our prayer."

◆ All may add their own prayers here.

Let us pray: **Our Father . . . Amen.**

Heavenly Father,
we praise you for your generous love.
Help us to be as generous and loving to others.
We ask this through Christ our Lord.

Amen.

✚ All make the Sign of the Cross.

38

OPENING

Today we celebrate two friends, Sts. Cornelius and Cyprian. St. Cyprian was a bishop who helped the poor and supported the election of his friend Cornelius to the papacy. Both used their gifts in service to God and his people. In today's Gospel, Jesus tells a parable of three people (the "slaves" referred to here are "servants") who do different things with their "talents." A talent is a large sum of money. The one who used his talents wisely was praised as trustworthy.

✦ All make the Sign of the Cross.

In the name of the Father, and of the Son, and of the Holy Spirit. Amen.

PSALM

(For a longer psalm, see page xi.)
Psalm 66:1–3a

Make a joyful noise to God, all the earth.

Make a joyful noise to God, all the earth.

Make a joyful noise to God, all the earth;
   sing the glory of his name;
   give to him glorious praise.
Say to God, "How awesome are your deeds!"

Make a joyful noise to God, all the earth.

◆ All stand and sing **Alleluia.**

GOSPEL

Matthew 25:14–15, 19–21

A reading from the holy Gospel according to Matthew.

Jesus said, "For it is as if a man, going on a journey, summoned his slaves and entrusted his property to them; to one he gave five talents, to another two, to another one, to each according to his ability. Then he went away. After a long time the master of those slaves came and settled accounts with them. Then the one who had received the five talents came forward, bringing five more talents, saying, 'Master, you handed over to me five talents; see, I have made five more talents.' His master said to him, 'Well done, good and trustworthy slave; you have been trustworthy in a few things, I will put you in charge of many things; enter into the joy of your master.'"

The Gospel of the Lord.

◆ All sit and observe silence.

FOR SILENT REFLECTION

Think about this silently in your heart. What gifts has God given you? How can we use our gifts to praise God?

CLOSING PRAYER

Let us pray to God for our needs and the needs of others: our family, neighborhood, and the world. For each need we say, "Lord, hear our prayer."

◆ All may add their own prayers here.

Let us pray: **Our Father . . . Amen.**

Dear God,
thank you for your many gifts.
Help us to use them wisely and carefully.
We ask this in the name of Jesus Christ
our Lord.

Amen.

✦ All make the Sign of the Cross.

OPENING

Today we remember St. Robert Bellarmine, a great scholar on Scripture and Catholic teaching. By the example of his life, we understand that the root of our faith is Jesus Christ himself. In today's Gospel, Jesus tells a parable to remind us to be humble. To be humble is not to be proud or think we are better than someone else, to know that we are not perfect. In the parable, the Pharisee—a religious leader in Jesus' time—thought he was better than other people.

✚ All make the Sign of the Cross.

In the name of the Father, and of the Son, and of the Holy Spirit. Amen.

PSALM

(For a longer psalm, see page xi.)

Psalm 66:1–3a

Make a joyful noise to God, all the earth.

Make a joyful noise to God, all the earth.

Make a joyful noise to God, all the earth;
sing the glory of his name;
give to him glorious praise.
Say to God, "How awesome are your deeds!"

Make a joyful noise to God, all the earth.

◆ All stand and sing **Alleluia.**

GOSPEL

Luke 18:9–14

A reading from the holy Gospel according to Luke.

He also told this parable to some who trusted in themselves that they were righteous and regarded others with contempt: "Two men went up to the temple to pray, one a Pharisee and the other a tax collector. The Pharisee, standing by himself, was praying thus, 'God, I thank you that I am not like other people: thieves, rogues, adulterers, or even like this tax collector. I fast twice a week; I give a tenth of all my income.' But the tax collector, standing far off, would not even look up to heaven, but was beating his breast and saying, 'God, be merciful to me, a sinner!' I tell you, this man went down to his home justified rather than the other; for all who exalt themselves will be humbled, but all who humble themselves will be exalted."

The Gospel of the Lord.

◆ All sit and observe silence.

FOR SILENT REFLECTION

Think about this silently in your heart. How can you become humble before God?

CLOSING PRAYER

Let us pray to God for our needs and the needs of others: our family, neighborhood, and the world. For each need we say, "Lord, hear our prayer."

◆ All may add their own prayers here.

Let us pray: **Our Father . . . Amen.**

God our Father,
forgive us when we treat others poorly.
Help us to see you in one another,
to be humble and forgiving,
and to heed the teachings of your Son
our Savior, Jesus Christ.

Amen.

✚ All make the Sign of the Cross.

OPENING

In today's Gospel, Jesus tells us a parable of a rich man who is building many barns so that he can rest and enjoy his life. The man is foolish because he has stored up treasures for himself but has not put enough trust in God.

✦ All make the Sign of the Cross.

In the name of the Father, and of the Son, and of the Holy Spirit. Amen.

PSALM
(For a longer psalm, see page xi.)
Psalm 66:1–3a

Make a joyful noise to God, all the earth.

Make a joyful noise to God, all the earth.

Make a joyful noise to God, all the earth;
  sing the glory of his name;
  give to him glorious praise.
Say to God, "How awesome are your deeds!"

Make a joyful noise to God, all the earth.

◆ All stand and sing **Alleluia.**

GOSPEL
Luke 12:16–21

A reading from the holy Gospel according to Luke.

Jesus told his disciples a parable: "The land of a rich man produced abundantly. And he thought to himself, 'What should I do, for I have no place to store my crops?' Then he said, 'I will do this: I will pull down my barns and build larger ones, and there I will store all my grain and my goods. And I will say to my soul, Soul, you have ample goods laid up for many years; relax, eat, drink, be merry.' But God said to him, 'You fool! This very night your life

is being demanded of you. And the things you have prepared, whose will they be?' So it is with those who store up treasures for themselves but are not rich toward God."

The Gospel of the Lord.

◆ All sit and observe silence.

FOR SILENT REFLECTION

Think about this silently in your heart. How can you be rich toward God?

CLOSING PRAYER

Let us pray to God for our needs and the needs of others: our family, neighborhood, and the world. For each need we say, "Lord, hear our prayer."

◆ All may add their own prayers here.

Let us pray: **Our Father . . . Amen.**

Dear God,
let us be kind and caring toward others.
Help us share our abundance with
those in need
and remember all that we have,
and all that we give to others,
is because of your generous heart.
We ask this in Christ's name.

Amen.

✦ All make the Sign of the Cross.

PRAYER FOR THE WEEK

WITH A READING FROM THE GOSPEL FOR **SUNDAY, SEPTEMBER 20, 2020**

OPENING

The parable in today's Gospel tells us about the fairness and generosity of God. We may think the landowner is unfair in not paying more to the laborers who had worked all day, or less to those who had worked only a small portion of the day. But the landowner has chosen to be overly generous to his workers, just as God is with each of us.

✛ All make the Sign of the Cross.

In the name of the Father, and of the Son, and of the Holy Spirit. Amen.

PSALM

(For a longer psalm, see page xi.)
Psalm 66:1–3a

Make a joyful noise to God, all the earth.

Make a joyful noise to God, all the earth.

Make a joyful noise to God, all the earth;
  sing the glory of his name;
  give to him glorious praise.
Say to God, "How awesome are your deeds!"

Make a joyful noise to God, all the earth.

◆ All stand and sing **Alleluia.**

GOSPEL

Matthew 20:1–2, 5, 7c–8b, 10, 11b–13, 15b

A reading from the holy Gospel according to Matthew.

"The kingdom of heaven is like a landowner who went out early in the morning to hire laborers for his vineyard. After agreeing with the laborers for the usual daily wage, he sent them into his vineyard. When he went out again about noon and about three o'clock, he did the same. He said to them, 'You also go into the vineyard.' When evening came, the owner of the vineyard said to his manager, 'Call the laborers and give them their pay.' Now when the first came, they thought they would receive more; but each of them also received the usual daily wage. They grumbled against the landowner, saying, 'These last worked only one hour, and you have made them equal to us who have borne the burden of the day and the scorching heat.' But he replied to one of them, 'Friend, I am doing you no wrong; did you not agree with me for the usual daily wage? Are you envious because I am generous?'"

The Gospel of the Lord.

◆ All sit and observe silence.

FOR SILENT REFLECTION

Think about this silently in your heart. How can you be more generous with others?

CLOSING PRAYER

Let us pray to God for our needs and the needs of others: our family, neighborhood, and the world. For each need we say, "Lord, hear our prayer."

◆ All may add their own prayers here.

Let us pray: **Our Father . . . Amen.**

O God,
we thank you and praise you.
Help us to share your gifts with others.
We ask this in the name of Jesus Christ,
our Lord.

Amen.

✛ All make the Sign of the Cross.

OPENING

Today is the feast day of St. Matthew, one of the Twelve Apostles. St. Matthew was a tax collector before he met Jesus. In Jesus' time, a tax collector was not considered a good person. St. Matthew, however, left his old life behind and chose to follow Jesus. Today's reading is from the first book of the Bible, Genesis. There are two creation stories in Genesis. This week we will hear the second story.

✜ All make the Sign of the Cross.

In the name of the Father, and of the Son, and of the Holy Spirit. Amen.

PSALM

(For a longer psalm, see page xi.)
Psalm 66:1–3a

Make a joyful noise to God, all the earth.

Make a joyful noise to God, all the earth.

Make a joyful noise to God, all the earth;
  sing the glory of his name;
  give to him glorious praise.
Say to God, "How awesome are your deeds!"

Make a joyful noise to God, all the earth.

READING

Genesis 2:4–7

A reading from the Book of Genesis.

These are the generations of the heavens and the earth when they were created. In the day that the LORD God made the earth and the heavens, when no plant of the field was yet in the earth and no herb of the field had yet sprung up—for the LORD God had not caused it to rain upon the earth, and there was no one to till the ground; but a stream would rise from the earth, and water the whole face of the ground—then the LORD God formed man from the dust of the ground, and breathed into his nostrils the breath of life; and the man became a living being.

The Word of the Lord.

◆ All observe silence.

FOR SILENT REFLECTION

Think about this silently in your heart. How can we help care for this earth that God has made?

CLOSING PRAYER

Let us pray to God for our needs and the needs of others: our family, neighborhood, and the world. For each need we say, "Lord, hear our prayer."

◆ All may add their own prayers here.

Let us pray: **Our Father . . . Amen.**

God of all creation,
help us to be stewards of this earth,
of the seas, and of all your creatures.
We praise you for your beautiful work!
May we be mindful of the care of
your creation.
We pray in the name of Jesus Christ,
our Lord and Savior.

Amen.

✜ All make the Sign of the Cross.

PRAYER FOR
TUESDAY, SEPTEMBER 22, 2020

OPENING

We continue to hear the creation story in Genesis. After God created a man, he created trees, which provided both beauty and nourishment. We are then told of a river that flows into four branches. The river waters the trees and gardens. We hear the names of the rivers, two of which exist today in western Asia, the Tigris and Euphrates [yoo-FRAY-teez].

✚ All make the Sign of the Cross.

In the name of the Father, and of the Son, and of the Holy Spirit. Amen.

PSALM

(For a longer psalm, see page xi.)
Psalm 66:1–3a

Make a joyful noise to God, all the earth.

Make a joyful noise to God, all the earth.

Make a joyful noise to God, all the earth;
  sing the glory of his name;
  give to him glorious praise.
Say to God, "How awesome are your deeds!"

Make a joyful noise to God, all the earth.

READING

Genesis 2:8–11a, 13–14

A reading from the Book of Genesis.

And the Lord God planted a garden in Eden, in the east; and there he put the man whom he had formed. Out of the ground the Lord God made to grow every tree that is pleasant to the sight and good for food, the tree of life also in the midst of the garden, and the tree of the knowledge of good and evil. A river flows out of Eden to water the garden, and from there it divides and becomes four branches. The name of the first is Pishon. The name of the second river is Gihon; it is the one that flows around the whole land of Cush. The name of the third river is Tigris, which flows east of Assyria. And the fourth river is the Euphrates.

The Word of the Lord.

◆ All observe silence.

FOR SILENT REFLECTION

Think about this silently in your heart. How do we use God's gifts of trees, plants, and water? How can we take care of and preserve these creations?

CLOSING PRAYER

Let us pray to God for our needs and the needs of others: our family, neighborhood, and the world. For each need we say, "Lord, hear our prayer."

◆ All may add their own prayers here.

Let us pray: **Our Father . . . Amen.**

Lord God,
we praise you for your wondrous creation.
You give us food to eat and water to
nourish us.
Help us take care of, preserve, and clean our
water that you have provided for us.
Help us tend to our earth and our gardens,
for they sustain us and make your
world beautiful.
We pray in the name of Jesus Christ,
our Lord.

Amen.

✚ All make the Sign of the Cross.

OPENING

God put the man in Eden to care for and tend the garden. God then created every animal and bird so that the man would not be alone. But none of these animals was enough to be called a helper or companion. Today is the feast day of St. Pio of Pietrelcina, also called Padre Pio (1887–1968). St. Pio helped open a hospital in Italy called Home for the Relief of the Suffering.

✚ All make the Sign of the Cross.

In the name of the Father, and of the Son, and of the Holy Spirit. Amen.

PSALM
(For a longer psalm, see page xi.)
Psalm 66:1–3a

Make a joyful noise to God, all the earth.

Make a joyful noise to God, all the earth.

Make a joyful noise to God, all the earth;
  sing the glory of his name;
  give to him glorious praise.
Say to God, "How awesome are your deeds!"

Make a joyful noise to God, all the earth.

READING
Genesis 2:15, 18–20

A reading from the Book of Genesis.

The LORD God took the man and put him in the garden of Eden to till it and keep it. Then the LORD God said, "It is not good that the man should be alone; I will make him a helper as his partner." So out of the ground the LORD God formed every animal of the field and every bird of the air, and brought them to the man to see what he would call them; and whatever the man called every living creature, that was its name. The man gave names to all cattle, and to the birds of the air, and to every animal of the field; but for the man there was not found a helper as his partner.

The Word of the Lord.

◆ All observe silence.

FOR SILENT REFLECTION

Think about this silently in your heart. What was missing from the man's life that the animals were not enough for companionship?

CLOSING PRAYER

Let us pray to God for our needs and the needs of others: our family, neighborhood, and the world. For each need we say, "Lord, hear our prayer."

◆ All may add their own prayers here.

Let us pray: **Our Father . . . Amen.**

Creator God,
St. Padre Pio teaches us to have compassion for
those who are ill and who suffer.
Help us to care for all you have created,
including those who need our help.
We thank you for all the blessings of nature.
We ask you to hear us
in Christ's name.

Amen.

✚ All make the Sign of the Cross.

PRAYER FOR
THURSDAY, SEPTEMBER 24, 2020

OPENING

We hear today how God created a woman, who became a partner for the man. Made by God's hands, the man and woman are brought into a relationship with each other and with God.

✛ *All make the Sign of the Cross.*

In the name of the Father, and of the Son, and of the Holy Spirit. Amen.

PSALM

(For a longer psalm, see page xi.)
Psalm 66:1–3a

Make a joyful noise to God, all the earth.

Make a joyful noise to God, all the earth.

Make a joyful noise to God, all the earth;
   sing the glory of his name;
   give to him glorious praise.
Say to God, "How awesome are your deeds!"

Make a joyful noise to God, all the earth.

READING

Genesis 2:21–24

A reading from the Book of Genesis.

So the LORD God caused a deep sleep to fall upon the man, and he slept; then he took one of his ribs and closed up its place with flesh. And the rib that the LORD God had taken from the man he made into a woman and brought her to the man. Then the man said, "This at last is bone of my bones and flesh of my flesh; this one shall be called Woman, for out of Man this one was taken." Therefore a man leaves his father and his mother and clings to his wife, and they become one flesh.

The Word of the Lord.

◆ *All observe silence.*

FOR SILENT REFLECTION

Think about this silently in your heart. How do our relationships with others also reflect our relationship with God?

CLOSING PRAYER

Let us pray to God for our needs and the needs of others: our family, neighborhood, and the world. For each need we say, "Lord, hear our prayer."

◆ *All may add their own prayers here.*

Let us pray: **Our Father . . . Amen.**

Creator God,
we thank you for the many relationships
that we have
with those we love,
with friends and classmates,
and even with those we don't know very well.
Help us to be honest, caring, respectful, and
loving to all.
Through Christ our Lord.

Amen.

✛ *All make the Sign of the Cross.*

OPENING

Today's reading from the book of Sirach tells us more about creation. God filled the earth with human beings in God's own image. He created humans with strength, with knowledge, and with understanding.

✠ All make the Sign of the Cross.

In the name of the Father, and of the Son, and of the Holy Spirit. Amen.

PSALM

(For a longer psalm, see page xi.)
Psalm 66:1–3a

Make a joyful noise to God, all the earth.

Make a joyful noise to God, all the earth.

Make a joyful noise to God, all the earth;
   sing the glory of his name;
   give to him glorious praise.
Say to God, "How awesome are your deeds!"

Make a joyful noise to God, all the earth.

READING

Sirach 16:24, 26a, 27a, 29; 17:1a, 3, 6–7, 9–10, 13

A reading from the Book of Sirach.

Listen to me my child, and acquire knowledge, and pay close attention to my words. When the Lord created his works from the beginning, he arranged his works in an eternal order. Then the Lord looked upon the earth, and filled it with his good things. The Lord created human beings out of earth. He endowed them with strength like his own, and made them in his own image. Discretion and tongue and eyes, ears and a mind for thinking he gave them. He filled them with knowledge and understanding, and showed them good and evil. And they will praise God's holy name, to proclaim the grandeur of his works. Their eyes saw his glorious majesty, and their ears heard the glory of his voice.

The Word of the Lord.

◆ All observe silence.

FOR SILENT REFLECTION

Think about this silently in your heart. How can we respect the dignity of life?

CLOSING PRAYER

Let us pray to God for our needs and the needs of others: our family, neighborhood, and the world. For each need we say, "Lord, hear our prayer."

◆ All may add their own prayers here.

Let us pray: **Our Father . . . Amen.**

Holy God,
help us to respect all life,
for we are made wonderfully in your image.
Help us to bring life to others,
that we may all live in happiness and peace.
We ask this in the name of Jesus Christ
our Lord.

Amen.

✠ All make the Sign of the Cross.

PRAYER FOR THE WEEK

OPENING

In today's Gospel, Jesus makes a point about those who promise to do something but then do not and those who argue that they won't do something but change their minds and decide to do it. God wants us to honor our word and to change our minds when we have first rejected God. We can always turn to God.

✝ All make the Sign of the Cross.

In the name of the Father, and of the Son, and of the Holy Spirit. Amen.

PSALM

(For a longer psalm, see page xi.)
Psalm 66:1–3a

Make a joyful noise to God, all the earth.

Make a joyful noise to God, all the earth.

Make a joyful noise to God, all the earth;
  sing the glory of his name;
  give to him glorious praise.
Say to God, "How awesome are your deeds!"

Make a joyful noise to God, all the earth.

◆ All stand and sing **Alleluia.**

GOSPEL

Matthew 21:28–32

A reading from the holy Gospel according to Matthew.

Jesus said to the chief priests and elders of the people, "What do you think? A man had two sons; he went to the first and said, 'Son, go and work in the vineyard today.' He answered, 'I will not'; but later he changed his mind and went. The father went to the second and said the same; and he answered, 'I go, sir'; but he did not go. Which of the two did the will of his father?" They said, "The first." Jesus said to them, "Truly I tell you, the tax collectors and the prostitutes are going into the kingdom of God ahead of you. For John came to you in the way of righteousness and you did not believe him, but the tax collectors and the prostitutes believed him; and even after you saw it, you did not change your minds and believe him."

The Gospel of the Lord.

◆ All sit and observe silence.

FOR SILENT REFLECTION

Think about this silently in your heart. Have you ever said something that you didn't mean? Did you try to make things right?

CLOSING PRAYER

Let us pray to God for our needs and the needs of others: our family, neighborhood, and the world. For each need we say, "Lord, hear our prayer."

◆ All may add their own prayers here.

Let us pray: **Our Father . . . Amen.**

O Lord,
help us when we are uncertain or afraid to do what is right.
Show us the path that leads us to you.
May we joyfully accept our discipleship.
In Christ's name we pray.

Amen.

✝ All make the Sign of the Cross.

OPENING

Today is the feast day of Sts. Wenceslaus and Lorenzo Ruiz and his companions. King Wenceslaus ruled Bohemia (Czech Republic) in the tenth century. He stood up for Christian values and was martyred for the faith. St. Lorenzo Ruiz was also martyred, along with fifteen others, when they would not give up their Christian faith. He is the first Filipino martyr. This week, we will hear Scripture readings praising God. David invited ministers to sing and to play their instruments in praise of God.

✝ All make the Sign of the Cross.

In the name of the Father, and of the Son, and of the Holy Spirit. Amen.

PSALM

(For a longer psalm, see page xi.)
Psalm 66:1–3a

Make a joyful noise to God, all the earth.

Make a joyful noise to God, all the earth.

Make a joyful noise to God, all the earth;
sing the glory of his name;
give to him glorious praise.
Say to God, "How awesome are your deeds!"

Make a joyful noise to God, all the earth.

READING

1 Chronicles 16:4–5ab, 6–10

A reading from the First Book of Chronicles.

David appointed certain of the Levites [LEE-vīts] as ministers before the ark of the LORD, to invoke, to thank, and to praise the LORD, the God of Israel. Asaph [AY-saf] was the chief. Asaph was to sound the cymbals, and the priests Benaiah [ben-uh-Ī-ah] and Jahaziel [jay-HAZ-ee-el] were to blow trumpets regularly, before the ark of the covenant of God. Then on that day David first appointed the singing of praises to the LORD by Asaph and his kindred. O give thanks to the LORD, call on his name, make known his deeds among the peoples. Sing to him, sing praises to him, tell of all his wonderful works. Glory in his holy name; let the hearts of those who seek the LORD rejoice.

The Word of the Lord.

◆ All observe silence.

FOR SILENT REFLECTION

Think about this silently in your heart. We often sing in Mass to praise God. In what other ways do you praise God?

CLOSING PRAYER

Let us pray to God for our needs and the needs of others: our family, neighborhood, and the world. For each need we say, "Lord, hear our prayer."

◆ All may add their own prayers here.

Let us pray: **Our Father . . . Amen.**

Holy Lord,
we sing your praise and make known your wonderful deeds. Alleluia!
We glorify your holy name. Alleluia!
We pray in Christ's name.

Amen.

✝ All make the Sign of the Cross.

PRAYER FOR
TUESDAY, SEPTEMBER 29, 2020

OPENING

Today is the feast day of the three archangels [AHRK-ayn-jihlz] mentioned in the Bible. In the book of Daniel, St. Michael stands guard over God's people. St. Gabriel is portrayed as a messenger of God. St. Raphael is seen as a companion and healer in the Old Testament. We continue hearing stories about praising God. We are reminded to praise him with our hearts, minds, and voices.

◆ All make the Sign of the Cross.

In the name of the Father, and of the Son, and of the Holy Spirit. Amen.

PSALM

(For a longer psalm, see page xi.)
Psalm 66:1–3a

Make a joyful noise to God, all the earth.

Make a joyful noise to God, all the earth.

Make a joyful noise to God, all the earth;
    sing the glory of his name;
    give to him glorious praise.
Say to God, "How awesome are your deeds!"

Make a joyful noise to God, all the earth.

READING

Sirach 39:13a, 14–16a, 32–33, 35

A reading from the Book of Sirach [SEER-ak].

Listen to me, my faithful children. Send out fragrance like incense, and put forth blossoms like a lily. Scatter the fragrance, and sing a hymn of praise; bless the Lord for all his works. Ascribe majesty to his name and give thanks to him with praise, with songs on your lips, and with harps; this is what you shall say in thanksgiving: "All the works of the Lord are very good." So from the beginning I have been convinced of all this and have thought it out and left it in writing: All the works of the Lord are good, and he will supply every need in its time. So now sing praise with all your heart and voice, and bless the name of the Lord.

The Word of the Lord.

◆ All observe silence.

FOR SILENT REFLECTION

Think about this silently in your heart. The angels remind us that God is with us. How can we use song to thank God for being among us?

CLOSING PRAYER

Let us pray to God for our needs and the needs of others: our family, neighborhood, and the world. For each need we say, "Lord, hear our prayer."

◆ All may add their own prayers here.

Let us pray: **Our Father . . . Amen.**

O wondrous God,
we praise you and thank you
with all our hearts, minds, and voices
for your many blessings and love.
May we trust in you.
May we listen for your voice.
May we know you are near.
We ask this through Christ our Lord.

Amen.

✛ All make the Sign of the Cross.

OPENING

Today is the feast day of St. Jerome (340–420). Because of his great love and understanding of Scripture, St. Jerome wrote the first translation of the Bible from Hebrew and Greek into Latin. He is the patron saint of librarians. In today's Gospel, you will hear the word *Hosanna*, which is a shout of joy and praise.

✚ All make the Sign of the Cross.

In the name of the Father, and of the Son, and of the Holy Spirit. Amen.

PSALM

(For a longer psalm, see page xi.)
Psalm 66:1–3a

Make a joyful noise to God, all the earth.

Make a joyful noise to God, all the earth.

Make a joyful noise to God, all the earth;
    sing the glory of his name;
    give to him glorious praise.
Say to God, "How awesome are your deeds!"

Make a joyful noise to God, all the earth.

◆ All stand and sing **Alleluia.**

GOSPEL

Matthew 21:12a, 13ab, 14–16

A reading from the holy Gospel according to Matthew.

Then Jesus entered the temple and drove out all who were selling and buying in the temple. He said to them, "It is written, 'My house shall be called a house of prayer.'" The blind and the lame came to him in the temple, and he cured them. But when the chief priests and the scribes saw the amazing things that he did, and heard the children crying out in the temple, "Hosanna to the Son of David," they became angry and said to him, "Do you hear what these are saying?" Jesus said to them, "Yes; have you never read, 'Out of the mouths of infants and nursing babies you have prepared praise for yourself'?"

The Gospel of the Lord.

◆ All sit and observe silence.

FOR SILENT REFLECTION

Think about this silently in your heart. Have you ever shouted with joy for Jesus?

CLOSING PRAYER

Let us pray to God for our needs and the needs of others: our family, neighborhood, and the world. For each need we say, "Lord, hear our prayer."

◆ All may add their own prayers here.

Let us pray: **Our Father . . . Amen.**

Glory to you, O Lord!
We praise you with hearts full of joy!
We love and adore you.
May we sing your praise forever.
May we always be grateful for
your generous love.
In Christ Jesus' name we pray.

Amen.

✚ All make the Sign of the Cross.

OPENING

Today we remember the "Little Flower," St. Thérèse of Lisieux (1873–1897). St. Thérèse was only fifteen when she entered religious life, and she died from illness when she was just twenty-four. St. Thérèse followed what became known as the "Little Way," which is to live her life doing every small and ordinary act for the love of God. In today's reading, St. Paul praises Jesus Christ, who was made in the image of God and through whom all things were made.

✚ All make the Sign of the Cross.

In the name of the Father, and of the Son, and of the Holy Spirit. Amen.

PSALM

(For a longer psalm, see page xi.)
Psalm 66:1–3a

Make a joyful noise to God, all the earth.

Make a joyful noise to God, all the earth.

Make a joyful noise to God, all the earth;
   sing the glory of his name;
   give to him glorious praise.
Say to God, "How awesome are your deeds!"

Make a joyful noise to God, all the earth.

READING

Colossians 1:15–20

A reading from the Letter of Paul to the Colossians.

Christ is the image of the invisible God, the firstborn of all creation; for in him all things in heaven and on earth were created, things visible and invisible, whether thrones or dominions or rulers or powers—all things have been created through him and for him.

He himself is before all things, and in him all things hold together. He is the head of the body, the church; he is the beginning, the firstborn from the dead, so that he might come to have first place in everything. For in him all the fullness of God was pleased to dwell, and through him God was pleased to reconcile to himself all things, whether on earth or in heaven, by making peace through the blood of his cross.

The Word of the Lord.

◆ All observe silence.

FOR SILENT REFLECTION

Think about this silently in your heart. How can we do ordinary, simple things, like washing dishes or feeding a pet, in a way that shows we love God?

CLOSING PRAYER

Let us pray to God for our needs and the needs of others: our family, neighborhood, and the world. For each need we say, "Lord, hear our prayer."

◆ All may add their own prayers here.

Let us pray: **Our Father . . . Amen.**

O loving God our Father,
help us to live and serve
with loving and joyful hearts,
and to follow the "Little Way" of St. Thérèse.
We ask this through Christ our Lord.

Amen.

✚ All make the Sign of the Cross.

OPENING

Today we celebrate the feast of the Guardian Angels. The angels watch over us and guide us. Like all our readings this week, today's is about praising God. The author hears loud voices from heaven singing Hallelujah and praising God. Even those in heaven sing God's praises!

✚ All make the Sign of the Cross.

In the name of the Father, and of the Son, and of the Holy Spirit. Amen.

PSALM

(For a longer psalm, see page xi.)
Psalm 66:1–3a

Make a joyful noise to God, all the earth.

Make a joyful noise to God, all the earth.

Make a joyful noise to God, all the earth;
    sing the glory of his name;
    give to him glorious praise.
Say to God, "How awesome are your deeds!"

Make a joyful noise to God, all the earth.

READING

Revelation 19:1–2a, 3ab, 4–5abc, 6–7a

A reading from the Book of Revelation.

After this I heard what seemed to be the loud voice of a great multitude in heaven, saying, "Hallelujah! Salvation and glory and power to our God, for his judgments are true and just." Once more they said, "Hallelujah!" And the twenty-four elders and the four living creatures fell down and worshiped God who is seated on the throne, saying, "Amen. Hallelujah!" And from the throne came a voice saying, "Praise our God, all you his servants." Then I heard what seemed to be the voice of a great multitude, like the sound of many waters and like the sound of mighty thunderpeals, crying out, "Hallelujah! For the Lord our God the Almighty reigns. Let us rejoice and exult and give him the glory."

The Word of the Lord.

◆ All observe silence.

FOR SILENT REFLECTION

Think about this silently in your heart. *Hallelujah* means "praise God." How can your actions today praise God?

CLOSING PRAYER

Let us pray to God for our needs and the needs of others: our family, neighborhood, and the world. For each need we say, "Lord, hear our prayer."

◆ All may add their own prayers here.

Let us pray: **Our Father . . . Amen.**

Hear our songs of praise, O God Almighty!
We glorify your holy name.
We sing your praises as the heavenly host did.
Our hearts seek you always,
We pray in the name of Jesus Christ,
our Lord.

Amen.

✚ All make the Sign of the Cross.

OPENING

Today's Gospel is a parable of the Kingdom of God. Jesus uses this parable to tell of those who hear the Word of God but reject it. The Kingdom of God will be taken from them and given to those who will share the fruits of the Kingdom.

✦ All make the Sign of the Cross.

In the name of the Father, and of the Son, and of the Holy Spirit. Amen.

PSALM

(For a longer psalm, see page xi.)
Psalm 145:2–3

I will praise your name for ever, LORD.

I will praise your name for ever, LORD.

Every day I will bless you,
  and praise your name forever and ever.
Great is the LORD, and greatly to be praised;
  his greatness is unsearchable.

I will praise your name for ever, LORD.

◆ All stand and sing **Alleluia.**

GOSPEL

Matthew 21:33b, 33f, 34–35, 37–38, 39c–41a, 41c–42a, 43

A reading from the holy Gospel according to Matthew.

Jesus said to his disciples, "There was a landowner who planted a vineyard. Then he leased it to tenants. When the harvest time had come, he sent his slaves to the tenants to collect his produce. But the tenants seized his slaves and beat one, killed another, and stoned another. Finally he sent his son to them, saying, 'They will respect my son.' But when the tenants saw the son, they said to themselves, 'This is the heir; come, let us kill him and get his inheritance.' So they killed him. Now when the owner of the vineyard comes, what will he do to those tenants?" They said to him, "He will lease the vineyard to other tenants who will give him the produce at the harvest time." Jesus said to them, "Therefore I tell you, the kingdom of God will be taken away from you and given to a people that produces the fruits of the kingdom."

The Gospel of the Lord.

◆ All sit and observe silence.

FOR SILENT REFLECTION

Think about this silently in your heart. In the Gospel, who are the tenants? Who is the landowner? What are the fruits of the vineyard?

CLOSING PRAYER

Let us pray to God for our needs and the needs of others: our family, neighborhood, and the world. For each need we say, "Lord, hear our prayer."

◆ All may add their own prayers here.

Let us pray: **Our Father . . . Amen.**

Holy God,
we thank you for Jesus,
who cares for us and teaches us how to live.
May everything we do and say show you
our love.
We pray in the name of your Son,
Jesus Christ, our Lord.

Amen.

✦ All make the Sign of the Cross.

OPENING

Over the next two weeks, we will learn the story of Abraham from the Book of Genesis. His name was Abram before God changed it to Abraham. His wife was called Sarai [SAYR-ī]. In today's reading, we learn of Abram's ancestors as they travel from Ur to the land of Canaan.

✦ All make the Sign of the Cross.

In the name of the Father, and of the Son, and of the Holy Spirit. Amen.

PSALM

(For a longer psalm, see page xi.)
Psalm 145:2–3

I will praise your name for ever, LORD.

I will praise your name for ever, LORD.

Every day I will bless you,
  and praise your name forever and ever.
Great is the LORD, and greatly to be praised;
  his greatness is unsearchable.

I will praise your name for ever, LORD.

READING

Genesis 11:27–29c, 30–32

A reading from the Book of Genesis.

Now these are the descendants of Terah [TER-uh]. Terah was the father of Abram, Nahor [NAY-hohr], and Haran [HAYR-uhn]; and Haran was the father of Lot. Haran died before his father Terah in the land of his birth, in Ur [oor] of the Chaldeans [kal-DEE-uhnz]. Abram and Nahor took wives; the name of Abram's wife was Sarai, and the name of Nahor's wife was Milcah. Now Sarai was barren; she had no child. Terah took his son Abram and his grandson Lot son of Haran, and his daughter-in-law Sarai, his son Abram's wife, and they went out together from Ur of the Chaldeans to go into the land of Canaan [KAY-nin]; but when they came to Haran, they settled there. The days of Terah were two hundred and five years; and Terah died in Haran.

The Word of the Lord.

◆ All observe silence.

FOR SILENT REFLECTION

Think about this silently in your heart. Why do you think the Bible shares information about our ancestors?

CLOSING PRAYER

Let us pray to God for our needs and the needs of others: our family, neighborhood, and the world. For each need we say, "Lord, hear our prayer."

◆ All may add their own prayers here.

Let us pray: **Our Father . . . Amen.**

Dear God,
you have been with us through all of time.
May we forever be grateful for your love
and mercy.
We ask this through Jesus Christ, your Son.

Amen.

✦ All make the Sign of the Cross.

PRAYER FOR
TUESDAY, OCTOBER 6, 2020

OPENING

When he was seventy-five years old, Abram was told by God to go to a new land, Canaan. Abram listened to and obeyed God. Today we remember St. Bruno and Blessed Marie-Rose Durocher, both of whom founded religious orders. At the age of sixteen, Blessed Marie-Rose Durocher felt called by God to become a religious. She listened to God and later founded the Sisters of the Holy Names of Jesus and Mary. The order is devoted to religious education for children.

✚ All make the Sign of the Cross.

In the name of the Father, and of the Son, and of the Holy Spirit. Amen.

PSALM

(For a longer psalm, see page xi.)
Psalm 145:2–3

I will praise your name for ever, LORD.

I will praise your name for ever, LORD.

Every day I will bless you,
  and praise your name forever and ever.
Great is the LORD, and greatly to be praised;
  his greatness is unsearchable.

I will praise your name for ever, LORD..

READING

Genesis 12:1–4a, 4c–5c

A reading from the Book of Genesis.

Now the LORD said to Abram, "Go from your country and your kindred and your father's house to the land that I will show you. I will make of you a great nation, and I will bless you, and make your name great, so that you will be a blessing. I will bless those who bless you, and the one who curses you I will curse; and in you all the families of the earth shall be blessed." So Abram went, as the LORD had told him. Abram was seventy-five years old when he departed from Haran. Abram took his wife Sarai and his brother's son Lot, and all the possessions that they had gathered, and the persons whom they had acquired in Haran; and they set forth to go to the land of Canaan.

The Word of the Lord.

◆ All observe silence.

FOR SILENT REFLECTION

Think about this silently in your heart. Abram had great faith in God. How can we also put our trust in God so completely?

CLOSING PRAYER

Let us pray to God for our needs and the needs of others: our family, neighborhood, and the world. For each need we say, "Lord, hear our prayer."

◆ All may add their own prayers here.

Let us pray: **Our Father . . . Amen.**

Dear God,
may we be as faithful to you as Abram,
trust in your word and love,
and go wherever you send us.
May we be open to your call to service,
as your servant Blessed Marie-Rose Durocher.
Through Christ our Lord.

Amen.

✚ All make the Sign of the Cross.

OPENING

Abram and his nephew Lot continued their journey. Lot then traveled east, while the Lord gave Abram many lands and promised that he would have many descendants. Today we celebrate the feast of Our Lady of the Rosary. Praying the Rosary helps us to reflect on the mysteries of our salvation.

✦ All make the Sign of the Cross.

In the name of the Father, and of the Son, and of the Holy Spirit. Amen.

PSALM

(For a longer psalm, see page xi.)
Psalm 145:2–3

I will praise your name for ever, LORD.

I will praise your name for ever, LORD.

Every day I will bless you,
   and praise your name forever and ever.
Great is the LORD, and greatly to be praised;
   his greatness is unsearchable.

I will praise your name for ever, LORD.

READING

Genesis 13:5–6a, 11, 14–16, 18bd

A reading from the Book of Genesis.

Now Lot, who went with Abram, also had flocks and herds and tents, so that the land could not support both of them living together. So Lot chose for himself all the plain of the Jordan, and Lot journeyed eastward; thus they separated from each other.
The LORD said to Abram, after Lot had separated from him, "Raise your eyes now, and look from the place where you are, northward and southward and eastward and westward; for all the land that you see I will give to you and to your offspring forever. I will make your offspring like the dust of the earth; so that if one can count the dust of the earth, your offspring also can be counted." So Abram settled by the oaks of Mamre [MAM-ree], and there he built an altar to the LORD.

The Word of the Lord.

◆ All observe silence.

FOR SILENT REFLECTION

Think about this silently in your heart. Abram made an altar for God in his new land. Is there a space in your life that you devote to God?

CLOSING PRAYER

Let us pray to God for our needs and the needs of others: our family, neighborhood, and the world. For each need we say, "Lord, hear our prayer."

◆ All may add their own prayers here.

Let us pray: **Our Father . . . Amen.**

Lord God,
you have kept your promise to be faithful to your people.
May we be faithful to you.
Into your hands we entrust ourselves.
We pray in the name of Jesus Christ our Lord.

Amen.

✦ All make the Sign of the Cross.

PRAYER SERVICE
MEMORIAL OF OUR LADY OF THE ROSARY

Prepare eight leaders for this service. The third and fourth leaders will need Bibles for the Scripture passages and may need help practicing the readings. You may wish to begin by singing "The Servant Song" and end with "We Have Been Told." If the group will sing, prepare a song leader.

FIRST LEADER:

✠ All make the Sign of the Cross.

May the grace and peace of our Lord Jesus Christ be with us, now and forever.

Amen.

SECOND LEADER:

Today we celebrate Mary,
the Mother of our Lord Jesus,
whose life of holiness always pointed
toward Christ our Savior.
And today we honor her with this feast
in thanksgiving for the Rosary
that highlights the mysteries of
the life and Death of our Messiah.
May we say yes to God
as she did throughout her life.
We ask this through Christ our Lord.

Amen.

◆ All stand and sing Alleluia.

THIRD LEADER: Luke 1:39–45

A reading from the holy Gospel according to Luke.

◆ Read the passage from a Bible.

The Gospel of the Lord.

Response: **Praise to you, Lord Jesus Christ.**

CHILDREN'S DAILY PRAYER 2020–2021, © 2020 Archdiocese of Chicago: Liturgy Training Publications. All rights reserved. Orders: 800-933-1800 or www.LTP.org.

FOURTH LEADER: Luke 1:46–56

A reading from the holy Gospel according to Luke.

◆ Read the passage from a Bible.

The Gospel of the Lord.

Response: Praise to you, Lord Jesus Christ.

◆ All sit and observe silence.

FIFTH LEADER:

Lord Jesus,
your Mother's life
was centered around you.
Through the gift of the Rosary,
we can reflect on the key events
in your life filled with
joy, sorrow, and glory.
Guide us toward living as fully
as Mary did as we meditate on
your mysteries.
In your name we pray.

Amen.

SIXTH LEADER:

Together let us pray one decade of
the Rosary in honor of this
feast of our Mother Mary:

Hail Mary, full of grace
the Lord is with you,
blessed are you among women
and blessed is the fruit of your womb, Jesus.
Holy Mary, Mother of God,
pray for us sinners,
now and at the hour of our death.

Amen.

Glory be to the Father,
and to the Son,
and to the Holy Spirit.
As it was in the beginning,
is now and ever shall be
world without end.

Amen.

SEVENTH LEADER:

Loving Jesus,
fill our hearts with the same
loving response as Mary had
when the angel Gabriel asked her
to be the Mother of our Lord.
May we be mindful of how you
also remained faithful to God's will
through the tragedies and joys
of your life.
Help us to be vessels of your grace.
In your name we pray.

Amen.

EIGHTH LEADER:

May the love of God,

✟ All make the Sign of the Cross.

Father, Son, and Holy Spirit,
keep us connected with the help of
our Mother Mary,
now and forever.

Amen.

OPENING

Abram rescues his nephew Lot from another tribe. In Abram's time, those who had defeated a tribe or warring clan were entitled to take all of their possessions. But Abram would not take any of the spoils of the war because he had vowed to God that he would not.

✝ All make the Sign of the Cross.

In the name of the Father, and of the Son, and of the Holy Spirit. Amen.

PSALM
(For a longer psalm, see page xi.)
Psalm 145:2–3

I will praise your name for ever, LORD.

I will praise your name for ever, LORD.

Every day I will bless you,
and praise your name forever and ever.
Great is the LORD, and greatly to be praised;
his greatness is unsearchable.

I will praise your name for ever, LORD.

READING
Genesis 14:14a, 14d, 16b–c, 17ac, 18–19a, 21–23a, 24ab

A reading from the Book of Genesis.

When Abram heard that his nephew Lot had been taken captive, he led forth his trained men, and went in pursuit. He brought back his nephew Lot with his goods, and the women and the people.
After his return the kings of Sodom and Salem went out to meet him. And King Melchizedek [mehl-KEEZ-uh-dehk] of Salem brought out bread and wine; he was priest of God Most High. He blessed Abram. Then the king of Sodom said to Abram, "Give me the people, but take the goods for yourself." But Abram said to the king of Sodom, "I have sworn to the LORD, God Most High, maker of heaven and earth, that I would not take a thread or a sandal-thong or anything that is yours. I will take nothing but what the young men have eaten, and the share of the men who went with me."

The Word of the Lord.

◆ All observe silence.

FOR SILENT REFLECTION

Think about this silently in your heart. Has there ever been a promise you made that was hard to keep?

CLOSING PRAYER

Let us pray to God for our needs and the needs of others: our family, neighborhood, and the world. For each need we say, "Lord, hear our prayer."

◆ All may add their own prayers here.

Let us pray: **Our Father . . . Amen.**

Lord God Most High,
thank you for keeping your promise to
your people.
May we follow the example of our
father Abram
to trust in you always
and to be faithful to the promises we make.
We ask this through Christ our Lord.

Amen.

✝ All make the Sign of the Cross.

OPENING

Abram had listened to and followed God. Because of Abram's great faith, God made a covenant with him. A covenant is a promise, or agreement. God changed his name from *Abram*, which means "noble father," to *Abraham*, or "father of many." Today is the feast day of Sts. Denis (the patron saint of France) and John Leonardi, who spent his life in ministry to the ill and imprisoned.

✦ All make the Sign of the Cross.

In the name of the Father, and of the Son, and of the Holy Spirit. Amen.

PSALM

(For a longer psalm, see page xi.)
Psalm 145:2–3

I will praise your name for ever, LORD.

I will praise your name for ever, LORD.

Every day I will bless you,
and praise your name forever and ever.
Great is the LORD, and greatly to be praised;
his greatness is unsearchable.

I will praise your name for ever, LORD.

READING

Genesis 17:1–5a, 6–7

A reading from the Book of Genesis.

When Abram was ninety-nine years old, the LORD appeared to Abram, and said to him, "I am God Almighty; walk before me, and be blameless. And I will make my covenant between me and you, and will make you exceedingly numerous." Then Abram fell on his face; and God said to him, "As for me, this is my covenant with you: You shall be the ancestor of a multitude of nations. No longer shall your name be Abram, but your name shall be Abraham. I will make you exceedingly fruitful; and I will make nations of you, and kings shall come from you. I will establish my covenant between me and you, and your offspring after you throughout their generations, for an everlasting covenant, to be God to you and to your offspring after you."

The Word of the Lord.

◆ All observe silence.

FOR SILENT REFLECTION

Think about this silently in your heart. What promise can you make with God today?

CLOSING PRAYER

Let us pray to God for our needs and the needs of others: our family, neighborhood, and the world. For each need we say, "Lord, hear our prayer."

◆ All may add their own prayers here.

Let us pray: **Our Father . . . Amen.**

God of our fathers,
help us to open our hearts to you
and faithfully follow you as Abraham did.
Through Christ our Lord.

Amen.

✦ All make the Sign of the Cross.

PRAYER FOR THE WEEK
WITH A READING FROM THE GOSPEL FOR **SUNDAY, OCTOBER 11, 2020**

OPENING

Today we hear a parable from Jesus about a king who hosted a wedding banquet for his son. The people he invited to the banquet did not come. Instead, the king invites all who want to come to the feast. Think about what Jesus might be teaching us about the Kingdom of God.

✦ All make the Sign of the Cross.

In the name of the Father, and of the Son, and of the Holy Spirit. Amen.

PSALM

(For a longer psalm, see page xi.)
Psalm 145:2–3

I will praise your name for ever, LORD.

I will praise your name for ever, LORD.

Every day I will bless you,
   and praise your name forever and ever.
Great is the LORD, and greatly to be praised;
   his greatness is unsearchable.

I will praise your name for ever, LORD.

◆ All stand and sing **Alleluia.**

GOSPEL

Matthew 22:1–4c, 4e–5, 8–10

A reading from the holy Gospel according to Matthew.

Once more Jesus spoke to them in parables, saying: "The kingdom of heaven may be compared to a king who gave a wedding banquet for his son. He sent his slaves to call those who had been invited to the wedding banquet, but they would not come. Again he sent other slaves, saying, 'Tell those who have been invited: Look, I have prepared my dinner and everything is ready; come to the wedding banquet.' But they made light of it and went away, one to his farm, another to his business. Then the kings said to his slaves, 'The wedding is ready, but those invited were not worthy. Go therefore into the main streets, and invite everyone you find to the wedding banquet.' Those slaves went out into the streets and gathered all whom they found, both good and bad; so the wedding hall was filled with guests."

The Gospel of the Lord.

◆ All sit and observe silence.

FOR SILENT REFLECTION

Think about this silently in your heart. What does this parable tell us about the Kingdom of God? Who is invited into the Kingdom?

CLOSING PRAYER

Let us pray to God for our needs and the needs of others: our family, neighborhood, and the world. For each need we say, "Lord, hear our prayer."

◆ All may add their own prayers here.

Let us pray: **Our Father . . . Amen.**

Loving God,
we praise and thank you for your great glory.
Thank you for inviting us into the Kingdom.
Be with us as we celebrate your holy name,
and open our hearts to your Word.
Through Christ our Lord.

Amen.

✦ All make the Sign of the Cross.

OPENING

In the United States, we observe Columbus Day. We continue the story of Abraham in today's reading. Abraham invites three men into his tent, and he goes to great lengths to welcome them. They surprise Abraham and his wife Sarah with some unexpected news.

✛ All make the Sign of the Cross.

In the name of the Father, and of the Son, and of the Holy Spirit. Amen.

PSALM
(For a longer psalm, see page xi.)
Psalm 145:2–3

I will praise your name for ever, LORD.

I will praise your name for ever, LORD.

Every day I will bless you,
 and praise your name forever and ever.
Great is the LORD, and greatly to be praised;
 his greatness is unsearchable.

I will praise your name for ever, LORD.

READING
Genesis 18:1ac, 2a, 4, 6–8b, 9, 10ab, 11a

A reading from the Book of Genesis.

The LORD appeared to Abraham, as he sat at the entrance of his tent. Abraham looked up and saw three men standing near him. "Let a little water be brought, and wash your feet, and rest yourselves under the tree." And Abraham hastened into the tent to Sarah, and said, "Make ready quickly three measures of choice flour, knead it, and make cakes." Abraham ran to the herd, and took a calf, tender and good, and gave it to the servant, who hastened to prepare it. Then he took curds and milk and the calf that he had prepared, and set it before them. They said to him, "Where is your wife Sarah?" And he said, "There, in the tent." Then one said, "I will surely return to you in due season, and your wife Sarah shall have a son." Now Abraham and Sarah were old, advanced in age.

The Word of the Lord.

◆ All observe silence.

FOR SILENT REFLECTION

Think about this silently in your heart. How can we welcome others, as Abraham welcomed his three visitors?

CLOSING PRAYER

Let us pray to God for our needs and the needs of others: our family, neighborhood, and the world. For each need we say, "Lord, hear our prayer."

◆ All may add their own prayers here.

Let us pray: **Our Father . . . Amen.**

Dear Lord,
thank you for your love and devotion.
Help us to be kind and welcoming to all those we meet,
especially to those who are lost, afraid, or lonely.
In Christ Jesus' name we pray.

Amen.

✛ All make the Sign of the Cross.

PRAYER FOR
TUESDAY, OCTOBER 13, 2020

OPENING

In today's reading, Abraham has a conversation with God. He tries to understand God's love and faithfulness to the people by questioning God as to how far he would go to save a few of the faithful.

✚ All make the Sign of the Cross.

In the name of the Father, and of the Son, and of the Holy Spirit. Amen.

PSALM

(For a longer psalm, see page xi.)
Psalm 145:2–3

I will praise your name for ever, Lord.

I will praise your name for ever, Lord.

Every day I will bless you,
   and praise your name forever and ever.
Great is the Lord, and greatly to be praised;
   his greatness is unsearchable.

I will praise your name for ever, Lord.

READING

Genesis 18:20, 23–24, 26, 27a, 29b–30, 32abc

A reading from the Book of Genesis.

The Lord said, "How great is the outcry against Sodom and Gomorrah and how very grave their sin!" Then Abraham came near and said, "Will you indeed sweep away the righteous with the wicked? Suppose there are fifty righteous within the city; will you not forgive it for the fifty righteous who are in it?" And the Lord said, "If I find at Sodom fifty righteous in the city, I will forgive the whole place for their sake." Abraham answered, "Suppose forty righteous are found there?" The Lord answered, "For the sake of forty I will not do it." Then Abraham said, "Oh do

not let the Lord be angry if I speak. Suppose thirty are found there?" The Lord answered, "I will not do it, if I find thirty there." Then Abraham said, "Suppose ten are found there?" The Lord answered, "For the sake of ten I will not destroy it."

The Word of the Lord.

◆ All observe silence.

FOR SILENT REFLECTION

Think about this silently in your heart. Have you ever had a conversation with God? Did you listen closely for God's answer?

CLOSING PRAYER

Let us pray to God for our needs and the needs of others: our family, neighborhood, and the world. For each need we say, "Lord, hear our prayer."

◆ All may add their own prayers here.

Let us pray: **Our Father . . . Amen.**

Loving and merciful God,
we praise you for your goodness.
Help us to forgive those who have wronged us
and to ask for forgiveness
when we have hurt someone.
We ask this in Christ Jesus' name.

Amen.

✚ All make the Sign of the Cross.

OPENING

Today, God puts Abraham to a difficult test. He tells Abraham to go to the mountains and offer his only and beloved son Isaac as a burnt offering. It is a hard to understand why God would ask this of Abraham, but we do know that Abraham trusts God completely and prepares to do what he is asked.

✚ All make the Sign of the Cross.

In the name of the Father, and of the Son, and of the Holy Spirit. Amen.

PSALM

(For a longer psalm, see page xi.)
Psalm 145:2–3

I will praise your name for ever, LORD.

I will praise your name for ever, LORD.

Every day I will bless you,
    and praise your name forever and ever.
Great is the LORD, and greatly to be praised;
    his greatness is unsearchable.

I will praise your name for ever, LORD.

READING

Genesis 22:1a, 2–3, 5, 7a, 7c–8a

A reading from the Book of Genesis.

God tested Abraham. He said, "Take your son, your only son Isaac, whom you love, and go to the land of Moriah, and offer him there as a burnt offering on one of the mountains that I shall show you." So Abraham rose early in the morning, saddled his donkey, and took two of his young men with him, and his son Isaac; he cut the wood for the burnt offering, and set out and went to the place in the distance that God had shown him. Then Abraham said to his young men, "Stay here with the donkey; the boy and I will go over there; we will worship, and then we will come back to you." Isaac said to his father Abraham, "Father! The fire and the wood are here, but where is the lamb for a burnt offering?" Abraham said, "God himself will provide the lamb for a burnt offering, my son."

The Word of the Lord.

◆ All observe silence.

FOR SILENT REFLECTION

Think about this silently in your heart. What do you think Abraham meant when he said, "God himself will provide the lamb"?

CLOSING PRAYER

Let us pray to God for our needs and the needs of others: our family, neighborhood, and the world. For each need we say, "Lord, hear our prayer."

◆ All may add their own prayers here.

Let us pray: **Our Father . . . Amen.**

O God,
help us to trust you
and have faith in you,
even when it is difficult
or when we do not understand.
Be with us, and lead us to
wherever you may be.
We ask this through Christ our Lord.

Amen.

✚ All make the Sign of the Cross.

OPENING

Today we celebrate St. Teresa of Avila, one of the Doctors of the Church. She lived a prayerful and disciplined life and dedicated herself completely to God. Abraham also followed God's instructions and readied his son to be offered as a sacrifice. We hear how much courage and complete trust Abraham had in God's plan.

✝ All make the Sign of the Cross.

In the name of the Father, and of the Son, and of the Holy Spirit. Amen.

PSALM
(For a longer psalm, see page xi.)
Psalm 145:2–3

I will praise your name for ever, LORD.

I will praise your name for ever, LORD.

Every day I will bless you,
   and praise your name forever and ever.
Great is the LORD, and greatly to be praised;
   his greatness is unsearchable.

I will praise your name for ever, LORD.

READING
Genesis 22:9b, 11a, 12–13, 15, 16a, 17a

A reading from the Book of Genesis.

Abraham built an altar and laid the wood. He bound his son Isaac, and laid him on the altar, on top of the wood. But the angel of the LORD called to him from heaven, and said, "Abraham, do not lay your hand on the boy or do anything to him; for now I know that you fear God, since you have not withheld your son, your only son, from me." And Abraham looked up and saw a ram, caught in a thicket by its horns. Abraham went and took the ram and offered it up as a burnt offering instead of his son. The angel of the LORD called to Abraham a second time from heaven, and said, "I will indeed bless you, and I will make your offspring as numerous as the stars of heaven and as the sand on the seashore."

The Word of the Lord.

◆ All observe silence.

FOR SILENT REFLECTION

Think about this silently in your heart. It can be difficult to follow and trust in God completely. Reflect on how Abraham did.

CLOSING PRAYER

Let us pray to God for our needs and the needs of others: our family, neighborhood, and the world. For each need we say, "Lord, hear our prayer."

◆ All may add their own prayers here.

Let us pray: **Our Father . . . Amen.**

O Lord,
in times when we are afraid,
or uncertain,
help us to keep our faith in you.
Be with us always,
that we might know your presence
everywhere we go.
We ask this through your Son, Jesus Christ our Lord.

Amen.

✝ All make the Sign of the Cross.

OPENING

Today we celebrate two feast days. St. Hedwig (1174–1243) was a queen of Silesia, which is now part of Poland. She was beloved for her kindness to the poor, the homeless, and the sick and dying. St. Margaret Mary Alacoque [al-uh-KOHK] (1647–1690) was devoted to the Sacred Heart of Jesus. In today's reading, we hear of Abraham's death after a long life of faithfulness and trust in God.

✦ All make the Sign of the Cross.

In the name of the Father, and of the Son, and of the Holy Spirit. Amen.

PSALM

(For a longer psalm, see page xi.)
Psalm 145:2–3

I will praise your name for ever, LORD.

I will praise your name for ever, LORD.

Every day I will bless you,
and praise your name forever and ever.
Great is the LORD, and greatly to be praised;
his greatness is unsearchable.

I will praise your name for ever, LORD.

READING

Genesis 25:7–11

A reading from the Book of Genesis.

This is the length of Abraham's life, one hundred and seventy-five years. Abraham breathed his last and died in a good old age, an old man and full of years, and was gathered to his people. His sons Isaac and Ishmael [ISH-may-uhl] buried him in the cave of Machpelah [mak-PEE-luh], in the field of Ephron son of Zohar the Hittite [HIT-tīt], east of Mamre [MAM-ree], the field that Abraham purchased from the Hittites. There Abraham was buried, with his wife Sarah. After the death of Abraham God blessed his son Isaac. And Isaac settled at Beer-lahai-roi.

The Word of the Lord.

◆ All observe silence.

FOR SILENT REFLECTION

Think about this silently in your heart. Abraham was an important person in the history of our faith. What qualities do you wish to be remembered for?

CLOSING PRAYER

Let us pray to God for our needs and the needs of others: our family, neighborhood, and the world. For each need we say, "Lord, hear our prayer."

◆ All may add their own prayers here.

Let us pray: **Our Father . . . Amen.**

Dear God,
we thank you for your servant Abraham.
Help us to love and trust in you,
just as Abraham did.
We thank you for the example of the saints,
especially St. Hedwig and St. Margaret Mary Alacoque [al-uh-KOHK],
whose feast days we celebrate today.
Help us to live our lives
so that we may also be remembered as your faithful followers.
We ask this in Christ's name.

Amen.

✦ All make the Sign of the Cross.

PRAYER FOR THE WEEK

OPENING

In today's Gospel, the religious leaders are trying to trick Jesus. They asked him whether it was lawful to pay taxes. Jesus' followers do not like the Roman taxes and laws, but the Romans would not stand for Jesus rebelling against the taxes. Jesus is mindful of how they were intending to trap him.

✦ All make the Sign of the Cross.

In the name of the Father, and of the Son, and of the Holy Spirit. Amen.

PSALM

(For a longer psalm, see page xi.)
Psalm 145:2–3

I will praise your name for ever, LORD.

I will praise your name for ever, LORD.

Every day I will bless you,
and praise your name forever and ever.
Great is the LORD, and greatly to be praised;
his greatness is unsearchable.

I will praise your name for ever, LORD.

◆ All stand and sing **Alleluia.**

GOSPEL

Matthew 22:15–16a, 16c–21

A reading from the holy Gospel according to Matthew.

The Pharisees [FAYR-uh-seez] went and plotted to entrap Jesus in what he said. So they sent their disciples to him, saying, "Teacher, we know that you are sincere, and teach the way of God in accordance with truth, and show deference to no one; for you do not regard people with partiality. Tell us, then, what you think. Is it lawful to pay taxes to the emperor, or not?" But Jesus, aware of their malice, said, "Why are you putting me to the test, you hypocrites? Show me the coin used for the tax." And they brought him a denarius [dih-NAHR-ee-uhs]. Then he said to them, "Whose head is this, and whose title?" They answered, "The emperor's." Then he said to them, "Give therefore to the emperor the things that are the emperor's, and to God the things that are God's."

The Gospel of the Lord.

◆ All sit and observe silence.

FOR SILENT REFLECTION

Think about this silently in your heart. How can we give to God what is God's? What do we give God?

CLOSING PRAYER

Let us pray to God for our needs and the needs of others: our family, neighborhood, and the world. For each need we say, "Lord, hear our prayer."

◆ All may add their own prayers here.

Let us pray: **Our Father . . . Amen.**

Holy Spirit,
be with us in our struggles,
and inspire us to make thoughtful decisions.
Fill us with your grace.
Through Christ our Lord.

Amen.

✦ All make the Sign of the Cross.

OPENING

Each reading this week speaks of a covenant between God and humankind. A covenant is an agreement or promise entered into freely by two parties. Today we remember Sts. Isaac Jogues [Ī-zik johgz] and John de Brébeuf [BRAY-buhf] and their companions. St. Isaac Jogues was a Jesuit missionary who left France for America to evangelize to the native people. He was martyred in 1646. St. John de Brébeuf was also a French Jesuit who was a missionary in Canada. He was able to convert thousands of native people to Christianity before he was martyred in 1649.

✦ All make the Sign of the Cross.

In the name of the Father, and of the Son, and of the Holy Spirit. Amen.

PSALM
(For a longer psalm, see page xi.)
Psalm 145:2–3

I will praise your name for ever, LORD.

I will praise your name for ever, LORD.

Every day I will bless you,
    and praise your name forever and ever.
Great is the LORD, and greatly to be praised;
    his greatness is unsearchable.

I will praise your name for ever, LORD.

READING
Genesis 26:2, 3b–c, 3e–5, 25

A reading from the Book of Genesis.

The LORD appeared to Isaac and said, "Do not go down to Egypt; settle in the land that I shall show you. I will be with you, and will bless you. I will fulfill the oath that I swore to your father Abraham. I will make your offspring as numerous as the stars of heaven, and will give to your offspring all these lands; and all the nations of the earth shall gain blessing for themselves through your offspring, because Abraham obeyed my voice and kept my charge, my commandments, my statutes, and my laws." So Isaac built an altar there, called on the name of the LORD, and pitched his tent there. And there Isaac's servants dug a well.

The Word of the Lord.

◆ All observe silence.

FOR SILENT REFLECTION

Think about this silently in your heart. Abraham and Isaac both made altars for God. Can you make a space for God in your home or room?

CLOSING PRAYER

Let us pray to God for our needs and the needs of others: our family, neighborhood, and the world. For each need we say, "Lord, hear our prayer."

◆ All may add their own prayers here.

Let us pray: **Our Father . . . Amen.**

Most loving God,
speak to us as a friend.
May we listen, speak, and act
in ways that will keep our friendship with you strong.
We ask this in the name of Jesus Christ our Lord.

Amen.

✦ All make the Sign of the Cross.

OPENING

St. Paul of the Cross, whose feast day we celebrate today, was a popular preacher. He founded the Congregation of the Passion, also known as the Passionists. In today's reading, God appears to Jacob, Isaac's son. As he did with Abraham, God makes a covenant with Jacob and gives him a new name, Israel. The name means "God prevails" (or "triumphs"). Jacob builds an altar to God where God spoke to him, just as Abraham and Isaac did before him.

◆ All make the Sign of the Cross.

In the name of the Father, and of the Son, and of the Holy Spirit. Amen.

PSALM

(For a longer psalm, see page xi.)
Psalm 145:2–3

I will praise your name for ever, LORD.

I will praise your name for ever, LORD.

Every day I will bless you,
   and praise your name forever and ever.
Great is the LORD, and greatly to be praised;
   his greatness is unsearchable.

I will praise your name for ever, LORD.

READING

Genesis 35:9–12, 14–15

A reading from the Book of Genesis.

God appeared to Jacob again when he came from Paddan-aram, and he blessed him. God said to him, "Your name is Jacob; no longer shall you be called Jacob, but Israel shall be your name." So he was called Israel. God said to him, "I am God Almighty: be fruitful and multiply; a nation and a company of nations shall come from you, and kings shall spring from you. The land that I gave to Abraham and Isaac I will give to you, and I will give the land to your offspring after you." Jacob set up a pillar in the place where God had spoken with him, a pillar of stone; and he poured out a drink offering on it, and poured oil on it. So Jacob called the place where God had spoken with him Bethel.

The Word of the Lord.

◆ All observe silence.

FOR SILENT REFLECTION

Think about this silently in your heart. Why do you think God gave Abram and Jacob new names?

CLOSING PRAYER

Let us pray to God for our needs and the needs of others: our family, neighborhood, and the world. For each need we say, "Lord, hear our prayer."

◆ All may add their own prayers here.

Let us pray: **Our Father . . . Amen.**

Dearest Jesus,
we know how much you love us
because by your passion and death
we have been saved.
May we always make room in our hearts
for you.
Who live and reign with God the Father, in the unity of the Holy Spirit, one God, for ever and ever.

Amen.

✦ All make the Sign of the Cross.

OPENING

We move from Genesis to the second book of the Bible, Exodus. Around five hundred years after Abraham, God formed a new covenant with the prophet Moses. Moses led the Hebrew people out of slavery in Egypt and into the Promised Land.

✚ All make the Sign of the Cross.

In the name of the Father, and of the Son, and of the Holy Spirit. Amen.

PSALM

(For a longer psalm, see page xi.)
Psalm 145:2–3

I will praise your name for ever, LORD.

I will praise your name for ever, LORD.

Every day I will bless you,
 and praise your name forever and ever.
Great is the LORD, and greatly to be praised;
 his greatness is unsearchable.

I will praise your name for ever, LORD.

READING

Exodus 19:1–2, 3c–5a, 7–8

A reading from the Book of Exodus.

On the third new moon after the Israelites had gone out of the land of Egypt, on that very day, they came into the wilderness of Sinai. They had journeyed from Rephidim [REF-ih-dim], entered the wilderness of Sinai [SĪ-nī], and camped in the wilderness; Israel camped there in front of the mountain. The LORD called to Moses from the mountain, saying, "Thus you shall say to the house of Jacob, and tell the Israelites: You have seen what I did to the Egyptians, and how I bore you on eagles' wings and brought you to myself. Now therefore, if you obey my voice and keep my covenant, you shall be my treasured possession out of all the peoples." So Moses came, summoned the elders of the people, and set before them all these words that the LORD had commanded him. The people all answered as one: "Everything that the LORD has spoken we will do." Moses reported the words of the people to the LORD.

The Word of the Lord.

◆ All observe silence.

FOR SILENT REFLECTION

Think about this silently in your heart. The Israelites spoke in unison, "Everything the Lord has spoken we will do." Repeat this to yourself. Is that an easy promise to make to God?

CLOSING PRAYER

Let us pray to God for our needs and the needs of others: our family, neighborhood, and the world. For each need we say, "Lord, hear our prayer."

◆ All may add their own prayers here.

Let us pray: **Our Father . . . Amen.**

God our Father,
thank you for your faithfulness to your people throughout the ages.
We promise to love, follow, and trust in you.
Help us to be examples of your light to all we meet.
Through Christ our Lord.

Amen.

✚ All make the Sign of the Cross.

OPENING

Today is the feast day of St. John Paul II (1920–2005). He was pope from 1978 to 2005. He helped to improve the Catholic Church's relationship with other religions and was the patron of World Youth Day, which became a yearly event hosted in different countries. We hear today from Jeremiah, a prophet who lived many years after Moses. He preached at a time when the Israelites had stopped worshiping God. The word *iniquity* means "sinful behavior."

✛ All make the Sign of the Cross.

In the name of the Father, and of the Son, and of the Holy Spirit. Amen.

PSALM

(For a longer psalm, see page xi.)
Psalm 145:2–3

I will praise your name for ever, LORD.

I will praise your name for ever, LORD.

Every day I will bless you,
    and praise your name forever and ever.
Great is the LORD, and greatly to be praised;
    his greatness is unsearchable.

I will praise your name for ever, LORD.

READING

Jeremiah 31:31, 33b–34

A reading from the Book of the prophet Jeremiah.

The days are surely coming, says the LORD, when I will make a new covenant with the house of Israel and the house of Judah. I will put my law within them, and I will write it on their hearts; and I will be their God, and they shall be my people. No longer shall they teach one another, or say to each other, "Know the LORD," for they shall all know me, from the least of them to the greatest, says the LORD; for I will forgive their iniquity, and remember their sin no more.

The Word of the Lord.

◆ All observe silence.

FOR SILENT REFLECTION

Think about this silently in your heart. How can we turn back to God when we have sinned?

CLOSING PRAYER

Let us pray to God for our needs and the needs of others: our family, neighborhood, and the world. For each need we say, "Lord, hear our prayer."

◆ All may add their own prayers here.

Let us pray: **Our Father . . . Amen.**

Deepen our faith in you, O God.
We sometimes commit sin and
turn away from you.
Help us to see our faults and where we did
wrong and turn back to you.
Thank you for loving and forgiving us always.
We pray in the name of Christ our Lord.

Amen.

✛ All make the Sign of the Cross.

OPENING

Today we hear about a new covenant, this time in the New Testament. In the Last Supper, Jesus formed a new covenant with us when he broke the bread and shared the wine and offered them as his Body and Blood. We are part of the covenant with him every time we share in the Eucharist. Today we also remember St. John of Capistrano, who is the patron saint of judges.

◆ All make the Sign of the Cross.

In the name of the Father, and of the Son, and of the Holy Spirit. Amen.

PSALM

(For a longer psalm, see page xi.)
Psalm 145:2–3

I will praise your name for ever, LORD.

I will praise your name for ever, LORD.

Every day I will bless you,
    and praise your name forever and ever.
Great is the LORD, and greatly to be praised;
    his greatness is unsearchable.

I will praise your name for ever, LORD.

◆ All stand and sing **Alleluia.**

GOSPEL

Matthew 26:17a, 19–20, 26–29

A reading from the holy Gospel according to Matthew.

On the first day of Unleavened Bread the disciples did as Jesus had directed them, and they prepared the Passover meal. When it was evening, Jesus took his place with the twelve; and while they were eating, Jesus took a loaf of bread, and after blessing it he broke it, gave it to the disciples, and said, "Take, eat; this is my body." Then he took a cup, and after giving thanks he gave it to them, saying, "Drink from it, all of you; for this is my blood of the covenant, which is poured out for many for the forgiveness of sins. I tell you, I will never again drink of this fruit of the vine until that day when I drink it new with you in my Father's kingdom."

The Gospel of the Lord.

◆ All sit and observe silence.

FOR SILENT REFLECTION

Think about this silently in your heart. We are part of a covenant with God through Jesus Christ. How can we participate in that covenant every day?

CLOSING PRAYER

Let us pray to God for our needs and the needs of others: our family, neighborhood, and the world. For each need we say, "Lord, hear our prayer."

◆ All may add their own prayers here.

Let us pray: **Our Father . . . Amen.**

Loving God, our Father,
we thank you for your son Jesus
and for your many gifts.
Help us to fulfill our promise to you by
living our lives in the ways Jesus taught us.
We ask this in the name of Jesus Christ
our Lord.

Amen.

◆ All make the Sign of the Cross.

OPENING

In today's Gospel, Jesus tells us what the two greatest commandments are. They are so important that the ministry of Jesus can be summarized with these commandments: love God and love your neighbor.

✦ All make the Sign of the Cross.

In the name of the Father, and of the Son, and of the Holy Spirit. Amen.

PSALM

(For a longer psalm, see page xi.)
Psalm 145:2–3

I will praise your name for ever, LORD.

I will praise your name for ever, LORD.

Every day I will bless you,
    and praise your name forever and ever.
Great is the LORD, and greatly to be praised;
    his greatness is unsearchable.

I will praise your name for ever, LORD.

◆ All stand and sing **Alleluia.**

GOSPEL

Matthew 22:34–40

A reading from the holy Gospel according to Matthew.

When the Pharisees [FAYR-uh-seez] heard that he had silenced the Sadducees, they gathered together, and one of them, a lawyer, asked him a question to test him. "Teacher, which commandment in the law is the greatest?" He said to him, "'You shall love the Lord your God with all your heart, and with all your soul, and with all your mind.' This is the greatest and first commandment. And a second is like it: 'You shall love your neighbor as yourself.' On these two commandments hang all the law and the prophets."

The Gospel of the Lord.

◆ All sit and observe silence.

FOR SILENT REFLECTION

Think about this silently in your heart. The two greatest commandments are about love. How can we love as Jesus wants us to?

CLOSING PRAYER

Let us pray to God for our needs and the needs of others: our family, neighborhood, and the world. For each need we say, "Lord, hear our prayer."

◆ All may add their own prayers here.

Let us pray: **Our Father . . . Amen.**

Dearest God,
we thank you for your never-ending
and abundant love.
Help us to love you,
and to love others,
as you have loved us.
Through Christ our Lord.

Amen.

✦ All make the Sign of the Cross.

OPENING

This week we hear the story of Joseph, the second-youngest son of Jacob, from Genesis. Joseph was known for his dreams and his interpretation of them. His brothers hated him for his dreams and because their father loved him more.

✚ All make the Sign of the Cross.

In the name of the Father, and of the Son, and of the Holy Spirit. Amen.

PSALM

(For a longer psalm, see page xi.)
Psalm 145:2–3

I will praise your name for ever, LORD.

I will praise your name for ever, LORD.

Every day I will bless you,
and praise your name forever and ever.
Great is the LORD, and greatly to be praised;
his greatness is unsearchable.

I will praise your name for ever, LORD.

READING

Genesis 37:3–4b, 5–8b, 8d

A reading from the Book of Genesis.

Now Jacob loved Joseph more than any other of his children, because he was the son of his old age; and he had made him a long robe with sleeves. But when his brothers saw that their father loved Joseph more than all his brothers, they hated him. Once Joseph had a dream, and when he told it to his brothers, they hated him even more. He said to them, "Listen to this dream that I dreamed. There we were, binding sheaves in the field. Suddenly my sheaf rose and stood upright; then your sheaves gathered around it, and bowed down to my sheaf." His brothers said to him, "Are you indeed to reign over us?" So they hated him even more because of his dreams and his words.

The Word of the Lord.

◆ All observe silence.

FOR SILENT REFLECTION

Think about this silently in your heart. Sometimes when we think someone has more than we do, we are jealous. But jealousy often turns to hatred. How can we remove jealousy from our hearts?

CLOSING PRAYER

Let us pray to God for our needs and the needs of others: our family, neighborhood, and the world. For each need we say, "Lord, hear our prayer."

◆ All may add their own prayers here.

Let us pray: **Our Father . . . Amen.**

Loving God,
you have called us
to love and care for one another.
Help us to listen for your words
and to follow your teachings.
We ask this in Christ's name.
Amen.

✚ All make the Sign of the Cross.

OPENING

Because of their hatred and jealousy, Joseph's brothers conspired to take away Joseph's robe. They threw him into a pit with the intention of killing him. The brothers decided to sell him into slavery to rid themselves of him.

✚ All make the Sign of the Cross.

In the name of the Father, and of the Son, and of the Holy Spirit. Amen.

PSALM

(For a longer psalm, see page xi.)
Psalm 145:2–3

I will praise your name for ever, LORD.

I will praise your name for ever, LORD.

Every day I will bless you,
  and praise your name forever and ever.
Great is the LORD, and greatly to be praised;
  his greatness is unsearchable.

I will praise your name for ever, LORD.

READING

Genesis 37:14a–b, 17e–18a, 19–20, 23b, 24a, 25a–b, 26a–b, 27a, 28b–d

A reading from the Book of Genesis.

Jacob said to Joseph, "Go now, see if it is well with your brothers and with the flock." So Joseph went after his brothers, and found them at Dothan. They saw him from a distance and said to one another, "Here comes this dreamer. Come now, let us kill him and throw him into one of the pits; then we shall say that a wild animal has devoured him, and we shall see what will become of his dreams." They stripped Joseph of his robe, and they took him and threw him into a pit. Then they sat down to eat; and looking up they saw a caravan of Ishmaelites [ISH-may-uh-lītz]. Then Judah said to his brothers, "What profit is it if we kill our brother? Come, let us sell him to the Ishmaelites." They lifted Joseph out of the pit, and sold him to the Ishmaelites for twenty pieces of silver.

The Word of the Lord.

◆ All observe silence.

FOR SILENT REFLECTION

Think about this silently in your heart. How must Joseph's father have felt to lose his son?

CLOSING PRAYER

Let us pray to God for our needs and the needs of others: our family, neighborhood, and the world. For each need we say, "Lord, hear our prayer."

◆ All may add their own prayers here.

Let us pray: **Our Father . . . Amen.**

Dear God,
may we be people who choose what is right
and love and care for one another
rather than hurt and destroy.
Be with us and heal us when our hearts
feel lost, confused, and angry.
We ask this in Christ's name.

Amen.

✚ All make the Sign of the Cross.

OPENING

Today is the feast day of Sts. Simon and Jude Thaddeus, who were part of Jesus' Twelve Apostles. You can ask St. Jude for help in hopeless cases. Today, we hear how God was with Joseph, even after being sold into slavery and then being wronged by his master's wife and thrown into jail. Help the children understand how Joseph resisted temptation.

✚ All make the Sign of the Cross.

In the name of the Father, and of the Son, and of the Holy Spirit. Amen.

PSALM

(For a longer psalm, see page xi.)
Psalm 145:2–3

I will praise your name for ever, LORD.

I will praise your name for ever, LORD.

Every day I will bless you,
    and praise your name forever and ever.
Great is the LORD, and greatly to be praised;
    his greatness is unsearchable.

I will praise your name for ever, LORD.

READING

Genesis 39:1a, 2, 6d–8a, 11–12a, 12c,
16, 17b–18, 19a, 19c, 20b, 21a, c

A reading from the Book of Genesis.

Joseph was taken down to Egypt. The Lord was with him, and he became a successful man; he was in the house of his Egyptian master. Joseph was handsome and good-looking. And after a time his master's wife cast her eyes on Joseph and said, "Lie with me." But Joseph refused. One day, however, when he went into the house to do his work, and while no one else was in the house, she caught hold of his garment. He ran outside. Then she kept his garment by her until his master came home, and she told him, "The Hebrew servant, whom you have brought among us, came in to me to insult me; but as soon as I raised my voice and cried out, he left his garment beside me, and fled outside." When Joseph's master heard the words that his wife spoke, he became enraged and put Joseph into the prison. But the LORD was with Joseph; he gave him favor in sight of the chief jailer.

The Word of the Lord.

◆ All observe silence.

FOR SILENT REFLECTION

Think about this silently in your heart. Have you ever gotten someone into trouble by lying? What should you do?

CLOSING PRAYER

Let us pray to God for our needs and the needs of others: our family, neighborhood, and the world. For each need we say, "Lord, hear our prayer."

◆ All may add their own prayers here.

Let us pray: **Our Father . . . Amen.**

Holy God,
even in our darkest days,
you are always with us.
Help us to feel your presence and strength
when we are alone or afraid.
We pray in the name of Jesus Christ, our Lord.

Amen.

✚ All make the Sign of the Cross.

THURSDAY, OCTOBER 29, 2020

OPENING

In today's reading, the Pharaoh, or king, of Egypt, had a troubling dream that he could not understand. Word had spread about Joseph's abilities to interpret dreams, even though he was still in prison, so the Pharaoh sent for him. Joseph was able to interpret Pharaoh's dream.

✛ All make the Sign of the Cross.

In the name of the Father, and of the Son, and of the Holy Spirit. Amen.

PSALM

(For a longer psalm, see page xi.)
Psalm 145:2–3

I will praise your name for ever, LORD.

I will praise your name for ever, LORD.

Every day I will bless you,
   and praise your name forever and ever.
Great is the LORD, and greatly to be praised;
   his greatness is unsearchable.

I will praise your name for ever, LORD.

READING

Genesis 41:5b–7a, 8, 14a, 15a, 15c, 29a, 30a, 33, 34b, 36a

A reading from the Book of Genesis.

Pharaoh dreamed: seven ears of grain, plump and good, were growing on one stalk. Then seven ears, thin and blighted by the east wind, sprouted after them. The thin ears swallowed up the seven plump and full ears. In the morning Pharaoh's spirit was troubled; so he sent and called for all the magicians of Egypt and all its wise men. Pharaoh told them his dreams, but there was no one who could interpret them to Pharaoh. Then Pharaoh sent for Joseph and said to him, "I have heard it said of you that when you hear a dream you can interpret it." Joseph said, "There will come seven years of great plenty. After them will arise seven years of famine. Now therefore let Pharaoh select a man who is discerning and wise, and set him over the land of Egypt. Take one-fifth of the produce of the land of Egypt during the seven plenteous years. That food shall be a reserve for the land against the seven years of famine."

The Word of the Lord.

◆ All observe silence.

FOR SILENT REFLECTION

Think about this silently in your heart. Have you heard God speak to you in prayer?

CLOSING PRAYER

Let us pray to God for our needs and the needs of others: our family, neighborhood, and the world. For each need we say, "Lord, hear our prayer."

◆ All may add their own prayers here.

Let us pray: **Our Father . . . Amen.**

Dear God,
thank you for helping us
when we are uncertain or confused.
Help us as you helped Joseph,
to grow in wisdom and understanding.
We ask this in Christ's name.

Amen.

✛ All make the Sign of the Cross.

OPENING

Even after Joseph is sold into slavery by his brothers and had spent years in jail, he was given a high-ranking position by the Pharaoh—the highest position in Egypt, apart from the Pharaoh himself. The Pharaoh knew that God was with Joseph and planned for the famine ahead.

✦ All make the Sign of the Cross.

In the name of the Father, and of the Son, and of the Holy Spirit. Amen.

PSALM

(For a longer psalm, see page xi.)
Psalm 145:2–3

I will praise your name for ever, LORD.

I will praise your name for ever, LORD.

Every day I will bless you,
    and praise your name forever and ever.
Great is the LORD, and greatly to be praised;
    his greatness is unsearchable.

I will praise your name for ever, LORD.

READING

Genesis 41:39–40, 47–48a, 53–54, 57a

A reading from the Book of Genesis.

So Pharaoh said to Joseph, "Since God has shown you all this, there is no one so discerning and wise as you. You shall be over my house, and all my people shall order themselves as you command; only with regard to the throne will I be greater than you." During the seven plenteous years the earth produced abundantly. Joseph gathered up all the food of the seven years when there was plenty in the land of Egypt, and stored up food in the cities. The seven years of plenty that prevailed in the land of Egypt came to an end; and the seven years of famine began to come, just as Joseph had said. There was famine in every country, but throughout the land of Egypt there was bread. All the world came to Joseph in Egypt to buy grain.

The Word of the Lord.

◆ All observe silence.

FOR SILENT REFLECTION

Think about this silently in your heart. Find time today to sit quietly and listen to what God is telling you.

CLOSING PRAYER

Let us pray to God for our needs and the needs of others: our family, neighborhood, and the world. For each need we say, "Lord, hear our prayer."

◆ All may add their own prayers here.

Let us pray: **Our Father . . . Amen.**

Holy God of Wisdom,
open our ears that we may hear your words.
Open our minds that we may understand your plan for us.
Open our hearts so that we may know your goodness.
We ask this through Christ our Lord.

Amen.

✦ All make the Sign of the Cross.

HOME PRAYER
CELEBRATING THE SAINTS, REMEMBERING THE DEAD

Find the reading (1 Thessalonians 4:13–18) in your Bible, ask for a volunteer to read it, and encourage the reader to practice reading it a few times. Then gather the household in one room. You may want to light a candle to create an even more prayerful environment.

LEADER:
Saints live among us today as well as with Christ in heaven. These heroes of our faith persevere in troubled times as they follow the path of Jesus. Their unselfish actions, as well as their talents, skills, and virtuous living inspire us as they pray for us.

✚ All make the Sign of the Cross.

ALL: In the name of the Father, and of the Son, and of the Holy Spirit. Amen.

LEADER: Psalm 112: 1–6
Let us pray the psalm response:
Happy are those who fear the LORD.

ALL: Happy are those who fear the LORD.

LEADER:
Praise the LORD!
  Happy are those who fear the LORD,
    who greatly delight in his commandments.
Their descendants will be mighty in the land;
  the generation of the upright will
      be blessed.

ALL: Happy are those who fear the LORD.

LEADER:
Wealth and riches are in their houses,
  and their righteousness endures forever.
They rise in the darkness as a light for
      the upright;
  they are gracious, merciful, and righteous.

ALL: Happy are those who fear the LORD.

LEADER: 1 Thessalonians 4:13–18
A reading from the First Letter of Paul to the Thessalonians.

◆ Read the Scripture passage from the Bible.

The Word of the Lord.

◆ All observe a brief silence.

LEADER:
And now let us remember family members and friends who have died:

◆ The leader begins, then pauses so others may add names too.

LEADER:
Lord God,
we ask you to bring these and all
those who have gone before us
into your beloved presence.

◆ Leader pauses, then continues.

Jesus, our Savior,
you are the Source of all life.
We are grateful for our leaders in faith,
as well as our family members and friends
who are with you now in heaven.
Their goodness reveals your holy truth.
Help us to honor your Spirit within us in
everything we do.
We ask this in your name.

ALL: Amen.

✚ All make the Sign of the Cross.

CHILDREN'S DAILY PRAYER 2020–2021 © 2020 Archdiocese of Chicago: Liturgy Training Publications, 3949 South Racine Avenue, Chicago, IL 60609. All rights reserved. Orders: 800-933-1800 or www.LTP.org. Scripture excerpts are taken from *The New Revised Standard Version Bible: Catholic Edition*, copyright © 1989, Division of Christian Education of the National Council of the Churches of Christ in the United States of America. Used with permission. All rights reserved.

PRAYER FOR THE WEEK

OPENING

Today is the Solemnity of All Saints. We celebrate those men and women who have followed the path of Jesus. Today we hear Jesus pray the Beatitudes—the blessings in the Sermon on the Mount. The Beatitudes focus on love and humility and help lead us to a life in Jesus Christ.

✝ All make the Sign of the Cross.

In the name of the Father, and of the Son, and of the Holy Spirit. Amen.

PSALM

(For a longer psalm, see page xii.)

Psalm 98:1

The LORD has made known his victory.

The LORD has made known his victory.

O sing to the Lord a new song,
for he has done marvelous things.
His right hand and his holy arm
have gotten him victory.

The LORD has made known his victory.

◆ All stand and sing **Alleluia.**

GOSPEL

Matthew 5:2–12

A reading from the holy Gospel according to Matthew.

Then Jesus began to speak, and taught them, saying:

"Blessed are the poor in spirit, for theirs is the kingdom of heaven. Blessed are those who mourn, for they will be comforted. Blessed are the meek, for they will inherit the earth. Blessed are those who hunger and thirst for righteousness, for they will be filled. Blessed are the merciful, for they will receive mercy. Blessed are the pure in heart, for they will see God. Blessed are the peacemakers, for they will be called children of God. Blessed are those who are persecuted for righteousness' sake, for theirs is the kingdom of heaven. Blessed are you when people revile you and persecute you and utter all kinds of evil against you falsely on my account. Rejoice and be glad, for your reward is great in heaven, for in the same way they persecuted the prophets who were before you."

The Gospel of the Lord.

◆ All sit and observe silence.

FOR SILENT REFLECTION

Think about this silently in your heart. The Beatitudes can be difficult to understand and follow. Which one seems the most difficult to you?

CLOSING PRAYER

Let us pray to God for our needs and the needs of others: our family, neighborhood, and the world. For each need we say, "Lord, hear our prayer."

◆ All may add their own prayers here.

Let us pray: **Our Father . . . Amen.**

We are grateful for the example of all the holy men and women
who are with you now in heaven, O God our Father.
May we live our lives as they did.
Through Christ our Lord.

Amen.

✝ All make the Sign of the Cross.

PRAYER FOR
MONDAY, NOVEMBER 2, 2020

OPENING

Today we celebrate All Souls' Day. We remember all who have died before us. In today's reading from Genesis, we continue the story of Joseph. His brothers who had sold him into slavery came to Egypt, and to Joseph, for help. The did not recognize their brother Joseph.

✛ All make the Sign of the Cross.

In the name of the Father, and of the Son, and of the Holy Spirit. Amen.

PSALM

(For a longer psalm, see page xii.)
Psalm 98:1

The LORD has made known his victory.

The LORD has made known his victory.

O sing to the Lord a new song,
   for he has done marvelous things.
His right hand and his holy arm
   have gotten him victory.

The LORD has made known his victory.

READING

Genesis 42:1a–b, 2b–4, 6a, 7a–b,
8b, 9b, 17, 21a–b, 23a, 24a, 25a

A reading from the Book of Genesis.

When Jacob learned that there was grain in Egypt, he said to his sons, "Go down and buy grain for us there, that we may live and not die." So ten of Joseph's brothers went down to buy grain in Egypt. But Jacob did not send Joseph's youngest brother Benjamin with his brothers, for he feared that harm might come to him. Joseph was governor over the land. When Joseph saw his brothers, he recognized them, but he treated them like strangers and spoke harshly. They did not recognize him. Joseph said to them, "You are spies," and he put them all together in prison for three days. They said to one another, "Alas, we are paying the penalty for what we did to our brother. They did not know that Joseph understood them. He turned away from them and wept. Joseph then gave orders to fill their bags with grain.

The Word of the Lord.

◆ All observe silence.

FOR SILENT REFLECTION

Think about this silently in your heart. The brothers came to Egypt with humility, knowing what they did to their brother was wrong. Have you ever felt badly after you have wronged someone? What did you do?

CLOSING PRAYER

Let us pray to God for our needs and the needs of others: our family, neighborhood, and the world. For each need we say, "Lord, hear our prayer."

◆ All may add their own prayers here.

Let us pray: **Our Father . . . Amen.**

O God of love and forgiveness,
help us to empty our hearts of anger
and resentment.
Heal our hearts and make us open to
loving one another.
We ask this in Christ's name.

Amen.

✛ All make the Sign of the Cross.

OPENING

Today is the feast day of St. Martin de Porres (1579–1639). Born of mixed race in Peru, St. Martin became the patron saint of interracial justice and spent his life providing for the sick and poor. We hear that Joseph's brothers travel back to Egypt, this time with their youngest brother Benjamin.

✝ All make the Sign of the Cross.

In the name of the Father, and of the Son, and of the Holy Spirit. Amen.

PSALM

(For a longer psalm, see page xii.)
Psalm 98:1

The LORD has made known his victory.

The LORD has made known his victory.

O sing to the Lord a new song,
   for he has done marvelous things.
His right hand and his holy arm
   have gotten him victory.

The LORD has made known his victory.

READING

Genesis 42:29a; 43:2–3, 15a, c–d,
29a–c, 30a–b, 30d–31, 34c

A reading from the Book of Genesis.

Joseph's brothers came to their father Jacob in the land of Canaan. And when they had eaten up the grain they had brought from Egypt, their father said to them, "Go again, buy us a little more food." But Judah said to him, "The man solemnly warned us, saying, 'You shall not see my face unless your brother Benjamin is with you.'" So the men took Benjamin. Then they went on their way down to Egypt, and stood before Joseph. Then Joseph looked up and saw his brother Benjamin, his mother's son, and said, "Is this your youngest brother?" With that, Joseph hurried out, because he was overcome with affection for his brother. So he went into a private room and wept there. Then he washed his face and came out; and controlling himself he said, "Serve the meal." So they drank and were merry with him.

The Word of the Lord.

◆ All observe silence.

FOR SILENT REFLECTION

Think about this silently in your heart. Just as in St. Martin's and Joseph's times, many people today do not have access to food. How can you help those in your community who are hungry?

CLOSING PRAYER

Let us pray to God for our needs and the needs of others: our family, neighborhood, and the world. For each need we say, "Lord, hear our prayer."

◆ All may add their own prayers here.

Let us pray: **Our Father . . . Amen.**

You are the Living Bread from heaven,
Savior God.
We pray that we can love our brothers
and sisters,
and help feed those who hunger.
Who live and reign with God the Father, in
the unity of the Holy Spirit, one God, for
ever and ever.

Amen.

✝ All make the Sign of the Cross.

WEDNESDAY, NOVEMBER 4, 2020

OPENING

Today is the feast day of St. Charles Borromeo (1538–1584). St. Charles was a bishop in Milan who set up orphanages, hospitals, seminaries, and colleges. During a plague, he sold all he had to feed and care for the sick. St. Charles was a model for practicing the works of mercy. In today's reading, Joseph holds his brother Benjamin back.

✦ All make the Sign of the Cross.

In the name of the Father, and of the Son, and of the Holy Spirit. Amen.

PSALM

(For a longer psalm, see page xii.)

Psalm 98:1

The Lord has made known his victory.

The Lord has made known his victory.

O sing to the Lord a new song,
   for he has done marvelous things.
His right hand and his holy arm
   have gotten him victory.

The Lord has made known his victory.

READING

Genesis 44:1a–b, 2a–c, 3–4, 6a, 10c–d, 12–13

A reading from the Book of Genesis.

Joseph commanded the steward of his house, "Fill the men's sacks with food. Put my cup, the silver cup, in the top of the sack of the youngest." As soon as the morning was light, the men were sent away to Canaan [KAY-nuhn] with their donkeys. When they had gone only a short distance from the city, Joseph said to his steward, "Go, follow after the men; and when you overtake them, say to them, 'Why have you returned evil for good? Why have you stolen my silver cup?'" When the steward overtook them, he said, "He with whom the cup is found shall become my lord's slave but the rest of you shall go free." The steward searched, beginning with the eldest and ending with the youngest; and the cup was found in Benjamin's sack. At this the brothers tore their clothes. Then each one loaded his donkey and they returned to the city.

The Word of the Lord.

◆ All observe silence.

FOR SILENT REFLECTION

Think about this silently in your heart. Why do you think Joseph set a trap for his brothers, rather than just telling them who he was?

CLOSING PRAYER

Let us pray to God for our needs and the needs of others: our family, neighborhood, and the world. For each need we say, "Lord, hear our prayer."

◆ All may add their own prayers here.

Let us pray: **Our Father . . . Amen.**

God of Wisdom,
help us be repentant of our wrongdoings,
and help those we have wronged to heal.
May we be worthy of your grace and love
and of your presence in our lives.
Through Christ our Lord.

Amen.

✦ All make the Sign of the Cross.

OPENING

Joseph's brothers fell to the ground and begged him for the life of their brother Benjamin. Joseph recognizes that his brothers, in their humility in trying to save Benjamin, are no longer the same men that sold him into slavery. Joseph reveals himself to them.

✚ All make the Sign of the Cross.

In the name of the Father, and of the Son, and of the Holy Spirit. Amen.

PSALM

(For a longer psalm, see page xii.)
Psalm 98:1

The Lord has made known his victory.

The Lord has made known his victory.

O sing to the Lord a new song,
   for he has done marvelous things.
His right hand and his holy arm
   have gotten him victory.

The Lord has made known his victory.

READING

Genesis 44:14ac, 18a, 19b,
20b–20e; 45:3a–b, 3d–e, 7, 9, 11a, 15

A reading from the Book of Genesis.

Judah and his brothers came to Joseph's house. They fell to the ground before him. Then Judah stepped up to him and said, "O my lord, have you a father or a brother? We have a father, an old man, and a young brother, the child of his old age. His brother Joseph is dead." Joseph said to his brothers, "I am Joseph." But his brothers could not answer him, so dismayed were they at his presence. Joseph said, "God sent me before you to preserve for you a remnant on earth, and to keep alive for you many survivors.

Hurry and go up to my father and say to him, 'Thus says your son Joseph, God has made me lord of all Egypt; come down to me, do not delay. I will provide for you there.'" And he kissed all his brothers and wept upon them; and after that his brothers talked with him.

The Word of the Lord.

◆ All observe silence.

FOR SILENT REFLECTION

Think about this silently in your heart. Joseph forgave his brothers for treating him so badly. Is there someone you should forgive?

CLOSING PRAYER

Let us pray to God for our needs and the needs of others: our family, neighborhood, and the world. For each need we say, "Lord, hear our prayer."

◆ All may add their own prayers here.

Let us pray: **Our Father . . . Amen.**

Dear Lord,
we offer you praise for your great glory.
We thank you for showing us your mercy.
Help us to do the same for our brothers
and sisters.
Help us to show kindness for wrongs done
to us.
We ask this in Christ Jesus' name.

Amen.

✚ All make the Sign of the Cross.

PRAYER FOR
FRIDAY, NOVEMBER 6, 2020

OPENING

In today's reading, Jacob travels to Egypt with all his belongings. Joseph meets his father once again. They were both overcome with emotion at seeing each other. Joseph provides for his family and gives them land in Egypt.

✠ All make the Sign of the Cross.

In the name of the Father, and of the Son, and of the Holy Spirit. Amen.

PSALM

(For a longer psalm, see page xii.)
Psalm 98:1

The LORD has made known his victory.

The LORD has made known his victory.

O sing to the Lord a new song,
   for he has done marvelous things.
His right hand and his holy arm
   have gotten him victory.

The LORD has made known his victory.

READING

Genesis 46:5–6b, 28b–30; 47:11

A reading from the Book of Genesis.

Jacob set out from Beer-sheba [SHEE-buh]; and the sons of Jacob carried their father, their little ones, and their wives, in the wagons that Pharaoh had sent to carry him. They also took their livestock and the goods that they had acquired in the land of Canaan. When they came to the land of Goshen [GOH-shuhn], Joseph made ready his chariot and went up to meet his father Jacob. He presented himself to him, fell on his neck, and wept on his neck a good while. Jacob said to Joseph, "I can die now, having seen for myself that you are still alive." Joseph settled his father and his broth-ers, and granted them a holding in the land of Egypt, in the best part of the land, in the land of Rameses, as Pharaoh had instructed.

The Word of the Lord.

◆ All observe silence.

FOR SILENT REFLECTION

Think about this silently in your heart. Is there someone you haven't talked to or with whom you had a disagreement? How can you repair your relationship?

CLOSING PRAYER

Let us pray to God for our needs and the needs of others: our family, neighborhood, and the world. For each need we say, "Lord, hear our prayer."

◆ All may add their own prayers here.

Let us pray: **Our Father . . . Amen.**

Faithful and loving God,
you helped Joseph through difficult times.
Help us know that you are with us always.
Protect us from harm.
We ask this through Christ our Lord.

Amen.

✠ All make the Sign of the Cross.

PRAYER FOR THE WEEK

OPENING

In today's Gospel, we hear the parable of the ten bridesmaids. We should remember that in Jesus' times, there were no streetlights to light the roads. Only lanterns were used. Doors to cities, villages, and homes were locked at night. We learn from this parable that the doors to the Kingdom of heaven are open to all who are prepared, ready, and waiting to enter.

✚ All make the Sign of the Cross.

In the name of the Father, and of the Son, and of the Holy Spirit. Amen.

PSALM

(For a longer psalm, see page xii.)

Psalm 98:1

The LORD has made known his victory.

The LORD has made known his victory.

O sing to the Lord a new song,
    for he has done marvelous things.
His right hand and his holy arm
    have gotten him victory.

The LORD has made known his victory.

◆ All stand and sing **Alleluia.**

GOSPEL

Matthew 25:1–6, 8–10

A reading from the holy Gospel according to Matthew.

Jesus said, "Then the kingdom of heaven will be like this. Ten bridesmaids took their lamps and went to meet the bridegroom. Five of them were foolish, and five were wise. When the foolish took their lamps, they took no oil with them; but the wise took flasks of oil with their lamps. As the bridegroom was delayed, all of them became drowsy and slept. But at midnight there was a shout, 'Look! Here is the bridegroom! Come out to meet him.' The foolish said to the wise, 'Give us some of your oil, for our lamps are going out.' But the wise replied, 'No! there will not be enough for you and for us; you had better go to the dealers and buy some for yourselves.' And while they went to buy it, the bridegroom came, and those who were ready went with him into the wedding banquet; and the door was shut."

The Gospel of the Lord.

◆ All sit and observe silence.

FOR SILENT REFLECTION

Think about this silently in your heart. Why didn't the bridesmaids with enough oil share it with those that had none?

CLOSING PRAYER

Let us pray to God for our needs and the needs of others: our family, neighborhood, and the world. For each need we say, "Lord, hear our prayer."

◆ All may add their own prayers here.

Let us pray: **Our Father . . . Amen.**

Loving God,
help us to be prepared to enter your Kingdom.
May we be wise, thoughtful, and ready.
We ask this in Christ's name.

Amen.

✚ All make the Sign of the Cross.

PRAYER FOR
MONDAY, NOVEMBER 9, 2020

OPENING

Today we remember the Dedication of the Lateran Basilica in Rome. St. John Lateran is the pope's cathedral in the Diocese of Rome, but we may also consider her to be the church of all Catholics. This cathedral reminds us of God our Father and all that he does for us through the Church. Over the next few days, we will learn about some of the women in the Bible, starting with the prophet Huldah.

✚ All make the Sign of the Cross.

In the name of the Father, and of the Son, and of the Holy Spirit. Amen.

PSALM

(For a longer psalm, see page xii.)
Psalm 98:1

The LORD has made known his victory.

The LORD has made known his victory.

O sing to the Lord a new song,
    for he has done marvelous things.
His right hand and his holy arm
    have gotten him victory.

The LORD has made known his victory.

READING

2 Chronicles 34:21a–b, 22a, d,
23a, 26d–e, 27–28a, c

A reading from the Second Book of Chronicles.

King Josiah [joh-SĪ-uh] said, "Go, inquire of the LORD for me and for those who are left in Israel and in Judah, concerning the words of the book that has been found." So Hilkiah [hil-KĪ-uh] and those whom the king had sent went to the prophet Huldah, and spoke to her to that effect. She declared to them, "Thus says the LORD, the God of Israel: Regarding the words that you have heard, because your heart was penitent and you humbled yourself before God when you heard his words against this place and its inhabitants, and you have humbled yourself before me, and have torn your clothes and wept before me, I also have heard you, says the LORD. I will gather you to your ancestors and you shall be gathered to your grave in peace." They took the message back to the king.

The Word of the Lord.

◆ All observe silence.

FOR SILENT REFLECTION

Think about this silently in your heart. What does it mean to humble yourself before God?

CLOSING PRAYER

Let us pray to God for our needs and the needs of others: our family, neighborhood, and the world. For each need we say, "Lord, hear our prayer."

◆ All may add their own prayers here.

Let us pray: **Our Father . . . Amen.**

Faithful God,
we thank you for all the holy women you have sent to teach us.
Help us to be like King Josiah.
Help us to listen and learn from their words of wisdom
and from their good deeds.
We pray in Christ's name.

Amen.

✚ All make the Sign of the Cross.

OPENING

Today we remember St. Leo the Great, an early pope of the Church and considered one of the best because of his care and concern for Christ's flock. Today, we hear about Miriam. Miriam saved her brother Moses from the Pharaoh's men by hiding him in the reeds when he was just a baby. Miriam, her brother Aaron, and Moses led the Hebrew people out of Egypt. Miriam is recognized as a prophet and as one of the first cantors, or song leaders, in the Bible. Listen to today's reading as though you were listening to a song being sung.

✦ All make the Sign of the Cross.

In the name of the Father, and of the Son, and of the Holy Spirit. Amen.

PSALM

(For a longer psalm, see page xii.)
Psalm 98:1

The Lord has made known his victory.

The Lord has made known his victory.

O sing to the Lord a new song,
   for he has done marvelous things.
His right hand and his holy arm
   have gotten him victory.

The Lord has made known his victory.

READING

Exodus 15:1–2, 13, 18, 20–21

A reading from the Book of Exodus.

Then Moses and the Israelites sang this song to the Lord: "I will sing to the Lord, for he has triumphed gloriously; horse and rider he has thrown into the sea. The Lord is my strength and my might, and he has become my salvation; this is my God, and I will praise him, my father's God, and I will exalt him. In your steadfast love you led the people whom you redeemed; you guided them by your strength to your holy abode. The Lord will reign forever and ever." Then the prophet Miriam, Aaron's sister, took a tambourine in her hand; and all the women went out after her with tambourines and with dancing. And Miriam sang to them: "Sing to the Lord, for he has triumphed gloriously; horse and rider he has thrown into the sea."

The Word of the Lord.

◆ All observe silence.

FOR SILENT REFLECTION

Think about this silently in your heart. How is music, dancing, and singing used to praise God in our Church?

CLOSING PRAYER

Let us pray to God for our needs and the needs of others: our family, neighborhood, and the world. For each need we say, "Lord, hear our prayer."

◆ All may add their own prayers here.

Let us pray: **Our Father . . . Amen.**

O Lord,
we praise and bless you for your
wondrous deeds.
You are our strength and our salvation.
We will sing your praise forever.
We pray in Christ's name.

Amen.

✦ All make the Sign of the Cross.

PRAYER FOR
WEDNESDAY, NOVEMBER 11, 2020

OPENING

Today is the feast of St. Martin of Tours, who is the patron saint of soldiers and horses. He served in the Italian army and then later declared himself a "soldier of Christ." Today we hear about a woman who bathed and anointed Jesus' feet. Anointing someone's feet in Jesus' time was a sign of honor. She wished to show Jesus how sorry she was for her sins.

✛ All make the Sign of the Cross.

In the name of the Father, and of the Son, and of the Holy Spirit. Amen.

PSALM

(For a longer psalm, see page xii.)
Psalm 98:1

The LORD has made known his victory.

The LORD has made known his victory.

O sing to the Lord a new song,
   for he has done marvelous things.
His right hand and his holy arm
   have gotten him victory.

The LORD has made known his victory.

◆ All stand and sing **Alleluia.**

GOSPEL

Luke 7:36–37a–b, 37d–39, 48, 50b

A reading from the holy Gospel according to Luke.

One of the Pharisees [FAYR-uh-seez] asked Jesus to eat with him, and he went into the Pharisee's house and took his place at the table. And a woman in the city, who was a sinner, brought an alabaster jar of ointment. She stood behind him at his feet, weeping, and began to bathe his feet with her tears and to dry them with her hair. Then she continued kissing his feet and anointing them with the ointment. Now when the Pharisee who had invited him saw it, he said to himself, "If this man were a prophet, he would have known who and what kind of woman this is who is touching him—that she is a sinner." Then Jesus said to her, "Your sins are forgiven. Your faith has saved you; go in peace."

The Gospel of the Lord.

◆ All sit and observe silence.

FOR SILENT REFLECTION

Think about this silently in your heart. How can we show Jesus how sorry we are when we have sinned?

CLOSING PRAYER

Let us pray to God for our needs and the needs of others: our family, neighborhood, and the world. For each need we say, "Lord, hear our prayer."

◆ All may add their own prayers here.

Let us pray: **Our Father . . . Amen.**

Loving God,
help us be like this woman.
May we recognize when we have sinned against you,
and humble ourselves before you,
and ask for your forgiveness.
We ask this in the name of your Son, Jesus Christ,
through whom we are saved from sin.
Amen.

✛ All make the Sign of the Cross.

OPENING

In today's reading, we hear about the women who went to Jesus' tomb to prepare him properly for burial. Two angels appeared to them and told them that Jesus would rise on the third day. The women spread the angel's message, making them among the first evangelists of the Good News. Today is the feast day of St. Josaphat [JOS-uh-fat] (1580–1623). St. Josaphat fought for more unity among Christians.

✚ All make the Sign of the Cross.

In the name of the Father, and of the Son, and of the Holy Spirit. Amen.

PSALM

(For a longer psalm, see page xii.)
Psalm 98:1

The Lord has made known his victory.

The Lord has made known his victory.

O sing to the Lord a new song,
    for he has done marvelous things.
His right hand and his holy arm
    have gotten him victory.

The Lord has made known his victory.

◆ All stand and sing **Alleluia.**

GOSPEL

Luke 24:1–3, 4b–5b, 5d–e, 6a, 7–10

A reading from the holy Gospel according to Luke.

On the first day of the week, at early dawn, the women came to the tomb, taking the spices that they had prepared. They found the stone rolled away from the tomb, but when they went in, they did not find the body. Suddenly two men in dazzling clothes stood beside them.

The women were terrified and bowed their faces to the ground, but the men said to them, "He is not here, but has risen. Remember how he told you that the Son of Man must be handed over to sinners, and be crucified, and on the third day rise again." Then they remembered his words, and returning from the tomb, they told all this to the eleven and to all the rest. Now it was Mary Magdalene, Joanna, Mary the mother of James, and the other women with them who told this to the apostles.

The Gospel of the Lord.

◆ All sit and observe silence.

FOR SILENT REFLECTION

Think about this silently in your heart. Can you spread good news to others? What kind of good news would you share?

CLOSING PRAYER

Let us pray to God for our needs and the needs of others: our family, neighborhood, and the world. For each need we say, "Lord, hear our prayer."

◆ All may add their own prayers here.

Let us pray: **Our Father . . . Amen.**

O God, we wish to be like these women,
strong in our faith and devoted to you.
Help us share your Good News with others
and to help promote unity among Christians.
We ask this in the name of the Risen Christ.

Amen.

✚ All make the Sign of the Cross.

OPENING

Today is the feast day of St. Frances Xavier Cabrini, the patron saint of immigrants (1850–1917). Born in Italy, Mother Cabrini went to New York and founded nearly seventy institutions (hospitals, schools, and orphanages) that helped poor and sick immigrants. She lived her life in service to God and those in need. We hear St. Paul talking about all who have helped him and served God, including nine women.

✦ All make the Sign of the Cross.

In the name of the Father, and of the Son, and of the Holy Spirit. Amen.

PSALM
(For a longer psalm, see page xii.)
Psalm 98:1

The LORD has made known his victory.

The LORD has made known his victory.

O sing to the Lord a new song,
    for he has done marvelous things.
His right hand and his holy arm
    have gotten him victory.

The LORD has made known his victory.

READING
Romans 16:1–2ac, 3–4a, 6–7c, 12a, 13, 15a, 16

A reading from the Letter of Paul to the Romans.

I commend to you our sister Phoebe [FEE-bee], a deacon of the church at Cenchreae [SEN-kruh-ee], so that you may welcome her in the Lord as is fitting for the saints, for she has been a benefactor of many and of myself as well. Greet Prisca [PRIS-kuh] and Aquila [AK-wih-luh], who work with me in Christ Jesus, and who risked their necks for my life. Greet Mary, who has worked very hard among you. Greet Andronicus [an-DRAHN-uh-kuhs] and Junia, my relatives who were in prison with me; they are prominent among the apostles. Greet those workers in the Lord, Tryphaena [try-FE-nuh] and Tryphosa [try-FŌ-suh]. Greet Rufus [ROO-fuhs], chosen in the Lord; and greet his mother—a mother to me also. Greet Philologus [fi-LOL-o-gus], Julia, Nereus [NEE-rih-yoos] and his sister. Greet one another with a holy kiss. All the churches of Christ greet you.

The Word of the Lord.

◆ All observe silence.

FOR SILENT REFLECTION

Think about this silently in your heart. How can you help immigrant families in your community?

CLOSING PRAYER

Let us pray to God for our needs and the needs of others: our family, neighborhood, and the world. For each need we say, "Lord, hear our prayer."

◆ All may add their own prayers here.

Let us pray: **Our Father . . . Amen.**

Dear Lord,
thank you for all who have gone before us who have served the most vulnerable of your people.
Help us live our lives with love and justice.
We ask this in Christ's name.

Amen.

✦ All make the Sign of the Cross.

PRAYER FOR THE WEEK

OPENING

In today's Gospel, we are reminded that each of us are given gifts, talents, skills, and abilities. God wants us to use our gifts to make this world a better place. The "slaves" referred to in the Gospel passage are "servants."

✚ All make the Sign of the Cross.

In the name of the Father, and of the Son, and of the Holy Spirit. Amen.

PSALM

(For a longer psalm, see page xii.)
Psalm 98:1

The LORD has made known his victory.

The LORD has made known his victory.

O sing to the Lord a new song,
    for he has done marvelous things.
His right hand and his holy arm
    have gotten him victory.

The LORD has made known his victory.

◆ All stand and sing **Alleluia.**

GOSPEL

Matthew 25:14–15, 19–21

A reading from the holy Gospel according to Matthew.

"For it is as if a man, going on a journey, summoned his slaves and entrusted his property to them; to one he gave five talents, to another two, to another one, to each according to his ability. Then he went away. After a long time the master of those slaves came and settled accounts with them. Then the one who had received the five talents came forward, bringing five more talents, saying, 'Master, you handed over to me five talents; see, I have made five more talents.' His master said to him, 'Well done, good and trustworthy slave; you have been trustworthy in a few things, I will put you in charge of many things; enter into the joy of your master.'"

The Gospel of the Lord.

◆ All sit and observe silence.

FOR SILENT REFLECTION

Think about this silently in your heart. What talents or skills do you have? How can you use them to serve God and others?

CLOSING PRAYER

Let us pray to God for our needs and the needs of others: our family, neighborhood, and the world. For each need we say, "Lord, hear our prayer."

◆ All may add their own prayers here.

Let us pray: **Our Father . . . Amen.**

Loving God,
you have blessed us all with so many gifts
and talents.
May we recognize our special abilities
and use them to care for and love one another
and to give you glory.
We ask this in the name of Jesus Christ,
our Lord.

Amen.

✚ All make the Sign of the Cross.

PRAYER FOR
MONDAY, NOVEMBER 16, 2020

OPENING

We celebrate two saints today. St. Margaret (1045–1093) was queen of Scotland, known for her life of prayer and charity for the poor. St. Gertrude (1256–1301) also lived a life of prayer and studied God and the Church. This week we will look at the many names used to describe Jesus in the New Testament. In today's Gospel, Jesus is called the Messiah, or "anointed one."

✦ All make the Sign of the Cross.

In the name of the Father, and of the Son, and of the Holy Spirit. Amen.

PSALM

(For a longer psalm, see page xii.)
Psalm 98:1

The LORD has made known his victory.

The LORD has made known his victory.

O sing to the Lord a new song,
   for he has done marvelous things.
His right hand and his holy arm
   have gotten him victory.

The LORD has made known his victory.

◆ All stand and sing **Alleluia.**

GOSPEL

Matthew 1:1–2, 5c–6a, 12a, 15bc, 16–17

A reading from the holy Gospel according to Matthew.

An account of the genealogy [jee-nee-AH-luh-jEE] of Jesus the Messiah, the son of David, the son of Abraham. Abraham was the father of Isaac, and Isaac the father of Jacob, and Jacob the father of Judah and his brothers. And Obed the father of Jesse, and Jesse the father of King David. And after the deportation to Babylon:

Eleazar [el-ee-AY-zehr] the father of Matthan [MATH-uhn], and Matthan the father of Jacob, and Jacob the father of Joseph the husband of Mary, of whom Jesus was born, who is called the Messiah. So all the generations from Abraham to David are fourteen generations; and from David to the deportation to Babylon, fourteen generations; and from the deportation to Babylon to the Messiah, fourteen generations.

The Gospel of the Lord.

◆ All sit and observe silence.

FOR SILENT REFLECTION

Think about this silently in your heart. Why do you think it was important for the Gospel writer to write about Jesus' ancestors?

CLOSING PRAYER

Let us pray to God for our needs and the needs of others: our family, neighborhood, and the world. For each need we say, "Lord, hear our prayer."

◆ All may add their own prayers here.

Let us pray: **Our Father . . . Amen.**

You have given us so many faithful leaders throughout the generations, Almighty God, They have helped pave the way for your Son, the Messiah, Jesus Christ, who came to redeem us.
We thank you in his name.

Amen.

✦ All make the Sign of the Cross.

OPENING

In today's Gospel, we hear Jesus being called the King of the Jews, although this was a title Jesus never called himself. To be called King was treason against the Roman rulers. The Romans used this as an excuse to crucify Jesus. A queen of Hungary, St. Elizabeth (1207–1231) gave what she could to the poor. We celebrate the feast day of this patroness of Catholic Charities.

✦ All make the Sign of the Cross.

In the name of the Father, and of the Son, and of the Holy Spirit. Amen.

PSALM

(For a longer psalm, see page xii.)
Psalm 98:1

The LORD has made known his victory.

The LORD has made known his victory.

O sing to the Lord a new song,
 for he has done marvelous things.
His right hand and his holy arm
 have gotten him victory.

The LORD has made known his victory.

✦ All stand and sing **Alleluia.**

GOSPEL

Matthew 27:11, 27a, 28–29, 31c, 33ab, 35a, 37

A reading from the holy Gospel according to Matthew.

Now Jesus stood before the governor; and the governor asked him, "Are you the King of the Jews?" Jesus said, "You say so." Then the soldiers of the governor took Jesus into the governor's headquarters. They stripped him and put a scarlet robe on him, and after twisting some thorns into a crown, they put it on his head. They put a reed in his right hand and knelt before him and mocked him, saying, "Hail, King of the Jews!" Then they led him away to crucify him. They came to a place called Golgotha (which means Place of a Skull), and when they had crucified him, over his head they put the charge against him, which read, "This is Jesus, the King of the Jews."

The Gospel of the Lord.

◆ All sit and observe silence.

FOR SILENT REFLECTION

Think about this silently in your heart. Have you ever been called names or accused of something you didn't do? Who can you go to for help if you are bullied?

CLOSING PRAYER

Let us pray to God for our needs and the needs of others: our family, neighborhood, and the world. For each need we say, "Lord, hear our prayer."

◆ All may add their own prayers here.

Let us pray: **Our Father . . . Amen.**

Almighty and powerful God,
we praise you for your glory and majesty.
We hail your Son Jesus
not just as King of the Jews
but as king of our hearts.
We pray to you in his name.

Amen.

✦ All make the Sign of the Cross.

OPENING

We hear more names for Jesus today: the Lamb of God and Son of God. The *Agnus Dei*, or Lamb of God, is used in our Mass, often sung, as a form of prayer. Jesus is a servant of God who came to take away the sins of the world. Two of his Apostles, Sts. Peter and Paul, are remembered today; we celebrate the Dedication of the Basilicas of St. Peter and St. Paul.

✛ All make the Sign of the Cross.

In the name of the Father, and of the Son, and of the Holy Spirit. Amen.

PSALM

(For a longer psalm, see page xii.)
Psalm 98:1

The LORD has made known his victory.

The LORD has made known his victory.

O sing to the Lord a new song,
for he has done marvelous things.
His right hand and his holy arm
have gotten him victory.

The LORD has made known his victory.

◆ All stand and sing **Alleluia.**

GOSPEL

John 1:29, 32–36

A reading from the holy Gospel according to John.

The next day John the Baptist saw Jesus coming toward him and declared, "Here is the Lamb of God who takes away the sin of the world!" And John testified, "I saw the Spirit descending from heaven like a dove, and it remained on him. I myself did not know him, but the one who sent me to baptize with water said to me, 'He on whom you see the Spirit descend and remain is the one who baptizes with the Holy Spirit.' And I myself have seen and have testified that this is the Son of God." The next day John again was standing with two of his disciples, and as he watched Jesus walk by, he exclaimed, "Look, here is the Lamb of God!"

The Gospel of the Lord.

◆ All sit and observe silence.

FOR SILENT REFLECTION

Think about this silently in your heart. Why do you think that Jesus is called the Lamb of God?

CLOSING PRAYER

Let us pray to God for our needs and the needs of others: our family, neighborhood, and the world. For each need we say, "Lord, hear our prayer."

◆ All may add their own prayers here.

Let us pray: **Our Father . . . Amen.**

Lamb of God,
you take away the sins of the world,
have mercy on us.
Lamb of God,
you take away the sins of the world,
have mercy on us.
Lamb of God,
you take away the sins of the world,
grant us peace.

Amen.

✛ All make the Sign of the Cross.

OPENING

We hear today that Jesus is called *Rabbi*, the Hebrew name for "teacher." The disciples are worried about Jesus not eating, but Jesus responds that doing God's work is fulfilling enough for him. Jesus reminds us that we are all called to serve God, find opportunities to share God's love, and care for all of creation.

✦ All make the Sign of the Cross.

In the name of the Father, and of the Son, and of the Holy Spirit. Amen.

PSALM

(For a longer psalm, see page xii.)
Psalm 98:1

The Lord has made known his victory.

The Lord has made known his victory.

O sing to the Lord a new song,
  for he has done marvelous things.
His right hand and his holy arm
  have gotten him victory.

The Lord has made known his victory.

✦ All stand and sing **Alleluia.**

GOSPEL

John 4:31–35, 37–38

A reading from the holy Gospel according to John.

Meanwhile the disciples were urging him, "Rabbi, eat something." But he said to them, "I have food to eat that you do not know about." So the disciples said to one another, "Surely no one has brought him something to eat?" Jesus said to them, "My food is to do the will of him who sent me and to complete his work. Do you not say, 'Four months more, then comes the harvest'? But I tell you, look around you, and see how the fields are ripe for harvesting. For here the saying holds true, 'One sows and another reaps.' I sent you to reap that for which you did not labor. Others have labored, and you have entered into their labor."

The Gospel of the Lord.

✦ All sit and observe silence.

FOR SILENT REFLECTION

Think about this silently in your heart. You have many teachers in your life. What do they teach you about Jesus?

CLOSING PRAYER

Let us pray to God for our needs and the needs of others: our family, neighborhood, and the world. For each need we say, "Lord, hear our prayer."

✦ All may add their own prayers here.

Let us pray: **Our Father . . . Amen.**

God of Wisdom,
open our ears to listen to your teachings.
Open our hearts that we will follow
your commands.
May our lives give you honor and glory.
We pray this in the name
of our Master Teacher,
Jesus Christ our Lord.

Amen.

✦ All make the Sign of the Cross.

PRAYER FOR
FRIDAY, NOVEMBER 20, 2020

OPENING

In today's Gospel, Jesus reminds his disciples to practice what they preach. The religious leaders of Jesus' time were false teachers—they preached but did not do God's work. This is considered hypocritical, or insincere. Jesus calls himself the true Rabbi, or instructor, and Messiah.

✦ All make the Sign of the Cross.

In the name of the Father, and of the Son, and of the Holy Spirit. Amen.

PSALM

(For a longer psalm, see page xii.)
Psalm 98:1

The LORD has made known his victory.

The LORD has made known his victory.

O sing to the Lord a new song,
    for he has done marvelous things.
His right hand and his holy arm
    have gotten him victory.

The LORD has made known his victory.

◆ All stand and sing **Alleluia.**

GOSPEL

Matthew 23:1–5a, 6, 7b–8, 10

A reading from the holy Gospel according to Matthew.

Then Jesus said to the crowds and to his disciples, "The scribes and the Pharisees [FAYR-uh-seez] sit on Moses' seat; therefore, do whatever they teach you and follow it; but do not do as they do, for they do not practice what they teach. They tie up heavy burdens, hard to bear, and lay them on the shoulders of others; but they themselves are unwilling to lift a finger to move them. They do all their deeds to be seen by others. They love to have the place of honor at banquets and the best seats in the synagogues, and to have people call them rabbi. But you are not to be called rabbi, for you have one teacher, and you are all students. Nor are you to be called instructors, for you have one instructor, the Messiah."

The Gospel of the Lord.

◆ All sit and observe silence.

FOR SILENT REFLECTION

Think about this silently in your heart. We often know what Jesus wants us to do, but we do not always make the effort to do it. How can we remind ourselves to make the effort, and not be hypocritical?

CLOSING PRAYER

Let us pray to God for our needs and the needs of others: our family, neighborhood, and the world. For each need we say, "Lord, hear our prayer."

◆ All may add their own prayers here.

Let us pray: **Our Father . . . Amen.**

O Jesus,
help us to remember that being your disciple takes time and effort.
Help us when we struggle to follow your teachings.
Who live and reign with God the Father, in the unity of the Holy Spirit, one God, for ever and ever.

Amen.

✦ All make the Sign of the Cross.

PRAYER FOR THE WEEK

OPENING

Today we celebrate the solemnity of Christ the King. Jesus is not like a human king, who reigns on a throne over his people and lands. Jesus reigns in our hearts and over all of creation, and he is the humble servant of all. Today we hear that all that we do for any person in need, we do for him.

✦ All make the Sign of the Cross.

In the name of the Father, and of the Son, and of the Holy Spirit. Amen.

PSALM

(For a longer psalm, see page xii.)

Psalm 98:1

The LORD has made known his victory.

The LORD has made known his victory.

O sing to the Lord a new song,
    for he has done marvelous things.
His right hand and his holy arm
    have gotten him victory.

The LORD has made known his victory.

◆ All stand and sing **Alleluia.**

GOSPEL

Matthew 25:34b–38, 40

A reading from the holy Gospel according to Matthew.

The king will say to those at his right hand, "Come, you that are blessed by my Father, inherit the kingdom prepared for you from the foundation of the world; for I was hungry and you gave me food, I was thirsty and you gave me something to drink, I was a stranger and you welcomed me. I was naked and you gave me clothing, I was sick and you took care of me, I was in prison and you visited me." Then the righteous will answer him, "Lord, when was it that we saw you hungry and gave you food, or thirsty and gave you something to drink? And when was it that we saw you a stranger and welcomed you or naked and gave you clothing?" And the king will answer them, "Truly I tell you, just as you did it to one of the least of these who are members of my family, you did it to me."

The Gospel of the Lord.

◆ All sit and observe silence.

FOR SILENT REFLECTION

Think about this silently in your heart. How is doing something good for someone else an action done in Jesus' name?

CLOSING PRAYER

Let us pray to God for our needs and the needs of others: our family, neighborhood, and the world. For each need we say, "Lord, hear our prayer."

◆ All may add their own prayers here.

Let us pray: **Our Father . . . Amen.**

Jesus Christ our King,
we honor and praise you.
May you rule in our hearts and in our minds.
May we be worthy to serve you and
your people.
Who live and reign with God the Father,
in the unity of the Holy Spirit, one God,
for ever and ever.

Amen.

✦ All make the Sign of the Cross.

OPENING

We celebrate three holy men today. St. Clement I was the third pope after St. Peter (d. 100), St. Columbian was an Irish missionary (d. 615), and Blessed Miguel Augustín Pro (d. November 23, 1927) was a priest who continued to celebrate Mass, defying those who outlawed the Catholic Church in Mexico. All three stood against division and challenged those behaviors that went against Christ's teachings. We hear in today's reading that the prophet Jeremiah challenges the king of Judah.

✦ All make the Sign of the Cross.

In the name of the Father, and of the Son, and of the Holy Spirit. Amen.

PSALM

(For a longer psalm, see page xii.)
Psalm 98:1

The LORD has made known his victory.

The LORD has made known his victory.

O sing to the Lord a new song,
    for he has done marvelous things.
His right hand and his holy arm
    have gotten him victory.

The LORD has made known his victory.

READING

Jeremiah 22:2b, 3ab; 23:2acdfg, 3ab, 4abe

A reading from the Book of the prophet Jeremiah.

Hear the word of the LORD, O King of Judah sitting on the throne of David. Thus says the LORD: Act with justice and righteousness. Therefore thus says the LORD, concerning the shepherds who shepherd my people: It is you who have scattered my flock. So I will attend to you for your evil doings. Then I myself will gather the remnant of my flock out of all the lands where I have driven them, and I will bring them back to their fold. I will raise up shepherds over them who will shepherd them, and they shall not fear any longer, says the LORD.

The Word of the Lord.

◆ All observe silence.

FOR SILENT REFLECTION

Think about this silently in your heart. How is Jesus like a shepherd who unites his flock?

CLOSING PRAYER

Let us pray to God for our needs and the needs of others: our family, neighborhood, and the world. For each need we say, "Lord, hear our prayer."

◆ All may add their own prayers here.

Let us pray: **Our Father . . . Amen.**

Jesus our Good Shepherd,
so much divides your people.
Help us do our part to bring your
Kingdom to earth.
May we look to the three holy men we
remember today as models for how we can
stand up for Christian values.
Who live and reign with God the Father,
in the unity of the Holy Spirit, one God,
for ever and ever.

Amen.

✦ All make the Sign of the Cross.

OPENING

Today we remember St. Andrew Dūng-Lạc and his companions, who were martyred in Vietnam. On this day, Pope St. John Paul II beatified (and later canonized) 117 Vietnamese martyrs, including St. Andrew, who were persecuted and killed for their Catholic faith. In today's reading, Zechariah describes what will happen when people allow God to become king over all the earth.

✝ *All make the Sign of the Cross.*

In the name of the Father, and of the Son, and of the Holy Spirit. Amen.

PSALM

(For a longer psalm, see page xii.)
Psalm 98:1

The LORD has made known his victory.

The LORD has made known his victory.

O sing to the Lord a new song,
   for he has done marvelous things.
His right hand and his holy arm
   have gotten him victory.

The LORD has made known his victory.

READING

Zechariah 14:1a, 5d, 6–9, 20ab

A reading from the Book of the prophet Zechariah.

See, a day is coming for the LORD. Then the LORD my God will come. On that day there shall not be either cold or frost. And there shall be continuous day (it is known to the LORD), not day and not night, for at evening time there shall be light. On that day living waters shall flow out from Jerusalem, half of them to the eastern sea and half of them to the western sea;

it shall continue in summer as in winter. And the LORD will become king over all the earth; on that day the LORD will be one and his name one. On that day there shall be inscribed on the bells of the horses, "Holy to the LORD."

The Word of the Lord.

◆ *All observe silence.*

FOR SILENT REFLECTION

Think about this silently in your heart. Contemplate and imagine what such a day that Zechariah describes would actually look like.

CLOSING PRAYER

Let us pray to God for our needs and the needs of others: our family, neighborhood, and the world. For each need we say, "Lord, hear our prayer."

◆ *All may add their own prayers here.*

Let us pray: **Our Father . . . Amen.**

Holy God,
may we all imagine a day when all your people live together in peace, love, and justice. We need your guidance and love so that we can make your Kingdom a reality on earth.
St. Andrew Dūng-Lạc and his companions gave their lives to promote your Kingdom. We remember them and we pray in the name of Jesus Christ, our Savior and Lord.

Amen.

✝ *All make the Sign of the Cross.*

PRAYER FOR
WEDNESDAY, NOVEMBER 25, 2020

OPENING

Today we remember St. Catherine of Alexandria, the patroness of teachers, librarians, and students. She was young but clever enough to debate pagan philosophers. Today we read how the three Wise Men journeyed to find Jesus, the King of the Jews, in Bethlehem. They knelt before him and paid him homage, or treated him with great reverence and honor.

✦ All make the Sign of the Cross.

In the name of the Father, and of the Son, and of the Holy Spirit. Amen.

PSALM

(For a longer psalm, see page xii.)

Psalm 98:1

The LORD has made known his victory.

The LORD has made known his victory.

O sing to the Lord a new song,
  for he has done marvelous things.
His right hand and his holy arm
  have gotten him victory.

The LORD has made known his victory.

◆ All stand and sing **Alleluia.**

GOSPEL

Matthew 2:1ac–3a, 4, 5ab, 9b–11c

A reading from the holy Gospel according to Matthew.

In the time of King Herod, wise men from the East came to Jerusalem, asking, "Where is the child who has been born king of the Jews? For we observed his star at its rising, and have come to pay him homage." When King Herod heard this, he called together all the chief priests and scribes of the people, and inquired of them where the Messiah was to be born. They told him, "In Bethlehem of Judea." They set out; and there, ahead of them, went the star that they had seen at its rising, until it stopped over the place where the child was. When they saw that the star had stopped, they were overwhelmed with joy. On entering the house, they saw the child with Mary his mother; and they knelt down and paid him homage.

The Gospel of the Lord.

◆ All sit and observe silence.

FOR SILENT REFLECTION

Think about this silently in your heart. How might you give Jesus homage?

CLOSING PRAYER

Let us pray to God for our needs and the needs of others: our family, neighborhood, and the world. For each need we say, "Lord, hear our prayer."

◆ All may add their own prayers here.

Let us pray: **Our Father . . . Amen.**

O God our heavenly Father,
we thank you for the gift of your Son Jesus.
Show us signs of truth
so that we may follow in the right paths always.
We pray in the name of Jesus Christ,
your Son and our Savior.

Amen.

✦ All make the Sign of the Cross.

Find the reading (John 15:12–17) in your Bible, ask for a volunteer to read the Scripture passage, and encourage the reader to practice reading it a few times. If practical, light candles for your Thanksgiving table. You may wish to begin with a simple song of thanksgiving or a favorite "Alleluia." Then an older child or an adult reads the leader parts.

LEADER:

Almighty God,
look at the abundance here before us!
It fills us with joy and gratitude.
Let us begin our prayer with the
        Sign of the Cross.

✚ All make the Sign of the Cross.

In the name of the Father, and of the Son, and of the Holy Spirit. Amen.

◆ All stand and sing **Alleluia.**

READER: John 15:12–17

A reading from the holy Gospel according to John.

◆ Read the Gospel passage from the Bible.

The Gospel of the Lord.

◆ All sit and observe silence.

LEADER:

We come to this table,
grateful for the delicious meal we're about to share,
as well as the family and friends who surround us here.
Let us pray:
Heavenly Father,
we thank you for the love and friendship that envelops us today.
Help us to nurture one another
with your peace and serenity in the midst of our busy lives.
We thank all those who helped prepare
        this meal.
We are mindful of people in our
        community and
in other regions who may not have enough to
        eat today.
May we appreciate all that you provide for us
        now, and
we look forward to our heavenly banquet
        with you.
We ask this through our Lord Jesus Christ,
your Son, who lives and reigns with you
in the unity of the Holy Spirit, one God,
        for ever and ever.

ALL: Amen.

✚ All make the Sign of the Cross.

CHILDREN'S DAILY PRAYER 2020–2021 © 2020 Archdiocese of Chicago: Liturgy Training Publications, 3949 South Racine Avenue, Chicago, IL 60609. All rights reserved. Orders: 800-933-1800 or www.LTP.org. Scripture excerpts are taken from *The New Revised Standard Version Bible: Catholic Edition*, © 1989, Division of Christian Education of the National Council of the Churches of Christ in the United States of America. Used with permission. All rights reserved.

PRAYER SERVICE
FOR THANKSGIVING

Prepare seven leaders for this service. The fourth leader will need a Bible to read the Gospel passage and may need help finding and practicing the reading. You may want to begin by singing "One Bread, One Body," and end with "Table of Plenty." If the group will sing, prepare a song leader.

FIRST LEADER:

✝ All make the Sign of the Cross.

In the name of the Father, and of the Son, and of the Holy Spirit. Amen.

Let us pray:

Almighty God,
you bless us every day with the
signs and wonders of your creation.
We thank you for the fresh air,
trees, stars, and planets, as well as
all the animals and creatures that live on
      land and in the sea.
We are grateful that you have entrusted us
with care of your environment.

SECOND LEADER: Psalm 136:1–9
Our refrain is: For his steadfast love
endures forever.

ALL: For his steadfast love endures forever.

LEADER: O give thanks to the LORD,
for he is good,

ALL: For his steadfast love endures forever;

LEADER: Who alone does great wonders,

ALL: For his steadfast love endures forever;

LEADER: Who by understanding made
the heavens,

ALL: For his steadfast love endures forever;

CHILDREN'S DAILY PRAYER 2020–2021, © 2020 Archdiocese of Chicago: Liturgy Training Publications. All rights reserved. Orders: 800-933-1800 or www.LTP.org.

LEADER: Who spread out the earth on the waters,

ALL: For his steadfast love endures forever;

LEADER: Who made the great lights,

ALL: For his steadfast love endures forever;

LEADER: The sun to rule over the day,

ALL: For his steadfast love endures forever;

LEADER: The moon and stars to rule over the night,

ALL: For his steadfast love endures forever.

THIRD LEADER:
Creator God,
your presence is with us
today and always.
We are grateful for the
gift of your Son Jesus,
who lived and walked among us,
and whose Spirit fills our hearts
with gratitude and joy.

ALL: Amen.

FOURTH LEADER: 1 John 4:7–16
A reading from the first Letter of John.

◆ Read the Scripture passage from the Bible.

The Word of the Lord.

FIFTH LEADER: Psalm 100:1–5
Our refrain is: Make a joyful noise to the Lord.

ALL: Make a joyful noise to the Lord.

LEADER: Make a joyful noise to the Lord,
all the earth,
  Worship the Lord with gladness;
  Come into his presence with singing.

ALL: Make a joyful noise to the Lord.

LEADER: Know that the Lord is God.
  It is he that made us, and we are his;
  We are his people, and the sheep of
    his pasture.

ALL: Make a joyful noise to the Lord.

LEADER: Enter his gates with thanksgiving,
  and his courts with praise.
Give thanks to him, bless his name.

ALL: Make a joyful noise to the Lord.

SIXTH LEADER:
Loving God,
we thank you for all that you
provide for us.
We are grateful for all the loved ones
in our lives now,
and those who have gone before us.
You nurture us in so many ways.
May we always remember to praise you
and love others as you love us.
We ask this through Christ our Lord.

SEVENTH LEADER:
May the love of God,

✝ All make the Sign of the Cross.

Father, Son, and Holy Spirit,

always surround us in faith,
now and forever.

ALL: Amen.

HOME PRAYER
GATHERING AROUND AN ADVENT WREATH FOR PRAYER

Saturday evening before the First Sunday of Advent, gather the household around the wreath. Point out that the wreath is circular, with no beginning or end, like God's love. Explain that there are four candles, one for each Sunday of Advent. The third candle is rose because on the third Sunday we celebrate the joy of waiting for Christmas.

Use this service the first time you light your wreath and then on the following three Sundays when you light each new candle after the psalm response.

During the first week of Advent, light the first violet candle. During the second week of Advent, light two violet candles. For the third week, light two violet candles and one rose candle. During the final week of Advent, light all four candles. For your weekday celebration, simply light the candle(s), read one verse from Isaiah 40:1–5 and 9–11 (choose a different verse each time), and then say grace.

Before you begin, find the reading (John 1:1–5) in your Bible, ask a volunteer to read it, and encourage the reader to practice reading it a few times.

You may wish to begin with a simple Advent song, such as "O Come, O Come, Emmanuel," or "Soon and Very Soon." Then an older child or adult reads the leader parts.

LEADER:

Since ancient times, people have marked the passage of time with the light of the sun. In this holy season of Advent, we observe the passage of time through the light of this wreath, for each candle represents another week closer to the radiance of the newborn Son Jesus. Our anticipation for his glorious arrival can teach us much about patience as well as sharing the flame of our faith. So let us begin our time of prayer with the Sign of the Cross:

✚ All make the Sign of the Cross.

ALL: In the name of the Father, and of the Son, and of the Holy Spirit. Amen.

◆ Light the candle(s). Then all stand and sing **Alleluia**.

READER: John 1:1–5

A reading from the holy Gospel according to John.

◆ Read the Gospel passage from the Bible.

The Gospel of the Lord.

◆ All sit and observe silence.

LEADER:

God our Creator,
bless us as we gather around this
     Advent wreath,
ever anxious for the arrival of your Son, Jesus.
Renew us with your patience and
the light of your promise.
Help us to prepare our hearts
so that we are open to
your coming into our lives.
We ask this through Jesus Christ, our Lord.

ALL: Amen.

✚ All make the Sign of the Cross.

106 CHILDREN'S DAILY PRAYER 2020–2021 © 2020 Archdiocese of Chicago: Liturgy Training Publications, 3949 South Racine Avenue, Chicago, IL 60609. All rights reserved. Orders: 800-933-1800 or www.LTP.org. Scripture excerpts are taken from *The New Revised Standard Version Bible: Catholic Edition*, copyright © 1989, Division of Christian Education of the National Council of the Churches of Christ in the United States of America. Used with permission. All rights reserved.

ADVENT

SUNDAY, NOVEMBER 29 — THURSDAY, DECEMBER 24

ADVENT

THE MEANING OF ADVENT

"A shoot shall come out from the stump of Jesse, and a branch shall grow out of his roots" (Isaiah 11:1).

Jesse was the father of King David, a great leader of the Jewish people. But then Jesse's descendants became weak and scattered. The Jewish people no longer had a strong ruler and they suffered many periods of darkness, misery, and despair. The people of Israel had become like a great tree cut down to its stump. Yet God did not forsake the people. God, Israel's faithful protector, promised to make a new plant sprout. The people waited and prayed and hoped for many years, knowing God would keep this promise. We too are a people to whom God has made a solemn promise.

Advent is our time of waiting in "devout and joyful expectation" (*General Norms for the Liturgical Year*, 39) for the celebration of Christ's Incarnation and also for his Second Coming. We prepare as we wait by giving a little more to the poor and taking stock of our souls, as well as baking cookies and thinking about gifts for those we love. We wait, as did our spiritual ancestors, to celebrate the nativity of the Messiah. The first Sunday of Advent is also when the Church begins her new calendar year.

We begin our Advent with a week of Scriptures called the Messianic Prophecies. The prophets foretell where Jesus would be born and who his mother would be. They also predict Jesus' triumphant entry into Jerusalem on a donkey, his title of Good Shepherd, and that he will suffer. In the second and third week of our waiting we hear encouraging words that the Messiah would be the Light that breaks the darkness of injustice and brings peace. We'll hear the call of John the Baptist to "Prepare the Way of the Lord" (Luke 3:4). Our final week tells the great Infancy Narrative stories of the angel's announcement to Mary and reassurance to Joseph, and Mary's visit to Elizabeth with her joyful hymn of praise for God's wonderful work, the *Magnificat*.

PREPARING TO CELEBRATE ADVENT IN THE CLASSROOM

SACRED SPACE

During Advent create a mood of anticipation in the classroom. Use purples and violets on the bulletin boards instead of red and green since we are an Advent people. You can place the empty manger from a Christmas Nativity scene on your classroom prayer table. Slowly add elements like straw and animals and, in the last week, the Holy Family and shepherds. You might wait to add the star and the Magi after Christmas vacation, but it is not necessary.

You can also use an Advent wreath, which has a circular candleholder usually decorated with pine branches. It has four candles: three violet and one rose-colored (but you can use all violet or even white). When you first introduce the wreath to your class, wonder together with the children about why it's circular, why use pine boughs, why four candles. Children will often come up with beautiful answers to these questions: the wreath is round because God's love has no beginning and no end; the pine branches never lose their leaves or color just as God's love for us can never die; and the four candles represent the four Sundays of Advent, the four points of the compass, the four branches of the cross, the four Gospels, and so on. Explain that each day you will light one candle for each week in Advent; when all the candles are lit, then Christmas will be right around the corner! The children may be curious about the rose-colored candle. Explain that it is the third one that we light, for the third Sunday in Advent, which is called Gaudete [gow-DAY-tay] (Latin for "rejoice") because our wait is almost over!

MOVEMENT AND GESTURE

Children of all ages love solemn processions. Consider organizing an Advent procession. After sharing some of the material in "The Meaning of Advent" with them, explain that Advent has a new color, violet. Suggest to the children that you have a procession to change the color of your prayer tablecloth. You will want to speak with the children about processions they have participated in or have seen in church. Explain that a procession is a prayerful way to walk, and stress the importance of silence (or singing along if you plan to sing). You'll need children to place the Bible, Advent wreath, and other elements after the cloth is laid and, finally, someone to light the first candle. If you are not singing the procession could be accompanied by a wind chime.

FESTIVITY IN SCHOOL AND HOME

There are two wonderful feasts to celebrate in Advent, St. Nicholas (you may wish to hand out candy canes or "gold" chocolate coins) on December 6, and on December 13, St. Lucy (you may wish hand out cookies and hot chocolate). You might celebrate them in the week even if their day comes on a Saturday or Sunday. Please consider saving your celebration of Christmas until true Christmas time *after* December 25. The time of Advent is a great spiritual gift that helps us grow in the beautiful theological virtue of hope. Also, if you wait until you return from Christmas break to celebrate the great Christmas feast of Epiphany, the children will have settled down and may be more able to listen to the glad tidings of great joy.

In this book you will find special prayer services that may be used in the classroom or with a larger group. One is a service for Advent, pages 112–113, which could be used at any time; the other is for the Solemnity of the Immaculate Conception of the Blessed Virgin Mary on December 8, pages 122–123.

SACRED MUSIC

Discover which songs your parish will be singing during Advent. Sometimes the setting for the sung parts of the Mass will change with the liturgical time. Other Advent songs that children love include "The King of Glory Comes," "People Look East," and "O Come, O Come, Emmanuel."

PRAYERS FOR ADVENT

A wonderful prayer to become acquainted with during Advent is Mary's prayer of praise, the *Magnificat* (Luke 1:46–55). All those who pray the Liturgy of the Hours recite this beautiful prayer each evening to remember Mary's joy as she prayed to God, the Mighty One. It has been set to various tunes and may be sung. Two lovely sung versions are the Taizé "Magnificat" (canon) and "Holy Is Your Name."

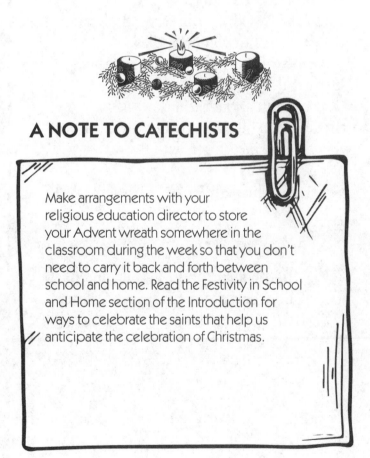

A NOTE TO CATECHISTS

Make arrangements with your religious education director to store your Advent wreath somewhere in the classroom during the week so that you don't need to carry it back and forth between school and home. Read the Festivity in School and Home section of the Introduction for ways to celebrate the saints that help us anticipate the celebration of Christmas.

GRACE BEFORE MEALS

ADVENT

LEADER:
Let the clouds rain down the Just One,
and the earth bring forth a Savior.

✚ All make the Sign of the Cross.

In the name of the Father, and of the Son, and of the Holy Spirit. Amen.

LEADER:
Lord God,
you provide for us in so many ways.
You have given us the earth,
full of so much goodness.
You have blessed us with water to drink
and food to nourish our bodies.
As we look forward to your gift of the
Christ child,
we also think about the day
when we will be with you in heaven,
where everyone is filled with the joy
of your glorious presence.
We ask this through Jesus Christ our Lord.

ALL: Amen.

✚ All make the Sign of the Cross.

In the name of the Father, and of the Son, and of the Holy Spirit. Amen.

PRAYER AT DAY'S END

ADVENT

LEADER:

O Wisdom of our God Most High,
guiding creation with power and love,
come to teach us the path of knowledge!

✚ All make the Sign of the Cross.

In the name of the Father, and of the Son, and of the Holy Spirit. Amen.

LEADER:

Holy God,
we thank you for this day
with all of its adventures, big and small.
May our days continue to be filled
with the light of your Son, our Lord,
your gift to us,
who shows us the way of
patience and forgiveness and love.
We ask this in his name.

ALL: Amen.

✚ All make the Sign of the Cross.

In the name of the Father, and of the Son, and of the Holy Spirit. Amen.

PRAYER SERVICE

ADVENT

Prepare a leader, reader, intercessor, and (if possible) a music leader for the service. Go over the intercessions with the class, and mention they are based on some Old Testament titles for Jesus we call the O Antiphons. Practice singing the refrain to "O Come, O Come Emmanuel" as the response, if possible. Place an Advent wreath on the table with a Bible and a purple cloth. Place the reading into the Bible and mark it with a ribbon or book mark. Review the reading with the reader and note that some verses are omitted. Decide who will light and extinguish the candles on the wreath. You might sing "Soon and Very Soon" at the end of the service.

LEADER:

- ◆ Gesture for all to stand.

- ✚ All make the sign of the Cross.

  In the name of the Father, and of the Son, and of the Holy Spirit. Amen.

LEADER:
Let us pray:
O God of wonder,
as we are busy preparing for Christmas
help us prepare our hearts for Jesus.
We are grateful for your simple words
    of hope
and the gift of new life in the Christ child.
May we follow the true light of Jesus
that shines for all people
through the darkness of sin and sorrow.
We ask this through Christ our Lord.

ALL: Amen.

CHILDREN'S DAILY PRAYER 2020–2021, © 2020 Archdiocese of Chicago: Liturgy Training Publications. All rights reserved. Orders: 800-933-1800 or www.LTP.org.

◆ Gesture for all to sit. An adult lights the appropriate number of candles on the Advent wreath. Allow a moment of silence to enjoy the beauty of the lit wreath. (For a discussion of the significance of the Advent wreath and a prayer for blessing it, see Preparing to Celebrate Advent in the Classroom, the section on Sacred Space on page 112.)

LEADER: Isaiah 40:5a, 11

Let us pray the psalm response:

The glory of the Lord shall be revealed.

ALL: The glory of the Lord shall be revealed.

LEADER:

He will feed his flock like a shepherd;
   he will gather the lambs in his arms,
and carry them in his bosom,
   and gently lead the mother sheep.

ALL: The glory of the Lord shall be revealed.

READER: Isaiah 11:1–10

A reading from the Book of the prophet Isaiah.

◆ Read the Scripture passage from a Bible.

The Word of the Lord.

◆ All observe silence.

INTERCESSOR:

O come, Emmanuel, free people who are held captive by racism, prejudice, and bullying. We sing:

ALL: "Rejoice! Rejoice! Emmanuel shall come to you, O Israel."

O come, Wisdom. Teach us how to be good
   to one another. We sing (say):

O come, Lord. Rule our hearts and minds in
   goodness. We sing (say):

O come, Shoot of Jesse's Stem. Forgive us our
   sins. We sing (say):

O come, Key of David. Open heaven for us.
   We sing (say):

O come, Dayspring. Replace the darkness of
   sin. We sing (say):

O come, Desire of Nations. Unite all the
   world's people. We sing (say):

LEADER:

Come quickly, Lord Jesus,
and guide us in God's way
of peace and justice.
Fill us with your gentle love
as we look forward to celebrating Christmas
with our family and friends.
You are our light and joy!

✛ All make the Sign of the Cross.

In the name of the Father, and of the Son and of the Holy Spirit.

◆ After the service someone extinguishes the candles on the Advent wreath.

PRAYER FOR THE WEEK

OPENING

Today is the First Sunday of Advent, a time of preparation and waiting for the birth of baby Jesus. We also wait for Jesus Christ to come again, so we light the first candle of our Advent wreath to symbolize the hope we have in anticipation of the coming Messiah. Today's parable reminds us that we must be alert and prepared for Jesus' coming.

✦ All make the Sign of the Cross.

In the name of the Father, and of the Son, and of the Holy Spirit. Amen.

PSALM

(For a longer psalm, see page xii.)

Psalm 85:8

Restore us again, O God of our salvation!

Restore us again, O God of our salvation!

Let me hear what God the LORD will speak,
for he will speak peace to his people,
to his faithful, to those who turn to him in
their hearts.

Restore us again, O God of our salvation!

✦ All stand and sing **Alleluia.**

GOSPEL

Mark 13:33–37

A reading from the holy Gospel according to Mark.

Beware, keep alert; for you do not know when the time will come. It is like a man going on a journey, when he leaves home and puts his slaves in charge, each with his work, and commands the doorkeeper to be on the watch. Therefore, keep awake—for you do not know when the master of the house will come, in the evening, or at midnight, or at cockcrow, or at dawn, or else he may find you asleep when he comes suddenly. And what I say to you I say to all: Keep awake.

The Gospel of the Lord.

✦ All sit and observe silence.

FOR SILENT REFLECTION

Think about this silently in your heart. How can you prepare for the coming of Jesus this Advent season?

CLOSING PRAYER

Let us pray to God for our needs and the needs of others: our family, neighborhood, and the world. For each need we say, "Lord, hear our prayer."

✦ All may add their own prayers here.

Let us pray: **Our Father . . . Amen.**

Dear God,
we eagerly await the birth of your
Son, Jesus,
with a hopeful heart.
Help us to stay awake and alert to
your presence
in our lives,
and may we see Jesus in one another this
Advent season.
We ask this through Jesus Christ, our Lord.

Amen.

✦ All make the Sign of the Cross.

OPENING

Today is the feast day of St. Andrew, a fisherman and one of the Twelve Apostles. This week we will hear prophecies from the Old Testament about the coming of the Messiah. These prophecies give hope to the people of Israel. The prophet Micah says the Messiah will come from the city of Bethlehem and will be a good shepherd.

✦ All make the Sign of the Cross.

In the name of the Father, and of the Son, and of the Holy Spirit. Amen.

PSALM

(For a longer psalm, see page xii.)

Psalm 85:8

Restore us again, O God of our salvation!

Restore us again, O God of our salvation!

Let me hear what God the LORD will speak,
for he will speak peace to his people,
to his faithful, to those who turn to him in
their hearts.

Restore us again, O God of our salvation!

READING

Micah 1:2a; 5:1–2, 4–5a

A reading from the Book of the prophet Micah.

Hear, you peoples, all of you. Now you are walled around with a wall; siege is laid against us; with a rod they strike the ruler of Israel upon the cheek. But you, O Bethlehem of Ephrathah [EF-ruh-thuh], who are one of the little clans of Judah, from you shall come forth for me one who is to rule in Israel, whose origin is from of old, from ancient days. And he shall stand and feed his flock in the strength of the LORD, in the majesty of the name of the LORD his God. And they shall live secure, for now he shall be great to the ends of the earth; and he shall be the one of peace.

The Word of the Lord.

◆ All observe silence.

FOR SILENT REFLECTION

Think about this silently in your heart. The prophet Micah says the Messiah will be one of peace. Pray today for peace in the world.

CLOSING PRAYER

Let us pray to God for our needs and the needs of others: our family, neighborhood, and the world. For each need we say, "Lord, hear our prayer."

◆ All may add their own prayers here.

Let us pray: **Our Father . . . Amen.**

Dear God,
we eagerly await the birth of your Son, Jesus,
with a hopeful heart.
Help us to stay awake and alert to
your presence
in our lives,
and may we see Jesus in one another this
Advent season.
We ask this through Jesus Christ, our Lord.
Amen.

✦ All make the Sign of the Cross.

OPENING

In today's reading, King Ahaz refuses to ask God for a sign of God's faithfulness because he does not want to test the Lord. Despite this, the prophet Isaiah [ī-ZAY-uh] tells the people of Israel there will be a sign: a young pregnant woman who bears a son named Immanuel, or "God with us."

✝ All make the Sign of the Cross.

In the name of the Father, and of the Son, and of the Holy Spirit. Amen.

PSALM

(For a longer psalm, see page xii.)
Psalm 85:8

Restore us again, O God of our salvation!

Restore us again, O God of our salvation!

Let me hear what God the LORD will speak,
for he will speak peace to his people,
to his faithful, to those who turn to him in their hearts.

Restore us again, O God of our salvation!

READING

Isaiah 7:3a, 4abc, 10–14

A reading from the Book of the prophet Isaiah.

Then the LORD said to Isaiah, Go out to meet Ahaz, and say to him, Take heed, be quiet, do not fear. Again the LORD spoke to Ahaz, saying, Ask a sign of the LORD your God; let it be deep as Sheol or high as heaven. But Ahaz said, I will not ask, and I will not put the LORD to the test. Then Isaiah said: "Hear then, O house of David! Is it too little for you to weary mortals, that you weary my God also? Therefore the Lord himself will give you a sign. Look, the young woman is with child and shall bear a son, and shall name him Immanuel."

The Word of the Lord.

◆ All observe silence.

FOR SILENT REFLECTION

Think about this silently in your heart. Jesus is called Immanuel. How does knowing that God is always with us make you feel?

CLOSING PRAYER

Let us pray to God for our needs and the needs of others: our family, neighborhood, and the world. For each need we say, "Lord, hear our prayer."

◆ All may add their own prayers here.

Let us pray: **Our Father . . . Amen.**

Dear God,
we eagerly await the birth of your Son, Jesus,
with a hopeful heart.
Help us to stay awake and alert to your presence
in our lives,
and may we see Jesus in one another this Advent season.
We ask this through Jesus Christ, our Lord.

Amen.

✝ All make the Sign of the Cross.

OPENING

The prophet Ezekiel foretold that God would be a good shepherd to the people of Israel. God will take care of all the sheep, even those who are scattered, lost, or injured. Let us reflect a moment on God's promise.

✢ All make the Sign of the Cross.

In the name of the Father, and of the Son, and of the Holy Spirit. Amen.

PSALM

(For a longer psalm, see page xii.)
Psalm 85:8

Restore us again, O God of our salvation!

Restore us again, O God of our salvation!

Let me hear what God the LORD will speak,
    for he will speak peace to his people,
to his faithful, to those who turn to him in
    their hearts.

Restore us again, O God of our salvation!

READING

Ezekiel 34:11, 12c, 14–16

A reading from the Book of the prophet Ezekiel.

For thus says the Lord GOD: I myself will search for my sheep, and will seek them out. I will rescue them from all the places to which they have been scattered on a day of clouds and thick darkness. I will feed them with good pasture, and the mountain heights of Israel shall be their pasture; there they shall lie down in good grazing land, and they shall feed on rich pasture on the mountains of Israel. I myself will be the shepherd of my sheep, and I will make them lie down, says the Lord GOD. I will seek the lost, and I will bring back the strayed, and I will bind up the injured, and I will strengthen the weak, but the fat and the strong I will destroy. I will feed them with justice.

The Word of the Lord.

◆ All observe silence.

FOR SILENT REFLECTION

Think about this silently in your heart. How does Jesus our Good Shepherd care for us, his sheep?

CLOSING PRAYER

Let us pray to God for our needs and the needs of others: our family, neighborhood, and the world. For each need we say, "Lord, hear our prayer."

◆ All may add their own prayers here.

Let us pray: **Our Father . . . Amen.**

Dear God,
we eagerly await the birth of your Son, Jesus,
with a hopeful heart.
Help us to stay awake and alert to
your presence
in our lives,
and may we see Jesus in one another this
Advent season.
We ask this through Jesus Christ, our Lord.

Amen.

✢ All make the Sign of the Cross.

OPENING

Today we remember St. Francis Xavier, one of the founding members of the Society of Jesus, or the Jesuits (1506–1552). Forsaking a life in academia and wealth, St. Francis Xavier decided to spread the Good News throughout the East. We hear in today's reading that the savior will be different from the earthly kings of the time. He will be riding on a donkey rather than on a noble warhorse. Jesus rode into Jerusalem on a donkey and the people waved palm branches and cheered to welcome him.

✚ All make the Sign of the Cross.

In the name of the Father, and of the Son, and of the Holy Spirit. Amen.

PSALM

(For a longer psalm, see page xii.)
Psalm 85:8

Restore us again, O God of our salvation!

Restore us again, O God of our salvation!

Let me hear what God the Lord will speak,
for he will speak peace to his people,
to his faithful, to those who turn to him in
their hearts.

Restore us again, O God of our salvation!

READING

Zechariah 9:9–10bd, 11, 16–17a

A reading from the Book of the prophet Zechariah.

Rejoice greatly, O daughter Zion! Shout aloud, O daughter Jerusalem! Lo, your king comes to you; triumphant and victorious is he, humble and riding on a donkey, on a colt, the foal of a donkey. The battle bow shall be cut off, and he shall command peace to the nations; his dominion shall be from sea to sea. As for you also, because of the blood of my covenant with you, I will set your prisoners free from the waterless pit. On that day the Lord their God will save them for they are the flock of his people; for like the jewels of a crown they shall shine on his land. For what goodness and beauty are his!

The Word of the Lord.

◆ All observe silence.

FOR SILENT REFLECTION

Think about this silently in your heart. Why would the Messiah arrive on a humble donkey?

CLOSING PRAYER

Let us pray to God for our needs and the needs of others: our family, neighborhood, and the world. For each need we say, "Lord, hear our prayer."

◆ All may add their own prayers here.

Let us pray: **Our Father . . . Amen.**

Dear God,
we eagerly await the birth of your Son, Jesus, with a hopeful heart.
Help us to stay awake and alert to
your presence
in our lives,
and may we see Jesus in one another this Advent season.
We ask this through Jesus Christ, our Lord.

Amen.

✚ All make the Sign of the Cross.

OPENING

We celebrate the feast of St. John, a monk from Damascus, who was a prolific writer in defense of the Christian faith (676–749). We hear today that the prophet Isaiah [ī-ZAY-uh] speaks of how the Messiah will take on the sins of the world and will suffer greatly even though he is blameless. The word *infirmities* means "frailties"; *transgressions* means "violations of law, command, or duty"; and *iniquities* means "wicked acts or sins"

✝ All make the Sign of the Cross.

In the name of the Father, and of the Son, and of the Holy Spirit. Amen.

PSALM

(For a longer psalm, see page xii.)
Psalm 85:8

Restore us again, O God of our salvation!

Restore us again, O God of our salvation!

Let me hear what God the LORD will speak,
    for he will speak peace to his people,
to his faithful, to those who turn to him in
    their hearts.

Restore us again, O God of our salvation!

READING

Isaiah 52:13a; 53:3ac, 4ac, 5ab, 7ab, 9

A reading from the Book of the prophet Isaiah.

See, my servant shall prosper. He was despised and rejected by others; and we held him of no account. Surely he has borne our infirmities and carried our diseases; yet we accounted him stricken, and afflicted. But he was wounded for our transgressions, crushed for our iniquities; upon him was the punishment that made us whole, and by his bruises we are healed. He was oppressed, and he was afflicted, yet he did not open his mouth. They made his grave with the wicked and his tomb with the rich, although he had done no violence, and there was no deceit in his mouth.

The Word of the Lord.

◆ All observe silence.

FOR SILENT REFLECTION

Think about this silently in your heart. Have you ever been blamed for something you did not do? What did you do?

CLOSING PRAYER

Let us pray to God for our needs and the needs of others: our family, neighborhood, and the world. For each need we say, "Lord, hear our prayer."

◆ All may add their own prayers here.

Let us pray: **Our Father . . . Amen.**

Dear God,
we eagerly await the birth of your Son, Jesus,
with a hopeful heart.
Help us to stay awake and alert to
your presence
in our lives,
and may we see Jesus in one another this
Advent season.
We ask this through Jesus Christ, our Lord.

Amen.

✝ All make the Sign of the Cross.

PRAYER FOR THE WEEK

OPENING

On this Second Sunday of Advent, we light two violet candles to symbolize the peace of God that we welcome into our hearts this season. We learn today from the Gospel of Mark about John the Baptist. St. John spread a message of Baptism and turning our hearts back to God and away from sin. Baptism with water symbolizes the washing away of our sins. St. John is the fulfillment of Isaiah's prophecy that a messenger would be sent ahead of the Messiah.

✝ All make the Sign of the Cross.

In the name of the Father, and of the Son, and of the Holy Spirit. Amen.

PSALM

(For a longer psalm, see page xii.)
Psalm 85:8

Restore us again, O God of our salvation!

Restore us again, O God of our salvation!

Let me hear what God the LORD will speak,
    for he will speak peace to his people,
to his faithful, to those who turn to him in
    their hearts.

Restore us again, O God of our salvation!

◆ All stand and sing **Alleluia.**

GOSPEL

Mark 1:1–5

A reading from the holy Gospel according to Mark.

The beginning of the good news of Jesus Christ, the Son of God. As it is written in the prophet Isaiah, "See, I am sending my messenger ahead of you, who will prepare your way; the voice of one crying out in the wilderness: 'Prepare the way of the Lord, make his paths straight,'" John the baptizer appeared in the wilderness, proclaiming a baptism of repentance for the forgiveness of sins. And people from the whole Judean countryside and all the people of Jerusalem were going out to him, and were baptized by him in the river Jordan, confessing their sins.

The Gospel of the Lord.

◆ All sit and observe silence.

FOR SILENT REFLECTION

Think about this silently in your heart. How can asking God for forgiveness when we are sorry bring us peace in our hearts?

CLOSING PRAYER

Let us pray to God for our needs and the needs of others: our family, neighborhood, and the world. For each need we say, "Lord, hear our prayer."

◆ All may add their own prayers here.

Let us pray: **Our Father . . . Amen.**

O God of Peace,
as we prepare for the birth of Jesus,
make our hearts and minds ready to
welcome your Son.
May we ask for forgiveness when we have
done wrong, and may we forgive others when
they have wronged us.
In Christ's name, we pray.

Amen.

✝ All make the Sign of the Cross.

OPENING

Our readings this week are all prophecies by Isaiah about the coming of the Messiah. They are known as the Messianic prophecies. In today's reading, we hear that, through sin, we experience darkness. We await light that only the Messiah can bring. We remember that Jesus is the Light of the World. Today we celebrate the feast of St. Ambrose, a bishop who opened the eyes of St. Augustine, helping him turn from his former ways. St. Augustine went on to become one of the Doctors of the Church.

✝ All make the Sign of the Cross.

In the name of the Father, and of the Son, and of the Holy Spirit. Amen.

PSALM

(For a longer psalm, see page xii.)

Psalm 85:8

Restore us again, O God of our salvation!

Restore us again, O God of our salvation!

Let me hear what God the LORD will speak,
   for he will speak peace to his people,
to his faithful, to those who turn to him in
   their hearts.

Restore us again, O God of our salvation!

READING

Isaiah 59:9–12

A reading from the Book of the prophet Isaiah.

Therefore justice is far from us, and righteousness does not reach us; we wait for light, and lo! there is darkness; and for brightness, but we walk in gloom. We grope like the blind along a wall, groping like those who have no eyes; we stumble at noon as in the twilight, among the vigorous as though we were dead. We all growl like bears; like doves we moan mournfully. We wait for justice, but there is none; for salvation, but it is far from us. For our transgressions before you are many, and our sins testify against us. Our transgressions indeed are with us, and we know our iniquities.

The Word of the Lord.

◆ All observe silence.

FOR SILENT REFLECTION

Think about this silently in your heart. How does Jesus transform our darkness into light?

CLOSING PRAYER

Let us pray to God for our needs and the needs of others: our family, neighborhood, and the world. For each need we say, "Lord, hear our prayer."

◆ All may add their own prayers here.

Let us pray: **Our Father . . . Amen.**

O God of Peace,
as we prepare for the birth of Jesus,
make our hearts and minds ready to
welcome your Son.
May we ask for forgiveness when we have
done wrong, and may we forgive others
when they have wronged us.
In Christ's name, we pray.

Amen.

✝ All make the Sign of the Cross.

PRAYER SERVICE
SOLEMNITY OF THE IMMACULATE CONCEPTION OF MARY

Prepare six leaders for this service. The third leader will need a Bible for the passages from Luke. Help the third leader practice the readings. You may wish to sing "Sing of Mary" as the opening song. If the group will sing, prepare someone to lead it.

FIRST LEADER:

We remember Mary, the Mother of Jesus, on this special day. We celebrate her Immaculate Conception and believe she was conceived with God's special grace in her mother's womb so that one day she would bear Jesus, her Son, our Lord and Savior. She was filled with God's grace and the guidance of the Holy Spirit as she continually followed God's will. She nurtured Jesus in her womb, guided her Son in his youth, and stood by him in his ministry, even through his death and Resurrection. She is the patroness of the United States because of her constant courage. Let us begin our prayer service in her honor by singing the opening song.

SONG LEADER:

◆ Gesture for all to stand, and lead the first few verses of the song.

SECOND LEADER:

✝ All make the Sign of the Cross.

In the name of the Father, and of the Son, and of the Holy Spirit. Amen.

Let us pray:
Almighty Father,
you gave Mary special grace
when she was conceived
in her mother's womb.
You chose for her a unique role
to bring salvation to the world.
She is a sign of hope

CHILDREN'S DAILY PRAYER 2020–2021, © 2020 Archdiocese of Chicago: Liturgy Training Publications. All rights reserved. Orders: 800-933-1800 or www.LTP.org.

because of her courage to say yes to you,
every moment of her life.
We pray with her to your Son Jesus,
our Lord and Savior,
in union with the Holy Spirit.

Amen.

◆ Remain standing and sing **Alleluia.**

THIRD LEADER: Luke 1:26–38
A reading from the holy Gospel according
to Luke.

◆ Read the Gospel passage from the Bible.

The Gospel of the Lord.

◆ All sit and observe silence.

FOURTH LEADER:

◆ Gesture for all to stand.

Let us bring our hopes and needs to God as
we pray, "Lord, hear our prayer."

For the courage to say, "yes" to God
as Mary did throughout her life,
we pray to the Lord.

For all who are struggling with
tough decisions in life,
may they look to Mary as
a true friend on their journey,
we pray to the Lord.

For all married people,
may they continue to be an example
of the love and devotion that
Mary and Joseph shared,
we pray to the Lord.

For all mothers
and those who nurture others,

help us to respect and protect life
from conception until natural death,
we pray to the Lord.

For those throughout the world
who are suffering from
hunger, lack of shelter, or disease,
and for those who have died,
may we have the compassion of Mary
to give us hope and the promise
of new life through Jesus,
we pray to the Lord.

FIFTH LEADER:
Let us pray the Hail Mary:

ALL: Hail Mary, full of grace . . .

◆ Pause, and then say:

Let us offer one another the sign of
Christ's peace.

◆ All offer one another a sign of peace.

SIXTH LEADER:
Let us pray Mary's special prayer,
the *Magnificat*:
"My soul magnifies the Lord,
    and my spirit rejoices in God my Savior,
for he has looked with favor on the lowliness
        of his servant.
    Surely, from now on all generations will
        call me blessed;
for the Mighty One has done great things
        for me,
    and holy is his name."

✚ All make the Sign of the Cross.

**In the name of the Father, and of the
Son, and of the Holy Spirit. Amen.**

OPENING

Today we celebrate the Immaculate Conception of the Blessed Virgin Mary, a title that recognizes that Mary came into the world free from sin. Her sinless nature helps Jesus to redeem humanity. In today's reading, Isaiah [ī-ZAY-uh] says that although there is great darkness in the world, we are called to arise and shine and let God's light shine in and through our lives.

✦ All make the Sign of the Cross.

In the name of the Father, and of the Son, and of the Holy Spirit. Amen.

PSALM

(For a longer psalm, see page xii.)

Psalm 85:8

Restore us again, O God of our salvation!

Restore us again, O God of our salvation!

Let me hear what God the LORD will speak,
    for he will speak peace to his people,
to his faithful, to those who turn to him in
    their hearts.

Restore us again, O God of our salvation!

READING

Isaiah 60:1–5b

A reading from the Book of the prophet Isaiah.

Arise, shine; for your light has come, and the glory of the LORD has risen upon you. For darkness shall cover the earth, and thick darkness the peoples; but the LORD will arise upon you, and his glory will appear over you. Nations shall come to your light, and kings to the brightness of your dawn. Lift up your eyes and look around; they all gather together, they come to you; your sons shall come from far away, and your daughters shall be carried on their nurses' arms. Then you shall see and be radiant; your heart shall thrill and rejoice.

The Word of the Lord.

◆ All observe silence.

FOR SILENT REFLECTION

Think about this silently in your heart. How can the light of Christ within you shine outward?

CLOSING PRAYER

Let us pray to God for our needs and the needs of others: our family, neighborhood, and the world. For each need we say, "Lord, hear our prayer."

◆ All may add their own prayers here.

Let us pray: **Our Father . . . Amen.**

O God of Peace,
as we prepare for the birth of Jesus,
make our hearts and minds ready to
welcome your Son.
May we ask for forgiveness when we have
done wrong, and may we forgive others
when they have wronged us.
We also remember our Mother Mary,
who came into the world without sin.
May she be a shining example for us.
In Christ's name, we pray.

Amen.

✦ All make the Sign of the Cross

OPENING

Isaiah talks of a "shoot," or branch, that came from the stump of Jesse. Jesse was the father of King David. Jesus traces his lineage from the family of King David. We use a Jesse Tree to show Jesus' family tree. Today is the feast of St. Juan Diego, a Native American who converted to Christianity. Our Lady of Guadalupe appeared to him to ask him to build a church in her honor.

✚ All make the Sign of the Cross.

In the name of the Father, and of the Son, and of the Holy Spirit. Amen.

PSALM

(For a longer psalm, see page xii.)

Psalm 85:8

Restore us again, O God of our salvation!

Restore us again, O God of our salvation!

Let me hear what God the LORD will speak, for he will speak peace to his people,
to his faithful, to those who turn to him in their hearts.

Restore us again, O God of our salvation!

READING

Isaiah 11:1–3a, 5, 10

A reading from the Book of the prophet Isaiah.

A shoot shall come out from the stump of Jesse, and a branch shall grow out of his roots. The spirit of the LORD shall rest on him, the spirit of wisdom and understanding, the spirit of counsel and might, the spirit of knowledge and the fear of the LORD. His delight shall be in the fear of the LORD. Righteousness shall be the belt around his waist, and faithfulness the belt around his loins. On that day the root of Jesse shall stand as a signal to the peoples; the nations shall inquire of him, and his dwelling shall be glorious.

The Word of the Lord.

◆ All observe silence.

FOR SILENT REFLECTION

Think about this silently in your heart. Why do you think it was important for the people of Israel to know that the Messiah would come from a royal line?

CLOSING PRAYER

Let us pray to God for our needs and the needs of others: our family, neighborhood, and the world. For each need we say, "Lord, hear our prayer."

◆ All may add their own prayers here.

Let us pray: **Our Father . . . Amen.**

We wait in joyful hope, O God,
for the coming of your Son Jesus.
As Isaiah promised,
your spirit will rest upon him,
and he will show us the way to you.
In Christ's name, we pray.

Amen.

✚ All make the Sign of the Cross.

OPENING

In today's prophecy from Isaiah, when the Messiah rules over the earth, the world will be a peaceful place where there is no violence, pain, or conflict.

✚ All make the Sign of the Cross.

In the name of the Father, and of the Son, and of the Holy Spirit. Amen.

PSALM

(For a longer psalm, see page xii.)
Psalm 85:8

Restore us again, O God of our salvation!

Restore us again, O God of our salvation!

Let me hear what God the LORD will speak,
  for he will speak peace to his people,
to his faithful, to those who turn to him in
  their hearts.

Restore us again, O God of our salvation!

READING

Isaiah 11:6–9

A reading from the Book of the
prophet Isaiah.

The wolf shall live with the lamb, the leopard shall lie down with the kid, the calf and the lion and the fatling together, and a little child shall lead them. The cow and the bear shall graze, their young shall lie down together; and the lion shall eat straw like the ox. The nursing child shall play over the hole of the asp, and the weaned child shall put its hand on the adder's den. They will not hurt or destroy on all my holy mountain; for the earth will be full of the knowledge of the LORD as the waters cover the sea.

The Word of the Lord.

◆ All observe silence.

FOR SILENT REFLECTION

Think about this silently in your heart. Isaiah presents many images that seem impossible. Reflect on how the world might be like if we could live harmoniously in the same way.

CLOSING PRAYER

Let us pray to God for our needs and the needs of others: our family, neighborhood, and the world. For each need we say, "Lord, hear our prayer."

◆ All may add their own prayers here.

Let us pray: **Our Father . . . Amen.**

O God of Peace,
as we prepare for the birth of Jesus,
make our hearts and minds ready to
welcome your Son.
May we ask for forgiveness when we have
done wrong, and may we forgive others
when they have wronged us.
May we live together in your Creation
in peace and harmony.
In Christ's name, we pray.

Amen.

✚ All make the Sign of the Cross.

OPENING

Today we hear a vision of the reign of God, in which the Messiah would sit on the throne. Isaiah describes a world in which the righteousness and justice of God rules. Righteousness in the Old Testament speaks of behavior that is morally just. When righteousness abides, there will be peace, quietness, and justice. St. Damasus I, whose feast day we celebrate today, defended the faith during a turbulent time in Church history.

✝ All make the Sign of the Cross.

In the name of the Father, and of the Son, and of the Holy Spirit. Amen.

PSALM

(For a longer psalm, see page xii.)
Psalm 85:8

Restore us again, O God of our salvation!

Restore us again, O God of our salvation!

Let me hear what God the LORD will speak,
for he will speak peace to his people,
to his faithful, to those who turn to him in
their hearts.

Restore us again, O God of our salvation!

READING

Isaiah 32:1, 16–18

A reading from the Book of the prophet Isaiah.

See, a king will reign in righteousness, and princes will rule with justice. Then justice will dwell in the wilderness, and righteousness abide in the fruitful field. The effect of righteousness will be peace, and the result of righteousness, quietness and trust forever. My people will abide in a peaceful habitation, in secure dwellings, and in quiet resting places.

The Word of the Lord.

◆ All observe silence.

FOR SILENT REFLECTION

Think about this silently in your heart. Can you find some quiet each day to rest in God's presence?

CLOSING PRAYER

Let us pray to God for our needs and the needs of others: our family, neighborhood, and the world. For each need we say, "Lord, hear our prayer."

◆ All may add their own prayers here.

Let us pray: **Our Father . . . Amen.**

O God of Peace,
as we prepare for the birth of Jesus,
make our hearts and minds ready to welcome your Son.
May we ask for forgiveness when we have done wrong, and may we forgive others when they have wronged us.
In Christ's name, we pray.

Amen.

✝ All make the Sign of the Cross.

PRAYER FOR THE WEEK
WITH A READING FROM THE GOSPEL FOR **SUNDAY, DECEMBER 13, 2020**

OPENING

Today is the third week of Advent, known as Gaudete [Gow-DAY-tay] Sunday. *Gaudete* means "rejoice." We rejoice that the birth of our Lord is near! We light the two violet candles and the rose-colored candle today. Because we are celebrating the coming of the Lord, the liturgical colors at Mass include rose. In today's reading, we hear John the Baptist proclaiming the coming of the Messiah.

✠ All make the Sign of the Cross.

In the name of the Father, and of the Son, and of the Holy Spirit. Amen.

PSALM

(For a longer psalm, see page xii.)
Psalm 85:8

Restore us again, O God of our salvation!

Restore us again, O God of our salvation!

Let me hear what God the LORD will speak,
for he will speak peace to his people,
to his faithful, to those who turn to him in their hearts.

Restore us again, O God of our salvation!

◆ All stand and sing **Alleluia.**

GOSPEL

John 1:6, 19, 23–27

A reading from the holy Gospel according to John.

There was a man sent from God, whose name was John. This the testimony given by John when the Jews sent priests and Levites from Jerusalem to ask him, "Who are you?" He said, "I am the voice of one crying out in the wilderness, 'Make straight the way of the Lord,'" as the prophet Isaiah said. Now they had been sent from the Pharisees [FAYR-uh-seez]. They asked him, "Why then are you baptizing if you are neither the Messiah, nor Elijah, nor the prophet?" John answered them, "I baptize with water. Among you stands one whom you do not know, the one who is coming after me; I am not worthy to untie the thong of his sandal."

The Gospel of the Lord.

◆ All sit and observe silence.

FOR SILENT REFLECTION

Think about this silently in your heart. This week, how might you show and share your joy for Jesus' coming?

CLOSING PRAYER

Let us pray to God for our needs and the needs of others: our family, neighborhood, and the world. For each need we say, "Lord, hear our prayer."

◆ All may add their own prayers here.

Let us pray: **Our Father . . . Amen.**

May our hearts be open to signs of your presence among us, O Lord.
May we, like John the Baptist, be faithful witnesses to your good works.
We pray in the name of Jesus Christ,
for whom we wait in hope.

Amen.

✠ All make the Sign of the Cross.

OPENING

Today is the memorial for St. John of the Cross (1542–1591). He was a Spanish priest known for his many writings and poems, written during dark days of his imprisonment. This week we hear more from the prophet Isaiah, who speaks about the great rejoicing that will occur when the Messiah comes.

✦ All make the Sign of the Cross.

In the name of the Father, and of the Son, and of the Holy Spirit. Amen.

PSALM

(For a longer psalm, see page xii.)
Psalm 85:8

Restore us again, O God of our salvation!

Restore us again, O God of our salvation!

Let me hear what God the LORD will speak,
for he will speak peace to his people,
to his faithful, to those who turn to him in
their hearts.

Restore us again, O God of our salvation!

READING

Isaiah 35:1–2b, 4–6

A reading from the Book of the prophet Isaiah.

The wilderness and the dry land shall be glad, the desert shall rejoice and blossom; like the crocus it shall blossom abundantly, and rejoice with joy and singing. Say to those who are of a fearful heart, "Be strong, do not fear! Here is your God. He will come with vengeance, with terrible recompense. He will come and save you." Then the eyes of the blind shall be opened, and the ears of the deaf unstopped; then the lame shall leap like a deer, and the tongue of the speechless sing for joy. For waters shall break forth in the wilderness, and streams in the desert.

The Word of the Lord.

✦ All observe silence.

FOR SILENT REFLECTION

Think about this silently in your heart. How does your family rejoice and celebrate Christmas Day?

CLOSING PRAYER

Let us pray to God for our needs and the needs of others: our family, neighborhood, and the world. For each need we say, "Lord, hear our prayer."

✦ All may add their own prayers here.

Let us pray: **Our Father . . . Amen.**

We long for the day, O Lord,
when the dry land shall be glad
and the desert shall rejoice and blossom.
Keep us faithful to you as we await
the coming of your Son,
our Lord Jesus Christ,
in whose name we pray.

Amen.

✦ All make the Sign of the Cross.

PRAYER FOR
TUESDAY, DECEMBER 15, 2020

OPENING

As we await the birth of Jesus, Isaiah describes the coming of the Lord as a day of rejoicing. The Lord God will come as a shepherd who will care for his flock.

✤ All make the Sign of the Cross.

In the name of the Father, and of the Son, and of the Holy Spirit. Amen.

PSALM

(For a longer psalm, see page xii.)

Psalm 85:8

Restore us again, O God of our salvation!

Restore us again, O God of our salvation!

Let me hear what God the LORD will speak,
   for he will speak peace to his people,
to his faithful, to those who turn to him in
   their hearts.

Restore us again, O God of our salvation!

READING

Isaiah 40:9–11

A reading from the Book of the prophet Isaiah.

Get you up to a high mountain, O Zion, herald of good tidings; lift up your voice with strength, O Jerusalem, herald of good tidings, lift it up, do not fear; say to the cities of Judah, "Here is your God!" See, the Lord GOD comes with might, and his arm rules for him; his reward is with him, and his recompense before him. He will feed his flock like a shepherd; he will gather the lambs in his arms, and carry them in his bosom, and gently lead the mother sheep.

The Word of the Lord.

◆ All observe silence.

FOR SILENT REFLECTION

Think about this silently in your heart. Why do you think that Jesus is like a Good Shepherd?

CLOSING PRAYER

Let us pray to God for our needs and the needs of others: our family, neighborhood, and the world. For each need we say, "Lord, hear our prayer."

◆ All may add their own prayers here.

Let us pray: **Our Father . . . Amen.**

As we wait for the celebration of
Jesus' birth, O God,
show us how to use this time
to make our hearts ready.
May we ask for forgiveness when we have
done wrong, and may we forgive others
when they have wronged us.
We pray in the name of the Good Shepherd,
Jesus Christ our Lord.

Amen.

✤ All make the Sign of the Cross.

OPENING

We hear Isaiah's reminder that God helped the Israelites cross the Red Sea out of Egypt. God will return to them again through the Messiah. Isaiah says the Messiah will come to Zion, also known as Jerusalem. When the Messiah comes, Isaiah says, there will be great rejoicing and singing. Christmas Day is near; we too will rejoice and sing.

✝ All make the Sign of the Cross.

In the name of the Father, and of the Son, and of the Holy Spirit. Amen.

PSALM

(For a longer psalm, see page xii.)
Psalm 85:8

Restore us again, O God of our salvation!

Restore us again, O God of our salvation!

Let me hear what God the LORD will speak,
    for he will speak peace to his people,
to his faithful, to those who turn to him in
    their hearts.

Restore us again, O God of our salvation!

READING

Isaiah 51:9ab, 10–11

A reading from the Book of the prophet Isaiah.

Awake, awake, put on strength, O arm of the LORD! Awake, as in days of old, the generations of long ago! Was it not you who dried up the sea, the waters of the great deep; who made the depths of the sea a way for the redeemed to cross over? So the ransomed of the LORD shall return, and come to Zion with singing; everlasting joy shall be upon their heads; they shall obtain joy and gladness, and sorrow and sighing shall flee away.

The Word of the Lord.

◆ All observe silence.

FOR SILENT REFLECTION

Think about this silently in your heart. Isaiah says that there will be no sorrow when the Messiah comes. Do you have any sorrows? Pray that Jesus can lift them from your heart.

CLOSING PRAYER

Let us pray to God for our needs and the needs of others: our family, neighborhood, and the world. For each need we say, "Lord, hear our prayer."

◆ All may add their own prayers here.

Let us pray: **Our Father . . . Amen.**

Almighty God,
you led the Israelites to freedom.
Jesus will free us from the bonds of sin
and death.
You are faithful to the promise you make to
your people,
and we wait in hope for the day of
Christ's return.
Through Christ our Lord.

Amen.

✝ All make the Sign of the Cross.

PRAYER FOR
THURSDAY, DECEMBER 17, 2020

OPENING

We hear more from the prophet Isaiah, who reminds us of the words of John the Baptist. Listen closely—you will hear similar words in tomorrow's Gospel passage.

✛ All make the Sign of the Cross.

In the name of the Father, and of the Son, and of the Holy Spirit. Amen.

PSALM

(For a longer psalm, see page xii.)

Psalm 85:8

Restore us again, O God of our salvation!

Restore us again, O God of our salvation!

Let me hear what God the LORD will speak,
  for he will speak peace to his people,
to his faithful, to those who turn to him in
  their hearts.

Restore us again, O God of our salvation!

READING

Isaiah 40:3–5

A reading from the Book of the prophet Isaiah.

A voice cries out: "In the wilderness prepare the way of the LORD, make straight in the desert a highway for our God. Every valley shall be lifted up, and every mountain and hill be made low; the uneven ground shall become level, and the rough places a plain. Then the glory of the LORD shall be revealed, and all people shall see it together, for the mouth of the LORD has spoken."

The Word of the Lord.

◆ All observe silence.

FOR SILENT REFLECTION

Think about this silently in your heart. What do you think of Isaiah's prophecy? What would be different if mountains are made low and valleys rise up? What do level grounds signify?

CLOSING PRAYER

Let us pray to God for our needs and the needs of others: our family, neighborhood, and the world. For each need we say, "Lord, hear our prayer."

◆ All may add their own prayers here.

Let us pray: **Our Father . . . Amen.**

O God of Peace,
as we prepare for the birth of Jesus,
make our hearts and minds ready to
welcome your Son.
May we ask for forgiveness when we have
done wrong, and may we forgive others
when they have wronged us.
In Christ's name, we pray.

Amen.

✛ All make the Sign of the Cross.

OPENING

In today's Gospel according to Mark, John the Baptist fulfills the prophecy of Isaiah by proclaiming the coming of the Messiah, Jesus. We have been preparing our hearts and homes to welcome Jesus. Rejoice—only one more week until the birth of our Savior.

✛ All make the Sign of the Cross.

In the name of the Father, and of the Son, and of the Holy Spirit. Amen.

PSALM

(For a longer psalm, see page xii.)
Psalm 85:8

Restore us again, O God of our salvation!

Restore us again, O God of our salvation!

Let me hear what God the LORD will speak,
for he will speak peace to his people,
to his faithful, to those who turn to him in
their hearts.

Restore us again, O God of our salvation!

◆ All stand and sing **Alleluia.**

GOSPEL

Mark 1:1–4

A reading from the holy Gospel according to Mark.

The beginning of the good news of Jesus Christ, the Son of God. As it is written in the prophet Isaiah, "See, I am sending my messenger ahead of you, who will prepare your way; the voice of one crying out in the wilderness: 'Prepare the way of the Lord, make his paths straight,'" John the baptizer appeared in the wilderness, proclaiming a baptism of repentance for the forgiveness of sins.

The Gospel of the Lord.

◆ All sit and observe silence.

FOR SILENT REFLECTION

Think about this silently in your heart. How have you prepared for Jesus' birth in your home?

CLOSING PRAYER

Let us pray to God for our needs and the needs of others: our family, neighborhood, and the world. For each need we say, "Lord, hear our prayer."

◆ All may add their own prayers here.

Let us pray: **Our Father . . . Amen.**

Almighty God,
we rejoice that the birth of your Son is near!
In these last days of Advent,
we look forward with joy to his birth.
May we be ready to welcome him.
Through Christ our Lord.

Amen.

✛ All make the Sign of the Cross.

PRAYER FOR THE WEEK

WITH A READING FROM THE GOSPEL **FOR SUNDAY, DECEMBER 20, 2020**

OPENING

On this Fourth Sunday of Advent, we light all four candles on our wreath. Our preparation and waiting are almost at an end. We eagerly anticipate the arrival of the blessed baby Jesus. In today's Gospel, we hear about Jesus' mother, Mary, and God's invitation to her.

✦ All make the Sign of the Cross.

In the name of the Father, and of the Son, and of the Holy Spirit. Amen.

PSALM

(For a longer psalm, see page xii.)
Psalm 85:8

Restore us again, O God of our salvation!

Restore us again, O God of our salvation!

Let me hear what God the LORD will speak,
  for he will speak peace to his people,
to his faithful, to those who turn to him in
  their hearts.

Restore us again, O God of our salvation!

◆ All stand and sing **Alleluia.**

GOSPEL

Luke 1:26–32

A reading from the holy Gospel according to Luke.

In the sixth month the angel Gabriel was sent by God to a town in Galilee called Nazareth, to a virgin engaged to a man whose name was Joseph, of the house of David. The virgin's name was Mary. And he came to her and said, "Greetings, favored one! The Lord is with you." But she was much perplexed by his words and pondered what sort of greeting this might be. The angel said to her, "Do not be afraid, Mary, for you have found favor with God. And now, you will conceive in your womb and bear a son, and you will name him Jesus. He will be great, and will be called the Son of the Most High, and the Lord God will give to him the throne of his ancestor David."

The Gospel of the Lord.

◆ All sit and observe silence.

FOR SILENT REFLECTION

Think about this silently in your heart. Mary was perplexed, or uncertain, at the angel's words. Have you ever been perplexed by what God calls you to do?

CLOSING PRAYER

Let us pray to God for our needs and the needs of others: our family, neighborhood, and the world. For each need we say, "Lord, hear our prayer."

◆ All may add their own prayers here.

Let us pray: **Our Father . . . Amen.**

Dear God,
you love us so much that you gave us
your son, Jesus,
to become one of us
and to teach us how to live as you wish us to.
May we trust in you,
as Joseph and Mary did,
and welcome Jesus into the world.
This we pray in his name.

Amen.

✦ All make the Sign of the Cross.

OPENING

As we prepare for the arrival of Jesus, we focus on the infancy narratives today. An angel named Gabriel, which means "God is my strength," appeared to Mary. Gabriel tells Mary of the great responsibility she will bear.

✚ All make the Sign of the Cross.

In the name of the Father, and of the Son, and of the Holy Spirit. Amen.

PSALM

(For a longer psalm, see page xii.)
Psalm 85:8

Restore us again, O God of our salvation!

Restore us again, O God of our salvation!

Let me hear what God the LORD will speak,
for he will speak peace to his people,
to his faithful, to those who turn to him in
their hearts.

Restore us again, O God of our salvation!

◆ All stand and sing **Alleluia.**

GOSPEL

Luke 1:26–32

A reading from the holy Gospel according to Luke.

In the sixth month the angel Gabriel was sent by God to a town in Galilee called Nazareth, to a virgin engaged to a man whose name was Joseph, of the house of David. The virgin's name was Mary. And he came to her and said, "Greetings, favored one! The Lord is with you." But she was much perplexed by his words and pondered what sort of greeting this might be. The angel said to her, "Do not be afraid, Mary, for you have found favor with God. And now, you will conceive in your womb and bear a son, and you will name him Jesus. He will be great, and will be called the Son of the Most High, and the Lord God will give to him the throne of his ancestor David."

The Gospel of the Lord.

◆ All sit and observe silence.

FOR SILENT REFLECTION

Think about this silently in your heart. The angel Gabriel told Mary, "Do not be afraid." When you are afraid or confused, can you imagine God with you, telling you to not be afraid?

CLOSING PRAYER

Let us pray to God for our needs and the needs of others: our family, neighborhood, and the world. For each need we say, "Lord, hear our prayer."

◆ All may add their own prayers here.

Let us pray: **Our Father . . . Amen.**

Holy Mary, Mother of God,
you were asked to bring forth the Light of the World.
Give us the courage to follow you and to bring Christ's light into the world today.
We ask your prayers in the name of your Son, Jesus Christ our Lord.

Amen.

✚ All make the Sign of the Cross.

OPENING

Today we continue hearing Mary's conversation with Gabriel. Mary is uncertain, and she questions Gabriel. Gabriel reminds her that nothing is impossible with God. Although she still may be uncertain, Mary accepts her responsibility and trusts in God.

✚ All make the Sign of the Cross.

In the name of the Father, and of the Son, and of the Holy Spirit. Amen.

PSALM
(For a longer psalm, see page xii.)
Psalm 85:8

Restore us again, O God of our salvation!

Restore us again, O God of our salvation!

Let me hear what God the LORD will speak,
    for he will speak peace to his people,
to his faithful, to those who turn to him in
    their hearts.

Restore us again, O God of our salvation!

◆ All stand and sing **Alleluia.**

GOSPEL
Luke 1:34–38

A reading from the holy Gospel according to Luke.

Mary said to the angel, "How can this be, since I am a virgin?" The angel said to her, "The Holy Spirit will come upon you, and the power of the Most High will overshadow you; therefore the child to be born will be holy; he will be called Son of God. And now, your relative Elizabeth in her old age has also conceived a son; and this is the sixth month for her who was said to be barren. For nothing will be impossible with God." Then Mary said, "Here am I, the servant of the Lord; let it be with me according to your word." Then the angel departed from her.

The Gospel of the Lord.

◆ All sit and observe silence.

FOR SILENT REFLECTION

Think about this silently in your heart. Do you trust in God?

CLOSING PRAYER

Let us pray to God for our needs and the needs of others: our family, neighborhood, and the world. For each need we say, "Lord, hear our prayer."

◆ All may add their own prayers here.

Let us pray: **Our Father . . . Amen.**

Dear God,
you love us so much that you gave us
your son, Jesus,
to become one of us
and to teach us how to live as you wish us to.
May we trust in you,
as Joseph and Mary did,
and welcome Jesus into the world.
This we pray in his name.

Amen.

✚ All make the Sign of the Cross.

OPENING

We learn today that an angel also appeared to Joseph to tell him about Mary and to prepare him for the birth of Jesus. The angel tells him to name the baby Jesus, or Emmanuel, which means "God is with us." Joseph, like Mary, accepts and trusts what the angel has told him.

✦ All make the Sign of the Cross.

In the name of the Father, and of the Son, and of the Holy Spirit. Amen.

PSALM

(For a longer psalm, see page xii.)
Psalm 85:8

Restore us again, O God of our salvation!

Restore us again, O God of our salvation!

Let me hear what God the Lord will speak,
for he will speak peace to his people,
to his faithful, to those who turn to him in
their hearts.

Restore us again, O God of our salvation!

◆ All stand and sing **Alleluia.**

GOSPEL

Matthew 1:20b–24

A reading from the holy Gospel according to Matthew.

An angel of the Lord appeared to Joseph in a dream and said, "Joseph, son of David, do not be afraid to take Mary as your wife, for the child conceived in her is from the Holy Spirit. She will bear a son, and you are to name him Jesus, for he will save his people from their sins." All this took place to fulfill what had been spoken by the Lord through the prophet: "Look, the virgin shall conceive and bear a son, and they shall name him Emmanuel," which means, "God is with us." When Joseph awoke from sleep, he did as the angel of the Lord commanded him; he took Mary as his wife.

The Gospel of the Lord.

◆ All sit and observe silence.

FOR SILENT REFLECTION

Think about this silently in your heart. How can you, like Mary and Joseph, put your trust in God?

CLOSING PRAYER

Let us pray to God for our needs and the needs of others: our family, neighborhood, and the world. For each need we say, "Lord, hear our prayer."

◆ All may add their own prayers here.

Let us pray: **Our Father . . . Amen.**

Dear God,
you love us so much that you gave us
your son, Jesus,
to become one of us
and to teach us how to live as you wish us to.
May we trust in you,
as Joseph and Mary did,
and welcome Jesus into the world.
This we pray in his name.

Amen.

✦ All make the Sign of the Cross.

PRAYER FOR
THURSDAY, DECEMBER 24, 2020

OPENING

In today's Gospel, Mary travels to visit her cousin Elizabeth. Elizabeth and her husband Zechariah were old in age, but an angel appeared to them and Elizabeth became pregnant. Elizabeth's baby is to be John the Baptist. Elizabeth's child is filled with joy when Mary comes, carrying the baby Messiah.

✚ All make the Sign of the Cross.

In the name of the Father, and of the Son, and of the Holy Spirit. Amen.

PSALM

(For a longer psalm, see page xii.)
Psalm 85:8

Restore us again, O God of our salvation!

Restore us again, O God of our salvation!

Let me hear what God the LORD will speak,
for he will speak peace to his people,
to his faithful, to those who turn to him in
their hearts.

Restore us again, O God of our salvation!

◆ All stand and sing **Alleluia.**

GOSPEL

Luke 1:39–42, 44–45

A reading from the holy Gospel according to Luke.

In those days Mary set out and went with haste to a Judean town in the hill country, where she entered the house of Zechariah and greeted Elizabeth. When Elizabeth heard Mary's greeting, the child leaped in her womb. And Elizabeth was filled with the Holy Spirit and exclaimed with a loud cry, "Blessed are you among women, and blessed is the fruit of your womb. For as soon as I heard the sound of your greeting, the child in my womb leaped for joy. And blessed is she who believed that there would be a fulfillment of what was spoken to her by the Lord."

The Gospel of the Lord.

◆ All sit and observe silence.

FOR SILENT REFLECTION

Think about this silently in your heart. Even the baby in Elizabeth's womb leaped with joy at the presence of Jesus. How may our hearts leap with joy this Christmas season?

CLOSING PRAYER

Let us pray to God for our needs and the needs of others: our family, neighborhood, and the world. For each need we say, "Lord, hear our prayer."

◆ All may add their own prayers here.

Let us pray: **Our Father . . . Amen.**

We give you thanks and praise, O God,
for this season of Advent.
We have prepared our hearts and are ready
to welcome the gift of your Son, Jesus,
in whose name we pray.

Amen.

✚ All make the Sign of the Cross.

CHRISTMAS TIME

SUNDAY, JANUARY 3 — SUNDAY, JANUARY 10

THE MEANING OF CHRISTMAS

"For a child has been born for us,
　　a son given to us;
authority rests upon his shoulders;
　　and he is named
Wonderful Counselor, Mighty God,
　　Everlasting Father, Prince of Peace."

(Isaiah 9:6)

God keeps the great promise of the gift of Jesus! Of course, God amazes us with other gifts we never could have imagined or asked for. The earth is filled with God's gifts. Think of the solid ground that supports us, gravity that keeps us from floating away, the atmosphere that provides oxygen for breathing and a shield to protect us from the heat of the sun, and water that keeps our cells healthy. We need so many things just to stay alive. And yet the earth contains much more than is necessary to keep us going. Within the earth, precious metals and gems delight us with their shine. Seashells and spider webs amaze us with their geometry. Roses and lilacs fill the air with perfume. Peacocks and pinecones and pecans add to the world's great fascination. And every day our friends and family share new ways to love. What a world we have been given!

But God wants to give us something even more precious: a share in God's very own life. So Immanuel, God-with-us, came to us in Bethlehem. God, who was there before the universe, who was the Word that spoke the world into existence, gave himself to us as an infant who could do nothing for itself. This gift has changed everything. God's heart is opened for us. Out of the tree stump of despair, God has brought a flowering branch.

Our Scriptures are full of epiphanies or manifestations; that is, events that clearly show people that this baby, Jesus, is the promised Messiah. We will stand in front of the manger in Bethlehem this week and gaze in wonder with Mary, Joseph, the angels, the shepherds, and the Magi as we realize this holy child, Jesus, is our God.

PREPARING TO CELEBRATE CHRISTMAS IN THE CLASSROOM

SACRED SPACE

Replace the Advent wreath with a new, white pillar candle and change the purple cloth to a white one. You might add some gold tinsel or a gold cloth. Place the star and the Magi in the Nativity scene.

MOVEMENT AND GESTURE

If you have older students, they light and hold congregational candles (thin tapers) during the Epiphany Prayer Service.

FESTIVITY IN SCHOOL AND HOME

The prayer service for Epiphany on pages 144–145 provides a beautiful and prayerful way to celebrate the arrival of the Magi in Bethlehem.

SACRED MUSIC

Christmas Time is a time of music! Many beautiful carols, including "Joy to the World," "Angels We Have Heard on High," "O Come, All Ye Faithful," and "We Three Kings" can be sung with the children. You may even wish to organize a caroling party and go door to door through your school.

PRAYERS FOR CHRISTMAS

The opening verses of the Gospel according to St. John contain some of the most beautiful poetry in the world: "In the beginning was the Word, and the Word was with God, and the Word was God. He was in the beginning with God. All things came into being through him, and without him not one thing came into being. What has come into being in him was life, and the life was the light of all people. The light shines in the darkness, and the darkness did not overcome it" (John 1:1–5).

These verses beautifully express the mystery of the Incarnation, the mystery of God becoming a human being to be close to us. You might want to spend some time during religion class reading this beautiful hymn line by line. Ask the children whom St. John means when he speaks about the "Word of God." See what they say when you ask them how "all things came into being" through Christ when we know Jesus was born after the creation of the world. How can one person be the "light of all people"? What kind of light do people need? What do the children think St. John means when he says, "the darkness did not overcome" the Light of the World?

A NOTE TO CATECHISTS

See whether you can share a Christmas Nativity scene with the teacher who shares your classroom. Or take your students on a "field trip" to the church and let them pray in front of the parish Nativity scene! Perhaps families could share their Nativity sets, or pieces from them. This is especially wonderful if you have a variety of nationalities and ethnic groups among your children.

GRACE BEFORE MEALS

CHRISTMAS TIME

LEADER:
"For a child has been born for us,"

ALL: "a son given to us."

✚ All make the Sign of the Cross.

In the name of the Father, and of the Son, and of the Holy Spirit. Amen.

LEADER:
Heavenly Father,
may the food we are about to share
help to nourish our bodies and minds,
just as you nurture us always
with the gift of your Son
and your everlasting Spirit.
May we be a living sign of the
presence of Jesus,
who is hope for the world.
We ask this through Christ our Lord.

ALL: Amen.

✚ All make the Sign of the Cross.

In the name of the Father, and of the Son, and of the Holy Spirit. Amen.

PRAYER AT DAY'S END

CHRISTMAS TIME

LEADER:

Sing to the Lord a new song,

ALL: for he has done wondrous deeds!

✚ All make the Sign of the Cross.

In the name of the Father, and of the Son, and of the Holy Spirit. Amen.

LEADER:

Heavenly Father,
the gift of your Son
gives us so much joy!
We thank you for this day,
filled with wonder and small adventures.
May we always remember that you
are the source of all goodness
as we praise the miracle of Jesus,
whom you sent to us
to lead the way back to you.
We ask this through Christ our Lord
and Savior.

ALL: Amen.

✚ All make the Sign of the Cross.

In the name of the Father, and of the Son, and of the Holy Spirit. Amen.

PRAYER SERVICE
EPIPHANY

Prepare six leaders and a song leader for this service. The second and fourth leaders will need Bibles to read the Scripture passages and may need help finding and practicing them. Before you begin, remove the figures of shepherds and the three kings from your Nativity scene. Put the shepherds away until next year. Place the kings a short distance from the Nativity scene. Then gather the class near it. This service calls for two songs. Help the song leader prepare to lead the singing.

SONG LEADER:
Please stand and join in singing our opening song, "We Three Kings."

FIRST LEADER:

✚ All make the Sign of the Cross.

May the light of our Creator guide us in this prayer of praise.

ALL: Amen.

Let us pray:
Almighty God,
you are the light of the world!
Guide us with your radiance
as we reflect your goodness in our lives.
We ask this through Christ our Lord.

ALL: Amen.

◆ Gesture for all to sit.

SECOND LEADER: Isaiah 9:2–7
A reading from the Book of the Prophet Isaiah.

◆ Read the Scripture passage from the Bible.

The Word of the Lord.

◆ All observe silence.

CHILDREN'S DAILY PRAYER 2020–2021, © 2020 Archdiocese of Chicago: Liturgy Training Publications. All rights reserved. Orders: 800-933-1800 or www.LTP.org.

THIRD LEADER: Psalm 148:1–2, 3–4, 9–10, 11–12, 13

Our refrain is: Praise the LORD!

ALL: Praise the LORD!

Praise the LORD from the heavens;
   praise him in the heights!
Praise him, all his angels;
   praise him, all his host!

ALL: Praise the LORD!

Praise him, sun and moon;
   praise him, all you shining stars!
Praise him, you highest heavens,
   and you waters above the heavens!

ALL: Praise the LORD!

Mountains and all hills,
   fruit trees and all cedars!
Wild animals and all cattle,
   creeping things and flying birds!

ALL: Praise the LORD!

Kings of the earth and all peoples,
   princes and all rulers of the earth!
Young men and women alike,
   old and young together!

ALL: Praise the LORD!

◆ All stand and sing **Alleluia**.

FOURTH LEADER: Matthew 2:9b–12

A reading from the holy Gospel according
to Matthew.

◆ Read the Scripture passage from a Bible.

The Gospel of the Lord.

◆ All sit and observe silence.

◆ In silence, an adult slowly moves the three figures of the Wise Men, one at a time, into the stable.

SONG LEADER:
Let us stand and sing, "Joy to the World."

FIFTH LEADER:
Heavenly Father,
you created the sun, planets,
moon, and stars,
and everything that breathes
to give you glory.
You are almighty and powerful,
yet you are as close to us as our breath,
and you live within our hearts.
Inspire us more with your
gentle Spirit and direction
just as you did the wise men
who traveled far to
see your glory in the Christ child.
We ask this through your Son Jesus.

Amen.

Let us pray: **Our Father . . . Amen.**

SIXTH LEADER:
May God's love, found in the Trinity of
Father, Son, and Spirit,
always surround us on our journey.

ALL: Amen.

✚ All make the Sign of the Cross.

PRAYER FOR THE WEEK
WITH A READING FROM THE GOSPEL FOR **SUNDAY, JANUARY 3, 2021**

OPENING

Today we celebrate the Epiphany of the Lord. An epiphany is a moment of revelation, understanding, or insight. We remember the three Wise Men who came to seek the baby Jesus. The men were overcome with joy at meeting Jesus because they recognized he was a true king. We remember on Epiphany that Jesus came to the world for all people, not just the Jewish people.

✚ All make the Sign of the Cross.

In the name of the Father, and of the Son, and of the Holy Spirit. Amen.

PSALM

(For a longer psalm, see page xiii.)
Psalm 96:1–2a

Let the heavens be glad and the earth rejoice!

Let the heavens be glad and the earth rejoice!

O sing to the Lord a new song;
  sing to the Lord, all the earth.
Sing to the Lord; bless his name.

Let the heavens be glad and the earth rejoice!

◆ All stand and sing **Alleluia.**

GOSPEL

Matthew 2:1–2, 8ab, 9–11

A reading from the holy Gospel according to Matthew.

In the time of King Herod, after Jesus was born in Bethlehem of Judea, wise men from the East came to Jerusalem, asking, "Where is the child who has been born king of the Jews? For we observed his star at its rising, and have come to pay him homage." Then King Herod sent them to Bethlehem, saying, "Go and search diligently for the child." When they had heard the king,

they set out; and there, ahead of them, went the star that they had seen at its rising, until it stopped over the place where the child was. When they saw that the star had stopped, they were overwhelmed with joy. On entering the house, they saw the child with Mary his mother; and they knelt down and paid him homage. Then, opening their treasure chests, they offered him gifts of gold, frankincense, and myrrh.

The Gospel of the Lord.

◆ All sit and observe silence.

FOR SILENT REFLECTION

Think about this silently in your heart. We do not have expensive gifts of gold, frankincense, and myrrh for Jesus. What gifts might we give instead?

CLOSING PRAYER

Let us pray to God for our needs and the needs of others: our family, neighborhood, and the world. For each need we say, "Lord, hear our prayer."

◆ All may add their own prayers here.

Let us pray: **Our Father . . . Amen.**

Glory to you, O God!
We celebrate with you the birth
of your son Jesus.
Help us to seek Jesus, just as the Wise Men did.
May our whole lives, hearts, words, and deeds reflect the love we have for your Son.

Amen.

✚ All make the Sign of the Cross.

OPENING

This week we continue our Epiphany celebration by hearing more about epiphanies in the Bible. The prophet Isaiah [ī-ZAY-uh] tells us of a child who will be born and will bring great light and joy. The child will bring peace, justice, and righteousness to the world. Today we remember St. Elizabeth Ann Seton (1774–1821), who is the patron saint of Catholic schools.

✦ All make the Sign of the Cross.

In the name of the Father, and of the Son, and of the Holy Spirit. Amen.

PSALM

(For a longer psalm, see page xiii.)
Psalm 96:1–2a

Let the heavens be glad and the earth rejoice!

Let the heavens be glad and the earth rejoice!

O sing to the Lord a new song;
    sing to the Lord, all the earth.
Sing to the Lord; bless his name.

Let the heavens be glad and the earth rejoice!

READING

Isaiah 9:1a, 2b–3, 6–7

A reading from the Book of the prophet Isaiah.

But there will be no gloom for those who were in anguish. The people who walked in darkness have seen a great light; those who lived in a land of deep darkness—on them light has shined. You have multiplied the nation, you have increased its joy; they rejoice before you as with joy at the harvest, as people exult when dividing plunder. For a child has been born for us, a son given to us; authority rests upon his shoulders; and he is named Wonderful Counselor, Mighty God, Everlasting Father, Prince of Peace. His authority shall grow continually, and there shall be endless peace for the throne of David and his kingdom. He will establish and uphold it with justice and with righteousness from this time onwards and for evermore. The zeal of the Lord of hosts will do this.

The Word of the Lord.

✦ All observe silence.

FOR SILENT REFLECTION

Think about this silently in your heart. How is Jesus like a Wonderful Counselor, Mighty God, Everlasting Father, and Prince of Peace?

CLOSING PRAYER

Let us pray to God for our needs and the needs of others: our family, neighborhood, and the world. For each need we say, "Lord, hear our prayer."

✦ All may add their own prayers here.

Let us pray: **Our Father . . . Amen.**

O Wonderful Counselor,
Mighty God,
Everlasting Father,
Prince of Peace,
we thank you for bringing us light and joy.
Help us to sow peace and justice always.
Through Christ our Lord.

Amen.

✦ All make the Sign of the Cross.

OPENING

Today's epiphany is that of the shepherds in the field. An angel appeared to the shepherds and told them where to find the baby Messiah. We continue to commemorate Catholic schools by honoring St. John Newman (1811–1860). He was a bishop in Philadelphia who founded the first Catholic school system in the United States. He was a gifted organizer and used this ability to spread the Gospel.

✚ All make the Sign of the Cross.

In the name of the Father, and of the Son, and of the Holy Spirit. Amen.

PSALM

(For a longer psalm, see page xiii.)
Psalm 96:1–2a

Let the heavens be glad and the earth rejoice!

Let the heavens be glad and the earth rejoice!

O sing to the LORD a new song;
    sing to the LORD, all the earth.
Sing to the LORD; bless his name.

Let the heavens be glad and the earth rejoice!

◆ All stand and sing **Alleluia.**

GOSPEL

Luke 2:8–14

A reading from the holy Gospel according to Luke.

In that region there were shepherds living in the fields, keeping watch over their flock by night. Then an angel of the Lord stood before them, and the glory of the Lord shone around them, and they were terrified. But the angel said to them, "Do not be afraid; for see—I am bringing you good news of great joy for all the people: to you is born this day in the city of David a Savior, who is the Messiah, the Lord. This will be a sign for you: you will find a child wrapped in bands of cloth and lying in a manger." And suddenly there was with the angel a multitude of the heavenly host, praising God and saying, "Glory to God in the highest heaven, and on earth peace among those whom he favors!"

The Gospel of the Lord.

◆ All sit and observe silence.

FOR SILENT REFLECTION

Think about this silently in your heart. Why do you think the angels brought the news of Jesus' birth to the poor shepherds in the field?

CLOSING PRAYER

Let us pray to God for our needs and the needs of others: our family, neighborhood, and the world. For each need we say, "Lord, hear our prayer."

◆ All may add their own prayers here.

Let us pray: **Our Father . . . Amen.**

Glory to God in the Highest!
Because of your promise to your people,
O Lord,
we live in hope for a world of peace and joy.
We praise you as we sing with all the angels,
Glory to God in the Highest!
We pray in the name of Christ our Lord.

Amen.

✚ All make the Sign of the Cross.

OPENING

Today we remember St. Andre Bessette (1845–1937). St. Andre was a French-Canadian religious man devoted to St. Joseph. Due to his devotion to God, he is believed to have miraculously cured thousands and was canonized in 2010. We hear today that after seeing the heavenly choirs of angels the shepherds go to see the Messiah themselves. They are in awe of what they find.

✝ All make the Sign of the Cross.

In the name of the Father, and of the Son, and of the Holy Spirit. Amen.

PSALM

(For a longer psalm, see page xiii.)
Psalm 96:1–2a

Let the heavens be glad and the earth rejoice!

Let the heavens be glad and the earth rejoice!

O sing to the LORD a new song;
 sing to the LORD, all the earth.
Sing to the LORD; bless his name.

Let the heavens be glad and the earth rejoice!

◆ All stand and sing **Alleluia.**

GOSPEL

Luke 2:15–20

A reading from the holy Gospel according to Luke.

When the angels had left them and gone into heaven, the shepherds said to one another, "Let us go now to Bethlehem and see this thing that has taken place, which the Lord has made known to us." So they went with haste and found Mary and Joseph, and the child lying in the manger. When they saw this, they made known what had been told them about this child; and all who heard it were amazed at what the shepherds told them. But Mary treasured all these words and pondered them in her heart. The shepherds returned, glorifying and praising God for all they had heard and seen, as it had been told them.

The Gospel of the Lord.

◆ All sit and observe silence.

FOR SILENT REFLECTION

Think about this silently in your heart. How do you think Mary felt as she pondered all the things the shepherds told her?

CLOSING PRAYER

Let us pray to God for our needs and the needs of others: our family, neighborhood, and the world. For each need we say, "Lord, hear our prayer."

◆ All may add their own prayers here.

Let us pray: **Our Father . . . Amen.**

Faithful God,
we thank you for your gift of everlasting love,
for the treasure of your Son Jesus.
Help us to keep your Word close to our hearts,
as his Mother Mary did.
We ask this through Christ our Lord.

Amen.

✝ All make the Sign of the Cross.

PRAYER FOR
THURSDAY, JANUARY 7, 2021

OPENING

Today we remember St. Raymond of Peñafort, who is the patron saint of canon lawyers. We hear more today about Wise Men from the East who paid Jesus homage. Homage is a sign of respect or honor; we pay homage when we kneel or bow before the cross, for example. Jesus came for all nations and people, not just the Jews.

✛ All make the Sign of the Cross.

In the name of the Father, and of the Son, and of the Holy Spirit. Amen.

PSALM

(For a longer psalm, see page xiii.)
Psalm 96:1–2a

Let the heavens be glad and the earth rejoice!

Let the heavens be glad and the earth rejoice!

O sing to the LORD a new song;
   sing to the LORD, all the earth.
Sing to the LORD; bless his name.

Let the heavens be glad and the earth rejoice!

◆ All stand and sing **Alleluia.**

GOSPEL

Matthew 2:1–2, 8ab, 9–11

A reading from the holy Gospel according to Matthew.

In the time of King Herod, after Jesus was born in Bethlehem of Judea, wise men from the East came to Jerusalem, asking, "Where is the child who has been born king of the Jews? For we observed his star at its rising, and have come to pay him homage." Then King Herod sent them to Bethlehem, saying, "Go and search diligently for the child." When they had heard the king, they set out; and there, ahead of them, went the star that they had seen at its rising, until it stopped over the place where the child was. When they saw that the star had stopped, they were overwhelmed with joy. On entering the house, they saw the child with Mary his mother; and they knelt down and paid him homage. Then, opening their treasure chests, they offered him gifts of gold, frankincense, and myrrh.

The Gospel of the Lord.

◆ All sit and observe silence.

FOR SILENT REFLECTION

Think about this silently in your heart. How do you pay Jesus homage?

CLOSING PRAYER

Let us pray to God for our needs and the needs of others: our family, neighborhood, and the world. For each need we say, "Lord, hear our prayer."

◆ All may add their own prayers here.

Let us pray: **Our Father . . . Amen.**

Dear God,
may we honor you and seek your presence as the Wise Men did.
We offer you our love and faith
and our pledge to continue to follow you all our lives.
We pray in Christ's name.

Amen.

✛ All make the Sign of the Cross.

OPENING

In today's reading, Joseph, the husband of Mary and father to Jesus, had an epiphany in a dream. In his dream, an angel revealed a message from God that directed him on what to do. Joseph listened and followed his message from God.

✛ All make the Sign of the Cross.

In the name of the Father, and of the Son, and of the Holy Spirit. Amen.

PSALM

(For a longer psalm, see page xiii.)
Psalm 96:1–2a

Let the heavens be glad and the earth rejoice!

Let the heavens be glad and the earth rejoice!

O sing to the LORD a new song;
sing to the LORD, all the earth.
Sing to the LORD; bless his name.

Let the heavens be glad and the earth rejoice!

◆ All stand and sing **Alleluia.**

GOSPEL

Matthew 2:13abd, 14ac, 15a, 19–20ac, 23

A reading from the holy Gospel according to Matthew.

Now after the Magi had left, an angel of the Lord appeared to Joseph in a dream and said, "Get up, take the child and his mother, and flee to Egypt; for Herod is about to search for the child, to destroy him." Then Joseph got up, and went to Egypt, and remained there until the death of Herod. When Herod died, an angel of the Lord suddenly appeared in a dream to Joseph in Egypt and said, "Get up, and go to the land of Israel, for those who were seeking the child's life are dead." There he made his home in a town called Nazareth, so that what had been spoken through the prophets might be fulfilled, "He will be called a Nazorean."

The Gospel of the Lord.

◆ All sit and observe silence.

FOR SILENT REFLECTION

Think about this silently in your heart. Pray today for refugees who have to leave their countries to save their lives.

CLOSING PRAYER

Let us pray to God for our needs and the needs of others: our family, neighborhood, and the world. For each need we say, "Lord, hear our prayer."

◆ All may add their own prayers here.

Let us pray: **Our Father . . . Amen.**

We pray, O God,
for all those who seek safety and shelter.
We ask you to guide them to safety and peace,
as the Holy Spirit guided the Holy Family.
Help us to trust in you as St. Joseph did.
For this we pray
through Christ our Lord.
Amen.

✛ All make the Sign of the Cross.

OPENING

We end Christmas Time with the celebration of the solemnity of the Baptism of the Lord. We hear in the Gospel of Jesus' baptism by his cousin John. Our Baptisms signify our initiation, or welcome, into a relationship with God. Through his baptism, Jesus gave us an outward sign that he wanted to live according to God's way.

✚ All make the Sign of the Cross.

In the name of the Father, and of the Son, and of the Holy Spirit. Amen.

PSALM
(For a longer psalm, see page xiii.)
Psalm 96:1–2a

Let the heavens be glad and the earth rejoice!

Let the heavens be glad and the earth rejoice!

O sing to the LORD a new song;
sing to the LORD, all the earth.
Sing to the LORD; bless his name.

Let the heavens be glad and the earth rejoice!

◆ All stand and sing **Alleluia.**

GOSPEL
Mark 1:7–11

A reading from the holy Gospel according to Mark.

This is what John the Baptist proclaimed, "The one who is more powerful than I is coming after me; I am not worthy to stoop down and untie the thong of his sandals. I have baptized you with water; but he will baptize you with the Holy Spirit."
In those days Jesus came from Nazareth of Galilee and was baptized by John in the Jordan.

And just as he was coming up out of the water, he saw the heavens torn apart and the Spirit descending like a dove on him. And a voice came from heaven, "You are my Son, the Beloved; with you I am well pleased."

The Gospel of the Lord.

◆ All sit and observe silence.

FOR SILENT REFLECTION

Think about this silently in your heart. What do you know of your Baptism? How does this sacrament welcome you into a relationship with God and your community of faith?

CLOSING PRAYER

Let us pray to God for our needs and the needs of others: our family, neighborhood, and the world. For each need we say, "Lord, hear our prayer."

◆ All may add their own prayers here.

Let us pray: **Our Father . . . Amen.**

O God,
thank you for your great love
and for caring for us as your sons and daughters.
May our Baptisms remind us to live
in ways that are good and holy.
We pray this in the name of your Son
Jesus Christ, our Lord.

Amen.

✚ All make the Sign of the Cross.

ORDINARY TIME WINTER

MONDAY, JANUARY 11 — TUESDAY, FEBRUARY 16

WINTER **ORDINARY TIME**

THE MEANING OF ORDINARY TIME

We've just celebrated the two great seasons of Advent and Christmas and now move back into Ordinary Time. Our seasons celebrate certain aspects of what we call Christ's "Paschal Mystery." For example, during the four weeks of Advent we focused on preparing to celebrate Christ's first coming in the Incarnation and preparing for Christ's Second Coming at the Parousia [par-oo-SEE-u]. The several weeks of Christmas focus on the wonder and joy of that first reality of God-with-us in Jesus. Now we move into the beginning of this year's ordered—that is, counted—Sundays of Ordinary Time. Each celebrates the Paschal Mystery in its entirety: Christ has died and is risen and will come again. Winter Ordinary Time is usually quite short, lasting only a few weeks.

The Prayers for the Week will reflect the Sunday Gospels, but during the week we will again "walk through the Bible." In week one we'll hear about Jesus' early years with the great stories of the Presentation in the Temple (an epiphany for Simeon and Anna), the finding in the Temple, and Jesus' baptism. We end the week with Jesus' instruction to the Apostles and to us to go out and proclaim the Gospel, the "good news." Week two examines the theme of abundance, from the concrete need for water to God's ineffable Word. Week three looks at the Transfiguration of Jesus by introducing Elijah and Moses in the Old Testament, relating St. Luke's story of the Transfiguration and its implications for Jesus. Week four is about "light" and we look at its biblical varieties in the books of Proverbs and Baruch, the Gospel of Luke, and letters to the Romans and Ephesians.

PREPARING TO CELEBRATE ORDINARY TIME IN THE CLASSROOM

You will need to replace your white cloth with a green one, now that it is Ordinary Time again. Plan another procession with your students if they respond well to them. Otherwise, you might ask them if they have any ideas about how to change the cloths with care and dignity. You might be surprised at the depth of their suggestions.

SACRED SPACE

Place a clear bowl with water in the prayer space for the first week to honor the baptism of Jesus and our own.

A plain vase with a bunch of bare branches would be appropriate, or a potted plant. A spider plant or an ivy will withstand long weekends without too much attention. Give its care and watering to your students. Make a job chart and allow them to take turns watering the plant. Watching the plant grow will provide a concrete sign of the growth that can take place in our hearts during this liturgical season.

In February consider placing two candles tied with a red ribbon for St. Blaise (February 3) in the space.

MOVEMENT AND GESTURE

Integrate the bowl of water into the daily prayer by bringing the bowl to the children or having them go to the bowl to make the Sign of the Cross. You might get holy water from the parish church but using tap water is also fine. Water is intrinsically holy. If the water becomes dirty it should be used to water plants or poured into the earth because it is holy by God's creation and by our use. See the suggestions for February 2, the Presentation of the Lord, below.

FESTIVITY IN SCHOOL AND HOME

From January 18 through 25, the Church joins with our Protestant brothers and sisters in the Week of Prayer for Christian Unity. A special prayer service, which may be used anytime during the week, is provided on page 165.

On February 2 we celebrate the feast of the Presentation of the Lord, also known as Candlemas. This is a beautiful feast to celebrate with children. If your school does not attend Mass that day, you might use the Scriptures from Monday and Tuesday of the first week of Ordinary Time. Before you begin prayer that day, dim the classroom lights and light a candle. Help the student proclaiming the Scripture to practice so that it can be done well, and allow time for the class to ponder the story together. If the children are old enough they might light and hold congregational candles (tapers) during the Gospel. (See more, under Prayers for Ordinary Time and A Note to Catechists.)

SACRED MUSIC

This would be the perfect time to learn how to sing one of the psalms. Psalm 27 ("The Lord Is My Light and My Salvation") and Psalm 23 ("The Lord Is My Shepherd") are two beautiful psalms that have many different musical settings. Children might also enjoy "This Little Light of Mine" and "I Want to Walk as a Child of the Light." Invite children to share favorite spiritual songs from their ethnic backgrounds and try singing songs from other countries ("We are Marching in the Light," "Pan de Vida," the round "Shalom Chevarim"). Also, don't forget to sing Alleluia often during these days. When Lent arrives, we will have to wait a long time before Easter when we can sing it again. The best Alleluia to sing is the one your parish uses before the Sunday Gospel.

PRAYERS FOR ORDINARY TIME

A tradition from the Liturgy of the Hours is to pray the *Canticle of Simeon* before going to bed. This is the prayer of the elderly man Simeon, who met the Holy Family in the Temple of Jerusalem when Mary and Joseph brought Jesus there as a baby. God had promised Simeon he would not die before he saw the Messiah. Simeon took the child Jesus in his arms and said this prayer:

"Master, now you are dismissing your servant
in peace,
according to your word;
for my eyes have seen your salvation,
which you have prepared in the presence
of all peoples,
a light for revelation to the Gentiles
and for glory to your people Israel."
(Luke 2:29–32)

Introduce this prayer on February 2, the feast of the Presentation of the Lord. You may want to ask the children about certain key words in the prayer. Possible "wondering" questions could include: Why does Simeon call himself God's "servant"? Does the word "servant" recall anything that Mary once said? How did Simeon know that Jesus was a special baby? How is this small baby a "light" and a "glory"?

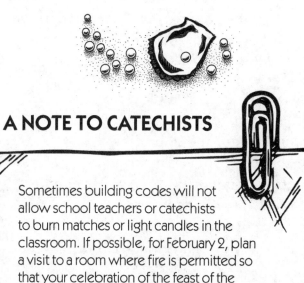

A NOTE TO CATECHISTS

Sometimes building codes will not allow school teachers or catechists to burn matches or light candles in the classroom. If possible, for February 2, plan a visit to a room where fire is permitted so that your celebration of the feast of the Presentation of the Lord will be set apart from the days surrounding it.

GRACE BEFORE MEALS

ORDINARY TIME • WINTER

LEADER:
Who is this King of glory?

ALL: The Lord, strong and mighty.

✚ All make the Sign of the Cross.

In the name of the Father, and of the Son, and of the Holy Spirit. Amen.

LEADER:
Heavenly Father,
we thank you for
the food we are about to share.
The abundance of this meal
reflects your goodness,
and how you provide for us
every day, in so many ways.
We ask this through Christ our Lord.

All: Amen.

✚ All make the Sign of the Cross.

In the name of the Father, and of the Son, and of the Holy Spirit. Amen.

PRAYER AT DAY'S END

ORDINARY TIME • WINTER

LEADER:
Your word is a light to my feet,

ALL: and a light to my path.

✚ All make the Sign of the Cross.

> **In the name of the Father, and of the Son, and of the Holy Spirit. Amen.**

LEADER:
Heavenly Father,
thank you for this day of learning.
As we make our way home or
to other activities,
help us turn to you
for guidance in everything we do.
Keep us safe as we respond
to your Word in our hearts
as we meet with family and friends.
We ask this through Christ our Lord.

All: Amen.

✚ All make the Sign of the Cross.

> **In the name of the Father, and of the Son, and of the Holy Spirit. Amen.**

OPENING

This week, we focus on Scripture stories of faithfulness. In today's Gospel, Mary and Joseph show great faithfulness in traveling to Jerusalem to present Jesus to God in the temple, in accordance with Jewish law. Simeon waited faithfully for Jesus to come, and his patience was rewarded.

✦ All make the Sign of the Cross.

In the name of the Father, and of the Son, and of the Holy Spirit. Amen.

PSALM
(For a longer psalm, see page xiii.) Psalm 23:1–3a

I shall dwell in the house of the LORD my whole life long.

I shall dwell in the house of the LORD my whole life long.

The LORD is my shepherd, I shall not want.
  He makes me lie down in green pastures;
he leads me beside still waters;
  he restores my soul.

I shall dwell in the house of the LORD my whole life long.

◆ All stand and sing **Alleluia.**

GOSPEL
Luke 2:21, 22b, 25ab, 26–27b, 28–32

A reading from the holy Gospel according to Luke.

After eight days had passed, it was time to circumcise the child; and he was called Jesus, the name given by the angel before he was conceived in the womb. Mary and Joseph brought Jesus up to Jerusalem to present him to the Lord. Now there was a man in Jerusalem whose name was Simeon; this man was righteous and devout. It had been revealed to him by the Holy Spirit that he would not see death before he had seen the Lord's Messiah. Guided by the Spirit, Simeon came into the temple; and when the parents brought in the child Jesus, Simeon took him in his arms and praised God, saying, "Master, now you are dismissing your servant in peace, according to your word; for my eyes have seen your salvation, which you have prepared in the presence of all peoples, a light for revelation to the Gentiles and for glory to your people Israel."

The Gospel of the Lord.

◆ All sit and observe silence.

FOR SILENT REFLECTION

Think about this silently in your heart. How do you show your faithfulness to God?

CLOSING PRAYER

Let us pray to God for our needs and the needs of others: our family, neighborhood, and the world. For each need we say, "Lord, hear our prayer."

◆ All may add their own prayers here.

Let us pray: **Our Father . . . Amen.**

Help us to welcome Jesus into our hearts, gracious God.
Help us always to be faithful to you.
Through Christ our Lord.

Amen.

✦ All make the Sign of the Cross.

OPENING

In today's Gospel, we hear about the prophet Anna. In faith, she never left the temple and worshiped and prayed there constantly. When she sees Jesus, she rejoices and praises God as Simeon did. She shares the Good News with all who were waiting for the Messiah.

✠ All make the Sign of the Cross.

In the name of the Father, and of the Son, and of the Holy Spirit. Amen.

PSALM   (For a longer psalm, see page xiii.) Psalm 23:1–3a

I shall dwell in the house of the LORD my whole life long.

I shall dwell in the house of the LORD my whole life long.

The LORD is my shepherd, I shall not want.
   He makes me lie down in green pastures;
he leads me beside still waters;
   he restores my soul.

I shall dwell in the house of the LORD my whole life long.

◆ All stand and sing **Alleluia.**

GOSPEL   Luke 2:36–38

A reading from the holy Gospel according to Luke.

In the temple, there was also a prophet, Anna the daughter of Phanuel, of the tribe of Asher. She was of a great age, having lived with her husband seven years after her marriage, then as a widow to the age of eighty-four. She never left the temple but worshiped there with fasting and prayer night and day. At that moment she came, and began to praise God and to speak about the child to all who were looking for the redemption of Jerusalem.

The Gospel of the Lord.

◆ All sit and observe silence.

FOR SILENT REFLECTION

Think about this silently in your heart. Anna shows her faithfulness by praying night and day. Think about how you can add moments of prayer throughout the day.

CLOSING PRAYER

Let us pray to God for our needs and the needs of others: our family, neighborhood, and the world. For each need we say, "Lord, hear our prayer."

◆ All may add their own prayers here.

Let us pray: **Our Father . . . Amen.**

Ever-present God,
we give thanks for the men and women who show us how to be devoted to you.
Help us to live in faith, hope, and love.
Help us to trust in you
even when our patience wears thin or when life presents us challenges.
We ask this in Christ's name.

Amen.

✠ All make the Sign of the Cross.

PRAYER FOR
WEDNESDAY, JANUARY 13, 2021

OPENING

We celebrate the feast day of St. Hilary of Poitiers, France (315–368). He converted into the faith by studying the Bible. He later wrote many works explaining the faith and converted many, so he is one of the Doctors of the Church. Today we hear a story of Jesus' childhood. Like many Jewish families, Mary, Joseph, and Jesus faithfully traveled every year to the temple in Jerusalem to celebrate the important Jewish feast of Passover.

✚ All make the Sign of the Cross.

In the name of the Father, and of the Son, and of the Holy Spirit. Amen.

PSALM
(For a longer psalm, see page xiii.) Psalm 23:1–3a

I shall dwell in the house of the LORD my whole life long.

I shall dwell in the house of the LORD my whole life long.

The LORD is my shepherd, I shall not want.
   He makes me lie down in green pastures;
he leads me beside still waters;
   he restores my soul.

I shall dwell in the house of the LORD my whole life long.

◆ All stand and sing **Alleluia.**

GOSPEL
Luke 2:41–47

A reading from the holy Gospel according to Luke.

Now every year Jesus' parents went to Jerusalem for the festival of the Passover. And when he was twelve years old, they went up as usual for the festival. When the festival was ended and they started to return, the boy Jesus stayed behind in Jerusalem, but his parents did not know it. Assuming that he was in the group of travelers, they went a day's journey. Then they started to look for him among their relatives and friends. When they did not find him, they returned to Jerusalem to search for him. After three days they found Jesus in the temple, sitting among the teachers, listening to them and asking them questions. And all who heard him were amazed at his understanding and his answers.

The Gospel of the Lord.

◆ All sit and observe silence.

FOR SILENT REFLECTION

Think about this silently in your heart. What emotions might Mary and Joseph have felt when they saw Jesus in the temple?

CLOSING PRAYER

Let us pray to God for our needs and the needs of others: our family, neighborhood, and the world. For each need we say, "Lord, hear our prayer."

◆ All may add their own prayers here.

Let us pray: **Our Father . . . Amen.**

Heavenly Father,
may we open our hearts and minds to your truth.
We ask this through Christ our Lord.

Amen.

✚ All make the Sign of the Cross.

OPENING

When Jesus was baptized by John, the heavens opened up and the Holy Spirit came down upon Jesus like a dove. A voice came from heaven and announced Jesus as the Son of God. Listen closely to the Gospel.

✦ All make the Sign of the Cross.

In the name of the Father, and of the Son, and of the Holy Spirit. Amen.

PSALM

(For a longer psalm, see page xiii.)
Psalm 23:1–3a

I shall dwell in the house of the LORD my whole life long.

I shall dwell in the house of the LORD my whole life long.

The LORD is my shepherd, I shall not want.
    He makes me lie down in green pastures;
he leads me beside still waters;
    he restores my soul.

I shall dwell in the house of the LORD my whole life long.

✦ All stand and sing **Alleluia.**

GOSPEL

Mark 1:7–11

A reading from the holy Gospel according to Mark.

John the Baptist proclaimed, "The one who is more powerful than I is coming after me; I am not worthy to stoop down and untie the thong of his sandals. I have baptized you with water; but he will baptize you with the Holy Spirit." In those days Jesus came from Nazareth of Galilee and was baptized by John in the Jordan.

And just as he was coming up out of the water, he saw the heavens torn apart and the Spirit descending like a dove on him. And a voice came from heaven, "You are my Son, the Beloved; with you I am well pleased."

The Gospel of the Lord.

◆ All sit and observe silence.

FOR SILENT REFLECTION

Think about this silently in your heart. Like Jesus, you are also God's beloved child. How does that make you feel?

CLOSING PRAYER

Let us pray to God for our needs and the needs of others: our family, neighborhood, and the world. For each need we say, "Lord, hear our prayer."

◆ All may add their own prayers here.

Let us pray: **Our Father . . . Amen.**

Heavenly Father,
thank you for calling us to be your children
and for the gift of our Advocate,
the Holy Spirit.
Help us to live
as your beloved sons and daughters.
Through Christ our Lord.

Amen.

✦ All make the Sign of the Cross.

OPENING

Today's Gospel recalls the moment when Jesus appears to the disciples before ascending into heaven. A disciple is a faithful follower of Jesus. When Jesus appears to his disciples, he tells them to go into the world and celebrate the Good News.

✦ All make the Sign of the Cross.

In the name of the Father, and of the Son, and of the Holy Spirit. Amen.

PSALM
(For a longer psalm, see page xiii.) Psalm 23:1–3a

I shall dwell in the house of the LORD my whole life long.

I shall dwell in the house of the LORD my whole life long.

The LORD is my shepherd, I shall not want.
  He makes me lie down in green pastures;
he leads me beside still waters;
  he restores my soul.

I shall dwell in the house of the LORD my whole life long.

◆ All stand and sing **Alleluia.**

GOSPEL
Mark 16:14a, 15–16a, 17, 19–20

A reading from the holy Gospel according to Mark.

Later Jesus appeared to the eleven disciples as they were sitting at the table. And he said to them, "Go into all the world and proclaim the good news to the whole creation. The one who believes and is baptized will be saved. And these signs will accompany those who believe: by using my name they will cast out demons; they will speak in new tongues." So then the Lord Jesus, after he had spoken to them, was taken up into heaven and sat down at the right hand of God. And they went out and proclaimed the good news everywhere, while the Lord worked with them and confirmed the message by the signs that accompanied it.

The Gospel of the Lord.

◆ All sit and observe silence.

FOR SILENT REFLECTION

Think about this silently in your heart. How do you proclaim the Good News? How do others know that you are a disciple of Jesus?

CLOSING PRAYER

Let us pray to God for our needs and the needs of others: our family, neighborhood, and the world. For each need we say, "Lord, hear our prayer."

◆ All may add their own prayers here.

Let us pray: **Our Father . . . Amen.**

Lord God,
may we be instruments of your peace.
Open our eyes,
our ears,
and our hearts to your Good News.
Help us to share our love for you with others.
Through Christ our Lord.

Amen.

✦ All make the Sign of the Cross.

PRAYER FOR THE WEEK

WITH A READING FROM THE GOSPEL FOR **SUNDAY, JANUARY 17, 2021**

OPENING

Today we move into Ordinary Time. While it is not a season of waiting like Advent or Lent, or a time of celebration like Christmas Time or Easter Time, Ordinary Time is an opportunity to grow in our faith. We learn more about Jesus' life and teachings. In today's reading, we learn about Jesus' first disciples.

✛ All make the Sign of the Cross.

In the name of the Father, and of the Son, and of the Holy Spirit. Amen.

PSALM

(For a longer psalm, see page xiii.)
Psalm 23:1–3a

I shall dwell in the house of the LORD my whole life long.

I shall dwell in the house of the LORD my whole life long.

The LORD is my shepherd, I shall not want.
He makes me lie down in green pastures;
he leads me beside still waters;
he restores my soul.

I shall dwell in the house of the LORD my whole life long.

◆ All stand and sing **Alleluia.**

GOSPEL

John 1:35–38c, 40–42

A reading from the holy Gospel according to John.

John was standing with two of his disciples, and as he watched Jesus walk by, he exclaimed, "Look, here is the Lamb of God!" The two disciples heard him say this, and they followed Jesus. When Jesus turned and saw them following, he said to them, "What are you looking for?" They said to him, "Rabbi" (which translated means Teacher). It was about four o'clock in the afternoon. One of the two who heard John speak and followed him was Andrew, Simon Peter's brother. He first found his brother Simon and said to him, "We have found the Messiah" (which is translated Anointed). He brought Simon to Jesus, who looked at him and said, "You are Simon son of John. You are to be called Cephas [SEE-fuhs]" (which is translated Peter).

The Gospel of the Lord.

◆ All sit and observe silence.

FOR SILENT REFLECTION

Think about this silently in your heart. How are you a disciple, or follower, of Jesus?

CLOSING PRAYER

Let us pray to God for our needs and the needs of others: our family, neighborhood, and the world. For each need we say, "Lord, hear our prayer."

◆ All may add their own prayers here.

Let us pray: **Our Father . . . Amen.**

Loving God,
you desire that we follow you and serve one another. Help us be your faithful disciples, serving you and our brothers and sisters in love. Through Christ our Lord.

Amen.

✛ All make the Sign of the Cross.

PRAYER SERVICE
DR. MARTIN LUTHER KING JR.

Place an image of Martin Luther King in the sacred space. Prepare a leader, four readers, and a song leader. If possible, sing the refrain of "We Are Called" or "Let Justice Roll Like a River," or some other suitable song. Be sure to keep some silence where it's indicated. Since the Scriptures are abridged, copy them and put them in the Bible marked with ribbons. Put the MLK quotes in a binder.

LEADER:

◆ Gesture for all to stand.

✝ All make the sign of the Cross.

> **In the name of the Father, and of the Son, and of the Holy Spirit. Amen**

LEADER:

We remember and celebrate Dr. Martin Luther King, who worked for the just treatment of African Americans. Even though he received many death threats, he spoke out courageously and taught us how to make changes through nonviolent protest.

◆ Gesture for all to sit.

READER 1

From Dr. King's "I Have a Dream" Speech.
"I have a dream that my four little children will one day live in a nation where they will not be judged by the color of their skin, but by the content of their character."

◆ Observe some silence.

READER 2

A quote from Dr. King's book *Strength to Love.*

"Returning hate for hate multiplies hate, adding deeper darkness to a night already devoid of stars. Darkness cannot drive out darkness; only light can do that. Hate cannot drive out hate; only love can do that."

◆ Observe some silence.

READER 3   Colossians 3:12, 14–15a

A reading from St. Paul's Letter to the Colossians.

As God's chosen ones, holy and beloved, clothe yourselves with compassion, kindness, humility, meekness, and patience. Above all, clothe yourselves with love, which binds everything together in perfect harmony. And let the peace of Christ rule in your hearts.

The Word of the Lord.

◆ Observe some silence.

LEADER:

◆ Gesture for all to stand.

◆ All stand to sing the song.

LEADER:

Let us pray.
O God of justice and love,
give us the courage
to challenge injustice wherever we see it.
Help us be open to all your children
and not let race, religion,
or anything else divide us.
We ask this in Jesus' name.

ALL: Amen

✝ All make the Sign of the Cross.

> **In the name of the Father, and of the Son, and of the Holy Spirit. Amen**

Prepare four leaders and a song leader for this service. The second leader will need a Bible to read the Scripture passage and may need help finding and practicing it.

FIRST LEADER:

May the peace of Christ, who unites brothers and sisters around the world in his name, be with us, now and for ever.

ALL: Amen.

✦ All make the Sign of the Cross.

Let us pray:
Almighty God,
Creator of all wisdom,
you have made each of us
in your image
to reflect your many gifts.
We have been blessed through the
waters of Baptism,
to join with all Christians in the
loving power of
Father, Son, and Spirit.
Send your Spirit to guide us
as we seek your truth
and become united with Jesus
as our leader in faith.
We ask this through Christ our Lord.

ALL: Amen.

◆ All stand and sing **Alleluia.**

SECOND LEADER: John 15:12–17

A reading from the holy Gospel according to John.

◆ Read the Gospel passage from the Bible.

The Gospel of the Lord.

Let us pause and pray in silence for peace and unity among all Christians.

◆ Observe a time of silence.

THIRD LEADER:

Lord God,
you have made yourself known
to all the nations.
We declare your handiwork through
acts of peace and social justice
that assist all in need.
Guide us with your ways of peace.
Give us the courage to seek solutions
that benefit all
and that serve people
to build dignity and respect
for one another.
We ask this through Christ our Lord.

ALL: Amen.

FOURTH LEADER:

Now let us offer to one another a sign of Christ's peace.

◆ All offer one another a sign of peace.

And may the Lord bless us,

✦ All make the Sign of the Cross.

protect us from all evil,
and bring us to everlasting life.

ALL: Amen.

OPENING

We will hear Scripture from the Old Testament today and tomorrow. The "ark of God" was a highly decorated wooden chest containing the tablets of the Ten Commandments. (Do you remember who King David was?) King David gave thanks to God because the ark had a new permanent home in Jerusalem. King David and the people of Israel celebrated by singing God's praises.

✝ All make the Sign of the Cross.

In the name of the Father, and of the Son, and of the Holy Spirit. Amen.

PSALM
(For a longer psalm, see page xiii.)
Psalm 23:1–3a

I shall dwell in the house of the LORD my whole life long.

I shall dwell in the house of the LORD my whole life long.

The LORD is my shepherd, I shall not want.
  He makes me lie down in green pastures;
he leads me beside still waters;
  he restores my soul.

I shall dwell in the house of the LORD my whole life long.

READING
1 Chronicles 16:1a, 4, 5c, 6a, 7–8a, 10, 31a, 32–33a

A reading from the First Book of Chronicles.

They brought in the ark of God. David appointed certain of the Levites [LEE-vīts] as ministers before the ark of the LORD, to invoke, to thank, and to praise the LORD, the God of Israel. Asaph [AY-saf] was to sound the cym-bals, and the priests Benaiah [ben-uh-I-ah] and Jahaziel [jay-HAZ-ee-el] were to blow trumpets regularly. Then on that day David first appointed the singing of praises to the LORD by Asaph and his kindred. O give thanks to the LORD. Glory in his holy name; let the hearts of those who seek the LORD rejoice. Let the heavens be glad, and let the earth rejoice! Let the sea roar, and all that fills it; let the field exult, and everything in it. Then shall the trees of the forest sing for joy before the LORD.

The Word of the Lord.

◆ All observe silence.

FOR SILENT REFLECTION

Think about this silently in your heart. How does your church community praise and thank God?

CLOSING PRAYER

Let us pray to God for our needs and the needs of others: our family, neighborhood, and the world. For each need we say, "Lord, hear our prayer."

◆ All may add their own prayers here.

Let us pray: **Our Father . . . Amen.**

Almighty God,
we praise and glorify you!
We thank you for all your creation.
May we keep your commands
and be good stewards of all your good gifts.
We ask this in Christ's name.

Amen.

✝ All make the Sign of the Cross.

OPENING

Today is the feast of Sts. Fabian and Sebastian. St. Sebastian was a Roman martyr. St. Fabian is famous for the miraculous way he was elected pope, in which a dove descended upon his head. We hear another passage of celebration today. Passover is a holy time in the Jewish faith. The Jewish people remember their enslavement and eventual freedom from Egypt.

✚ All make the Sign of the Cross.

In the name of the Father, and of the Son, and of the Holy Spirit. Amen.

PSALM
(For a longer psalm, see page xiii.)
Psalm 23:1–3a

II shall dwell in the house of the LORD my whole life long.

I shall dwell in the house of the LORD my whole life long.

The LORD is my shepherd, I shall not want.
  He makes me lie down in green pastures;
he leads me beside still waters;
  he restores my soul.

I shall dwell in the house of the LORD my whole life long.

READING
2 Chronicles 30:1acd, 13a, 21, 25

A reading from the Second Book of Chronicles.

King Hezekiah [hehz-eh-KĪ-uh] sent word to all Israel and Judah, that they should come to the house of the LORD at Jerusalem, to keep the passover to the LORD the God of Israel. Many people came together in Jerusalem to keep the festival of unleavened bread in the second month. The people of Israel who were present at Jerusalem kept the festival of unleavened bread seven days with great gladness; and the Levites [LEE-vīts] and the priests praised the LORD day by day, accompanied by loud instruments for the LORD. The whole assembly of Judah, the priests and the Levites, and the whole assembly that came out of Israel, and the resident aliens who came out of the land of Israel, and the resident aliens who lived in Judah, rejoiced.

The Word of the Lord.

◆ All observe silence.

FOR SILENT REFLECTION

Think about this silently in your heart. The Jewish people celebrate Passover with a Seder meal. We celebrate the Last Supper during the Liturgy of the Eucharist. Why are shared meals so important to our faiths?

CLOSING PRAYER

Let us pray to God for our needs and the needs of others: our family, neighborhood, and the world. For each need we say, "Lord, hear our prayer."

◆ All may add their own prayers here.

Let us pray: **Our Father . . . Amen.**

Holy God,
bless us when we gather together in your name. We ask this in Christ's name.

Amen.

✚ All make the Sign of the Cross.

PRAYER FOR
THURSDAY, JANUARY 21, 2021

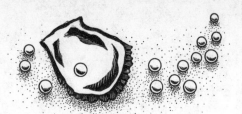

OPENING

We hear Jesus recount the Beatitudes in the Sermon on the Mount. *Beatitude* means "happy" or "blessed." Jesus says that if we follow these Beatitudes, we shall be blessed, and we should rejoice. Today is the memorial for the martyr St. Agnes of Rome, who is the patron saint of virtue.

✝ All make the Sign of the Cross.

In the name of the Father, and of the Son, and of the Holy Spirit. Amen.

PSALM

(For a longer psalm, see page xiii.)
Psalm 23:1–3a

I shall dwell in the house of the LORD my whole life long.

I shall dwell in the house of the LORD my whole life long.

The LORD is my shepherd, I shall not want.
    He makes me lie down in green pastures;
he leads me beside still waters;
    he restores my soul.

I shall dwell in the house of the LORD my whole life long.

◆ All stand and sing **Alleluia.**

GOSPEL

Matthew 5:2–12a

A reading from the holy Gospel according to Matthew.

Then Jesus began to speak, and taught them, saying: "Blessed are the poor in spirit, for theirs is the kingdom of heaven. Blessed are those who mourn, for they will be comforted. Blessed are the meek, for they will inherit the earth. Blessed are those who hunger and thirst for righteousness, for they will be filled. Blessed are the merciful, for they will receive mercy. Blessed are the pure in heart, for they will see God. Blessed are the peacemakers, for they will be called children of God. Blessed are those who are persecuted for righteousness' sake, for theirs is the kingdom of heaven. Blessed are you when people revile you and persecute you and utter all kinds of evil against you falsely on my account. Rejoice and be glad, for your reward is great in heaven."

The Gospel of the Lord.

◆ All sit and observe silence.

FOR SILENT REFLECTION

Think about this silently in your heart. Which of the Beatitudes offers you comfort today?

CLOSING PRAYER

Let us pray to God for our needs and the needs of others: our family, neighborhood, and the world. For each need we say, "Lord, hear our prayer."

◆ All may add their own prayers here.

Let us pray: **Our Father . . . Amen.**

Loving God,
thank you for teaching us the right ways.
May we accomplish the purpose
for which you created us.
We ask this in Christ's name.

Amen.

✝ All make the Sign of the Cross.

OPENING

We have heard of the joy of the Israelites. In today's reading, St. Paul tells us to rejoice as followers of Jesus. While rejoicing often comes with a great celebration, music, and singing, St. Paul tells us to rejoice through gentleness, prayer, and peace. Today we pray for the legal protection of unborn children.

✤ All make the Sign of the Cross.

In the name of the Father, and of the Son, and of the Holy Spirit. Amen.

PSALM
(For a longer psalm, see page xiii.)
Psalm 23:1–3a

I shall dwell in the house of the Lord my whole life long.

I shall dwell in the house of the Lord my whole life long.

The Lord is my shepherd, I shall not want.
  He makes me lie down in green pastures;
he leads me beside still waters;
  he restores my soul.

I shall dwell in the house of the Lord my whole life long.

READING
Philippians 3:17, 20; 4:1, 4–7

A reading from the Letter of Paul to the Philippians.

Brothers and sisters, join in imitating me, and observe those who live according to the example you have in us. But our citizenship is in heaven, and it is from there that we are expecting a Savior, the Lord Jesus Christ. Therefore, my brothers and sisters, whom I love and long for, my joy and crown, stand firm in the Lord in this way, my beloved. Rejoice in the Lord always; again I will say, Rejoice. Let your gentleness be known to everyone. The Lord is near. Do not worry about anything, but in everything by prayer and supplication with thanksgiving let your requests be made known to God. And the peace of God, which surpasses all understanding, will guard your hearts and your minds in Christ Jesus.

The Word of the Lord.

◆ All observe silence.

FOR SILENT REFLECTION

Think about this silently in your heart. How might you praise and thank God for the gift of life?

CLOSING PRAYER

Let us pray to God for our needs and the needs of others: our family, neighborhood, and the world. For each need we say, "Lord, hear our prayer."

◆ All may add their own prayers here.

Let us pray: **Our Father . . . Amen.**

We give you thanks, O loving God,
for the gift of life.
We pray for mothers, fathers, and all children,
those unborn and all who especially need
your protection.
We ask this in Christ's name.

Amen.

✤ All make the Sign of the Cross.

PRAYER FOR THE WEEK
WITH A READING FROM THE GOSPEL FOR **SUNDAY, JANUARY 24, 2021**

OPENING

We hear that Jesus went to the shore of the Sea of Galilee proclaiming the Good News. He calls out to Simon, Andrew, James, and John and invites them to follow him. They left everything—their jobs, families, and way of life—to be disciples of Jesus.

✚ All make the Sign of the Cross.

In the name of the Father, and of the Son, and of the Holy Spirit. Amen.

PSALM

(For a longer psalm, see page xiii.)
Psalm 23:1–3a

I shall dwell in the house of the LORD my whole life long.

I shall dwell in the house of the LORD my whole life long.

The LORD is my shepherd, I shall not want.
   He makes me lie down in green pastures;
he leads me beside still waters;
   he restores my soul.

I shall dwell in the house of the LORD my whole life long.

◆ All stand and sing **Alleluia.**

GOSPEL

Mark 1:14–20

A reading from the holy Gospel according to Mark.

Now after John was arrested, Jesus came to Galilee, proclaiming the good news of God, and saying, "The time is fulfilled, and the kingdom of God has come near; repent, and believe in the good news." As Jesus passed along the Sea of Galilee, he saw Simon and his brother Andrew casting a net into the sea—for they were fishermen. And Jesus said to them, "Follow me and I will make you fish for people." And immediately they left their nets and followed him. As he went a little farther, he saw James son of Zebedee and his brother John, who were in their boat mending the nets. Immediately he called them; and they left their father Zebedee in the boat with the hired men, and followed him.

The Gospel of the Lord.

◆ All sit and observe silence.

FOR SILENT REFLECTION

Think about this silently in your heart. Something about Jesus prompted these men to drop everything and follow him.

CLOSING PRAYER

Let us pray to God for our needs and the needs of others: our family, neighborhood, and the world. For each need we say, "Lord, hear our prayer."

◆ All may add their own prayers here.

Let us pray: **Our Father . . . Amen.**

Lord Jesus,
we wish to follow where you lead.
Open our hearts so that we may hear your call.
Who live and reign with God the Father,
in the unity of the Holy Spirit,
one God, for ever and ever.

Amen.

✚ All make the Sign of the Cross.

OPENING

Mountains are often thought of as places to be close to God, or where God is revealed. An angel told the prophet Elijah to go up the mountain to seek the Lord. Although there was great wind, earthquakes, and fire, Elijah heard God in the silence. To be zealous is to have great devotion or dedication.

✚ All make the Sign of the Cross.

In the name of the Father, and of the Son, and of the Holy Spirit. Amen.

PSALM

(For a longer psalm, see page xiii.)
Psalm 23:1–3a

I shall dwell in the house of the LORD my whole life long.

I shall dwell in the house of the LORD my whole life long.

The LORD is my shepherd, I shall not want.
   He makes me lie down in green pastures;
he leads me beside still waters;
   he restores my soul.

I shall dwell in the house of the LORD my whole life long.

READING

1 Kings 19:11–12, 13c–14c, 14fg

A reading from the First Book of Kings.

The angel of the LORD said to Elijah, "Go out and stand on the mountain before the LORD, for the LORD is about to pass by." Now there was a great wind, so strong that it was splitting mountains and breaking rocks in pieces before the LORD, but the LORD was not in the wind; and after the wind an earthquake, but the LORD was not in the earthquake; and after the earthquake a fire, but the LORD was not in the fire; and after the fire a sound of sheer silence. Then there came a voice to him that said, "What are you doing here, Elijah?" He answered, "I have been very zealous for the LORD, the God of hosts; for the Israelites have forsaken your covenant. I alone am left, and they are seeking my life, to take it away."

The Word of the Lord.

◆ All observe silence.

FOR SILENT REFLECTION

Think about this silently in your heart. Have you ever listened for God's voice? Take some time today to be still and listen.

CLOSING PRAYER

Let us pray to God for our needs and the needs of others: our family, neighborhood, and the world. For each need we say, "Lord, hear our prayer."

◆ All may add their own prayers here.

Let us pray: **Our Father . . . Amen.**

Holy God,
help us to hear the quiet of your voice
in the busyness of our day.
Increase our faith
during this Ordinary Time,
that it may grow deep roots and flourish.
We ask this through Christ our Lord.

Amen.

✚ All make the Sign of the Cross.

OPENING

Today we remember St. Timothy and St. Titus, two disciples St. Paul mentioned in the New Testament. In yesterday's reading, the prophet Elijah mentioned the covenant the Israelites had with God. A covenant is an agreement. God made a promise to the people and, through Moses, gave them the Ten Commandments. The word means the same as "laws," "statutes," and "ordinances."

✝ All make the Sign of the Cross.

In the name of the Father, and of the Son, and of the Holy Spirit. Amen.

PSALM

(For a longer psalm, see page xiii.)
Psalm 23:1–3a

I shall dwell in the house of the LORD my whole life long.

I shall dwell in the house of the LORD my whole life long.

The LORD is my shepherd, I shall not want.
   He makes me lie down in green pastures;
he leads me beside still waters;
   he restores my soul.

I shall dwell in the house of the LORD my whole life long.

READING

Deuteronomy 5:1–5

A reading from the Book of Deuteronomy.

Moses convened all Israel, and said to them: Hear, O Israel, the statutes and ordinances that I am addressing to you today; you shall learn them and observe them diligently. The LORD our God made a covenant with us at Horeb. Not with our ancestors did the LORD make this covenant, but with us, who are all of us here alive today. The LORD spoke with you face to face at the mountain, out of the fire. (At that time I was standing between the LORD and you to declare to you the words of the LORD; for you were afraid because of the fire and did not go up the mountain.)

The Word of the Lord.

◆ All observe silence.

FOR SILENT REFLECTION

Think about this silently in your heart. Which of the Ten Commandments do you have trouble keeping?

CLOSING PRAYER

Let us pray to God for our needs and the needs of others: our family, neighborhood, and the world. For each need we say, "Lord, hear our prayer."

◆ All may add their own prayers here.

Let us pray: **Our Father . . . Amen.**

Almighty God,
you brought Moses and the Israelites to your holy mountain
and gave them commandments to live by.
Help us to follow your commandments.
We ask this through your Son,
our Lord Jesus Christ.

Amen.

✝ All make the Sign of the Cross.

OPENING

We celebrate St. Angela Merici today. She dedicated her life to helping young girls have a Christian education. We hear more Scripture that takes place on a mountaintop. Jesus took Peter, James, and John to the top of a mountain. He transfigured, or revealed, his true self to them.

✛ All make the Sign of the Cross.

In the name of the Father, and of the Son, and of the Holy Spirit. Amen.

PSALM

(For a longer psalm, see page xiii.)
Psalm 23:1–3a

I shall dwell in the house of the LORD my whole life long.

I shall dwell in the house of the LORD my whole life long.

The LORD is my shepherd, I shall not want.
   He makes me lie down in green pastures;
he leads me beside still waters;
   he restores my soul.

I shall dwell in the house of the LORD my whole life long.

◆ All stand and sing **Alleluia.**

GOSPEL

Mark 9:2–8

A reading from the holy Gospel according to Mark.

Six days later, Jesus took with him Peter and James and John, and led them up a high mountain apart, by themselves. And he was transfigured before them, and his clothes became dazzling white, such as no one on earth could bleach them. And there appeared to them Elijah with Moses, who were talking with Jesus. Then Peter said to Jesus, "Rabbi, it is good for us to be here; let us make three dwellings, one for you, one for Moses, and one for Elijah." He did not know what to say, for they were terrified. Then a cloud overshadowed them, and from the cloud there came a voice, "This is my Son, the Beloved; listen to him!" Suddenly when they looked around, they saw no one with them anymore, but only Jesus.

The Gospel of the Lord.

◆ All sit and observe silence.

FOR SILENT REFLECTION

Think about this silently in your heart. Sometimes we know when God is clearly present in our lives. Reflect on that time.

CLOSING PRAYER

Let us pray to God for our needs and the needs of others: our family, neighborhood, and the world. For each need we say, "Lord, hear our prayer."

◆ All may add their own prayers here.

Let us pray: **Our Father . . . Amen.**

Loving God,
you have sent many men and women to help guide the way to you.
Help us to remember their teachings so that we may remain close and faithful to you.
We ask this in Christ's name.

Amen.

✛ All make the Sign of the Cross.

PRAYER FOR
THURSDAY, JANUARY 28, 2021

OPENING

Today we celebrate the feast of St. Thomas Aquinas. He was a scholar of philosophy and theology, and his works are studied today. In today's Gospel, Jesus tells his disciples about his death and Resurrection. They do not yet understand him and are afraid to ask him questions.

✚ All make the Sign of the Cross.

In the name of the Father, and of the Son, and of the Holy Spirit. Amen.

PSALM

(For a longer psalm, see page xiii.)
Psalm 23:1–3a

I shall dwell in the house of the LORD my whole life long.

I shall dwell in the house of the LORD my whole life long.

The LORD is my shepherd, I shall not want.
   He makes me lie down in green pastures;
he leads me beside still waters;
   he restores my soul.

I shall dwell in the house of the LORD my whole life long.

◆ All stand and sing **Alleluia.**

GOSPEL

Mark 9:9–10, 30–32

A reading from the holy Gospel according to Mark.

As Peter, James, John, and Jesus were coming down the mountain, Jesus ordered them to tell no one about what they had seen, until after the Son of Man had risen from the dead. So they kept the matter to themselves, questioning what this rising from the dead could mean.

Jesus and his disciples went on from there and passed through Galilee. He did not want anyone to know it; for he was teaching his disciples, saying to them, "The Son of Man is to be betrayed into human hands, and they will kill him, and three days after being killed, he will rise again." But they did not understand what he was saying and were afraid to ask him.

The Gospel of the Lord.

◆ All sit and observe silence.

FOR SILENT REFLECTION

Think about this silently in your heart. What questions do you have about your faith? Bring them to prayer and to your teacher, parents, or priest.

CLOSING PRAYER

Let us pray to God for our needs and the needs of others: our family, neighborhood, and the world. For each need we say, "Lord, hear our prayer."

◆ All may add their own prayers here.

Let us pray: **Our Father . . . Amen.**

Loving Jesus,
you reveal yourself in ways we don't always understand or recognize.
Be with us as we seek the truth.
Grant us wisdom to know your will.
Who live and reign with God the Father,
in the unity of the Holy Spirit,
one God, for ever and ever.

Amen.

✚ All make the Sign of the Cross.

OPENING

The disciples begin to argue about who among them is the greatest. Jesus responds to them by taking a child into his arms and challenging their understanding of greatness.

✜ All make the Sign of the Cross.

In the name of the Father, and of the Son, and of the Holy Spirit. Amen.

PSALM

(For a longer psalm, see page xiii.)

Psalm 23:1–3a

I shall dwell in the house of the LORD my whole life long.

I shall dwell in the house of the LORD my whole life long.

The LORD is my shepherd, I shall not want.
  He makes me lie down in green pastures;
he leads me beside still waters;
  he restores my soul.

I shall dwell in the house of the LORD my whole life long.

◆ All stand and sing **Alleluia.**

GOSPEL

Mark 9:33–37

A reading from the holy Gospel according to Mark.

Then Jesus and his disciples came to Capernaum [kuh-PER-n*m]; and when he was in the house he asked them, "What were you arguing about on the way?" But they were silent, for on the way they had argued with one another about who was the greatest. Jesus sat down, called the twelve, and said to them, "Whoever wants to be first must be last of all and servant of all." Then he took a little child and put it among them; and taking it in his arms, he said to them, "Whoever welcomes one such child in my name welcomes me, and whoever welcomes me welcomes not me but the one who sent me."

The Gospel of the Lord.

◆ All sit and observe silence.

FOR SILENT REFLECTION

Think about this silently in your heart. What does Jesus mean by "Whoever wants to be first must be last of all and servant of all"?

CLOSING PRAYER

Let us pray to God for our needs and the needs of others: our family, neighborhood, and the world. For each need we say, "Lord, hear our prayer."

◆ All may add their own prayers here.

Let us pray: **Our Father . . . Amen.**

God of love and mercy,
help us to know that putting others first
also means putting you first.
Help us to live as your obedient sons
and daughters.
In Jesus Christ's name we pray,

Amen.

✜ All make the Sign of the Cross.

PRAYER FOR THE WEEK
WITH A READING FROM THE GOSPEL FOR **SUNDAY, JANUARY 31, 2021**

OPENING

Jesus taught in a synagogue on the Sabbath day and expelled an unclean spirit from a man. A synagogue is the Jewish place of worship, instruction, and prayer. The Sabbath is the Jewish holy day of the week. The people in the synagogue were amazed that Jesus taught with authority, or "with power."

✝ All make the Sign of the Cross.

In the name of the Father, and of the Son, and of the Holy Spirit. Amen.

PSALM

(For a longer psalm, see page xiii.)
Psalm 23:1–3a

I shall dwell in the house of the LORD my whole life long.

I shall dwell in the house of the LORD my whole life long.

The LORD is my shepherd, I shall not want.
  He makes me lie down in green pastures;
he leads me beside still waters;
  he restores my soul.

I shall dwell in the house of the LORD my whole life long.

◆ All stand and sing **Alleluia.**

GOSPEL

Mark 1:21–27

A reading from the holy Gospel according to Mark.

Jesus and his disciples went to Capernaum [kuh-PER-n*m]; and when the sabbath came, Jesus entered the synagogue and taught. They were astounded at his teaching, for he taught them as one having authority, and not as the scribes. Just then there was in their synagogue a man with an unclean spirit, and he cried out, "What have you to do with us, Jesus of Nazareth? Have you come to destroy us? I know who you are, the Holy One of God." But Jesus rebuked him, saying, "Be silent, and come out of him!" And the unclean spirit, throwing him into convulsions and crying with a loud voice, came out of him. They were all amazed, and they kept on asking one another, "What is this? A new teaching—with authority! He commands even the unclean spirits, and they obey him."

The Gospel of the Lord.

◆ All sit and observe silence.

FOR SILENT REFLECTION

Think about this silently in your heart. How does Jesus amaze you?

CLOSING PRAYER

Let us pray to God for our needs and the needs of others: our family, neighborhood, and the world. For each need we say, "Lord, hear our prayer."

◆ All may add their own prayers here.

Let us pray: **Our Father . . . Amen.**

O God our Father,
thank you for sending us Jesus.
We are grateful for all that he taught us.
May we glorify you
and live according to your will.
We ask this in Christ's name.

Amen.

✝ All make the Sign of the Cross.

OPENING

In Jesus' day, the Jews did not like tax collectors because they were thought to be greedy and supporters of the Romans. But Jesus welcomed sinners and tax collectors—his ministry welcomed all into community with him. This was hard for some to understand.

✚ All make the Sign of the Cross.

In the name of the Father, and of the Son, and of the Holy Spirit. Amen.

PSALM

(For a longer psalm, see page xiii.)
Psalm 23:1–3a

I shall dwell in the house of the Lord my whole life long.

I shall dwell in the house of the Lord my whole life long.

The Lord is my shepherd, I shall not want.
  He makes me lie down in green pastures;
he leads me beside still waters;
  he restores my soul.

I shall dwell in the house of the Lord my whole life long.

◆ All stand and sing **Alleluia.**

GOSPEL

Mark 2:13–17

A reading from the holy Gospel according to Mark.

Jesus went out again beside the sea; the whole crowd gathered around him, and he taught them. As he was walking along, he saw Levi son of Alphaeus [AL-fee-uhs] sitting at the tax booth, and he said to him, "Follow me." And he got up and followed him. And as he sat at dinner in Levi's house, many tax collectors and sinners were also sitting with Jesus and his disciples—for there were many who followed him. When the scribes of the Pharisees [FAYR-uh-seez] saw that he was eating with sinners and tax collectors, they said to his disciples, "Why does he eat with tax collectors and sinners?" When Jesus heard this, he said to them, "Those who are well have no need of a physician, but those who are sick; I have come to call not the righteous but sinners."

The Gospel of the Lord.

◆ All sit and observe silence.

FOR SILENT REFLECTION

Think about this silently in your heart. Why do you think Jesus called sinners to him?

CLOSING PRAYER

Let us pray to God for our needs and the needs of others: our family, neighborhood, and the world. For each need we say, "Lord, hear our prayer."

◆ All may add their own prayers here.

Let us pray: **Our Father . . . Amen.**

God of all that is good,
we have been welcomed and called to you
through your son Jesus,
even though we are not perfect.
May we be as welcoming to others.
We ask this through Christ our Lord.

Amen.

✚ All make the Sign of the Cross.

PRAYER FOR
TUESDAY, FEBRUARY 2, 2021

OPENING

Today we celebrate the Presentation of the Lord. By Jewish law, the firstborn son would be presented at the temple forty days after his birth. Today's feast marks Jesus' presentation by his parents. We also traditionally bless candles today, so sometimes this feast day is called Candlemas. Mexican Catholics commemorate the day by bringing statues to church of "el Niño Dios," or "Child Jesus."

✚ All make the Sign of the Cross.

> **In the name of the Father, and of the Son, and of the Holy Spirit. Amen.**

PSALM

(For a longer psalm, see page xiii.)
Psalm 23:1–3a

I shall dwell in the house of the LORD my whole life long.

I shall dwell in the house of the LORD my whole life long.

The LORD is my shepherd, I shall not want.
  He makes me lie down in green pastures;
he leads me beside still waters;
  he restores my soul.

I shall dwell in the house of the LORD my whole life long.

READING

Exodus 30:22, 23a, 24c–26, 29, 31–32

A reading from the Book of Exodus.

The LORD spoke to Moses: Take the finest spices measured by the sanctuary shekel—and a hin of olive oil; and you shall make of these a sacred anointing oil blended as by the perfumer; it shall be a holy anointing oil. With it you shall anoint the tent of meeting and the ark of the covenant. You shall consecrate them, so that they may be most holy; whatever touches them will become holy. You shall say to the Israelites, "This shall be my holy anointing oil throughout your generations. It shall not be used in any ordinary anointing of the body, and you shall make no other like it in composition; it is holy, and it shall be holy to you."

The Word of the Lord.

◆ All observe silence.

FOR SILENT REFLECTION

Think about this silently in your heart. You were anointed with oils during Baptism to signify God's call and blessing. How do you answer that call today?

CLOSING PRAYER

Let us pray to God for our needs and the needs of others: our family, neighborhood, and the world. For each need we say, "Lord, hear our prayer."

◆ All may add their own prayers here.

Let us pray: **Our Father . . . Amen.**

God our Father,
you have called us to follow you
and have blessed us with gifts to share.
May we use your gifts to give you glory.
Help us to be a sign of your love to all.
In Christ's name we pray.

Amen.

✚ All make the Sign of the Cross.

OPENING

Today is the feast of St. Blaise. It is traditional to have our throats blessed and to pray for good health on this day. We hear that Jesus reads from the prophet Isaiah [ī-ZAY-uh] in the synagogue. Jesus states that the prophecy of the promised savior has been fulfilled through him.

✚ All make the Sign of the Cross.

In the name of the Father, and of the Son, and of the Holy Spirit. Amen.

PSALM

(For a longer psalm, see page xiii.)
Psalm 23:1–3a

I shall dwell in the house of the LORD my whole life long.

I shall dwell in the house of the LORD my whole life long.

The LORD is my shepherd, I shall not want.
   He makes me lie down in green pastures;
he leads me beside still waters;
   he restores my soul.

I shall dwell in the house of the LORD my whole life long.

◆ All stand and sing **Alleluia.**

GOSPEL

Luke 4:16–19, 21

A reading from the holy Gospel according to Luke.

When Jesus came to Nazareth, where he had been brought up, he went to the synagogue on the sabbath day, as was his custom. He stood up to read, and the scroll of the prophet Isaiah was given to him. He unrolled the scroll and found the place where it was written: "The Spirit of the Lord is upon me, because he has anointed me to bring good news to the poor. He has sent me to proclaim release to the captives and recovery of sight to the blind, to let the oppressed go free, to proclaim the year of the Lord's favor." Then he began to say to them, "Today this scripture has been fulfilled in your hearing."

The Gospel of the Lord.

◆ All sit and observe silence.

FOR SILENT REFLECTION

Think about this silently in your heart. If you were there in the synagogue, how would you have reacted to Jesus' proclamation?

CLOSING PRAYER

Let us pray to God for our needs and the needs of others: our family, neighborhood, and the world. For each need we say, "Lord, hear our prayer."

◆ All may add their own prayers here.

Let us pray: **Our Father . . . Amen.**

You, O Lord, are worthy of our
thanks and praise!
Help us to follow the example of your
Son Jesus,
our Master Teacher.
May we learn from him always.
Through Christ our Lord.

Amen.

✚ All make the Sign of the Cross.

PRAYER FOR
THURSDAY, FEBRUARY 4, 2021

OPENING

We hear more about discipleship in this passage about Philip, one of seven deacons mentioned by St. Paul. Philip cared for the poor Christian communities in Jerusalem and proclaimed the Good News in Samaria. He prepared the way for the Apostles Peter and John. The gesture of laying on of hands is to call forth the Holy Spirit.

✦ All make the Sign of the Cross.

In the name of the Father, and of the Son, and of the Holy Spirit. Amen.

PSALM

(For a longer psalm, see page xiii.)
Psalm 23:1–3a

I shall dwell in the house of the LORD my whole life long.

I shall dwell in the house of the LORD my whole life long.

The LORD is my shepherd, I shall not want.
  He makes me lie down in green pastures;
he leads me beside still waters;
  he restores my soul.

I shall dwell in the house of the LORD my whole life long.

READING

Acts 8:5–6, 14–17

A reading from the Acts of the Apostles.

Philip went down to the city of Samaria and proclaimed the Messiah to them. The crowds with one accord listened eagerly to what was said by Philip, hearing and seeing the signs that he did. Now when the apostles at Jerusalem heard that Samaria had accepted the word of God, they sent Peter and John to them. The two went down and prayed for them that they might receive the Holy Spirit (for as yet the Spirit had not come upon any of them; they had only been baptized in the name of the Lord Jesus). Then Peter and John laid their hands on them, and they received the Holy Spirit.

The Word of the Lord.

✦ All observe silence.

FOR SILENT REFLECTION

Think about this silently in your heart. Pray today that the Holy Spirit fills you with wisdom and understanding.

CLOSING PRAYER

Let us pray to God for our needs and the needs of others: our family, neighborhood, and the world. For each need we say, "Lord, hear our prayer."

✦ All may add their own prayers here.

Let us pray: **Our Father . . . Amen.**

O Holy Spirit,
we ask that you come upon us and flow through us.
Direct us by your wisdom and give us courage.
Lead us to make good judgments.
Through Christ our Lord.

Amen.

✦ All make the Sign of the Cross.

OPENING

St. Agatha, whose memorial we celebrate today, was tortured for choosing to live a virtuous life. She was martyred in 253. We hear about St. Paul guiding and mentoring Timothy about his ministry in Ephesus [EF-uh-suhs]. He tells Timothy to be an example to others, to continue reading Scripture, and to devote himself to the gift he was given.

✝ All make the Sign of the Cross.

In the name of the Father, and of the Son, and of the Holy Spirit. Amen.

PSALM

(For a longer psalm, see page xiii.)
Psalm 23:1–3a

I shall dwell in the house of the LORD my whole life long.

I shall dwell in the house of the LORD my whole life long.

The LORD is my shepherd, I shall not want.
  He makes me lie down in green pastures;
he leads me beside still waters;
  he restores my soul.

I shall dwell in the house of the LORD my whole life long.

READING

1 Timothy 4:11–16

A reading from the First Letter of Paul to Timothy.

These are the things you must insist on and teach. Let no one despise your youth, but set the believers an example in speech and conduct, in love, in faith, in purity. Until I arrive, give attention to the public reading of scripture, to exhorting, to teaching. Do not neglect the gift that is in you, which was given to you through prophecy with the laying on of hands by the council of elders. Put these things into practice, devote yourself to them, so that all may see your progress. Pay close attention to yourself and to your teaching; continue in these things, for in doing this you will save both yourself and your hearers.

The Word of the Lord.

◆ All observe silence.

FOR SILENT REFLECTION

Think about this silently in your heart. What gifts have you been blessed with?

CLOSING PRAYER

Let us pray to God for our needs and the needs of others: our family, neighborhood, and the world. For each need we say, "Lord, hear our prayer."

◆ All may add their own prayers here.

Let us pray: **Our Father . . . Amen.**

Good and gracious God,
we are grateful for your many gifts.
Help us to devote ourselves to strengthening them
so that we may serve your people in love.
This we ask through Christ our Lord.

Amen.

✝ All make the Sign of the Cross.

OPENING

We hear that Jesus began healing those who were ill. He cured Simon's mother-in-law, and soon the whole city was gathered at the door. Jesus continued to heal many during his ministry.

✝ All make the Sign of the Cross.

In the name of the Father, and of the Son, and of the Holy Spirit. Amen.

PSALM

(For a longer psalm, see page xiii.)
Psalm 23:1–3a

I shall dwell in the house of the LORD my whole life long.

I shall dwell in the house of the LORD my whole life long.

The LORD is my shepherd, I shall not want.
    He makes me lie down in green pastures;
he leads me beside still waters;
    he restores my soul.

I shall dwell in the house of the LORD my whole life long.

◆ All stand and sing **Alleluia.**

GOSPEL

Mark 1:29–34

A reading from the holy Gospel according to Mark.

As soon as they left the synagogue, Jesus entered the house of Simon and Andrew, with James and John. Now Simon's mother-in-law was in bed with a fever, and they told him about her at once. He came and took her by the hand and lifted her up. Then the fever left her, and she began to serve them. That evening, at sunset, they brought to him all who were sick or possessed with demons. And the whole city was gathered around the door. And he cured many who were sick with various diseases, and cast out many demons; and he would not permit the demons to speak, because they knew him.

The Gospel of the Lord.

◆ All sit and observe silence.

FOR SILENT REFLECTION

Think about this silently in your heart. What cure do you ask of Jesus? What sickness, sadness, loneliness, worries, or bad feelings can you lay before him? Pray to Jesus and ask for healing.

CLOSING PRAYER

Let us pray to God for our needs and the needs of others: our family, neighborhood, and the world. For each need we say, "Lord, hear our prayer."

◆ All may add their own prayers here.

Let us pray: **Our Father . . . Amen.**

Almighty Father,
in becoming human, Jesus the Son of God understood human weakness and suffering, Jesus has healed and cured many.
We ask that you heal our hearts, minds, and bodies from what ails and hurts us, so that we may do your good work in the world.
We ask this in Christ's name.

Amen.

✝ All make the Sign of the Cross.

OPENING

St. Paul tells us today that we are all given gifts from the Holy Spirit. Today we remember St. Jerome Emiliani (1486–1537), who is the patron saint of orphans and abandoned children, and St. Josephine Margaret Bakhita (1869–1947), who was kidnapped from Sudan in Africa into slavery. She suffered in captivity but eventually became a nun.

✛ All make the Sign of the Cross.

In the name of the Father, and of the Son, and of the Holy Spirit. Amen.

PSALM
(For a longer psalm, see page xiii.)
Psalm 23:1–3a

I shall dwell in the house of the LORD my whole life long.

I shall dwell in the house of the LORD my whole life long.

The LORD is my shepherd, I shall not want.
   He makes me lie down in green pastures;
he leads me beside still waters;
   he restores my soul.

I shall dwell in the house of the LORD my whole life long.

READING
1 Corinthians 12:4–11

A reading from the First Letter of Paul to the Corinthians [kohr-IN-thee-uhnz].

Now there are varieties of gifts, but the same Spirit; and there are varieties of services, but the same Lord; and there are varieties of activities, but it is the same God who activates all of them in everyone. To each is given the manifestation of the Spirit for the common good. To one is given through the Spirit the utterance of wisdom, and to another the utterance of knowledge according to the same Spirit, to another faith by the same Spirit, to another gifts of healing by the one Spirit, to another the working of miracles, to another prophecy, to another the discernment of spirits, to another various kinds of tongues, to another the interpretation of tongues. All these are activated by one and the same Spirit, who allots to each one individually just as the Spirit chooses.

The Word of the Lord.

◆ All observe silence.

FOR SILENT REFLECTION

Think about this silently in your heart. How do you use your God-given gifts?

CLOSING PRAYER

Let us pray to God for our needs and the needs of others: our family, neighborhood, and the world. For each need we say, "Lord, hear our prayer."

◆ All may add their own prayers here.

Let us pray: **Our Father . . . Amen.**

In your wisdom, O God,
you have given us various gifts.
May we honor you by using our talents and strengths to serve you and one another.
Through Christ our Lord.

Amen.

✛ All make the Sign of the Cross.

PRAYER FOR
TUESDAY, FEBRUARY 9, 2021

OPENING

St. Paul compares the Body of Christ to the human body. Just as our body has many parts, the Body of Christ has many members. All people, no matter their race, religion, or nationality are part of the Body of Christ. Jesus came for all people.

✦ All make the Sign of the Cross.

In the name of the Father, and of the Son, and of the Holy Spirit. Amen.

PSALM
(For a longer psalm, see page xiii.)
Psalm 23:1–3a

I shall dwell in the house of the LORD my whole life long.

I shall dwell in the house of the LORD my whole life long.

The LORD is my shepherd, I shall not want.
He makes me lie down in green pastures;
he leads me beside still waters;
he restores my soul.

I shall dwell in the house of the LORD my whole life long.

READING
1 Corinthians 12:12–13; 10:31–33c

A reading from the First Letter of Paul to the Corinthians [kohr-IN-thee-uhnz].

For just as the body is one and has many members, and all the members of the body, though many, are one body, so it is with Christ. For in the one Spirit we were all baptized into one body—Jews or Greeks, slaves or free—and we were all made to drink of one Spirit. So, whether you eat or drink, or whatever you do, do everything for the glory of God. Give no offence to Jews or to Greeks or to the church of God, just as I try to please everyone; in everything I do, not seeking my own advantage, but that of many.

The Word of the Lord.

◆ All observe silence.

FOR SILENT REFLECTION

Think about this silently in your heart. If all people are one in Christ, how should we treat people, especially those who are different from us?

CLOSING PRAYER

Let us pray to God for our needs and the needs of others: our family, neighborhood, and the world. For each need we say, "Lord, hear our prayer."

◆ All may add their own prayers here.

Let us pray: **Our Father . . . Amen.**

Holy and loving God,
though we are many, we are all one in you.
Help us recognize you in others.
May we practice love, compassion, and mercy.
We ask this in Christ's name.

Amen.

✦ All make the Sign of the Cross.

OPENING

St. Paul continues to teach using the metaphor for the Body of Christ. He tells us that we are all equal members. What happens to one member of the Body of Christ affects every member. A body works best when all parts are working. Christ's Body is best when each of us does our part and uses our gifts to serve others. St. Scholastica, the twin sister of St. Benedict, is celebrated today. Like her brother, St. Scholastica dedicated herself totally to God.

✛ All make the Sign of the Cross.

In the name of the Father, and of the Son, and of the Holy Spirit. Amen.

PSALM

(For a longer psalm, see page xiii.)
Psalm 23:1–3a

I shall dwell in the house of the LORD my whole life long.

I shall dwell in the house of the LORD my whole life long.

The LORD is my shepherd, I shall not want.
  He makes me lie down in green pastures;
he leads me beside still waters;
  he restores my soul.

I shall dwell in the house of the LORD my whole life long.

READING

1 Corinthians 12:14–17, 20, 26

A reading from the First Letter of Paul to the Corinthians [kohr-IN-thee-uhnz].

Indeed, the body does not consist of one member but of many. If the foot would say, "Because I am not a hand, I do not belong to the body," that would not make it any less a part of the body. And if the ear would say, "Because I am not an eye, I do not belong to the body," that would not make it any less a part of the body. If the whole body were an eye, where would the hearing be? If the whole body were hearing, where would the sense of smell be? As it is, there are many members, yet one body. If one member suffers, all suffer together with it; if one member is honored, all rejoice together with it.

The Word of the Lord.

◆ All observe silence.

FOR SILENT REFLECTION

Think about this silently in your heart. Even though we are all different, how are we connected?

CLOSING PRAYER

Let us pray to God for our needs and the needs of others: our family, neighborhood, and the world. For each need we say, "Lord, hear our prayer."

◆ All may add their own prayers here.

Let us pray: **Our Father . . . Amen.**

O holy and loving God,
we are all your sons and daughters.
May we celebrate our differences as well as
be united by what we have in common.
We ask this in Christ Jesus' name.

Amen.

✛ All make the Sign of the Cross.

PRAYER FOR
THURSDAY, FEBRUARY 11, 2021

OPENING

We hear from St. Paul that love, above all else, is the heart of the Christian message. Even though we may have other gifts, without love, they are nothing. St. Paul teaches us the many attributes of love. Today we celebrate Our Lady of Lourdes, to whom we ask help to be good Christians.

✦ All make the Sign of the Cross.

In the name of the Father, and of the Son, and of the Holy Spirit. Amen.

PSALM

(For a longer psalm, see page xiii.)

Psalm 23:1–3a

I shall dwell in the house of the LORD my whole life long.

I shall dwell in the house of the LORD my whole life long.

The LORD is my shepherd, I shall not want.
  He makes me lie down in green pastures;
he leads me beside still waters;
  he restores my soul.

I shall dwell in the house of the LORD my whole life long.

READING

1 Corinthians 13:1–2, 4–8a

A reading from the First Letter of Paul to the Corinthians [kohr-IN-thee-uhnz].

If I speak in the tongues of mortals and of angels, but do not have love, I am a noisy gong or a clanging cymbal. And if I have prophetic powers, and understand all mysteries and all knowledge, and if I have all faith, so as to remove mountains, but do not have love, I am

nothing. Love is patient; love is kind; love is not envious or boastful or arrogant or rude. It does not insist on its own way; it is not irritable or resentful; it does not rejoice in wrongdoing, but rejoices in the truth. It bears all things, believes all things, hopes all things, endures all things. Love never ends.

The Word of the Lord.

◆ All observe silence.

FOR SILENT REFLECTION

Think about this silently in your heart. How does St. Paul's description of love equal selflessness?

CLOSING PRAYER

Let us pray to God for our needs and the needs of others: our family, neighborhood, and the world. For each need we say, "Lord, hear our prayer."

◆ All may add their own prayers here.

Let us pray: **Our Father . . . Amen.**

Walk with us, O God, and guide us.
help us to seek your will,
to always act with love and compassion.
We ask this in the name of your Son
Jesus Christ our Lord,
who showed us by his own example
how much he loves us.

Amen.

✦ All make the Sign of the Cross.

OPENING

St. Paul continues to teach us about the Body of Christ and how we should live. He says that we should allow Christ to live deeply in our hearts. Our actions and our words should reflect the great love of Christ.

✢ All make the Sign of the Cross.

In the name of the Father, and of the Son, and of the Holy Spirit. Amen.

PSALM

(For a longer psalm, see page xiii.)
Psalm 23:1–3a

I shall dwell in the house of the LORD my whole life long.

I shall dwell in the house of the LORD my whole life long.

The LORD is my shepherd, I shall not want.
  He makes me lie down in green pastures;
he leads me beside still waters;
  he restores my soul.

I shall dwell in the house of the LORD my whole life long.

READING

Colossians 3:12–16

A reading from the Letter of Paul to the Colossians.

As God's chosen ones, holy and beloved, clothe yourselves with compassion, kindness, humility, meekness, and patience. Bear with one another, and if anyone has a complaint against another, forgive each other; just as the Lord has forgiven you, so you also must forgive. Above all, clothe yourselves with love, which binds everything together in perfect harmony.

And let the peace of Christ rule in your hearts, to which indeed you were called in the one body. And be thankful. Let the word of Christ dwell in you richly; teach and admonish one another in all wisdom; and with gratitude in your hearts sing psalms, hymns, and spiritual songs to God.

The Word of the Lord.

◆ All observe silence.

FOR SILENT REFLECTION

Think about this silently in your heart. Which of St. Paul's teachings can you start living out today?

CLOSING PRAYER

Let us pray to God for our needs and the needs of others: our family, neighborhood, and the world. For each need we say, "Lord, hear our prayer."

◆ All may add their own prayers here.

Let us pray: **Our Father . . . Amen.**

O God,
may we have loving and kind hearts.
May the peace and love of Christ rule our words and actions.
We ask this in the name of your Son
Jesus Christ our Lord.

Amen.

✢ All make the Sign of the Cross.

PRAYER FOR THE WEEK

WITH A READING FROM THE GOSPEL FOR **SUNDAY, FEBRUARY 14, 2021**

OPENING

Leprosy is a disease that often affects how someone looks. In Jesus' time, those infected were outcasts of society and called unclean. They were considered uncurable.

✦ All make the Sign of the Cross.

> **In the name of the Father, and of the Son, and of the Holy Spirit. Amen.**

PSALM

(For a longer psalm, see page xiii.)
Psalm 23:1–3a

I shall dwell in the house of the LORD my whole life long.

I shall dwell in the house of the LORD my whole life long.

The LORD is my shepherd, I shall not want.
   He makes me lie down in green pastures;
he leads me beside still waters;
   he restores my soul.

I shall dwell in the house of the LORD my whole life long.

◆ All stand and sing **Alleluia.**

GOSPEL

Mark 1:40–44a, 45

A reading from the holy Gospel according to Mark.

A leper came to Jesus begging him, and kneeling he said to him, "If you choose, you can make me clean." Moved with pity, Jesus stretched out his hand and touched him, and said to him, "I do choose. Be made clean!" Immediately the leprosy left him, and he was made clean. After sternly warning him Jesus sent him away at once, saying to him, "See that

you say nothing to anyone." But he went out and began to proclaim it freely, and to spread the word, so that Jesus could no longer go into a town openly, but stayed out in the country; and people came to him from every quarter.

The Gospel of the Lord.

◆ All sit and observe silence.

FOR SILENT REFLECTION

Think about this silently in your heart. Do you notice classmates or others who seem to be alone or outcast? What can you do to welcome them?

CLOSING PRAYER

Let us pray to God for our needs and the needs of others: our family, neighborhood, and the world. For each need we say, "Lord, hear our prayer."

◆ All may add their own prayers here.

Let us pray: **Our Father . . . Amen.**

O God of hope and healing,
each of us is called to minister to others,
especially those who are forgotten or alone.
We pray for all who are ill and suffering,
whether they are sick in body, mind, or spirit.
Please strengthen them and give them courage.
We ask this through Christ our Lord.

Amen.

✦ All make the Sign of the Cross.

OPENING

In today's reading, a religious leader named Jairus [JĪ-ruhs] came to Jesus and asked him to cure his daughter. Even though others had told Jairus not to bother Jesus, Jesus tells him not to fear and just believe.

✚ All make the Sign of the Cross.

In the name of the Father, and of the Son, and of the Holy Spirit. Amen.

PSALM

(For a longer psalm, see page xiii.)
Psalm 23:1–3a

I shall dwell in the house of the LORD my whole life long.

I shall dwell in the house of the LORD my whole life long.

The LORD is my shepherd, I shall not want.
   He makes me lie down in green pastures;
he leads me beside still waters;
   he restores my soul.

I shall dwell in the house of the LORD my whole life long.

◆ All stand and sing **Alleluia.**

GOSPEL Mark 5:22–23, 35b–d, 36b, 39a, 39c, 40c–41b, 41d–42c

A reading from the holy Gospel according to Mark.

Then one of the leaders of the synagogue named Jairus came and, when he saw Jesus, fell at his feet and begged him repeatedly, "My little daughter is at the point of death. Come and lay your hands on her, so that she may be made well, and live." Some people came from the leader's house to say, "Your daughter is dead. Why trouble the teacher any further?" Jesus said to the leader of the synagogue, "Do not fear, only believe." When Jesus had entered the house, he said to them, "The child is not dead but sleeping." Then he went in where the child was. He took her by the hand and said to her, "Little girl, get up!" And immediately the girl got up and began to walk about (she was twelve years of age). At this they were overcome with amazement.

The Gospel of the Lord.

◆ All sit and observe silence.

FOR SILENT REFLECTION

Think about this silently in your heart. How much faith in Jesus must the father of the sick girl have had!

CLOSING PRAYER

Let us pray to God for our needs and the needs of others: our family, neighborhood, and the world. For each need we say, "Lord, hear our prayer."

◆ All may add their own prayers here.

Let us pray: **Our Father . . . Amen.**

O God of hope and healing,
we pray for all who are ill and suffering,
whether they are sick in body, mind, or spirit.
Please strengthen them and give them courage.
We ask this through Christ our Lord.

Amen.

✚ All make the Sign of the Cross.

OPENING

Simon, called Peter, Andrew, James, and John were new disciples of Jesus. Already Jesus had amazed them by teaching with authority in the synagogue and rebuking an unclean spirit. In today's reading, Jesus heals Simon's mother-in-law and many others who came to him.

✛ All make the Sign of the Cross.

In the name of the Father, and of the Son, and of the Holy Spirit. Amen.

PSALM   (For a longer psalm, see page xiii.) Psalm 23:1–3a

I shall dwell in the house of the LORD my whole life long.

I shall dwell in the house of the LORD my whole life long.

The LORD is my shepherd, I shall not want.
   He makes me lie down in green pastures;
he leads me beside still waters;
   he restores my soul.

I shall dwell in the house of the LORD my whole life long.

◆ All stand and sing **Alleluia.**

GOSPEL   Mark 1:29–34

A reading from the holy Gospel according to Mark.

As soon as they left the synagogue, Jesus entered the house of Simon and Andrew, with James and John. Now Simon's mother-in-law was in bed with a fever, and they told him about her at once. He came and took her by the hand and lifted her up. Then the fever left her, and she began to serve them. That evening, at sunset, they brought to him all who were sick or possessed with demons. And the whole city was gathered around the door. And he cured many who were sick with various diseases, and cast out many demons; and he would not permit the demons to speak, because they knew him.

The Gospel of the Lord.

◆ All sit and observe silence.

FOR SILENT REFLECTION

Think about this silently in your heart. Imagine you were one of Jesus' disciples witnessing his miracles of healing. How would you feel?

CLOSING PRAYER

Let us pray to God for our needs and the needs of others: our family, neighborhood, and the world. For each need we say, "Lord, hear our prayer."

◆ All may add their own prayers here.

Let us pray: **Our Father . . . Amen.**

O Lord Jesus,
your disciples followed you and loved you.
May we be as willing to follow you
and amazed by your presence as they were.
Who live and reign with God the Father,
in the unity of the Holy Spirit,
one God for ever and ever.

Amen.

✛ All make the Sign of the Cross.

LENT

WEDNESDAY, FEBRUARY 17 — WEDNESDAY, MARCH 31

LENT

THE MEANING OF LENT

On Ash Wednesday the Church enters into her great retreat time called Lent. It is a time to reflect on how we are with God, with our neighbor, and with ourselves and to make some changes in our attitudes or speech or actions if we need to. We should do this often throughout the year, but we do it more consciously in Lent to prepare for the celebration of Easter when some people will be baptized and the rest of us will renew our Baptismal promises.

We have six weeks to concentrate on this conversion of heart, this turning back to or moving closer to God. During this time we might ask ourselves a simple question: "What do I need to stop doing or start doing to be the very good person God made me?" If we find we have some bad habits or have hurt someone (even ourselves) or have neglected to do something we should, we can express our sincere regret and willingness to change in the Sacrament of Reconciliation.

The three Lenten disciplines can help us to train our hearts in love. We are called to pray, fast, and give alms. We pray more regularly and perhaps for longer periods of time. Praying is a conversation with God and a way to be closer to God.

We fast to remind ourselves that there is nothing more important than God and the needs of God's people. Perhaps we give up a certain food and give the money we save to the poor. We might give up playing video games and use the time to help around the house. Part of fasting is abstaining from meat on Fridays of Lent so we eat simply and sparingly as poor people must.

The third discipline is almsgiving. The word comes from the Greek meaning "compassion" and is associated with giving food, money, or clothing to the poor. The money we save by giving up a favorite food or activity might be used this way. We may have a toy, games, or clothes we no longer use very often that we could give to someone else.

Lent's purpose of preparing us to celebrate Easter becomes more focused as we enter into Holy Week. Lent ends with the Mass of the Lord's Supper on Holy Thursday evening. At that moment we enter the Triduum, the three holiest days of the Church year.

PREPARING TO CELEBRATE LENT IN THE CLASSROOM

SACRED SPACE

Remember that on Ash Wednesday, you will need to change your prayer tablecloth from green to purple. If you have a growing plant in the prayer space, remove it. Ask the children to bring in their family's dried palms from last year and put them in a simple vase. A clear bowl full of ashes would be appropriate. They are available through local religious goods stores. (Use the same bowl to hold water in Easter.)

MOVEMENT AND GESTURE

You may want to use some incense during some of the prayers. Ask the parish priest or deacon for some charcoal and incense. You'll also need a pot full of sand to place the charcoal in. An altar server can help you light the charcoal about ten minutes before the prayer. Then the leader can place just enough incense on the charcoal before the Scripture is proclaimed. Be sure to have open windows and let people know you are using the incense. Ask the children with allergies and asthma to stand in the back of the space in case the smoke bothers them. At the end of the prayer cover the charcoal with sand to stop it from smoking.

FESTIVITY IN SCHOOL AND HOME

Lent is a more solemn time. Festivity is kept to a minimum, although there may be special feasts such as St. Joseph's Day or St. Patrick's Day, where it is the custom to celebrate and honor these saints. Because we are not in school during the three sacred days leading up to Easter, we have provided prayers the children can bring home. You will find Home Prayer pages to copy and send home so that families can keep Holy Thursday and Good Friday (pages 240–241). The Prayer Service for Ash Wednesday (pages 198–199) can be used for the classroom or for a larger group.

SACRED MUSIC

Lent is a more solemn time and our music reflects this. Our songs are more plaintive and contemplative. Children love to sing "Jesus, Remember Me," and "What Wondrous Love Is This?" Other songs for Lent are "Amazing Grace," the African American spiritual "Somebody's Knockin' at Your Door," and the Latin hymn "Ubi Caritas." We don't sing "Alleluia" during Lent. Tell the children we are saving all our Alleluia joy for Easter. For the Prayer for the Week, and during the week where there is a Gospel, we sing an acclamation, such as "Praise to you, Lord Jesus Christ" to whatever tune the parish is using.

PRAYERS FOR LENT

Lent is the perfect time to learn or to review an Act of Contrition. Psalm 51 is also a beautiful prayer for this season of penance and conversion.

A NOTE TO CATECHISTS

If any children in your group are preparing to celebrate the sacraments of initiation at the Easter Vigil, gather them to read the following three great accounts from the Gospel of John: (1) Jesus teaches the Woman at the Well who finally understands Jesus is the Messiah (John 4:5–15, 19b–26, 39a, 40–42); (2) Jesus cures the Man Born Blind of physical blindness and the man "sees" and follow him (John 9:1, 6–9, 13–17, 34–38); and (3) Jesus raises Lazarus from the dead (John 11:3–7, 17, 20–27, 33b–45). These are long passages and may require some time to read and discuss with your students, but fight the temptation to rush through them!

GRACE BEFORE MEALS

LENT

LEADER:

We adore you, O Christ, and we praise you

ALL: because by your holy Cross you have redeemed the world.

> ✝ All make the Sign of the Cross.
>
> **In the name of the Father, and of the Son, and of the Holy Spirit. Amen.**

LEADER:

God of compassion,
we thank you for this meal
and for those who prepared it.
May we be nourished by this food
and by the love and friendship we share.
Help us to be mindful of people
in our community and other regions
who will remain hungry today.
May we become your true food for others
through gifts of your Spirit and our works
      of charity.
We ask this through Christ our Lord.

All: Amen.

> ✝ All make the Sign of the Cross.
>
> **In the name of the Father, and of the Son, and of the Holy Spirit. Amen.**

PRAYER AT DAY'S END

LENT

LEADER:
Blessed be the Lord,

ALL: for he has heard the sound of my pleadings.

✙ All make the Sign of the Cross.

In the name of the Father, and of the Son, and of the Holy Spirit. Amen.

LEADER:
Merciful Lord,
sometimes we fail in what
we say or do.
As our school day ends,
help us to remember that
your mercy and love
are never-ending.
Guide us as we renew our
commitment
to deepen our relationship with you
throughout this season of Lent.
We ask this in your name.

All: Amen.

✙ All make the Sign of the Cross.

In the name of the Father, and of the Son, and of the Holy Spirit. Amen.

HOME PRAYER
KEEPING LENT

Before you begin, place a candle, an empty bowl, and a jar with a slit cut into the lid (for coins to give to the poor) where the household will gather in prayer. Find the reading (Matthew 7:7–12) in your Bible, ask for a volunteer to read it and encourage him/her to practice reading it a few times. You may wish to begin with a simple song, such as "Jesus, Remember Me," or "Amen" (but not "Alleluia" during Lent). An older child or adult reads the leader parts.

LEADER:

Lent is a time of reflection
and of turning our hearts to God.
We turn our attention to
growing spiritually
so that we can fully cherish the joy of Easter.
Lent helps us to listen more and pray,
just as Jesus did in the desert.

✚ All make the Sign of the Cross.

> **In the name of the Father, and of the Son, and of the Holy Spirit. Amen.**

LEADER: Psalm 37:5a, 3–4, 23–24, 27–28, 30–31

Let us repeat the psalm response:
Commit your way to the LORD.

ALL: Commit your way to the LORD.

Trust in the LORD, and do good;
   so you will live in the land, and
      enjoy security.
Take delight in the LORD,
   and he will give you the desires of
      your heart.

ALL: Commit your way to the LORD.

Our steps are made firm by the LORD,
   when he delights in our way;
though we stumble, we shall not fall headlong,
   for the LORD holds us by the hand.

ALL: Commit your way to the LORD.

◆ All stand and sing **Praise to you, Lord Jesus Christ** . . .

LEADER: Matthew 7:7–12

A reading from the holy Gospel according to Matthew

◆ Read the Gospel passage from the Bible.

The Gospel of the Lord.

◆ All sit and observe silence. An adult lights the candle.

LEADER:

Heavenly Father,
you sent your Son to us
to light the way back to you.
Guide us in this season of Lent
so that we can focus on you
and on others who may need our help.
We ask this through our Lord Jesus Christ,
your Son, who lives and reigns with you
in the unity of the Holy Spirit, one God,
forever and ever.

ALL: Amen.

LEADER:

Let us pray as Jesus taught us:
Our Father . . . Amen.

✚ All make the Sign of the Cross.

 CHILDREN'S DAILY PRAYER 2020–2021 © 2020 Archdiocese of Chicago: Liturgy Training Publications, 3949 South Racine Avenue, Chicago, IL 60609. All rights reserved. Orders: 800-933-1800 or www.LTP.org. Scripture excerpts are taken from *The New Revised Standard Version Bible: Catholic Edition*, copyright © 1989, Division of Christian Education of the National Council of the Churches of Christ in the United States of America. Used with permission. All rights reserved.

OPENING

Today is Ash Wednesday, the first day of Lent. Lent is a time of spiritual preparation for welcoming Jesus Christ into our lives in a new way at Easter. The readings for the remainder of the week focus on piety or humbling ourselves in prayer and deeds. Today Jesus tells us to humbly offer our prayers to God.

✚ All make the Sign of the Cross.

In the name of the Father, and of the Son, and of the Holy Spirit. Amen.

PSALM

(For a longer psalm, see page xiv.)
Psalm 34:4–5

The LORD saves the crushed in spirit.

The LORD saves the crushed in spirit.

I sought the LORD, and he answered me,
 and delivered me from all my fears.
Look to him, and be radiant;
 so your faces shall never be ashamed.

The LORD saves the crushed in spirit.

◆ All stand and sing **Praise to you, Lord Jesus Christ . . .**

GOSPEL

Matthew 6:2–3, 5–6

A reading from the holy Gospel according to Matthew.

Jesus said, "So whenever you give alms, do not sound a trumpet before you, as the hypocrites do in the synagogues and in the streets, so that they may be praised by others. Truly I tell you, they have received their reward. But when you give alms, do not let your left hand know what your right hand is doing. And whenever you pray, do not be like the hypocrites; for they love to stand and pray in the synagogues and at the street corners, so that they may be seen by others. Truly I tell you, they have received their reward. But whenever you pray, go into your room and shut the door and pray to your Father who is in secret; and your Father who sees in secret will reward you."

The Gospel of the Lord.

◆ All sit and observe silence.

FOR SILENT REFLECTION

Think about this silently in your heart. How can you welcome God into your heart this Lent?

CLOSING PRAYER

Let us pray to God for our needs and the needs of others: our family, neighborhood, and the world. For each need we say, "Lord, hear our prayer."

◆ All may add their own prayers here.

Let us pray: **Our Father . . . Amen.**

Loving God,
during this time of preparation,
may we turn our minds and hearts
toward you,
so that we might grow closer to you through prayer, fasting, and good deeds.
We pray in Christ's name.

Amen.

✚ All make the Sign of the Cross.

PRAYER SERVICE
ASH WEDNESDAY

Prepare eight leaders for this service. Before you begin, prepare a long piece of butcher-block paper or cloth banner with the word "Alleluia" written on it. The inside of the first three letters, "A-l-l" should be colored in, but you should only be able to see an outline of the rest of the word's letters, "e-l-u-i-a." Hang this banner for all to see, but make it accessible so that an additional letter can be colored each week of Lent. On Fridays during Lent, you may want to incorporate coloring the additional letters when you do Prayer at Day's End for Lent, found on page 195.

The fifth and sixth leaders of this Prayer Service will need Bibles for the Scripture passages and may need help practicing them. You may wish to begin by singing "From Ashes to the Living Font" and end with "Soon and Very Soon." If the group will sing, prepare a song leader.

FIRST LEADER:

✛ All make the sign of the Cross.

In the name of the Father, and of the Son, and of the Holy Spirit. Amen.

Today we embark together on a journey through Lent. It is a time for self-discovery as we remember how Jesus went into the desert for forty days and was tempted by the devil. During our Lenten experience, we pray more, eat less, and give to the poor to prepare ourselves for what is at the heart of our Christian faith—Christ's Resurrection at Easter! But we must make ready our hearts and minds, like an athlete trains for a key game or race. We need to strengthen our good habits as we remain God's sons and daughters through the waters of Baptism.

SECOND LEADER:

Each year, on Ash Wednesday, Catholics are marked with ashes in the Sign of the Cross as a reminder that we are entering into Lent. This ashen sign reminds us of our humanness, and that sometimes we fail. We need God's help to succeed. That's why prayer is so vital in our lives.

THIRD LEADER:

During Lent, we also fast from the word "Alleluia," which means "Praise the Lord" in Hebrew. We've prepared this banner with only three of the letters colored in. But you'll see that on this special day, we are *all* in this together! Lent can be a time for us *all* to get closer to Christ. Just like a team trains for a big game, we *all* can do this through prayer and sacrifice. So at the end of each week in Lent, we will color in one more letter to mark another week closer to our declaring this joyous word!

FOURTH LEADER:

Let us pray:
Almighty Father,
through the waters of Baptism,
you claimed us as
your sons and daughters.

CHILDREN'S DAILY PRAYER 2020–2021, © 2020 Archdiocese of Chicago: Liturgy Training Publications. All rights reserved. Orders: 800-933-1800 or www.LTP.org.

You love us without condition.
May our prayers, fasting, and
works of charity deepen
our connection with you
as we better understand the suffering of
our brothers and sisters around the world.
May we remember how
Jesus was tempted in the desert
and that *all* of us need to make
you our priority
in word and deed.
We ask this through Christ our Lord.

ALL: Amen.

◆ All stand and sing **Praise to you, Lord Jesus Christ** . . .

FIFTH LEADER: Matthew 4:1–11
A reading from the holy Gospel according
to Matthew.

◆ Read the Scripture passage from a Bible.

The Gospel of the Lord.

◆ All remain standing and observe silence.

SIXTH LEADER: Matthew 6:1–2
A reading from the holy Gospel according
to Matthew.

◆ Read the Scripture passage from a Bible.

The Gospel of the Lord.

◆ All sit and observe silence.

SEVENTH LEADER:
Let us pray as Jesus taught us:

ALL: Our Father . . . Amen.

Lord God,
help us to be one with you
during this season of Lent.
Guide us as you led
Jesus through the
trying times in his life.
May we let go of
our negative habits and thoughts
that make us feel distant
from your loving presence.
We look forward to
the joy of Easter,
for our hope is Jesus
in this time of preparation.
We ask this through Christ our Lord.

ALL: Amen.

EIGHTH LEADER:
Let us offer to one another a sign of
Christ's peace:

◆ All offer one another a sign of peace.

And may the Lord bless us,

✚ All make the Sign of the Cross.

protect us from all evil,
and bring us to everlasting life.

ALL: Amen.

CHILDREN'S DAILY PRAYER 2020–2021, © 2020 Archdiocese of Chicago: Liturgy Training Publications. All rights reserved. Orders: 800-933-1800 or www.LTP.org.

OPENING

Piety is our devotion or love of God. Piety helps us recognize that we belong to God. Jesus tells us that when we pray or fast, we must do so that only God might see our actions and hear our prayers and know that we are sincere.

✚ All make the Sign of the Cross.

In the name of the Father, and of the Son, and of the Holy Spirit. Amen.

PSALM

(For a longer psalm, see page xiv.)
Psalm 34:4–5

The LORD saves the crushed in spirit.

The LORD saves the crushed in spirit.

I sought the LORD, and he answered me,
    and delivered me from all my fears.
Look to him, and be radiant;
    so your faces shall never be ashamed.

The LORD saves the crushed in spirit.

◆ All stand and sing **Praise to you, Lord Jesus Christ . . .**

GOSPEL

Matthew 6:1, 7, 16–18

A reading from the holy Gospel according to Matthew.

Jesus said, "Beware of practicing your piety before others in order to be seen by them; for then you have no reward from your Father in heaven. When you are praying, do not heap up empty phrases as the Gentiles do; for they think that they will be heard because of their many words. And whenever you fast, do not look dismal, like the hypocrites, for they disfigure their faces so as to show others that they are fasting. Truly I tell you, they have received their reward. But when you fast, put oil on your head and wash your face, so that your fasting may be seen not by others but by your Father who is in secret; and your Father who sees in secret will reward you."

The Gospel of the Lord.

◆ All sit and observe silence.

FOR SILENT REFLECTION

Think about this silently in your heart. How can you show God your devotion through prayer?

CLOSING PRAYER

Let us pray to God for our needs and the needs of others: our family, neighborhood, and the world. For each need we say, "Lord, hear our prayer."

◆ All may add their own prayers here.

Let us pray: **Our Father . . . Amen.**

Loving God,
we desire to belong to you.
Draw us closer to you
so that when we speak to you in prayer,
we can hear your voice and feel your love.
We pray in Christ's name.

Amen.

✚ All make the Sign of the Cross.

OPENING

Fasting is a spiritual practice during Lent, along with prayer and almsgiving. Most people fast from food, but the prophet Isaiah [ī-ZAY-uh] reminds us of those who go without food, justice, and shelter because of injustice and oppression. Isaiah reminds us that Lent is a time to share what we have with those less fortunate than ourselves and to serve those who have very little.

◆ All make the Sign of the Cross.

In the name of the Father, and of the Son, and of the Holy Spirit. Amen.

PSALM

(For a longer psalm, see page xiv.)
Psalm 34:4–5

The LORD saves the crushed in spirit.

The LORD saves the crushed in spirit.

I sought the LORD, and he answered me,
  and delivered me from all my fears.
Look to him, and be radiant;
  so your faces shall never be ashamed.

The LORD saves the crushed in spirit.

READING

Isaiah 58:5acde, 6–7, 8ab, 9ab

A reading from the Book of the prophet Isaiah [ī-ZAY-uh].

Is such the fast that I choose, a day to humble oneself? And to lie in sackcloth and ashes? Will you call this a fast, a day acceptable to the LORD? Is not this the fast that I choose: to loose the bonds of injustice, to undo the thongs of the yoke, to let the oppressed go free, and to break every yoke? Is it not to share your bread with the hungry, and bring the homeless poor into your house; when you see the naked, to cover them, and not to hide yourself from your own kin? Then your light shall break forth like the dawn, and your healing shall spring up quickly. Then you shall call, and the LORD will answer; you shall cry for help, and he will say, Here I am.

The Word of the Lord.

◆ All observe silence.

FOR SILENT REFLECTION

Think about this silently in your heart. How might you serve the poor this Lent?

CLOSING PRAYER

Let us pray to God for our needs and the needs of others: our family, neighborhood, and the world. For each need we say, "Lord, hear our prayer."

◆ All may add their own prayers here.

Let us pray: **Our Father . . . Amen.**

Dear God,
may we recognize the needs of others this Lenten season
and dedicate ourselves to providing for them.
We want to share your blessings.
We pray in Christ's name.

Amen.

◆ All make the Sign of the Cross.

PRAYER FOR THE WEEK

OPENING

In biblical times, the wilderness was a harsh place, where there was great evil or temptation. But it was also a place to find the presence of God. In the Gospel according to Mark, Jesus overcame evil in the wilderness, guided by the Holy Spirit and angels. Jesus was clearly and deeply committed to proclaiming the Kingdom of God.

✛ All make the Sign of the Cross.

In the name of the Father, and of the Son, and of the Holy Spirit. Amen.

PSALM

(For a longer psalm, see page xiv.)

Psalm 34:4–5

The LORD saves the crushed in spirit.

The LORD saves the crushed in spirit.

I sought the LORD, and he answered me,
   and delivered me from all my fears.
Look to him, and be radiant;
   so your faces shall never be ashamed.

The LORD saves the crushed in spirit.

◆ All stand and sing **Praise to you, Lord Jesus Christ . . .**

GOSPEL

Mark 1:12–15

A reading from the holy Gospel according to Mark.

And the Spirit immediately drove Jesus out into the wilderness. He was in the wilderness forty days, tempted by Satan; and he was with the wild beasts; and the angels waited on him. Now after John was arrested, Jesus came to Galilee, proclaiming the good news of God, and saying, "The time is fulfilled, and the kingdom of God has come near; repent, and believe in the good news."

The Gospel of the Lord.

◆ All sit and observe silence.

FOR SILENT REFLECTION

Think about this silently in your heart. In what ways can we deepen our commitment to God during this time of preparation?

CLOSING PRAYER

Let us pray to God for our needs and the needs of others: our family, neighborhood, and the world. For each need we say, "Lord, hear our prayer."

◆ All may add their own prayers here.

Let us pray: **Our Father . . . Amen.**

Holy God,
during these days of preparation
and waiting,
help us renew and deepen our devotion.
May we commit ourselves to serving and
loving others during this time
so that we may rejoice in the Resurrection at
Easter. We ask this through Christ our Lord.

Amen.

✛ All make the Sign of the Cross.

OPENING

In today's Gospel, Jesus tells there are just two commandments we should live by: to love your God and to love your neighbor. As we focus on our spiritual preparation this Lent, we must listen closely to the instructions Jesus gives us and hold them close to our hearts.

✦ All make the Sign of the Cross.

In the name of the Father, and of the Son, and of the Holy Spirit. Amen.

PSALM

(For a longer psalm, see page xiv.)
Psalm 34:4–5

The LORD saves the crushed in spirit.

The LORD saves the crushed in spirit.

I sought the LORD, and he answered me,
   and delivered me from all my fears.
Look to him, and be radiant;
   so your faces shall never be ashamed.

The LORD saves the crushed in spirit.

◆ All stand and sing **Praise to you, Lord Jesus Christ . . .**

GOSPEL

Mark 12:28–31

A reading from the holy Gospel according to Mark.

One of the scribes came near and heard them disputing with one another, and seeing that Jesus answered them well, he asked him, "Which commandment is the first of all?" Jesus answered, "The first is, 'Hear, O Israel: the Lord our God, the Lord is one; you shall love the Lord your God with all your heart, and with all your soul, and with all your mind, and with all your strength.' The second is this, 'You shall love your neighbor as yourself.' There is no other commandment greater than these."

The Gospel of the Lord.

◆ All sit and observe silence.

FOR SILENT REFLECTION

Think about this silently in your heart. Are these commandments easy or hard to follow?

CLOSING PRAYER

Let us pray to God for our needs and the needs of others: our family, neighborhood, and the world. For each need we say, "Lord, hear our prayer."

◆ All may add their own prayers here.

Let us pray: **Our Father . . . Amen.**

O God,
help us to live your commandments.
Help us to love you with all our heart, soul, mind, and strength,
and help us to love our neighbors well.
We ask this in Christ's name.

Amen.

✦ All make the Sign of the Cross.

PRAYER FOR
TUESDAY, FEBRUARY 23, 2021

OPENING

Jesus instructs us today on how to address wrongs in community. Jesus wants us to confront our angers rather than having them dwell inside of us. Most important, Jesus tells us today how often we are to forgive others.

✤ All make the Sign of the Cross.

In the name of the Father, and of the Son, and of the Holy Spirit. Amen.

PSALM

(For a longer psalm, see page xiv.)
Psalm 34:4–5

The LORD saves the crushed in spirit.

The LORD saves the crushed in spirit.

I sought the LORD, and he answered me,
    and delivered me from all my fears.
Look to him, and be radiant;
    so your faces shall never be ashamed.

The LORD saves the crushed in spirit.

◆ All stand and sing **Praise to you, Lord Jesus Christ . . .**

GOSPEL

Matthew 18:15–16, 21–22

A reading from the holy Gospel according to Matthew.

Jesus said, "If another member of the church sins against you, go and point out the fault when the two of you are alone. If the member listens to you, you have regained that one. But if you are not listened to, take one or two others along with you, so that every word may be confirmed by the evidence of two or three witnesses." Then Peter came and said to him, "Lord, if another member of the church sins against me, how often should I forgive? As many as seven times?" Jesus said to him, "Not seven times, but, I tell you, seventy-seven times."

The Gospel of the Lord.

◆ All sit and observe silence.

FOR SILENT REFLECTION

Think about this silently in your heart. Have you ever held a grudge against someone for hurting you? Can you try to follow Jesus' instructions?

CLOSING PRAYER

Let us pray to God for our needs and the needs of others: our family, neighborhood, and the world. For each need we say, "Lord, hear our prayer."

◆ All may add their own prayers here.

Let us pray: **Our Father . . . Amen.**

Loving God,
we are often hurt by others,
and we know we sometimes are the one
to hurt others.
Help us to focus our hearts on forgiveness
and healing,
so that we are filled with your love
and compassion.
Through Christ our Lord.

Amen.

✤ All make the Sign of the Cross.

OPENING

Today we read the first part of the Parable of the Unforgiving Servant. Jesus uses this parable to teach us to forgive others as we are forgiven by God. The talent referred to in the Scripture is a piece of gold. It was a large sum of money during the time of Jesus. Tomorrow we will hear the second part of this parable.

✚ All make the Sign of the Cross.

In the name of the Father, and of the Son, and of the Holy Spirit. Amen.

PSALM

(For a longer psalm, see page xiv.)
Psalm 34:4–5

The LORD saves the crushed in spirit.

The LORD saves the crushed in spirit.

I sought the LORD, and he answered me,
and delivered me from all my fears.
Look to him, and be radiant;
so your faces shall never be ashamed.

The LORD saves the crushed in spirit.

◆ All stand and sing **Praise to you, Lord Jesus Christ . . .**

GOSPEL

Matthew 18:23–27

A reading from the holy Gospel according to Matthew.

Jesus said, "For this reason the kingdom of heaven may be compared to a king who wished to settle accounts with his slaves. When he began the reckoning, one who owed him ten thousand talents was brought to him; and, as he could not pay, his lord ordered him to be sold, together with his wife and children and all his possessions, and payment to be made. So the slave fell on his knees before him, saying, 'Have patience with me, and I will pay you everything.' And out of pity for him, the lord of that slave released him and forgave him the debt."

The Gospel of the Lord.

◆ All sit and observe silence.

FOR SILENT REFLECTION

Think about this silently in your heart. What does this parable teach you about God's Kingdom? How would we be treated by God?

CLOSING PRAYER

Let us pray to God for our needs and the needs of others: our family, neighborhood, and the world. For each need we say, "Lord, hear our prayer."

◆ All may add their own prayers here.

Let us pray: **Our Father . . . Amen.**

O Lord,
help us to be compassionate.
May we forgive others, as you forgive us.
Help us to know right from wrong and to be kind and caring toward others.
We ask this in Christ's name.

Amen.

✚ All make the Sign of the Cross.

PRAYER FOR
THURSDAY, FEBRUARY 25, 2021

OPENING

Today we continue the Parable of the Unforgiving Servant. Yesterday, a slave was forgiven his debts by the king. Today, that same slave does not forgive the debt of a fellow slave. Listen to what the king does when he heard of the slave's lack of forgiveness. A *denarius* is a Roman coin worth much less than a talent.

✝ All make the Sign of the Cross.

In the name of the Father, and of the Son, and of the Holy Spirit. Amen.

PSALM
(For a longer psalm, see page xiv.)
Psalm 34:4–5

The LORD saves the crushed in spirit.

The LORD saves the crushed in spirit.

I sought the LORD, and he answered me,
    and delivered me from all my fears.
Look to him, and be radiant;
    so your faces shall never be ashamed.

The LORD saves the crushed in spirit.

◆ All stand and sing **Praise to you, Lord Jesus Christ . . .**

GOSPEL
Matthew 18:28a, 28c–34

A reading from the holy Gospel according to Matthew.

Jesus continued, "That same slave came upon one of his fellow-slaves who owed him a hundred denarii; and seizing him by the throat, he said, 'Pay what you owe.' Then his fellow slave fell down and pleaded with him, 'Have patience with me, and I will pay you.' But he refused; then he went and threw him into prison until he would pay the debt. When his fellow slaves saw what had happened, they were greatly distressed, and they went and reported to their lord all that had taken place. Then his lord summoned him and said to him, 'You wicked slave! I forgave you all that debt because you pleaded with me. Should you not have had mercy on your fellow slave, as I had mercy on you?' And in anger his lord handed him over to be tortured until he should pay his entire debt."

The Gospel of the Lord.

◆ All sit and observe silence.

FOR SILENT REFLECTION

Think about this silently in your heart. How does God expect us to treat our neighbors?

CLOSING PRAYER

Let us pray to God for our needs and the needs of others: our family, neighborhood, and the world. For each need we say, "Lord, hear our prayer."

◆ All may add their own prayers here.

Let us pray: **Our Father . . . Amen.**

Merciful God,
you have taught us how to love and forgive.
Help us be compassionate and merciful to others as you are with us.
Through Christ our Lord.

Amen.

✝ All make the Sign of the Cross.

OPENING

We hear today the Parable of the True Vine. The word *abide* appears in this passage eight times. It means to "remain in" or "live in." Jesus is the True Vine, and we are the branches. We are called to live and remain close to Jesus, so that we might bear fruit.

✤ All make the Sign of the Cross.

In the name of the Father, and of the Son, and of the Holy Spirit. Amen.

PSALM

(For a longer psalm, see page xiv.)
Psalm 34:4–5

The Lord saves the crushed in spirit.

The Lord saves the crushed in spirit.

I sought the Lord, and he answered me,
and delivered me from all my fears.
Look to him, and be radiant;
so your faces shall never be ashamed.

The Lord saves the crushed in spirit.

◆ All stand and sing **Praise to you, Lord Jesus Christ . . .**

GOSPEL

John 15:1–2a, 4–7

A reading from the holy Gospel according to John.

"I am the true vine, and my Father is the vinegrower. He removes every branch in me that bears no fruit. Abide in me as I abide in you. Just as the branch cannot bear fruit by itself unless it abides in the vine, neither can you unless you abide in me. I am the vine, you are the branches. Those who abide in me and I in them bear much fruit, because apart from me you can do nothing. Whoever does not abide in me is thrown away like a branch and withers; such branches are gathered, thrown into the fire, and burned. If you abide in me, and my words abide in you, ask for whatever you wish, and it will be done for you."

The Gospel of the Lord.

◆ All sit and observe silence.

FOR SILENT REFLECTION

Think about this silently in your heart. How do you live in or remain in Jesus?

CLOSING PRAYER

Let us pray to God for our needs and the needs of others: our family, neighborhood, and the world. For each need we say, "Lord, hear our prayer."

◆ All may add their own prayers here.

Let us pray: **Our Father . . . Amen.**

Christ Jesus,
you have called us to keep you at the center of our lives.
Help our hearts flow with your goodness and grace,
so all that we do shows our love for you.
You live and reign with God the Father,
in the unity of the Holy Spirit,
one God, for ever and ever.

Amen.

✤ All make the Sign of the Cross.

OPENING

On this Second Sunday of Lent, we hear about the Transfiguration of Jesus. Jesus is changed, or revealed, into his true self to his disciples. During this season of penitence, this Gospel reminds us of what we look forward to: Easter.

✚ All make the Sign of the Cross.

In the name of the Father, and of the Son, and of the Holy Spirit. Amen.

PSALM

(For a longer psalm, see page xiv.)

Psalm 34:4–5

The LORD saves the crushed in spirit.

The LORD saves the crushed in spirit.

I sought the LORD, and he answered me,
   and delivered me from all my fears.
Look to him, and be radiant;
   so your faces shall never be ashamed.

The LORD saves the crushed in spirit.

◆ All stand and sing **Praise to you, Lord Jesus Christ . . .**

GOSPEL

Mark 9:2–5, 7–9b, 10a

A reading from the holy Gospel according to Mark.

Six days later, Jesus took with him Peter and James and John, and led them up a high mountain apart, by themselves. And he was transfigured before them, and his clothes became dazzling white, such as no one on earth could bleach them. And there appeared to them Elijah with Moses, who were talking with Jesus. Then Peter said to Jesus, "Rabbi, it is good for us to be here; let us make three dwellings, one for you, one for Moses, and one for Elijah." Then a cloud overshadowed them, and from the cloud there came a voice, "This is my Son, the Beloved; listen to him!" Suddenly when they looked around, they saw no one with them any more, but only Jesus. As they were coming down the mountain, he ordered them to tell no one about what they had seen. So they kept the matter to themselves.

The Gospel of the Lord.

◆ All sit and observe silence.

FOR SILENT REFLECTION

Think about this silently in your heart. Why do you think Jesus showed his divine self to his disciples but asked them to keep it to themselves?

CLOSING PRAYER

Let us pray to God for our needs and the needs of others: our family, neighborhood, and the world. For each need we say, "Lord, hear our prayer."

◆ All may add their own prayers here.

Let us pray: **Our Father . . . Amen.**

Merciful and loving God,
we want to be changed this Lent.
We want to turn our hearts to you.
Help us spend this time well
with prayer, fasting, and good works.
Through Christ our Lord.

Amen.

✚ All make the Sign of the Cross.

OPENING

This week we will hear parables about something that is lost. Jesus uses images that those listening to him would understand: a shepherd with his sheep, a woman with a coin, and a man who lost a son. In each of these parables, Jesus is responding to the Pharisees [FAYR-uh-seez], who disliked that Jesus was preaching to sinners.

✚ All make the Sign of the Cross.

In the name of the Father, and of the Son, and of the Holy Spirit. Amen.

PSALM

(For a longer psalm, see page xiv.)
Psalm 34:4–5

The LORD saves the crushed in spirit.

The LORD saves the crushed in spirit.

I sought the LORD, and he answered me,
    and delivered me from all my fears.
Look to him, and be radiant;
    so your faces shall never be ashamed.

The LORD saves the crushed in spirit.

◆ All stand and sing **Praise to you, Lord Jesus Christ . . .**

GOSPEL

Luke 15:1–7

A reading from the holy Gospel according to Luke.

Tax collectors and sinners were coming near to listen to Jesus. And the Pharisees and the scribes were grumbling and saying, "This fellow welcomes sinners and eats with them." So Jesus told them this parable: "Which one of you, having a hundred sheep and losing one of them, does not leave the ninety-nine in the wilderness and go after the one that is lost until he finds it? When he has found it, he lays it on his shoulders and rejoices. And when he comes home, he calls together his friends and neighbors, saying to them, 'Rejoice with me, for I have found my sheep that was lost.' Just so, I tell you, there will be more joy in heaven over one sinner who repents than over ninety-nine righteous persons who need no repentance."

The Gospel of the Lord.

◆ All sit and observe silence.

FOR SILENT REFLECTION

Think about this silently in your heart. Why would the heavens rejoice when one person comes back to God?

CLOSING PRAYER

Let us pray to God for our needs and the needs of others: our family, neighborhood, and the world. For each need we say, "Lord, hear our prayer."

◆ All may add their own prayers here.

Let us pray: **Our Father . . . Amen.**

Loving God,
we are sometimes lost, like a sheep.
Help us find our way back to you,
where we trust in your welcoming arms.
We ask this through our Good Shepherd.

Amen.

✚ All make the Sign of the Cross.

OPENING

Again, in today's Gospel, Jesus describes the joy and celebration in heaven over one sinner who has repented. Those listening to Jesus must have been familiar with losing a valuable coin and searching carefully for it. Jesus celebrates when someone has been lost and then found.

✝ All make the Sign of the Cross.

In the name of the Father, and of the Son, and of the Holy Spirit. Amen.

PSALM

(For a longer psalm, see page xiv.)
Psalm 34:4–5

The LORD saves the crushed in spirit.

The LORD saves the crushed in spirit.

I sought the LORD, and he answered me,
   and delivered me from all my fears.
Look to him, and be radiant;
   so your faces shall never be ashamed.

The LORD saves the crushed in spirit.

◆ All stand and sing **Praise to you, Lord Jesus Christ . . .**

GOSPEL

Luke 15:1–3a, 8–10

A reading from the holy Gospel according to Luke.

Now all the tax collectors and sinners were coming near to listen to him. And the Pharisees [FAYR-uh-seez] and the scribes were grumbling and saying, "This fellow welcomes sinners and eats with them." So he told them this parable: "What woman having ten silver coins, if she loses one of them, does not light a lamp, sweep the house, and search carefully until she finds it? When she has found it, she calls together her friends and neighbors, saying, 'Rejoice with me, for I have found the coin that I had lost.' Just so, I tell you, there is joy in the presence of the angels of God over one sinner who repents."

The Gospel of the Lord.

◆ All sit and observe silence.

FOR SILENT REFLECTION

Think about this silently in your heart. Jesus tells another story about God's mercy and love. Why do you think the Pharisees and scribes grumbled?

CLOSING PRAYER

Let us pray to God for our needs and the needs of others: our family, neighborhood, and the world. For each need we say, "Lord, hear our prayer."

◆ All may add their own prayers here.

Let us pray: **Our Father . . . Amen.**

Dear God,
your Word is for all people.
help us to listen closely to your Word,
that we might be changed this Lent.
May we spend this time wisely,
especially in prayer.
Through Christ our Lord.

Amen.

✝ All make the Sign of the Cross.

OPENING

As we listen to the Parable of the Prodigal Son and His Brother for the rest of the week, carefully listen to each person: the younger son, the father, and the eldest son. *Prodigal* means "to be reckless or wasteful, extravagant." Today we hear from the youngest son, who is the prodigal one. We also remember St. Katharine Drexel, who founded Xavier University in New Orleans.

✝ All make the Sign of the Cross.

In the name of the Father, and of the Son, and of the Holy Spirit. Amen.

PSALM
(For a longer psalm, see page xiv.)
Psalm 34:4–5

The LORD saves the crushed in spirit.

The LORD saves the crushed in spirit.

I sought the LORD, and he answered me,
and delivered me from all my fears.
Look to him, and be radiant;
so your faces shall never be ashamed.

The LORD saves the crushed in spirit.

◆ All stand and sing **Praise to you, Lord Jesus Christ . . .**

GOSPEL
Luke 15:11–13a, 14ac, 15–17a,18–19

A reading from the holy Gospel according to Luke.

Jesus said, "There was a man who had two sons. The younger of them said to his father, 'Father, give me the share of the property that will belong to me.' So the father divided his property between them. A few days later the younger son gathered all he had and traveled to a distant country. When he had spent everything, he began to be in need. So he went and hired himself out to one of the citizens of that country, who sent him to his fields to feed the pigs. He would gladly have filled himself with the pods that the pigs were eating; and no one gave him anything. But when he came to himself he said, 'I will get up and go to my father, and I will say to him, "Father, I have sinned against heaven and before you; I am no longer worthy to be called your son; treat me like one of your hired hands."'"

The Gospel of the Lord.

◆ All sit and observe silence.

FOR SILENT REFLECTION

Think about this silently in your heart. What does it say about the father that his son wanted to come back?

CLOSING PRAYER

Let us pray to God for our needs and the needs of others: our family, neighborhood, and the world. For each need we say, "Lord, hear our prayer."

◆ All may add their own prayers here.

Let us pray: **Our Father . . . Amen.**

Merciful God,
help us to know when we have gone wrong.
We trust you will welcome us back always.
Through Christ our Lord

Amen.

✝ All make the Sign of the Cross.

OPENING

We heard yesterday that the younger son was selfish and wasteful of his inheritance. Today we continue the story from the perspective of the Father. He calls for a celebration for his son who returned home. We also remember today the feast of St. Casimir, who ruled Poland and Lithuania. He was known for his service and generosity to the sick and poor.

✢ All make the Sign of the Cross.

In the name of the Father, and of the Son, and of the Holy Spirit. Amen.

PSALM
(For a longer psalm, see page xiv.)
Psalm 34:4–5

The Lord saves the crushed in spirit.

The Lord saves the crushed in spirit.

I sought the Lord, and he answered me,
and delivered me from all my fears.
Look to him, and be radiant;
so your faces shall never be ashamed.

The Lord saves the crushed in spirit.

◆ All stand and sing **Praise to you, Lord Jesus Christ . . .**

GOSPEL
Luke 15:20–24

A reading from the holy Gospel according to Luke.

Jesus said, "So the son set off and went to his father. But while he was still far off, his father saw him and was filled with compassion; he ran and put his arms around his son and kissed him. Then the son said to him, 'Father, I have sinned against heaven and before you; I am no longer worthy to be called your son.' But the father said to his slaves, 'Quickly, bring out a robe—the best one—and put it on him; put a ring on his finger and sandals on his feet. And get the fatted calf and kill it, and let us eat and celebrate; for this son of mine was dead and is alive again; he was lost and is found!' And they began to celebrate."

The Gospel of the Lord.

◆ All sit and observe silence.

FOR SILENT REFLECTION

Think about this silently in your heart. What do you think of the father's response to the younger son?

CLOSING PRAYER

Let us pray to God for our needs and the needs of others: our family, neighborhood, and the world. For each need we say, "Lord, hear our prayer."

◆ All may add their own prayers here.

Let us pray: **Our Father . . . Amen.**

O compassionate God,
help us to be like you.
We pray to grow closer to you this Lent.
We ask this in Christ's name.

Amen.

✢ All make the Sign of the Cross.

OPENING

Jesus told parables to teach us about the nature of God. Jesus' parable about the father and his sons reveals something about God. Today we hear from the elder son, the prodigal's brother. The elder son became angry and self-righteous. But again, the father shows great love and mercy because he loves both of his sons.

✚ *All make the Sign of the Cross.*

In the name of the Father, and of the Son, and of the Holy Spirit. Amen.

PSALM

(For a longer psalm, see page xiv.)
Psalm 34:4–5

The L‍ORD saves the crushed in spirit.

The L‍ORD saves the crushed in spirit.

I sought the L‍ORD, and he answered me,
  and delivered me from all my fears.
Look to him, and be radiant;
  so your faces shall never be ashamed.

The L‍ORD saves the crushed in spirit.

◆ *All stand and sing* **Praise to you, Lord Jesus Christ . . .**

GOSPEL

Luke 15:25–29, 31–32

A reading from the holy Gospel according to Luke.

"Now the elder son was in the field; and when he came and approached the house, he heard music and dancing. He called one of the slaves and asked what was going on. The slave replied, 'Your brother has come, and your father has killed the fatted calf, because he has got him back safe and sound.' Then the older brother became angry and refused to go in. His father came out and began to plead with him. The father said to him, 'Son, you are always with me, and all that is mine is yours. But we had to celebrate and rejoice, because this brother of yours was dead and has come to life; he was lost and has been found.'"

The Gospel of the Lord.

◆ *All sit and observe silence.*

FOR SILENT REFLECTION

Think about this silently in your heart. Have you ever felt like the older son sometimes? How does it make you feel to know that God loves all of us without conditions?

CLOSING PRAYER

Let us pray to God for our needs and the needs of others: our family, neighborhood, and the world. For each need we say, "Lord, hear our prayer."

◆ *All may add their own prayers here.*

Let us pray: **Our Father . . . Amen.**

O Lord,
rid our hearts of all jealousy and anger.
Help us realize how much you love us,
and lead us on the path of reconciliation.
We pray through Christ our Lord.

Amen.

✚ *All make the Sign of the Cross.*

PRAYER FOR THE WEEK
WITH A READING FROM THE GOSPEL FOR **SUNDAY, MARCH 7, 2021**

OPENING

The temple in Jerusalem was the holiest of places for the Jewish community. In Jesus' time, worship in the temple involved offering animal sacrifice. People believed that their sacrifice to God would grant them forgiveness of their sins or help them in various endeavors. Over time, merchants and moneylenders came into the temple and carried out all kinds of business. Jesus was angry at this and drove people out of the temple. As we get closer to Holy Week, we must remember that his actions caused many religious leaders of his day to plot against him.

◆ All make the Sign of the Cross.

In the name of the Father, and of the Son, and of the Holy Spirit. Amen.

PSALM

(For a longer psalm, see page xiv.)
Psalm 34:4–5

The LORD saves the crushed in spirit.

The LORD saves the crushed in spirit.

I sought the LORD, and he answered me,
   and delivered me from all my fears.
Look to him, and be radiant;
   so your faces shall never be ashamed.

The LORD saves the crushed in spirit.

◆ All stand and sing **Praise to you, Lord Jesus Christ . . .**

GOSPEL

John 2:13–17

A reading from the holy Gospel according to John.

The Passover of the Jews was near, and Jesus went up to Jerusalem. In the temple he found people selling cattle, sheep, and doves, and the money changers seated at their tables. Making a whip of cords, he drove all of them out of the temple, both the sheep and the cattle. He also poured out the coins of the money changers and overturned their tables. He told those who were selling the doves, "Take these things out of here! Stop making my Father's house a marketplace!" His disciples remembered that it was written, "Zeal for your house will consume me."

The Gospel of the Lord.

◆ All sit and observe silence.

FOR SILENT REFLECTION

Think about this silently in your heart. Do you like to be in church? Does it make you want to be silent and pray?

CLOSING PRAYER

Let us pray to God for our needs and the needs of others: our family, neighborhood, and the world. For each need we say, "Lord, hear our prayer."

◆ All may add their own prayers here.

Let us pray: **Our Father . . . Amen.**

Dear God,
as we near Holy Week,
may we be mindful of Jesus' ministry on earth.
May we live according to what he taught.
We ask this in Christ Jesus' name.

Amen.

◆ All make the Sign of the Cross.

OPENING

In today's reading, St. James teaches of the wisdom of God. He writes that wisdom from God can guide us to the works of mercy and peace. Today we remember St. John of God (1495–1550). He was forty years old when he realized he needed to change his life and serve God and his people. Because of his work with the sick and poor, he is the patron saint of hospitals and nurses.

✠ All make the Sign of the Cross.

In the name of the Father, and of the Son, and of the Holy Spirit. Amen.

PSALM

(For a longer psalm, see page xiv.)
Psalm 34:4–5

The LORD saves the crushed in spirit.

The LORD saves the crushed in spirit.

I sought the LORD, and he answered me,
    and delivered me from all my fears.
Look to him, and be radiant;
    so your faces shall never be ashamed.

The LORD saves the crushed in spirit.

READING

James 3:13, 16–18

A reading from the Letter of James.

Who is wise and understanding among you? Show by your good life that your works are done with gentleness born of wisdom. For where there is envy and selfish ambition, there will also be disorder and wickedness of every kind. But the wisdom from above is first pure, then peaceable, gentle, willing to yield, full of mercy and good fruits, without a trace of partiality or hypocrisy. And a harvest of righteousness is sown in peace for those who make peace.

The Word of the Lord.

◆ All observe silence.

FOR SILENT REFLECTION

Think about this silently in your heart. How can you contribute to peace in the world?

CLOSING PRAYER

Let us pray to God for our needs and the needs of others: our family, neighborhood, and the world. For each need we say, "Lord, hear our prayer."

◆ All may add their own prayers here.

Let us pray: **Our Father . . . Amen.**

O God of Wisdom,
sow in us seeds of wisdom,
so that we may bear the fruit of peace,
through prayer, fasting, and good deeds.
We ask this in the name of Jesus Christ,
your Son and the Prince of Peace.

Amen.

✠ All make the Sign of the Cross.

PRAYER FOR
TUESDAY, MARCH 9, 2021

OPENING

The Sixth Commandment is, "You shall not kill." Jesus explains that this commandment refers to many ways in which we treat one another disrespectfully when we are angry. The word *liable* means "to be responsible by law," which, in this reading, means God's law. To *reconcile* means "to restore friendly relations" with another person. Today is the memorial of St. Frances of Rome (1384–1440), who founded an order of women who shared a life of prayer and service.

✦ All make the Sign of the Cross.

In the name of the Father, and of the Son, and of the Holy Spirit. Amen.

PSALM
(For a longer psalm, see page xiv.)
Psalm 34:4–5

The LORD saves the crushed in spirit.

The LORD saves the crushed in spirit.

I sought the LORD, and he answered me,
    and delivered me from all my fears.
Look to him, and be radiant;
    so your faces shall never be ashamed.

The LORD saves the crushed in spirit.

◆ All stand and sing **Praise to you, Lord Jesus Christ . . .**

GOSPEL
Matthew 5:21–24

A reading from the holy Gospel according to Matthew.

Jesus said, "You have heard that it was said to those of ancient times, 'You shall not murder'; and 'whoever murders shall be liable to judg-ment.' But I say to you that if you are angry with a brother or sister, you will be liable to judgment; and if you insult a brother or sister, you will be liable to the council; and if you say, 'You fool,' you will be liable to the hell of fire. So when you are offering your gift at the altar, if you remember that your brother or sister has something against you, leave your gift there before the altar and go; first be reconciled to your brother or sister, and then come and offer your gift."

The Gospel of the Lord.

◆ All sit and observe silence.

FOR SILENT REFLECTION

Think about this silently in your heart. How do you handle your anger?

CLOSING PRAYER

Let us pray to God for our needs and the needs of others: our family, neighborhood, and the world. For each need we say, "Lord, hear our prayer."

◆ All may add their own prayers here.

Let us pray: **Our Father . . . Amen.**

Merciful God,
help us to see the ways in which we hold anger toward others.
Help us to ask for forgiveness so that we can be reconciled with them and with you.
Through Christ our Lord.

Amen.

✦ All make the Sign of the Cross.

OPENING

Jesus challenges us to love more than only those who love us back. He calls us to love our *enemies*. His vision of love was probably as radical to many of his followers as it is today. As we near Easter, we are reminded that Jesus loved those who persecuted him. We are called to love in the same way.

✚ All make the Sign of the Cross.

In the name of the Father, and of the Son, and of the Holy Spirit. Amen.

PSALM

(For a longer psalm, see page xiv.)
Psalm 34:4–5

The Lord saves the crushed in spirit.

The Lord saves the crushed in spirit.

I sought the Lord, and he answered me,
   and delivered me from all my fears.
Look to him, and be radiant;
   so your faces shall never be ashamed.

The Lord saves the crushed in spirit.

◆ All stand and sing **Praise to you, Lord Jesus Christ . . .**

GOSPEL

Luke 6:27b–32, 35

A reading from the holy Gospel according to Luke.

Jesus said, "Love your enemies, do good to those who hate you, bless those who curse you, pray for those who abuse you. If anyone strikes you on the cheek, offer the other also; and from anyone who takes away your coat do not withhold even your shirt. Give to everyone who begs from you; and if anyone takes away your goods, do not ask for them again. Do to others as you would have them do to you. If you love those who love you, what credit is that to you? For even sinners love those who love them. But love your enemies, do good, expecting nothing in return."

The Gospel of the Lord.

◆ All sit and observe silence.

FOR SILENT REFLECTION

Think about this silently in your heart. "Love your enemies" does not mean you shouldn't stand up for yourself if someone is mistreating you. It means you shouldn't hold hatred for that person in your heart or want to seek revenge.

CLOSING PRAYER

Let us pray to God for our needs and the needs of others: our family, neighborhood, and the world. For each need we say, "Lord, hear our prayer."

◆ All may add their own prayers here.

Let us pray: **Our Father . . . Amen.**

O Lord,
during this holy season
help us to pray often.
Help us to be kind and forgiving.
Help us to give generously.
We ask this in Christ's name.

Amen.

✚ All make the Sign of the Cross.

PRAYER FOR
THURSDAY, MARCH 11, 2021

OPENING

Jesus tells his disciples that they must not judge but rather show mercy. If we are to judge, we must judge ourselves first. We are reminded that forgiveness is central to Jesus' message. A *hypocrite* is someone who preaches one thing but does another.

✦ All make the Sign of the Cross.

In the name of the Father, and of the Son, and of the Holy Spirit. Amen.

PSALM

(For a longer psalm, see page xiv.)
Psalm 34:4–5

The LORD saves the crushed in spirit.

The LORD **saves the crushed in spirit.**

I sought the LORD, and he answered me,
    and delivered me from all my fears.
Look to him, and be radiant;
    so your faces shall never be ashamed.

The LORD **saves the crushed in spirit.**

✦ All stand and sing **Praise to you, Lord Jesus Christ . . .**

GOSPEL

Luke 6:37–38a, 41–42

A reading from the holy Gospel according to Luke.

Jesus said, "Do not judge, and you will not be judged; do not condemn, and you will not be condemned. Forgive, and you will be forgiven; give, and it will be given to you." Why do you see the speck in your neighbor's eye, but do not notice the log in your own eye? Or how can you say to your neighbor, 'Friend, let me take out the speck in your eye,' when you yourself do not see the log in your own eye? You hypocrite, first take the log out of your own eye, and then you will see clearly to take the speck out of your neighbor's eye."

The Gospel of the Lord.

✦ All sit and observe silence.

FOR SILENT REFLECTION

Think about this silently in your heart. You see the speck in your neighbor's eye and do not see the log in your own eye. What does this mean?

CLOSING PRAYER

Let us pray to God for our needs and the needs of others: our family, neighborhood, and the world. For each need we say, "Lord, hear our prayer."

✦ All may add their own prayers here.

Let us pray: **Our Father . . . Amen.**

Dear Lord,
help us avoid being judgmental.
May we learn to forgive others as you forgive us.
We ask this in the name of Jesus Christ, your Son
who teaches us all good things.

Amen.

✦ All make the Sign of the Cross.

218

OPENING

Jesus says that in welcoming and taking care of others, we are welcoming and caring for him. When we are loving to others, we are loving to Jesus. When we are unkind to others, we are unkind to Jesus. He reminds us what it means to follow him.

✜ All make the Sign of the Cross.

In the name of the Father, and of the Son, and of the Holy Spirit. Amen.

PSALM

(For a longer psalm, see page xiv.)
Psalm 34:4–5

The LORD saves the crushed in spirit.

The LORD saves the crushed in spirit.

I sought the LORD, and he answered me,
   and delivered me from all my fears.
Look to him, and be radiant;
   so your faces shall never be ashamed.

The LORD saves the crushed in spirit.

◆ All stand and sing **Praise to you, Lord Jesus Christ . . .**

GOSPEL

Matthew 25:34–35, 37–38ab, 40b

A reading from the holy Gospel according to Matthew.

Then the king will say to those at his right hand, "Come, you that are blessed by my Father, inherit the kingdom prepared for you from the foundation of the world; for I was hungry and you gave me food, I was thirsty and you gave me something to drink, I was a stranger and you welcomed me." Then the righteous will answer him, "Lord, when was it that we saw you hungry and gave you food, or thirsty and gave you something to drink? And when was it that we saw you a stranger and welcomed you?" And the king will answer them, "Truly I tell you, just as you did it to one of the least of these who are members of my family, you did it to me."

The Gospel of the Lord.

◆ All sit and observe silence.

FOR SILENT REFLECTION

Think about this silently in your heart. How can you welcome others into your church like you would welcome Jesus?

CLOSING PRAYER

Let us pray to God for our needs and the needs of others: our family, neighborhood, and the world. For each need we say, "Lord, hear our prayer."

◆ All may add their own prayers here.

Let us pray: **Our Father . . . Amen.**

God of love and compassion,
in caring for others we honor you.
May we each know how to respond
to the needs of those who are suffering.
For in serving them, we serve you.
We ask this in Christ's name.

Amen.

✜ All make the Sign of the Cross.

PRAYER FOR THE WEEK

OPENING

Today's Gospel tells us that those who believe and follow Jesus will have eternal life. As we enter the fourth week of Lent, we are reminded that we are brought into a relationship with God because God loves us. We must respond to his love by putting our faith into action.

✚ All make the Sign of the Cross.

In the name of the Father, and of the Son, and of the Holy Spirit. Amen.

PSALM

(For a longer psalm, see page xiv.)
Psalm 34:4–5

The LORD saves the crushed in spirit.

The LORD saves the crushed in spirit.

I sought the LORD, and he answered me,
    and delivered me from all my fears.
Look to him, and be radiant;
    so your faces shall never be ashamed.

The LORD saves the crushed in spirit.

◆ All stand and sing **Praise to you, Lord Jesus Christ . . .**

GOSPEL

John 3:16–18a, 19–21

A reading from the holy Gospel according to John.

For God so loved the world that he gave his only Son, so that everyone who believes in him may not perish but may have eternal life. Indeed, God did not send the Son into the world to condemn the world, but in order that the world might be saved through him. Those who believe in him are not condemned. And this is the judgment, that the light has come into the world, and people loved darkness rather than light because their deeds were evil. For all who do evil hate the light and do not come to the light, so that their deeds may not be exposed. But those who do what is true come to the light, so that it may be clearly seen that their deeds have been done in God.

The Gospel of the Lord.

◆ All sit and observe silence.

FOR SILENT REFLECTION

Think about this silently in your heart. Imagine eternity—endless time. That is how long we can enjoy life with God.

CLOSING PRAYER

Let us pray to God for our needs and the needs of others: our family, neighborhood, and the world. For each need we say, "Lord, hear our prayer."

◆ All may add their own prayers here.

Let us pray: **Our Father . . . Amen.**

Wondrous God,
you want us to believe
in your unending love for us.
Help us, when our faith is shaky,
to cling to Jesus' teachings.
Help us see and hear you
in all the good around us.
Through Christ our Lord.

Amen.

✚ All make the Sign of the Cross.

OPENING

In today's Gospel, Jesus speaks with a woman from Samaria [suh-MAYR-ee-uh]. It was unusual for Jews to talk with Samaritans and even more unlikely for a man to speak with a woman alone in public. But Jesus ministered to those who were considered outsiders. The woman had faith that the Messiah would come, and Jesus revealed himself.

✚ All make the Sign of the Cross.

In the name of the Father, and of the Son, and of the Holy Spirit. Amen.

PSALM
(For a longer psalm, see page xiv.)
Psalm 34:4–5

The LORD saves the crushed in spirit.

The LORD saves the crushed in spirit.

I sought the LORD, and he answered me,
    and delivered me from all my fears.
Look to him, and be radiant;
    so your faces shall never be ashamed.

The LORD saves the crushed in spirit.

◆ All stand and sing **Praise to you, Lord Jesus Christ . . .**

GOSPEL
John 4:7, 9–10, 11ac, 14b, 19, 25bc, 26

A reading from the holy Gospel according to John.

A Samaritan woman came to draw water, and Jesus said to her, "Give me a drink." The Samaritan woman said to him, "How is it that you, a Jew, ask a drink of me, a woman of Samaria?" (Jews do not share things in common with Samaritans.) Jesus answered her, "If you knew the gift of God, and who it is that is saying to you, 'Give me a drink,' you would have asked him, and he would have given you living water." The woman said to him, "Where do you get that living water?" Jesus said, "The water that I will give will become in them a spring of water gushing up to eternal life." The woman said to him, "Sir, I see that you are a prophet. I know that Messiah is coming (who is called Christ). When he comes, he will proclaim all things to us." Jesus said to her, "I am he, the one who is speaking to you."

The Gospel of the Lord.

◆ All sit and observe silence.

FOR SILENT REFLECTION

Think about this silently in your heart. We all need water to live. Jesus gives living water. What do you believe that means?

CLOSING PRAYER

Let us pray to God for our needs and the needs of others: our family, neighborhood, and the world. For each need we say, "Lord, hear our prayer."

◆ All may add their own prayers here.

Let us pray: **Our Father . . . Amen.**

Loving God,
our thirst is quenched
by the Living Water that is Jesus Christ,
in whose name we pray.

Amen.

✚ All make the Sign of the Cross.

OPENING

Many people in Jesus' time believed disease or illness was punishment for one's sins. When encountering a blind man, Jesus' disciples asked him who had sinned, the man or his parents. Jesus rejected the common understanding and told them that illness was not a result of sinfulness. Rather, illness is another way that God's work is revealed.

✦ All make the Sign of the Cross.

In the name of the Father, and of the Son, and of the Holy Spirit. Amen.

PSALM

(For a longer psalm, see page xiv.)

Psalm 34:4–5

The LORD saves the crushed in spirit.

The LORD saves the crushed in spirit.

I sought the LORD, and he answered me,
    and delivered me from all my fears.
Look to him, and be radiant;
    so your faces shall never be ashamed.

The LORD saves the crushed in spirit.

◆ All stand and sing **Praise to you, Lord Jesus Christ . . .**

GOSPEL

John 9:1–3, 5, 6b–7abd, 35b, 38

A reading from the holy Gospel according to John.

As Jesus walked along, he saw a man blind from birth. His disciples asked him, "Rabbi, who sinned, this man or his parents, that he was born blind?" Jesus answered, "Neither this man nor his parents sinned; he was born blind so that God's works might be revealed in him. As long as I am in the world, I am the light of the world." He spat on the ground and made mud with the saliva and spread the mud on the man's eyes, saying to him, "Go, wash in the pool of Siloam [sih-LOH-uhm]." Then the man went and washed and came back able to see. Jesus said, "Do you believe in the Son of Man?" He said, "Lord, I believe." And he worshiped him.

The Gospel of the Lord.

◆ All sit and observe silence.

FOR SILENT REFLECTION

Think about this silently in your heart. How is Jesus the Light of the World?

CLOSING PRAYER

Let us pray to God for our needs and the needs of others: our family, neighborhood, and the world. For each need we say, "Lord, hear our prayer."

◆ All may add their own prayers here.

Let us pray: **Our Father . . . Amen.**

Jesus our Light,
we believe in you.
Heal our hearts, bodies, and souls,
so that we are ready to welcome you into
every part of our lives.
You live and reign with God the Father,
in the unity of the Holy Spirit,
one God, for ever and ever.

Amen.

✦ All make the Sign of the Cross.

OPENING

Today we celebrate the Irish saint Patrick (385–431). St. Patrick was a missionary and bishop in Ireland. It is believed that St. Patrick taught the Irish about the Holy Trinity by showing them a shamrock, a three-leafed plant. In today's Gospel, we hear Jesus' power over death.

✚ All make the Sign of the Cross.

In the name of the Father, and of the Son, and of the Holy Spirit. Amen.

PSALM
(For a longer psalm, see page xiv.)
Psalm 34:4–5

The LORD saves the crushed in spirit.

The LORD saves the crushed in spirit.

I sought the LORD, and he answered me,
and delivered me from all my fears.
Look to him, and be radiant;
so your faces shall never be ashamed.

The LORD saves the crushed in spirit.

◆ All stand and sing **Praise to you, Lord Jesus Christ . . .**

GOSPEL
John 11:17, 20ab, 21, 23–25, 38ac, 43bc, 44

A reading from the holy Gospel according to John.

When Jesus arrived, he found that Lazarus had already been in the tomb four days. When Martha heard that Jesus was coming, she went and met him. Martha said to Jesus, "Lord, if you had been here, my brother would not have died." Jesus said to her, "Your brother will rise again." Martha said to him, "I know that he will rise again in the resurrection on the last day." Jesus said to her, "I am the resurrection and the life. Those who believe in me, even though they die, will live." Then Jesus came to the tomb. He cried with a loud voice, "Lazarus, come out!" The dead man came out, his hands and feet bound with strips of cloth, and his face wrapped in a cloth. Jesus said to them, "Unbind him, and let him go."

The Gospel of the Lord.

◆ All sit and observe silence.

FOR SILENT REFLECTION

Think about this silently in your heart. Why does Jesus call himself "the resurrection and the life"?

CLOSING PRAYER

Let us pray to God for our needs and the needs of others: our family, neighborhood, and the world. For each need we say, "Lord, hear our prayer."

◆ All may add their own prayers here.

Let us pray: **Our Father . . . Amen.**

Heavenly Father,
by raising Lazarus
Jesus revealed your power over death.
You desire that we have life here on earth
and someday with you in heaven.
For this we give you thanks and praise.
Through Christ our Lord.

Amen.

✚ All make the Sign of the Cross.

PRAYER SERVICE
MEMORIAL OF ST. PATRICK

Prepare six leaders for this service. The third reader will need a Bible for the Gospel passage and may need help finding it and practicing. After the story of St. Patrick, you may wish to begin by singing "Lord of All Hopefulness," and end with "Christ Be Beside Me" (to the tune of "Morning Has Broken") or "The Summons." If there will be singing, prepare a song leader.

◆ All make the Sign of the Cross.

In the name of the Father, and of the Son, and of the Holy Spirit. Amen.

FIRST LEADER:
Praise be to God,
who in every age sends great missionaries
    like St. Patrick
to preach the Good News of Jesus Christ!

ALL: Amen.

Listen now to the story of St. Patrick, who lived in the fifth century: As a teen, St. Patrick was kidnapped from Scotland and sold as a slave in Ireland. Several years later, with God's help, he escaped to Britain, where he studied to become a priest and later was ordained a bishop. Then he went back to Ireland and brought the faith of Jesus to all the Irish people. He helped them believe that God didn't live in the trees of the forest, but in the hearts of all people.

SONG LEADER:
Please join in singing our opening song.

CHILDREN'S DAILY PRAYER 2020–2021, © 2020 Archdiocese of Chicago: Liturgy Training Publications. All rights reserved. Orders: 800-933-1800 or www.LTP.org.

SECOND LEADER:

Let us pray:
Holy Trinity, one God in three persons,
we thank you for sending us holy men
     and women
who help people to know you.
May we always look for guides who will
     give us a deeper knowledge of
     your mysteries.
We ask this through Christ our Lord.

ALL: Amen.

◆ All stand and sing **Praise to you,
Lord Jesus Christ . . .**

THIRD LEADER: Matthew 28:18–20

A reading from the holy Gospel according
to Matthew.

◆ Read the Gospel passage from the Bible.

The Gospel of the Lord.

◆ All observe silence.

FOURTH LEADER:

Let us bring our hopes and needs to God as
we pray, "Lord, hear our prayer."

For all the children of the world, may we
find good guides and models of faith. May
we develop our talents and use them wisely,
we pray to the Lord.

For our Irish ancestors and all those who
came before us. May we live the faith they
passed on to us and treasure the heritage they
have given us, we pray to the Lord.

For the homeless and the hungry, for those
who are sick or suffering in any way, and for
those who have died, we pray to the Lord.

FIFTH LEADER:

Let us pray as Jesus taught us:
Our Father . . . Amen.

◆ Pause, and then say:

Let us offer one another a sign of
Christ's peace.

◆ All offer one another a sign of peace.

SIXTH LEADER:

Let us pray:
God of our ancestors,
give us the strength and courage
     of St. Patrick
so that we may bring the love and joy
     of your Kingdom
to all the world.
We ask this through Christ our Lord.

ALL: Amen.

✝ All make the Sign of the Cross.

**In the name of the Father, and of the
Son, and of the Holy Spirit. Amen.**

PRAYER FOR
THURSDAY, MARCH 18, 2021

OPENING

In today's letter to the Ephesians [ee-FEE-zhuhnz], St. Paul gives instructions on how to live as a follower of Jesus. He tells the Ephesians to be imitators of God, or to follow God's example. St. Cyril, whom we remember today, sold gifts from the emperor to raise money for the poor. He was well loved for his charity and generosity.

✦ All make the Sign of the Cross.

In the name of the Father, and of the Son, and of the Holy Spirit. Amen.

PSALM

(For a longer psalm, see page xiv.)
Psalm 34:4–5

The LORD saves the crushed in spirit.

The LORD saves the crushed in spirit.

I sought the LORD, and he answered me,
    and delivered me from all my fears.
Look to him, and be radiant;
    so your faces shall never be ashamed.

The LORD saves the crushed in spirit.

READING

Ephesians 4:25b–26, 28–29, 32; 5:1–2ab

A reading from the Letter of Paul to Ephesians.

Let all of us speak the truth to our neighbors, for we are members of one another. Be angry but do not sin; do not let the sun go down on your anger. Thieves must give up stealing; rather let them labor and work honestly with their own hands, so as to have something to share with the needy. Let no evil talk come out of your mouths, but only what is useful for building up, as there is need, so that your words may give grace to those who hear. And be kind to one another, tenderhearted, forgiving one another, as God in Christ has forgiven you. Therefore be imitators of God, as beloved children, and live in love, as Christ loved us and gave himself up for us.

The Word of the Lord.

◆ All observe silence.

FOR SILENT REFLECTION

Think about this silently in your heart. How can you speak in a way that builds people up, as St. Paul asks?

CLOSING PRAYER

Let us pray to God for our needs and the needs of others: our family, neighborhood, and the world. For each need we say, "Lord, hear our prayer."

◆ All may add their own prayers here.

Let us pray: **Our Father . . . Amen.**

O Christ our Lord,
help us learn from your example,
so that we may be more kind,
forgive others easily,
and love as you love.
You live and reign with God the Father,
in the unity of the Holy Spirit,
one God, for ever and ever.
Amen.

✦ All make the Sign of the Cross.

OPENING

Today we celebrate the feast of St. Joseph, the husband of Mary, the Mother of Jesus. St. Joseph was a carpenter and Jesus' father on earth. In the Gospels, St. Joseph obeyed God, married Mary, and later fled to Egypt with his family to protect them from Herod. We remember St. Joseph as a faithful follower of God. Today's reading is a gentle reminder that followers of Jesus must live in the Light.

✚ All make the Sign of the Cross.

In the name of the Father, and of the Son, and of the Holy Spirit. Amen.

PSALM

(For a longer psalm, see page xiv.)
Psalm 34:4–5

The Lord saves the crushed in spirit.

The Lord saves the crushed in spirit.

I sought the Lord, and he answered me,
  and delivered me from all my fears.
Look to him, and be radiant;
  so your faces shall never be ashamed.

The Lord saves the crushed in spirit.

READING

1 John 1:5; 2:9–11ac, 12, 14c

A reading from the First Letter of John.

This is the message we have heard from him and proclaim to you, that God is light and in him there is no darkness at all. Whoever says, "I am in the light," while hating a brother or sister, is still in the darkness. Whoever loves a brother or sister lives in the light, and in such a person there is no cause for stumbling. But whoever hates another believer is in the darkness, and does not know the way to go, because the darkness has brought on blindness.

I am writing to you, little children, because your sins are forgiven on account of his name. I write to you, young people, because you are strong and the word of God abides in you, and you have overcome the evil one.

The Word of the Lord.

◆ All observe silence.

FOR SILENT REFLECTION

Think about this silently in your heart. St. John is writing to young children because they are strong, and the word of God lives in them. How does God's Word live in you?

CLOSING PRAYER

Let us pray to God for our needs and the needs of others: our family, neighborhood, and the world. For each need we say, "Lord, hear our prayer."

◆ All may add their own prayers here.

Let us pray: **Our Father . . . Amen.**

Loving God,
help us to live in your Light
and reject the darkness,
so that we may be strong in our faith
and love of the Lord.
May we look to St. Joseph to trust in you.
We ask this through Christ our Lord.

Amen.

✚ All make the Sign of the Cross.

PRAYER SERVICE
SOLEMNITY OF ST. JOSEPH

Prepare six leaders for this service. The third leader will need a Bible for the passage from Matthew. Take time to help the third leader practice the readings. You may wish to sing "You Are the Light of the World," "Blest Are They," or "We Are Called," as opening or closing songs. If the group will sing, prepare someone to lead.

FIRST LEADER:

Today we remember St. Joseph, the husband of Mary and the foster father of Jesus here on earth. At several key times in his life, St. Joseph listened and followed special messengers that God directed to this humble carpenter. St. Joseph's faith led him to marry his fiancée, even though she became pregnant in a divinely inspired way. He courageously took them to Egypt to escape Herod's wrath. And St. Joseph raised Jesus as his own son, guiding his growth.

✝ All make the Sign of the Cross.

In the name of the Father, and of the Son, and of the Holy Spirit. Amen.

Let us remember St. Joseph as we begin by singing the opening song.

SONG LEADER:

◆ Gesture for all to stand, and lead the first few verses of the song.

SECOND LEADER:

Let us pray:
Almighty Father,
may we look to St. Joseph as our guide
as he responded to your call to be
a devoted husband and father.

CHILDREN'S DAILY PRAYER 2020–2021, © 2020 Archdiocese of Chicago: Liturgy Training Publications. All rights reserved. Orders: 800-933-1800 or www.LTP.org.

We pray with him to your Son Jesus,
our Lord and Savior,
in union with the Holy Spirit.

Amen.

◆ Remain standing and sing **Praise to you,
Lord Jesus Christ** . . .

THIRD LEADER: Matthew 2:13–15

A reading from the holy Gospel according
to Matthew.

◆ Read the Gospel passage from the Bible.

The Gospel of the Lord.

◆ All remain standing and observe silence.

FOURTH LEADER:

Let us bring our hopes and needs to God as we
pray, Lord, hear our prayer.

For the courage to live our faith
through word and action
as St. Joseph did throughout his days,
we pray to the Lord.

For all who are struggling with
tough decisions in life,
may they look to St. Joseph as
a brave friend,
we pray to the Lord.

For all married couples,
may they continue to be an example
of the love and devotion that
St. Joseph and Mary shared,
we pray to the Lord.

For all fathers
and those who nurture others.
Help us to respect and protect life
from conception until natural death,
we pray to the Lord.

May we have the conviction
to lead the way, as St. Joseph did
to hope and the promise
of new life through Jesus Christ,
we pray to the Lord.

FIFTH LEADER:

Let us pray as Jesus taught us:

Our Father . . . Amen.

◆ Pause, and then say:

Let us offer one another the sign of
Christ's peace.

◆ All offer one another a sign of peace.

SIXTH LEADER:

Let us pray:
Heavenly Father,
your servant St. Joseph
was a man of great faith.
He listened to you in prayer
and to angels whom you sent
in dreams.
He is a symbol for courage
in following God's will.
May we look to him
in times of trouble or doubt.
We ask this through Christ our Lord.

ALL: Amen.

✚ All make the Sign of the Cross.

PRAYER FOR THE WEEK
WITH A READING FROM THE GOSPEL FOR **SUNDAY, MARCH 21, 2021**

OPENING

On this Fifth Sunday of Lent, we are aware of how close we are to Easter. But before we celebrate Easter, we have Good Friday. In today's Gospel, Jesus prepares his disciples for his death and Resurrection. He reminds them that new life comes from death.

✚ All make the Sign of the Cross.

In the name of the Father, and of the Son, and of the Holy Spirit. Amen.

PSALM

(For a longer psalm, see page xiv.)
Psalm 34:4–5

The LORD saves the crushed in spirit.

The LORD **saves the crushed in spirit.**

I sought the LORD, and he answered me,
and delivered me from all my fears.
Look to him, and be radiant;
so your faces shall never be ashamed.

The LORD **saves the crushed in spirit.**

◆ All stand and sing **Praise to you, Lord Jesus Christ . . .**

GOSPEL

John 12:23–26

A reading from the holy Gospel according to John.

Jesus answered them, "The hour has come for the Son of Man to be glorified. Very truly, I tell you, unless a grain of wheat falls into the earth and dies, it remains just a single grain; but if it dies, it bears much fruit. Those who love their life lose it, and those who hate their life in this world will keep it for eternal life. Whoever serves me must follow me, and where I am, there will my servant be also. Whoever serves me, the Father will honor."

The Gospel of the Lord.

◆ All sit and observe silence.

FOR SILENT REFLECTION

Think about this silently in your heart. What fruit will our life bear if we love and follow Jesus?

CLOSING PRAYER

Let us pray to God for our needs and the needs of others: our family, neighborhood, and the world. For each need we say, "Lord, hear our prayer."

◆ All may add their own prayers here.

Let us pray: **Our Father . . . Amen.**

O Jesus,
as Good Friday draws closer,
may we reflect on your suffering
and sacrifice.
Let them fill us with meekness and consideration.
Help us let go of whatever is keeping us from you.
You live and reign with God the Father,
in the unity of the Holy Spirit,
one God, for ever and ever.

Amen.

✚ All make the Sign of the Cross.

OPENING

This week, we hear of Jesus' last entrance into Jerusalem, his celebration of Passover with his disciples, and his arrest in the Garden of Gethsemane. In today's Gospel according to Mark, Jesus enters Jerusalem, riding on a donkey, to the cheers and greetings of the people.

✚ All make the Sign of the Cross.

In the name of the Father, and of the Son, and of the Holy Spirit. Amen.

PSALM

(For a longer psalm, see page xiv.)
Psalm 34:4–5

The LORD saves the crushed in spirit.

The LORD saves the crushed in spirit.

I sought the LORD, and he answered me,
   and delivered me from all my fears.
Look to him, and be radiant;
   so your faces shall never be ashamed.

The LORD saves the crushed in spirit.

◆ All stand and sing **Praise to you, Lord Jesus Christ . . .**

GOSPEL

Mark 11:1a, 1c–2, 7–10

A reading from the holy Gospel according to Mark.

When they were approaching Jerusalem, Jesus sent two of his disciples and said to them, "Go into the village ahead of you, and immediately as you enter it, you will find tied there a colt that has never been ridden; untie it and bring it." Then they brought the colt to Jesus and threw their cloaks on it; and he sat on it. Many people spread their cloaks on the road, and others spread leafy branches that they had cut in the fields. Then those who went ahead and those who followed were shouting, "Hosanna! Blessed is the one who comes in the name of the Lord! Blessed is the coming kingdom of our ancestor David! Hosanna in the highest heaven!"

The Gospel of the Lord.

◆ All sit and observe silence.

FOR SILENT REFLECTION

Think about this silently in your heart. To shout or sing Hosanna is to express praise or joy. How do you express your joy to Jesus?

CLOSING PRAYER

Let us pray to God for our needs and the needs of others: our family, neighborhood, and the world. For each need we say, "Lord, hear our prayer."

◆ All may add their own prayers here.

Let us pray: **Our Father . . . Amen.**

O Jesus,
we praise and honor you! Hosanna in the highest!
As we hear the stories of your last days before your death,
let us walk with you and share in your journey.
You live and reign with God the Father,
in the unity of the Holy Spirit,
one God, for ever and ever.

Amen.

✚ All make the Sign of the Cross.

PRAYER FOR
TUESDAY, MARCH 23, 2021

OPENING

Today we remember St. Toribio de Mogrovejo (1538–1606). St. Toribio was a Spanish-born lawyer who did not plan to become archbishop of Lima. But once in Peru, he saw firsthand how much the people suffered oppression at the hands of the conquistadors. He built roads, schools, chapels, and hospitals. Today we hear how the religious leaders in Jerusalem were threatened by Jesus' popularity. Judas, one of the Twelve, betrays Jesus.

✦ All make the Sign of the Cross.

In the name of the Father, and of the Son, and of the Holy Spirit. Amen.

PSALM

(For a longer psalm, see page xiv.)
Psalm 34:4–5

The LORD saves the crushed in spirit.

The LORD saves the crushed in spirit.

I sought the LORD, and he answered me,
  and delivered me from all my fears.
Look to him, and be radiant;
  so your faces shall never be ashamed.

The LORD saves the crushed in spirit.

◆ All stand and sing **Praise to you, Lord Jesus Christ . . .**

GOSPEL

Mark 14:1–2, 10–11

A reading from the holy Gospel according to Mark.

It was two days before the Passover and the festival of Unleavened Bread. The chief priests and the scribes were looking for a way to arrest Jesus by stealth and kill him; for they said,

"Not during the festival, or there may be a riot among the people." Then Judas Iscariot, who was one of the twelve, went to the chief priests in order to betray Jesus to them. When they heard it, they were greatly pleased, and promised to give him money. So Judas began to look for an opportunity to betray Jesus.

The Gospel of the Lord.

◆ All sit and observe silence.

FOR SILENT REFLECTION

Think about this silently in your heart. Why do you think Judas would betray Jesus?

CLOSING PRAYER

Let us pray to God for our needs and the needs of others: our family, neighborhood, and the world. For each need we say, "Lord, hear our prayer."

◆ All may add their own prayers here.

Let us pray: **Our Father . . . Amen.**

O Jesus,
help us to resist temptations to evil.
Fill our hearts with your love, compassion, and mercy.
You live and reign with God the Father,
in the unity of the Holy Spirit,
one God, for ever and ever.

Amen.

✦ All make the Sign of the Cross.

OPENING

The feast of Unleavened Bread commemorates the time when the Hebrew people followed Moses out of Egypt so quickly that they were able to eat only unleavened, or unrisen, bread on their journey to the promised land of Israel. Jesus and his friends celebrate the Passover meal in today's Gospel. Jesus knows who will betray him.

✣ All make the Sign of the Cross.

In the name of the Father, and of the Son, and of the Holy Spirit. Amen.

PSALM

(For a longer psalm, see page xiv.)
Psalm 34:4–5

The LORD saves the crushed in spirit.

The LORD saves the crushed in spirit.

I sought the LORD, and he answered me,
    and delivered me from all my fears.
Look to him, and be radiant;
    so your faces shall never be ashamed.

The LORD saves the crushed in spirit.

◆ All stand and sing **Praise to you, Lord Jesus Christ . . .**

GOSPEL

Mark 14:12a–b, 13a, 15–20

A reading from the holy Gospel according to Mark.

On the first day of Unleavened Bread, when the Passover lamb is sacrificed, Jesus sent two of his disciples, saying to them, "Go into the city, and a man will show you a large room upstairs, furnished and ready. Make preparations for us there." So the disciples set out and went to the city, and found everything as he had told them; and they prepared the Passover meal. When it was evening, Jesus came with the twelve. And when they had taken their places and were eating, Jesus said, "Truly I tell you, one of you will betray me, one who is eating with me." They began to be distressed and to say to him one after another, "Surely, not I?" He said to them, "It is one of the twelve, one who is dipping bread into the bowl with me."

The Gospel of the Lord.

◆ All sit and observe silence.

FOR SILENT REFLECTION

Think about this silently in your heart. Why do you think Jesus allowed Judas to break bread with him even though he betrayed him?

CLOSING PRAYER

Let us pray to God for our needs and the needs of others: our family, neighborhood, and the world. For each need we say, "Lord, hear our prayer."

◆ All may add their own prayers here.

Let us pray: **Our Father . . . Amen.**

Holy God,
have mercy on us and forgive us our faults.
Never let us be separated from your love.
Through Christ our Lord.

Amen.

✣ All make the Sign of the Cross.

OPENING

Today is the feast of the Annunciation of the Lord. The Annunciation marks the day when the archangel Gabriel visited Mary and told her she would be the mother of the Messiah. It marks nine months before the birth of Jesus at Christmas. Today we hear the words that Jesus spoke during the Passover meal, which we remember as the Last Supper. These words of Jesus are spoken each week at Mass during the consecration of the bread and wine.

✝ All make the Sign of the Cross.

In the name of the Father, and of the Son, and of the Holy Spirit. Amen.

PSALM

(For a longer psalm, see page xiv.)
Psalm 34:4–5

The LORD saves the crushed in spirit.

The LORD saves the crushed in spirit.

I sought the LORD, and he answered me,
    and delivered me from all my fears.
Look to him, and be radiant;
    so your faces shall never be ashamed.

The LORD saves the crushed in spirit.

◆ All stand and sing **Praise to you, Lord Jesus Christ . . .**

GOSPEL

Mark 14:22–25

A reading from the holy Gospel according to Mark.

While they were eating, Jesus took a loaf of bread, and after blessing it he broke it, gave it to them, and said, "Take; this is my body." Then he took a cup, and after giving thanks he gave it to them, and all of them drank from it. He said to them, "This is my blood of the covenant, which is poured out for many. Truly I tell you, I will never again drink of the fruit of the vine until that day when I drink it new in the kingdom of God."

The Gospel of the Lord.

◆ All sit and observe silence.

FOR SILENT REFLECTION

Think about this silently in your heart. Jesus is with us—both in body and in spirit—when we celebrate the Eucharist.

CLOSING PRAYER

Let us pray to God for our needs and the needs of others: our family, neighborhood, and the world. For each need we say, "Lord, hear our prayer."

◆ All may add their own prayers here.

Let us pray: **Our Father . . . Amen.**

Lord God,
we praise and thank you for your Son, Jesus.
We celebrate his presence with us,
for all of time,
when we gather together in his name.
May we join our hearts together in
community when we celebrate the gifts he
has given us.
Through Jesus Christ our Lord.

Amen.

✝ All make the Sign of the Cross.

OPENING

After the Passover meal, Jesus and his disciples went to the Garden of Gethsemane to pray. Judas, who had left the meal, now arrives along with the elders of the Jewish religious community and betrays Jesus with a kiss. Jesus is arrested.

✚ All make the Sign of the Cross.

In the name of the Father, and of the Son, and of the Holy Spirit. Amen.

PSALM

(For a longer psalm, see page xiv.)
Psalm 34:4–5

The LORD saves the crushed in spirit.

The LORD saves the crushed in spirit.

I sought the LORD, and he answered me,
  and delivered me from all my fears.
Look to him, and be radiant;
  so your faces shall never be ashamed.

The LORD saves the crushed in spirit.

◆ All stand and sing **Praise to you, Lord Jesus Christ . . .**

GOSPEL

Mark 14:32, 43b–46, 48–50

A reading from the holy Gospel according to Mark.

After the Passover meal, Jesus and his disciples went to a place called Gethsemane; and he said to his disciples, "Sit here while I pray." Judas, one of the twelve, arrived; and with him there was a crowd with swords and clubs, from the chief priests, the scribes, and the elders. Now the betrayer had given them a sign, saying, "The one I will kiss is the man; arrest him and lead him away under guard." So when he came,

he went up to him at once and said, "Rabbi!" and kissed him. Then they laid hands on him and arrested him. Then Jesus said to them, "Have you come out with swords and clubs to arrest me as though I were a bandit? Day after day I was with you in the temple teaching, and you did not arrest me. But let the scriptures be fulfilled."

The Gospel of the Lord.

◆ All sit and observe silence.

FOR SILENT REFLECTION

Think about this silently in your heart. Judas later felt sorry for his betrayal of Jesus. God will always forgive us if we repent and ask for forgiveness.

CLOSING PRAYER

Let us pray to God for our needs and the needs of others: our family, neighborhood, and the world. For each need we say, "Lord, hear our prayer."

◆ All may add their own prayers here.

Let us pray: **Our Father . . . Amen.**

O Jesus,
our hearts ache knowing that you were betrayed by a friend.
May we be true friends to you and to others.
You live and reign with God the Father,
in the unity of the Holy Spirit,
one God, for ever and ever.

Amen.

✚ All make the Sign of the Cross.

PRAYER FOR THE WEEK
WITH A READING FROM THE GOSPEL FOR **SUNDAY, MARCH 28, 2021**

OPENING

Today is Palm Sunday of the Lord's Passion, and we now enter into the holiest of weeks of the Church year. The word *Passion* in this context means "suffering."

◆ All make the Sign of the Cross.

In the name of the Father, and of the Son, and of the Holy Spirit. Amen.

PSALM

(For a longer psalm, see page xiv.)
Psalm 34:4–5

The LORD saves the crushed in spirit.

The LORD saves the crushed in spirit.

I sought the LORD, and he answered me,
and delivered me from all my fears.
Look to him, and be radiant;
so your faces shall never be ashamed.

The LORD saves the crushed in spirit.

◆ All stand and sing **Praise to you, Lord Jesus Christ . . .**

GOSPEL

John 12:12–16

A reading from the holy Gospel according to John.

The next day the great crowd that had come to the festival heard that Jesus was coming to Jerusalem. So they took branches of palm trees and went out to meet him, shouting, "Hosanna! Blessed is the one who comes in the name of the Lord—the King of Israel!" Jesus found a young donkey and sat on it; as it is written: "Do not be afraid, daughter of Zion. Look, your king is coming, sitting on a donkey's colt!" His disciples did not understand these things at first; but when Jesus was glorified, then they remembered that these things had been written of him and had been done to him.

The Gospel of the Lord.

◆ All sit and observe silence.

FOR SILENT REFLECTION

Think about this silently in your heart. This week is Holy Week in our Church. How will you make God your priority this week?

CLOSING PRAYER

Let us pray to God for our needs and the needs of others: our family, neighborhood, and the world. For each need we say, "Lord, hear our prayer."

◆ All may add their own prayers here.

Let us pray: **Our Father . . . Amen.**

O loving God,
we thank you for the gift of your Son Jesus,
who taught us how to love, serve,
and forgive others.
May our Lenten disciplines of prayer, fasting, and almsgiving
lead us closer to your grace.
We ask this through Jesus Christ our Lord.

Amen.

✝ All make the Sign of the Cross.

OPENING

After Jesus was arrested in Gethsemane, the disciples all fled. Although Peter followed Jesus at a distance, he denied being Jesus' friend three times. When he realized what he had done, Peter wept and was overcome with his betrayal.

✢ All make the Sign of the Cross.

In the name of the Father, and of the Son, and of the Holy Spirit. Amen.

PSALM

(For a longer psalm, see page xiv.)
Psalm 34:4–5

The LORD saves the crushed in spirit.

The LORD saves the crushed in spirit.

I sought the LORD, and he answered me,
    and delivered me from all my fears.
Look to him, and be radiant;
    so your faces shall never be ashamed.

The LORD saves the crushed in spirit.

◆ All stand and sing **Praise to you, Lord Jesus Christ . . .**

GOSPEL

Mark 14:66, 67b, 68a–b, d, 69a, 69c–72

A reading from the holy Gospel according to Mark.

While Peter was below in the courtyard, one of the servant-girls of the high priest came by and said, "You also were with Jesus." But he denied it, saying, "I do not know or understand what you are talking about." Then the cock crowed. And the servant-girl began again to say to the bystanders, "This man is one of them." But again he denied it. Then after a little while the bystanders again said to Peter, "Certainly you are one of them; for you are a Galilean." But he began to curse, and he swore an oath, "I do not know this man you are talking about." At that moment the cock crowed for the second time. Then Peter remembered that Jesus had said to him, "Before the cock crows twice, you will deny me three times." And he broke down and wept.

The Gospel of the Lord.

◆ All sit and observe silence.

FOR SILENT REFLECTION

Think about this silently in your heart. Have you ever been so overcome with remorse over something that you wept? Jesus will forgive you if you ask.

CLOSING PRAYER

Let us pray to God for our needs and the needs of others: our family, neighborhood, and the world. For each need we say, "Lord, hear our prayer."

◆ All may add their own prayers here.

Let us pray: **Our Father . . . Amen.**

Lord Jesus,
as we end our time of Lent,
we pray never to abandon you.
You live and reign with God the Father,
in the unity of the Holy Spirit,
one God, for ever and ever.

Amen.

✢ All make the Sign of the Cross.

OPENING

Pontius Pilate was the prefect, or governor, of Judea. He presided over Jesus' trial. Although Pilate seems to believe Jesus was innocent, he is perhaps pressured by such a large angry crowd. He sends Jesus to his death.

✛ All make the Sign of the Cross.

In the name of the Father, and of the Son, and of the Holy Spirit. Amen.

PSALM

(For a longer psalm, see page xiv.)
Psalm 34:4–5

The LORD saves the crushed in spirit.

The LORD **saves the crushed in spirit.**

I sought the LORD, and he answered me,
   and delivered me from all my fears.
Look to him, and be radiant;
   so your faces shall never be ashamed.

The LORD **saves the crushed in spirit.**

◆ All stand and sing **Praise to you, Lord Jesus Christ . . .**

GOSPEL

Mark 15:1c–e, 3, 6–7, 9–13, 15

A reading from the holy Gospel according to Mark.

The soldiers bound Jesus, led him away, and handed him over to Pilate. Then the chief priests accused him of many things. Now at the festival Pilate used to release a prisoner for them, anyone for whom they asked. Now a man called Barabbas [buh-RAB-uhs] was in prison with the rebels who had committed murder during the insurrection. Pilate asked them, "Do you want me to release for you the King of the Jews?" For he realized that it was out of jealousy that the chief priests had handed him over. But the chief priests stirred up the crowd to have him release Barabbas for them instead. Pilate spoke to them again, "Then what do you wish me to do with the man you call the King of the Jews?" They shouted back, "Crucify him!" So Pilate, wishing to satisfy the crowd, released Barabbas for them; and after flogging Jesus, he handed him over to be crucified.

The Gospel of the Lord.

◆ All sit and observe silence.

FOR SILENT REFLECTION

Think about this silently in your heart. Do you feel peer pressure sometimes? How can you stand up for what is right?

CLOSING PRAYER

Let us pray to God for our needs and the needs of others: our family, neighborhood, and the world. For each need we say, "Lord, hear our prayer."

◆ All may add their own prayers here.

Let us pray: **Our Father . . . Amen.**

Holy Spirit,
guide us and give us wisdom
to defend what is right.
Through Christ our Lord.

Amen.

✛ All make the Sign of the Cross.

OPENING

As we listen to the final moments of Jesus' Passion, we hear how Jesus was tortured, mocked, and crucified by the Romans. As he was a political threat to the Romans as well as a threat to the Jewish leaders, they charged and addressed him as "The King of the Jews." Jesus was brought to a hill called Golgotha [GAWL-guh-thuh], also known as Calvary, outside the walls of Jerusalem to be crucified.

✦ All make the Sign of the Cross.

In the name of the Father, and of the Son, and of the Holy Spirit. Amen.

PSALM

(For a longer psalm, see page xiv.)
Psalm 34:4–5

The LORD saves the crushed in spirit.

The LORD saves the crushed in spirit.

I sought the LORD, and he answered me,
    and delivered me from all my fears.
Look to him, and be radiant;
    so your faces shall never be ashamed.

The LORD saves the crushed in spirit.

◆ All stand and sing **Praise to you, Lord Jesus Christ . . .**

GOSPEL

Mark 15:16a, 17–18, 20–21d, 22a, 23–25

A reading from the holy Gospel according to Mark.

Then the soldiers led Jesus into the courtyard of the palace. And they clothed him in a purple cloak; and after twisting some thorns into a crown, they put it on him. And they began saluting him, "Hail, King of the Jews!" After mocking him, they stripped him of the purple cloak and put his own clothes on him. Then they led him out to crucify him. They compelled a passer-by, who was coming in from the country, to carry his cross; it was Simon of Cyrene. Then they brought Jesus to the place called Golgotha. And they offered him wine mixed with myrrh; but he did not take it. And they crucified him, and divided his clothes among them, casting lots to decide what each should take. It was nine o'clock in the morning when they crucified him.

The Gospel of the Lord.

◆ All sit and observe silence.

FOR SILENT REFLECTION

Think about this silently in your heart. How can you help others carry their burdens, just as Simon of Cyrene helped Jesus carry his cross?

CLOSING PRAYER

Let us pray to God for our needs and the needs of others: our family, neighborhood, and the world. For each need we say, "Lord, hear our prayer."

◆ All may add their own prayers here.

Let us pray: **Our Father . . . Amen.**

Loving and merciful God,
we thank you for the gift of your Son Jesus.
We ask you to hear our prayers in his name.

Amen.

✦ All make the Sign of the Cross.

HOME PRAYER
HOLY THURSDAY

Before you begin, find the reading (John 13:3–5) in your Bible, ask for a volunteer to read it, and help the reader to practice reading it a few times. You could begin with a simple song, such as "Jesus, Remember Me," or "Amen." (We don't sing "Alleluia" until the Easter Vigil.) An older child or adult reads the leader parts.

LEADER

Today is Holy Thursday, and this evening we will remember two important things that Jesus did for his disciples and for us. On this night of the Last Supper, Jesus offered himself in the form of bread and wine and said, "This is my Body. . . . This is my Blood. Do this in memory of me." Later, he washed the feet of his followers, teaching them by example how we must be a servant for all.

✦ All make the Sign of the Cross.

In the name of the Father, and of the Son, and of the Holy Spirit. Amen.

LEADER: Psalm 27:1, 4, 11, 13–14

Let us repeat the psalm response:
Teach me your way, O Lord.

ALL: Teach me your way, O Lord.

The Lord is my light and my salvation;
   whom shall I fear?
The Lord is the stronghold of my life;
   of whom shall I be afraid?

ALL: Teach me your way, O Lord.

One thing I asked of the Lord,
   that will I seek after:
to live in the house of the Lord
   all the days of my life,
to behold the beauty of the Lord,
   and to inquire in his temple.

ALL: Teach me your way, O Lord.

I believe that I shall see the goodness
      of the Lord
   in the land of the living.
Wait for the Lord;
   be strong, and let your heart take courage;
   wait for the Lord!

ALL: Teach me your way, O Lord.

◆ All stand and sing **Praise to you, Lord Jesus Christ** . . .

LEADER: John 13:3–5

A reading from the holy Gospel according to John.

◆ Read the Gospel passage from the Bible.

The Gospel of the Lord.

◆ All sit and observe silence.

FOR SILENT REFLECTION

Why did Jesus, the disciples' leader, wish to be their servant?

LEADER:

Let us pray as Jesus taught us:

Our Father . . . Amen.

LEADER:

Almighty God,
we remember Jesus'
act of service of washing his friends' feet.
May we honor you with
our acts of love and service today and always.
We ask this through Christ our Lord.

ALL: Amen.

✦ All make the Sign of the Cross.

CHILDREN'S DAILY PRAYER 2020–2021 © 2020 Archdiocese of Chicago: Liturgy Training Publications, 3949 South Racine Avenue, Chicago, IL 60609. All rights reserved. Orders: 800-933-1800 or www.LTP.org. Scripture excerpts are taken from *The New Revised Standard Version Bible: Catholic Edition*, copyright © 1989, Division of Christian Education of the National Council of the Churches of Christ in the United States of America. Used with permission. All rights reserved.

Before you begin, find the reading (John 18:33–37) in your Bible, ask for a volunteer to read it, and help the reader to practice it a few times. You could begin with a simple song, such as "Jesus, Remember Me," or "Amen." (We don't sing "Alleluia" until the Easter Vigil.) An older child or adult reads the leader parts.

LEADER:

Today we remember Jesus' anguish and Death on the Cross. It is a sad time we don't understand. But Good Friday is also a day that we recall the goodness of God's Son who chose to die so that he could save us from sin and death. This day gives us so much hope because of the promise of new life!

✚ All make the Sign of the Cross.

In the name of the Father, and of the Son, and of the Holy Spirit. Amen.

LEADER: Psalm 31:1, 2, 5a, 21

Let us repeat the psalm response:
Into your hand I commit my spirit.

ALL: Into your hand I commit my spirit.

In you, O LORD, I seek refuge;
    do not let me ever be put to shame;
    in your righteousness deliver me.
Incline your ear to me;
    rescue me speedily.
Be a rock of refuge for me,
    a strong fortress to save me.

ALL: Into your hand I commit my spirit.

Blessed be the LORD,
    for he has wondrously shown his steadfast
        love to me
    when I was beset as a city under siege.

ALL: Into your hand I commit my spirit.

◆ All stand and sing **Praise to you, Lord Jesus Christ** . . .

LEADER: John 18:33–37

A reading from the holy Gospel according to John.

◆ Read the Gospel passage from the Bible.

The Gospel of the Lord.

◆ All sit and observe silence.

LEADER:

As I reflect on Jesus' love for me, how can I thank him?

LEADER:

Let us pray as Jesus taught us:

Our Father . . . **Amen.**

LEADER:

Today we remember Jesus' great love. Help us to honor him with our lives. We ask this in the name of the Father, the Son, and the Holy Spirit.

ALL: Amen.

CHILDREN'S DAILY PRAYER 2020–2021 © 2020 Archdiocese of Chicago: Liturgy Training Publications, 3949 South Racine Avenue, Chicago, IL 60609. All rights reserved. Orders: 800-933-1800 or www.LTP.org. Scripture excerpts are taken from *The New Revised Standard Version Bible: Catholic Edition*, © 1989, Division of Christian Education of the National Council of the Churches of Christ in the United States of America. Used with permission. All rights reserved.

EASTER TIME

SUNDAY, APRIL 4— SUNDAY, MAY 23

EASTER TIME

THE MEANING OF EASTER

The heart of Easter lies in the word *covenant*. A covenant is an agreement or contract between two parties. The history of salvation is the story of God's covenant with his people—God's promise to provide and care for humankind and humankind's response to return God's love and follow God's teachings to care for one another and all creation. In the Old Testament, God made covenants with Noah, Abraham, and Moses. In the New Testament, Jesus is the new covenant: "Whoever believes in me will never be thirsty" (John 6:35). With the Resurrection, God promises that the covenant of love will extend to all peoples for all time.

The Prayer for the Week will reflect the Sunday Gospels but during the week we will again "walk through the Bible." Scripture stories tell us of people throughout history from King David, to the Israelites, to the people of Jesus' time, to Paul and the early Christians who believed that faith and trust in God helped them to live joyfully in spite of difficulties.

As we read the stories of Jesus' appearances to his disciples after the Resurrection, we can reflect on how Jesus is always present in our lives. We will read stories of St. Paul and the early Christians who carried Jesus' teachings to people in many lands. Easter Time ends with the wonderful celebration of Pentecost. After Jesus died, his disciples were filled with fear and confusion. Jesus promised that he would send the Spirit to strengthen them. On Pentecost, we celebrate the Spirit that strengthened the disciples. This same Spirit fills us with wisdom, knowledge, courage, and love. These gifts make our lives and the world a better place for all God's creation.

PREPARING TO CELEBRATE EASTER IN THE CLASSROOM

SACRED SPACE

The liturgical color for Easter Time is white, so your prayer table cloth will need to change once more. You may want to add to your prayer table a vase of fresh daisies or lilies and a small glass bowl with a little water in it. When you introduce the water to your students you may say, "Jesus said, 'Let anyone who is thirsty come to me, and let the one who believes in me drink'" (John 7:37b–38a). Have children process in single file to the prayer table, carrying and placing the white cloth, a small white pillar candle, the flowers, and the bowl of water. Make sure you dim the lights before you begin. Then after all the objects have been placed on the prayer table, light the white pillar and chant the following phrase and response three times:

LEADER: The Light of Christ!

ALL: Thanks be to God!

Perhaps one of your students, or someone they know, received the Sacrament of Baptism at the Holy Saturday celebration of the Easter Vigil. If so, while standing before the water, you could explain that the water of Baptism recalls the great flood that Noah had to pass through to reach God's promise of peace, the Red Sea that Moses and the Israelites had to pass through to reach freedom, and the death that Jesus had to pass through to reach the life of the Resurrection. When we pass through (are baptized with) the water in the baptismal font, we enter into that same new life of the resurrected Christ.

Easter Time ends with the Solemnity of Pentecost. When you celebrate Pentecost as a group, make sure you exchange your white prayer table cloth for a red one.

MOVEMENT AND GESTURE

Children love this expanded form of the Easter Procession. After you have changed the color of the prayer cloth to white, carried in the white pillar candle, placed the objects on the prayer table, and lit the candle, sing "The Light of Christ" on one note. When you are finished singing, read a Gospel account of the Resurrection (such as John 20:11–18). Sing Alleluia and then announce the following: "Jesus has risen from the dead; Jesus, the Light of the World, has destroyed death. The light of the Risen Christ will never go out, for he shares his light and life with each of us. Not only that, but his light can spread and grow. Jesus shares his new life with each of us." Then call each child by name, one at a time, inviting them to come forward. For each child, light a small votive candle from the large pillar. As you give it to the child, say, "The Risen Christ shares his light with (child's name)." The child will then put the votive candle on the prayer table and sit down. Don't rush. Wait until the child is seated before you call the next child's name. If you are worried about fire, allow each child to hold his or her votive holder briefly, then you can place the candle on the table beside the lit pillar. Make sure you light a votive candle for yourself. When all the small candles are lit, sit in silence with the children and enjoy the beauty of the light. End your celebration by singing all the Alleluias that you know!

FESTIVITY IN SCHOOL AND HOME

You might want to engage some of the older children in making an Easter candle like the one that stands beside the altar in church. Use a tall white pillar candle. The Easter, or Paschal, candle has three symbols: a central cross identifies it as the Christ candle, and its flame burns despite the death Christ endured. The letters alpha and omega, which begin and end the Greek alphabet, signify that God is the beginning and the ending of all things. The current year indicates that God is present not just at the beginning and the end of time, but throughout history and among those gathered here and now around the candle. You can stand this candle on a candle holder beside the table in your prayer corner at school or at home.

In this book you will find special prayer services that may be used in the classroom or with a larger group. There is the service for Easter, pages 248–249; for the Ascension, pages 288–289; and for Pentecost, pages 296–297. There is also a special prayer service to honor May as the month of Mary, pages 274–275. In May, you might add pictures of Mary and fresh spring flowers to your prayer table. Invite children who know the Rosary to say a decade as part of your daily prayer.

SACRED MUSIC

Here are some Easter songs that children love: "Jesus Christ Is Risen Today," "What Wondrous Love Is This," "Alleluia, Sing to Jesus," "Come Down, O Love Divine," and "O Sons and Daughters." For Pentecost you might enjoy singing "Come, Holy Ghost" or "Veni Sancte Spiritus," or "Spirit of the Living God."

PRAYERS FOR EASTER

The following prayer is a beautiful psalm from the Easter Vigil:

Psalm 42:1–2, 43:3–4

As a deer longs for flowing streams,
    so my soul longs for you, O God.
My soul thirsts for God
    for the living God.
When shall I come and behold
    the face of God?
O send out your light and your truth;
    let them lead me;
let them bring me to your holy hill
    and to your dwelling.
Then I will go to the altar of God
    to God my exceeding joy;
and I will praise you with the harp,
    O God, my God.

A NOTE TO CATECHISTS

You may wish to study the prayers of Baptism with your students. The prayer of Blessing the Waters of Baptism is particularly rich in symbolism. You can recall with the children baptisms they remember seeing as well as stories and pictures of their own baptisms. You can find the Baptismal Rite online or ask your parish priest for a copy.

GRACE BEFORE MEALS

EASTER TIME

LEADER:

Jesus Christ is risen! He is truly risen!

ALL: Alleluia! Alleluia!

✦ All make the Sign of the Cross.

In the name of the Father, and of the Son, and of the Holy Spirit. Amen.

LEADER:

God, our Creator,
we are thankful for the
air we breathe and the
nourishment you offer
in our every moment on earth.
We are grateful for the meal
we are about to share,
for its nutrients sustain us and
give us energy for
working and playing for the glory
of Christ our Savior.
We ask this in his name.

ALL: Amen.

✦ All make the Sign of the Cross.

In the name of the Father, and of the Son, and of the Holy Spirit. Amen.

PRAYER AT DAY'S END

EASTER TIME

LEADER:

All the ends of the earth have seen

ALL: the victory of our God.

✚ All make the Sign of the Cross.

In the name of the Father, and of the Son, and of the Holy Spirit. Amen.

LEADER:

Heavenly Father,
we are grateful for
what we've learned today.
We thank you for our
teachers, assistants, coaches,
and friends who guide us
along our path.
Help us through the remainder of this day
as we are renewed by your Spirit
and the promise of an
eternal Easter.
We ask this through Christ our Lord.

ALL: Amen.

✚ All make the Sign of the Cross.

In the name of the Father, and of the Son, and of the Holy Spirit. Amen.

PRAYER SERVICE
EASTER

Prepare seven leaders for this prayer service. The third and fourth leaders will need Bibles for the Scripture passages and may need help finding them and practicing. You may wish to begin by singing "Jesus Christ Is Risen Today" and end with "Alleluia, Sing to Jesus." If there will be singing, prepare a song leader.

FIRST LEADER:
The grace, peace, and light of the Risen Christ be with us all.

ALL: Amen.

FIRST LEADER:
Today we celebrate Easter, the holiest, most important *solemnity* [suh-LEM-nuh-tee] of the Church, when we remember the Resurrection of Jesus Christ. Jesus won a great victory over death! He rose from death to new life and he will never die again! We can follow him and we too can rise from the dead and live forever with him. Easter is so important to us that one day could never contain all our joy, so we celebrate Easter for fifty days!

SECOND LEADER:

✚ All make the Sign of the Cross.

In the name of the Father, and of the Son, and of the Holy Spirit. Amen.

Let us pray:
Heavenly Father,
our hearts are filled with thankfulness
    and praise
as we think about Jesus' great love for us,
the sacrifice he made,

CHILDREN'S DAILY PRAYER 2019–2020, © 2019 Archdiocese of Chicago: Liturgy Training Publications. All rights reserved. Orders: 800-933-1800 or www.LTP.org.

and the never-ending life he lives and shares
with us now.
May we always thank you for the gift your
Son has given to us.
We ask this through the same Jesus Christ
our Lord.

ALL: Amen.

THIRD LEADER: Isaiah 42:10–12
A reading from the Book of the prophet Isaiah.

◆ Read the Scripture passage from the Bible.

The Word of the Lord.

◆ All observe silence. Then all stand and sing
Alleluia.

FOURTH LEADER: John 20:11–18
A reading from the holy Gospel according
to John.

◆ Read the Gospel passage from the Bible.

The Gospel of the Lord.

◆ All sit and observe silence.

FIFTH LEADER:
Let us stand and bring our hopes and needs
to God as we pray, "Lord, hear our prayer."

For all who live in fear or worry, may the
power of the Resurrection give them new
hope, we pray to the Lord.

For an end to hatred, divisions, and war,
we pray to the Lord.

For all who are unable to see the hand of
God at work in their lives, may God open
their eyes, we pray to the Lord.

For those who are sick and for those who
have died, we pray to the Lord.

SIXTH LEADER:
Let us pray as Jesus taught us.

ALL: Our Father . . . Amen.

◆ Pause, and then say the following.

Let us offer one another a sign of
Christ's peace.

◆ All offer one another a sign of peace.

SEVENTH LEADER:
Let us pray:
Lord God almighty,
in the Death and Resurrection of your Son,
Jesus Christ,
you have created a new heaven and
a new earth.
Bring the light and life of the Resurrection
into our hearts so that we too may be
renewed in holiness.
We ask this through our Lord Jesus Christ,
your Son, who lives and reigns with
you in the unity of the Holy Spirit,
one God, for ever and ever.

ALL: Amen.

✝ All make the Sign of the Cross.

PRAYER FOR THE WEEK
WITH A READING FROM THE GOSPEL FOR **SUNDAY, APRIL 4, 2021**

OPENING

Today we rejoice! Jesus is risen! Love has conquered hatred, and life has triumphed over death. Today begins our liturgical season of Easter Time. We celebrate the Resurrection of Jesus Christ for the next fifty days. Alleluia!

✝ All make the Sign of the Cross.

In the name of the Father, and of the Son, and of the Holy Spirit. Amen.

PSALM

(For a longer psalm, see page xiv.)
Psalm 105:1–2

The LORD saves the crushed in spirit.

The LORD saves the crushed in spirit.

I sought the LORD, and he answered me,
   and delivered me from all my fears.
Look to him, and be radiant;
   so your faces shall never be ashamed.

The LORD saves the crushed in spirit.

◆ All stand and sing **Alleluia.**

GOSPEL

John 20:1ac, 2acde–3, 4b, 6acd–8acd

A reading from the holy Gospel according to John.

Early on the first day of the week, Mary Magdalene came to the tomb and saw that the stone had been removed from the tomb. So she ran and went to Simon Peter and the other disciple, and said to them, "They have taken the Lord out of the tomb, and we do not know where they have laid him." Then Peter and the other disciple set out and went toward the tomb. The other disciple outran Peter and reached the tomb first. Then Simon Peter came, and went into the tomb. He saw the linen wrappings lying there, and the cloth that had been on Jesus' head, not lying with the linen wrappings but rolled up in a place by itself. Then the other disciple also went in, and he saw and believed.

The Gospel of the Lord.

◆ All sit and observe silence.

FOR SILENT REFLECTION

Think about this silently in your heart. If you were with the disciples at the tomb that morning, how would you feel?

CLOSING PRAYER

Let us pray to God for our needs and the needs of others: our family, neighborhood, and the world. For each need we say, "Lord, hear our prayer."

◆ All may add their own prayers here.

Let us pray: **Our Father . . . Amen.**

Glory to you, O Lord!
We sing Alleluia and praise your name!
We give you thanks!
Christ is risen!
Alleluia, Alleluia, Alleluia!

Amen.

✝ All make the Sign of the Cross.

OPENING

We continue to rejoice during this first week of Easter and for the next few weeks. We will be reminded of the salvation our Lord Jesus Christ brought us. In today's reading, the prophet Samuel shares King David's song of praise. David recognized God as the rock of his salvation. A rock in the Bible is a sign of stability, steadfastness, reliability, and security.

✦ All make the Sign of the Cross.

In the name of the Father, and of the Son, and of the Holy Spirit. Amen.

PSALM

(For a longer psalm, see page xiv.)
Psalm 105:1–2

Let the hearts of those who seek the LORD rejoice.

Let the hearts of those who seek the LORD rejoice.

O give thanks to the LORD, call on his name,
    make known his deeds among the peoples.
Sing to him, sing praises to him;
    tell of all his wonderful works.

Let the hearts of those who seek the LORD rejoice.

READING

2 Samuel 22:2–3, 4a, 7abd, 31ac, 32, 47bcd

A reading from the Second Book of Samuel.

David said: The LORD is my rock, my fortress, and my deliverer, my God, my rock, in whom I take refuge, my shield and the horn of my salvation, my stronghold and my refuge, my savior; you save me from violence. I call upon the LORD. In my distress I called upon the LORD; to my God I called. And my cry came to his ears. This God—his way is perfect; he is a shield for all who take refuge in him. For who is God, but the LORD? And who is a rock, except our God? Blessed be my rock, and exalted be my God, the rock of my salvation.

The Word of the Lord.

✦ All observe silence.

FOR SILENT REFLECTION

Think about this silently in your heart. How is Jesus Christ your rock?

CLOSING PRAYER

Let us pray to God for our needs and the needs of others: our family, neighborhood, and the world. For each need we say, "Lord, hear our prayer."

✦ All may add their own prayers here.

Let us pray: **Our Father . . . Amen.**

Blessed are you, O God.
Glory be to you.
You are our rock,
the rock of our salvation.
We thank you for the joy of Easter Time.
Alleluia, Alleluia, Alleluia!

Amen.

✦ All make the Sign of the Cross.

PRAYER FOR
TUESDAY, APRIL 6, 2021

OPENING

In today's Scripture reading, the prophet Isaiah [ī-ZAY-uh] tells the people of Israel how much God loves them. His words ring true for us today. God calls each of us by name, for we are God's. We are all precious and loved by God.

✚ All make the Sign of the Cross.

In the name of the Father, and of the Son, and of the Holy Spirit. Amen.

PSALM
(For a longer psalm, see page xiv.)
Psalm 105:1–2

Let the hearts of those who seek the LORD rejoice.

Let the hearts of those who seek the LORD rejoice.

O give thanks to the LORD, call on his name,
    make known his deeds among the peoples.
Sing to him, sing praises to him;
    tell of all his wonderful works.

Let the hearts of those who seek the LORD rejoice.

READING
Isaiah 43:1, 3a, 4, 5a, 10abc, 11–12ac

A reading from the Book of the prophet Isaiah [ī-ZAY-uh].

But now thus says the LORD, he who created you, O Jacob, he who formed you, O Israel: Do not fear, for I have redeemed you; I have called you by name, you are mine. For I am the LORD your God, the Holy One of Israel, your Savior. Because you are precious in my sight, and honored, and I love you, I give people in return for you, nations in exchange for your life. Do not fear, for I am with you. You are my witnesses, says the LORD, and my servant whom I have chosen, so that you may know and believe me and understand that I am he. I, I am the LORD, and besides me there is no savior. I declared and saved and proclaimed; and you are my witnesses, says the LORD.

The Word of the Lord.

◆ All observe silence.

FOR SILENT REFLECTION

Think about this silently in your heart. God honors and loves each of you. How can you respond to that love?

CLOSING PRAYER

Let us pray to God for our needs and the needs of others: our family, neighborhood, and the world. For each need we say, "Lord, hear our prayer."

◆ All may add their own prayers here.

Let us pray: **Our Father . . . Amen.**

Loving God,
thank you for loving us and calling us
by name.
You are our Lord and Savior;
there is no other but you.
We thank you for the joy of Easter Time.
Alleluia, Alleluia, Alleluia!

Amen.

✚ All make the Sign of the Cross.

252

OPENING

God sent Jesus to offer salvation for all people, not just a few. In today's Gospel, Jesus reveals himself as the Messiah [meh-SĪ-uh] to a Samaritan [suh-MAYR-uh-tuhn] woman. Jesus was the Messiah and Savior, not only of the Jews, but of the Samaritans and the world.

✦ All make the Sign of the Cross.

In the name of the Father, and of the Son, and of the Holy Spirit. Amen.

PSALM

(For a longer psalm, see page xiv.)
Psalm 105:1–2

Let the hearts of those who seek the LORD rejoice.

Let the hearts of those who seek the LORD rejoice.

O give thanks to the LORD, call on his name,
　　make known his deeds among the peoples.
Sing to him, sing praises to him;
　　tell of all his wonderful works.

Let the hearts of those who seek the LORD rejoice.

◆ All stand and sing **Alleluia.**

GOSPEL

John 4:25ab, 26, 28–30, 39a, 40–42ad

A reading from the holy Gospel according to John.

The woman said to Jesus, "I know that Messiah is coming" (who is called Christ). Jesus said to her, "I am he, the one who is speaking to you." Then the woman left her water jar and went back to the city. She said to the people, "Come and see a man who told me everything I have ever done! He cannot be the Messiah, can he?" They left the city and were on their way to him. Many Samaritans [suh-MAYR-uh-tuhnz] from that city believed in him because of the woman's testimony. So when the Samaritans came to him, they asked him to stay with them; and he stayed there two days. And many more believed because of his word. They said to the woman, "We know that this is truly the Savior of the world."

The Gospel of the Lord.

◆ All sit and observe silence.

FOR SILENT REFLECTION

Think about this silently in your heart. One woman brought many people to Jesus. How can you bring others to Jesus?

CLOSING PRAYER

Let us pray to God for our needs and the needs of others: our family, neighborhood, and the world. For each need we say, "Lord, hear our prayer."

◆ All may add their own prayers here.

Let us pray: **Our Father . . . Amen.**

O Savior of the world,
glory and praise to you!
We thank you for your love and faith in us.
Who live and reign with God the Father,
in the unity of the Holy Spirit,
one God, for ever and ever.

Amen.

✦ All make the Sign of the Cross.

PRAYER FOR
THURSDAY, APRIL 8, 2021

OPENING

Today's reading is from a letter St. Paul wrote to his younger colleague, Timothy, in the growing ministry in Ephesus [EF-uh-suhs]. St. Paul instructs Timothy to train in godliness. *Godliness* means to be devout and follow the laws and wishes of God. St. Paul recognizes that we all come from God and that the living God in Jesus is the Savior of all people.

✦ All make the Sign of the Cross.

In the name of the Father, and of the Son, and of the Holy Spirit. Amen.

PSALM

(For a longer psalm, see page xiv.)
Psalm 105:1–2

Let the hearts of those who seek the LORD rejoice.

Let the hearts of those who seek the LORD rejoice.

O give thanks to the LORD, call on his name,
 make known his deeds among the peoples.
Sing to him, sing praises to him;
 tell of all his wonderful works.

Let the hearts of those who seek the LORD rejoice.

READING

1 Timothy 4:6, 7b–8, 10–12

A reading from the First Letter of Paul to Timothy.

If you put these instructions before the brothers and sisters, you will be a good servant of Christ Jesus, nourished on the words of the faith and of the sound teaching that you have followed. Train yourself in godliness, for, while physical training is of some value, godliness is valuable in every way, holding promise for both the present life and the life to come. For to this end we toil and struggle, because we have our hope set on the living God, who is the Savior of all people, especially of those who believe. These are the things you must insist on and teach. Let no one despise your youth, but set the believers an example in speech and conduct, in love, in faith, in purity.

The Word of the Lord.

◆ All observe silence.

FOR SILENT REFLECTION

Think about this silently in your heart. St. Paul tells Timothy he is not too young to be an example to others. How can you be an example to others?

CLOSING PRAYER

Let us pray to God for our needs and the needs of others: our family, neighborhood, and the world. For each need we say, "Lord, hear our prayer."

◆ All may add their own prayers here.

Let us pray: **Our Father . . . Amen.**

O God,
help us to be servants of Jesus Christ by loving and serving others.
May we be faithful examples to all people.
We give you thanks for the gift of your Son Jesus,
in whose name we pray. Alleluia!

Amen.

✦ All make the Sign of the Cross.

OPENING

During Easter Time, we remember and celebrate God's great love for us. Today's reading reveals how important love is to the Easter message. God is love, anyone who loves is of God, and God loves us so much that he sent Jesus into the world. Jesus loved us very much; he gave his life for our salvation. To *abide* is to "live" or "stay."

✛ All make the Sign of the Cross.

In the name of the Father, and of the Son, and of the Holy Spirit. Amen.

PSALM

(For a longer psalm, see page xiv.)
Psalm 105:1–2

Let the hearts of those who seek the LORD rejoice.

Let the hearts of those who seek the LORD rejoice.

O give thanks to the LORD, call on his name,
   make known his deeds among the peoples.
Sing to him, sing praises to him;
   tell of all his wonderful works.

Let the hearts of those who seek the LORD rejoice.

READING

1 John 4:7, 9, 11–14, 16bcd

A reading from the First Letter of John.

Beloved, let us love one another, because love is from God; everyone who loves is born of God and knows God. God's love was revealed among us in this way: God sent his only Son into the world so that we might live through him. Beloved, since God loved us so much, we also ought to love one another. No one has ever seen God; if we love one another, God lives in us, and his love is perfected in us. By this we know that we abide in him and he in us, because he has given us of his Spirit. And we have seen and do testify that the Father has sent his Son as the Savior of the world. God is love, and those who abide in love abide in God, and God abides in them.

The Word of the Lord.

◆ All observe silence.

FOR SILENT REFLECTION

Think about this silently in your heart. "If we love one another, God lives in us."

CLOSING PRAYER

Let us pray to God for our needs and the needs of others: our family, neighborhood, and the world. For each need we say, "Lord, hear our prayer."

◆ All may add their own prayers here.

Let us pray: **Our Father . . . Amen.**

Dear God,
you are the source of love.
You have given us love.
Help us to be stewards of this great love,
so that we may help it grow throughout the world.
We thank you for the joy of Easter Time.
Alleluia, Alleluia, Alleluia!

Amen.

✛ All make the Sign of the Cross.

PRAYER FOR THE WEEK
WITH A READING FROM THE GOSPEL FOR **SUNDAY, APRIL 11, 2021**

OPENING

After the death of Jesus, the disciples were afraid of the Jewish authorities. Jesus appeared to his disciples many times after his Resurrection. He would often greet them, "Peace be with you," which must have reassured and comforted them. In today's reading, Jesus gives the gift of the Holy Spirit to the disciples. They will soon continue the work of Jesus.

✚ All make the Sign of the Cross.

In the name of the Father, and of the Son, and of the Holy Spirit. Amen.

PSALM

(For a longer psalm, see page xiv.)
Psalm 105:1–2

Let the hearts of those who seek the LORD rejoice.

Let the hearts of those who seek the LORD rejoice.

O give thanks to the LORD, call on his name,
   make known his deeds among the peoples.
Sing to him, sing praises to him;
   tell of all his wonderful works.

Let the hearts of those who seek the LORD rejoice.

◆ All stand and sing **Alleluia.**

GOSPEL

John 20:19–22

A reading from the holy Gospel according to John.

When it was evening on that day, the first day of the week, and the doors of the house where the disciples had met were locked for fear of the Jews, Jesus came and stood among them and said, "Peace be with you." After he said this, he showed them his hands and his side. Then the disciples rejoiced when they saw the Lord. Jesus said to them again, "Peace be with you. As the Father has sent me, so I send you." When he had said this, he breathed on them and said to them, "Receive the Holy Spirit."

The Gospel of the Lord.

◆ All sit and observe silence.

FOR SILENT REFLECTION

Think about this silently in your heart. We share the Sign of Peace during Mass. How might we share peace outside of church?

CLOSING PRAYER

Let us pray to God for our needs and the needs of others: our family, neighborhood, and the world. For each need we say, "Lord, hear our prayer."

◆ All may add their own prayers here.

Let us pray: **Our Father . . . Amen.**

Spirit of God,
fill us with peace and courage so that we too might spread the Good News with the world. We thank you for the joy of Easter Time. Alleluia, Alleluia, Alleluia!

Amen.

✚ All make the Sign of the Cross.

OPENING

This week we will hear accounts of what happened to Jesus' followers after his death and Resurrection. Today's reading from St. Mark tells us that three women were the first to learn that Christ had been raised. They had gone to Jesus' tomb to anoint his body with oils and spices, as was the Jewish custom.

✚ All make the Sign of the Cross.

In the name of the Father, and of the Son, and of the Holy Spirit. Amen.

PSALM

(For a longer psalm, see page xiv.)
Psalm 105:1–2

Let the hearts of those who seek the LORD rejoice.

Let the hearts of those who seek the LORD rejoice.

O give thanks to the LORD, call on his name,
  make known his deeds among the peoples.
Sing to him, sing praises to him;
  tell of all his wonderful works.

Let the hearts of those who seek the LORD rejoice.

◆ All stand and sing **Alleluia.**

GOSPEL

Mark 16:1, 2c, 4–7

A reading from the holy Gospel according to Mark.

When the sabbath was over, Mary Magdalene, and Mary the mother of James, and Salome bought spices, so that they might go and anoint Jesus. They went to the tomb. When they looked up, they saw that the stone, which was very large, had already been rolled back. As they entered the tomb, they saw a young man, dressed in a white robe, sitting on the right side; and they were alarmed. But he said to them, "Do not be alarmed; you are looking for Jesus of Nazareth, who was crucified. He has been raised; he is not here. Look, there is the place they laid him. But go, tell his disciples and Peter that he is going ahead of you to Galilee; there you will see him, just as he told you."

The Gospel of the Lord.

◆ All sit and observe silence.

FOR SILENT REFLECTION

Think about this silently in your heart. How must the women have felt not to find Jesus at the tomb and to be told they would see him in Galilee?

CLOSING PRAYER

Let us pray to God for our needs and the needs of others: our family, neighborhood, and the world. For each need we say, "Lord, hear our prayer."

◆ All may add their own prayers here.

Let us pray: **Our Father . . . Amen.**

We rejoice at your Resurrection, O Lord.
We rejoice that you have conquered death.
We thank you for the joy of Easter Time.
Alleluia, Alleluia, Alleluia!

Amen.

✚ All make the Sign of the Cross.

PRAYER FOR
TUESDAY, APRIL 13, 2021

OPENING

In today's reading, two disciples were walking to a village called Emmaus [eh-MAY-uhs]. Jesus appears to them, though they do not recognize him. The disciples share with Jesus all they know of him.

✚ All make the Sign of the Cross.

In the name of the Father, and of the Son, and of the Holy Spirit. Amen.

PSALM

(For a longer psalm, see page xiv.)
Psalm 105:1–2

Let the hearts of those who seek the Lord rejoice.

Let the hearts of those who seek the Lord rejoice.

O give thanks to the Lord, call on his name,
   make known his deeds among the peoples.
Sing to him, sing praises to him;
   tell of all his wonderful works.

Let the hearts of those who seek the Lord rejoice.

◆ All stand and sing **Alleluia.**

GOSPEL

Luke 24:13, 15b–17b, 18, 19c–20, 22b–23

A reading from the holy Gospel according to Luke.

Two of Jesus' disciples were going to a village called Emmaus, about seven miles from Jerusalem. Jesus himself came near and went with them, but their eyes were kept from recognizing him. Jesus said to them, "What are you discussing with each other?" Then one of them, whose name was Cleopas [KLEE-oh-puhs], answered him, "Are you the only stranger in Jerusalem who does not know the things that have taken place there in these days? The things about Jesus of Nazareth, who was a prophet mighty in deed and word before God and all the people, and how our chief priests and leaders handed him over to be condemned to death and crucified him. Some women of our group astounded us. They were at the tomb early this morning, and when they did not find his body there, they came back and told us that they had indeed seen a vision of angels who said that he was alive."

The Gospel of the Lord.

◆ All sit and observe silence.

FOR SILENT REFLECTION

Think about this silently in your heart. Why do you think the disciples were prevented from recognizing Jesus?

CLOSING PRAYER

Let us pray to God for our needs and the needs of others: our family, neighborhood, and the world. For each need we say, "Lord, hear our prayer."

◆ All may add their own prayers here.

Let us pray: **Our Father . . . Amen.**

O loving God,
help us recognize Jesus in all we meet.
Through Christ our Lord.

Amen.

✚ All make the Sign of the Cross.

OPENING

We continue the story of the two disciples who did not recognize Jesus on the road to Emmaus [eh-MAY-uhs]. The disciples still do not recognize Jesus, but they invite him to stay with them. They finally recognize him—listen for how their eyes were opened.

✝ All make the Sign of the Cross.

In the name of the Father, and of the Son, and of the Holy Spirit. Amen.

PSALM

(For a longer psalm, see page xiv.)
Psalm 105:1–2

Let the hearts of those who seek the LORD rejoice.

Let the hearts of those who seek the LORD rejoice.

O give thanks to the LORD, call on his name,
 make known his deeds among the peoples.
Sing to him, sing praises to him;
 tell of all his wonderful works.

Let the hearts of those who seek the LORD rejoice.

◆ All stand and sing **Alleluia.**

GOSPEL

Luke 24:28–33, 35

A reading from the holy Gospel according to Luke.

As they came near the village to which they were going, Jesus walked ahead as if he were going on. But they urged him strongly, saying, "Stay with us, because it is almost evening and the day is now nearly over." So he went in to stay with them. When he was at the table with them, he took bread, blessed and broke it, and gave it to them. Then their eyes were opened, and they recognized him; and he vanished from their sight. They said to each other, "Were not our hearts burning within us while he was talking to us on the road, while he was opening the scriptures to us?" That same hour they got up and returned to Jerusalem; and they found the eleven and their companions gathered together. Then they told what had happened on the road, and how Jesus had been made known to them in the breaking of the bread.

The Gospel of the Lord.

◆ All sit and observe silence.

FOR SILENT REFLECTION

Think about this silently in your heart. Why do you think Jesus revealed himself in the breaking of the bread?

CLOSING PRAYER

Let us pray to God for our needs and the needs of others: our family, neighborhood, and the world. For each need we say, "Lord, hear our prayer."

◆ All may add their own prayers here.

Let us pray: **Our Father . . . Amen.**

O loving God,
help us recognize Jesus' presence among us,
in your holy Word, and in the Eucharist.
Through Christ our Risen Lord.

Amen.

✝ All make the Sign of the Cross.

OPENING

Jesus again reveals himself to his disciples and offers them peace. The disciples are afraid and have a hard time believing. Jesus reassures them and shows that he is real.

✛ All make the Sign of the Cross.

In the name of the Father, and of the Son, and of the Holy Spirit. Amen.

PSALM

(For a longer psalm, see page xiv.)

Psalm 105:1–2

Let the hearts of those who seek the LORD rejoice.

Let the hearts of those who seek the LORD rejoice.

O give thanks to the LORD, call on his name,
  make known his deeds among the peoples.
Sing to him, sing praises to him;
  tell of all his wonderful works.

Let the hearts of those who seek the LORD rejoice.

◆ All stand and sing **Alleluia.**

GOSPEL

Luke 24:36–43

A reading from the holy Gospel according to Luke.

While the disciples were talking about what happened on the road and how Jesus was made known to them, Jesus himself stood among them and said to them, "Peace be with you." They were startled and terrified, and thought that they were seeing a ghost. He said to them, "Why are you frightened, and why do doubts arise in your hearts? Look at my hands and my feet; see that it is I myself. Touch me and see; for a ghost does not have flesh and bones as you see that I have." And when he had said this, he showed them his hands and his feet. While in their joy they were disbelieving and still wondering, he said to them, "Have you anything here to eat?" They gave him a piece of broiled fish, and he took it and ate in their presence.

The Gospel of the Lord.

◆ All sit and observe silence.

FOR SILENT REFLECTION

Think about this silently in your heart. We do not see Jesus as the disciples did, but he is with us always.

CLOSING PRAYER

Let us pray to God for our needs and the needs of others: our family, neighborhood, and the world. For each need we say, "Lord, hear our prayer."

◆ All may add their own prayers here.

Let us pray: **Our Father . . . Amen.**

God of peace,
thank you for filling our hearts with peace.
Thank you for reassuring us when we
are afraid.
We thank you for the joy of Easter Time.
Alleluia, Alleluia, Alleluia!

Amen.

✛ All make the Sign of the Cross.

OPENING

Today's reading is from St. Paul to the members of the church in Corinth [KOHR-ihnth]. St. Paul reminds the Corinthians [kohr-IN-thee-uhnz] of the many people, including himself, to whom Jesus appeared after his Resurrection.

✤ All make the Sign of the Cross.

> **In the name of the Father, and of the Son, and of the Holy Spirit. Amen.**

PSALM

(For a longer psalm, see page xiv.)
Psalm 105:1–2

Let the hearts of those who seek the LORD rejoice.

Let the hearts of those who seek the LORD rejoice.

O give thanks to the LORD, call on his name,
  make known his deeds among the peoples.
Sing to him, sing praises to him;
  tell of all his wonderful works.

Let the hearts of those who seek the LORD rejoice.

READING

1 Corinthians 15:1ab, 3b–8

A reading from the First Letter of Paul to the Corinthians.

Now I would remind you, brothers and sisters, of the good news that I proclaimed to you: that Christ died for our sins in accordance with the scriptures, and that he was buried, and that he was raised on the third day in accordance with the scriptures, and that he appeared to Cephas, then to the twelve. Then he appeared to more than five hundred brothers and sisters at one time, most of whom are still alive, though some have died. Then he appeared to James, then to all the apostles. Last of all, as to one untimely born, he appeared also to me.

The Word of the Lord.

◆ All observe silence.

FOR SILENT REFLECTION

Think about this silently in your heart. Why do you think Paul wanted to remind the early Christians of Christ's death and Resurrection?

CLOSING PRAYER

Let us pray to God for our needs and the needs of others: our family, neighborhood, and the world. For each need we say, "Lord, hear our prayer."

◆ All may add their own prayers here.

Let us pray: **Our Father . . . Amen.**

Glory to you, O Lord!
We sing Alleluia and praise your name!
We give you thanks!
Christ is risen!
Alleluia, Alleluia, Alleluia!

Amen.

✤ All make the Sign of the Cross.

PRAYER FOR THE WEEK

WITH A READING FROM THE GOSPEL FOR **SUNDAY, APRIL 18, 2021**

OPENING

On this Third Sunday of Easter, we again hear another post-Resurrection appearance by Jesus: he opened the minds of the disciples so that they might fully understand the Scriptures. He reminds them that repentance and forgiveness are both central to his message.

✚ All make the Sign of the Cross.

In the name of the Father, and of the Son, and of the Holy Spirit. Amen.

PSALM

(For a longer psalm, see page xiv.)
Psalm 105:1–2

Let the hearts of those who seek the Lord rejoice.

Let the hearts of those who seek the Lord rejoice.

O give thanks to the Lord, call on his name,
    make known his deeds among the peoples.
Sing to him, sing praises to him;
    tell of all his wonderful works.

Let the hearts of those who seek the Lord rejoice.

◆ All stand and sing **Alleluia.**

GOSPEL

Luke 24:36–38a, 39b–d, 44a–b, 45–48

A reading from the holy Gospel according to Luke.

While the disciples were talking about this, Jesus himself stood among them and said to them, "Peace be with you." They were startled and terrified, and thought that they were seeing a ghost. He said to them, "Why are you frightened? See that it is I myself. Touch me and see; for a ghost does not have flesh and bones as you see that I have." Then he said to them, "These are my words that I spoke to you while I was still with you." Then he opened their minds to understand the scriptures, and he said to them, "Thus it is written, that the Messiah is to suffer and to rise from the dead on the third day, and that repentance and forgiveness of sins is to be proclaimed in his name to all nations, beginning from Jerusalem. You are witnesses of these things."

The Gospel of the Lord.

◆ All sit and observe silence.

FOR SILENT REFLECTION

Think about this silently in your heart. You too are witnesses to Christ's message. How can you tell others about repentance and forgiveness?

CLOSING PRAYER

Let us pray to God for our needs and the needs of others: our family, neighborhood, and the world. For each need we say, "Lord, hear our prayer."

◆ All may add their own prayers here.

Let us pray: **Our Father . . . Amen.**

O Lord,
help us to follow in your ways
and to bear witness to your ministry on earth.
Through Christ our Risen Lord.

Amen.

✚ All make the Sign of the Cross.

OPENING

The readings this week focus on how the Apostles and the first Christians carried out Jesus' teachings. In today's reading, Peter bears witness to the life, death, and Resurrection of Christ to a large crowd. Peter tells them what they need to join in discipleship.

✚ All make the Sign of the Cross.

In the name of the Father, and of the Son, and of the Holy Spirit. Amen.

PSALM

(For a longer psalm, see page xiv.)
Psalm 105:1–2

Let the hearts of those who seek the LORD rejoice.

Let the hearts of those who seek the LORD rejoice.

O give thanks to the LORD, call on his name,
    make known his deeds among the peoples.
Sing to him, sing praises to him;
    tell of all his wonderful works.

Let the hearts of those who seek the LORD rejoice.

READING

Acts 2:14ac, 22bc, 23ac, 32, 37b–38b, 41

A reading from the Acts of the Apostles.

But Peter raised his voice and addressed them, "Listen to what I have to say: Jesus of Nazareth, a man attested to you by God with deeds of power, wonders, and signs that God did through him among you, as you yourselves know—this man, you crucified and killed by the hands of those outside the law. This Jesus God raised up, and of that all of us are witnesses." They were cut to the heart and said to Peter and to the other apostles, "Brothers, what should we do?" Peter said to them, "Repent, and be baptized every one of you in the name of Jesus Christ so that your sins may be forgiven." So those who welcomed his message were baptized, and that day about three thousand persons were added.

The Word of the Lord.

◆ All observe silence.

FOR SILENT REFLECTION

Think about this silently in your heart. Peter is establishing the Christian community. How does your faith community help you follow Jesus?

CLOSING PRAYER

Let us pray to God for our needs and the needs of others: our family, neighborhood, and the world. For each need we say, "Lord, hear our prayer."

◆ All may add their own prayers here.

Let us pray: **Our Father . . . Amen.**

Loving and merciful God,
your Son has done many wondrous deeds.
Help us to follow his path to love others,
to ask for forgiveness,
and to forgive others too.
We ask this in Christ's name.

Amen.

✚ All make the Sign of the Cross.

PRAYER FOR
TUESDAY, APRIL 20, 2021

OPENING

Listen closely to this passage to hear what these first Christians did as they followed Jesus' teachings.

✚ All make the Sign of the Cross.

In the name of the Father, and of the Son, and of the Holy Spirit. Amen.

PSALM

(For a longer psalm, see page xiv.)
Psalm 105:1–2

Let the hearts of those who seek the LORD rejoice.

Let the hearts of those who seek the LORD rejoice.

O give thanks to the LORD, call on his name,
  make known his deeds among the peoples.
Sing to him, sing praises to him;
  tell of all his wonderful works.

Let the hearts of those who seek the LORD rejoice.

READING

Acts 2:42–47

A reading from the Acts of the Apostles.

They devoted themselves to the apostles' teaching and fellowship, to the breaking of bread and the prayers. Awe came upon everyone, because many wonders and signs were being done by the apostles. All who believed were together and had all things in common; they would sell their possessions and goods and distribute the proceeds to all, as any had need. Day by day, as they spent much time together in the temple, they broke bread at home and ate their food with glad and generous hearts, praising God and having the goodwill of all the people. And day by day the Lord added to their number those who were being saved.

The Word of the Lord.

◆ All observe silence.

FOR SILENT REFLECTION

Think about this silently in your heart. How do you follow Jesus and live by his example?

CLOSING PRAYER

Let us pray to God for our needs and the needs of others: our family, neighborhood, and the world. For each need we say, "Lord, hear our prayer."

◆ All may add their own prayers here.

Let us pray: **Our Father . . . Amen.**

Loving God,
your Son taught us how to live in love.
Help us follow him in all we do and say.
May we share what we have with others,
devote ourselves to prayer,
and praise your name forever.
Through Christ our Risen Lord.

Amen.

✚ All make the Sign of the Cross.

OPENING

Today is the memorial of St. Anselm (1033–1109), a monk who eventually became Archbishop of Canterbury, England. His best-known work is the book *Cur Deus Homo* (Why God Became Man). We hear today the Apostles and early Christians continued the work of Jesus.

✚ All make the Sign of the Cross.

In the name of the Father, and of the Son, and of the Holy Spirit. Amen.

PSALM

(For a longer psalm, see page xiv.)
Psalm 105:1–2

Let the hearts of those who seek the LORD rejoice.

Let the hearts of those who seek the LORD rejoice.

O give thanks to the LORD, call on his name,
  make known his deeds among the peoples.
Sing to him, sing praises to him;
  tell of all his wonderful works.

Let the hearts of those who seek the LORD rejoice.

READING

Acts 4:32–36acd, 37

A reading from the Acts of the Apostles.

Now the whole group of those who believed were of one heart and soul, and no one claimed private ownership of any possessions, but everything they owned was held in common. With great power the apostles gave their testimony to the resurrection of the Lord Jesus, and great grace was upon them all. There was not a needy person among them, for as many as owned lands or houses sold them and brought the proceeds of what was sold. They laid it at the apostles' feet, and it was distributed to each as any had need. There was a Levite, Joseph, to whom the apostles gave the name Barnabas. He sold a field that belonged to him, then brought the money, and laid it at the apostles' feet.

The Word of the Lord.

◆ All observe silence.

FOR SILENT REFLECTION

Think about this silently in your heart. How does this Scripture remind you of why God became human?

CLOSING PRAYER

Let us pray to God for our needs and the needs of others: our family, neighborhood, and the world. For each need we say, "Lord, hear our prayer."

◆ All may add their own prayers here.

Let us pray: **Our Father . . . Amen.**

Dear God,
help us to share what we have with others:
our time,
our talents,
and our treasures.
May we learn to lift one another up,
for we are all your children.
We pray in the name of Jesus Christ,
our Risen Lord.

Amen.

✚ All make the Sign of the Cross.

PRAYER FOR
THURSDAY, APRIL 22, 2021

OPENING

Peter and the Apostles devoted themselves to spreading the Gospel. This made the religious leaders angry and jealous. They arrested Peter and the Apostles and "flogged," or whipped, them. But the Apostles did not waver in their faith and continued to proclaim the Good News.

✦ All make the Sign of the Cross.

In the name of the Father, and of the Son, and of the Holy Spirit. Amen.

PSALM
(For a longer psalm, see page xiv.)
Psalm 105:1–2

Let the hearts of those who seek the LORD rejoice.

Let the hearts of those who seek the LORD rejoice.

O give thanks to the LORD, call on his name,
    make known his deeds among the peoples.
Sing to him, sing praises to him;
    tell of all his wonderful works.

Let the hearts of those who seek the LORD rejoice.

READING
Acts 5:17bd, 18, 27c, 28a, 29, 33b, 40b–42

A reading from the Acts of the Apostles.

The high priest and all who were with him, being filled with jealousy, arrested Peter and the apostles and put them in the public prison. The high priest questioned them, saying, "We gave you strict orders not to teach in this name." But Peter and the apostles answered, "We must obey God rather than any human authority." They were enraged and wanted to kill them. They had them flogged. Then they ordered them not to speak in the name of Jesus, and let them go. As they left the council, the apostles rejoiced that they were considered worthy to suffer dishonor for the sake of the name. And every day in the temple and at home they did not cease to teach and proclaim Jesus as the Messiah.

The Word of the Lord.

◆ All observe silence.

FOR SILENT REFLECTION

Think about this silently in your heart. The early Christians were often punished for their faith. Think about how strong their faith in Jesus Christ must have been that they were willing to suffer imprisonment and punishment.

CLOSING PRAYER

Let us pray to God for our needs and the needs of others: our family, neighborhood, and the world. For each need we say, "Lord, hear our prayer."

◆ All may add their own prayers here.

Let us pray: **Our Father . . . Amen.**

Lord God,
help us to be strong and resolute in our faith.
May we never waver in our devotion and commitment to Jesus,
and continue to serve and love others.
In his name we pray.

Amen.

✦ All make the Sign of the Cross.

OPENING

We remember two saints today, one of whom is a beloved saint of England, St. George. Because he is popularly believed to have slayed a dragon, he is one of the better-known military saints. St. Adalbert was a bishop of Prague, Hungary. He and his companions spread the Good News around northern Europe. We have heard a great deal this week about those who came to follow Christ Jesus after his death. These new disciples spread Jesus' message throughout the Roman Empire and beyond. These new followers became known as Christians.

✚ All make the Sign of the Cross.

In the name of the Father, and of the Son, and of the Holy Spirit. Amen.

PSALM

(For a longer psalm, see page xiv.)
Psalm 105:1–2

Let the hearts of those who seek the LORD rejoice.

Let the hearts of those who seek the LORD rejoice.

O give thanks to the LORD, call on his name,
  make known his deeds among the peoples.
Sing to him, sing praises to him;
  tell of all his wonderful works.

Let the hearts of those who seek the LORD rejoice.

READING

Acts 11:20acd, 22–23, 24b, 26e

A reading from the Acts of the Apostles.

But among them were some men of Cyprus [SĪ-pruhs] and Cyrene [sī-REE-nee] who spoke to the Hellenists also proclaiming the Lord Jesus. News of this came to the ears of the church in Jerusalem, and they sent Barnabas to Antioch [AN-tee-ahk]. When he came and saw the grace of God, he rejoiced, and he exhorted them all to remain faithful to the Lord with steadfast devotion. And a great many people were brought to the Lord. So it was that for an entire year they met with the church and taught a great many people, and it was in Antioch that the disciples were first called "Christians."

The Word of the Lord.

◆ All observe silence.

FOR SILENT REFLECTION

Think about this silently in your heart. The early Christians showed steadfast devotion to Jesus. How might you do the same?

CLOSING PRAYER

Let us pray to God for our needs and the needs of others: our family, neighborhood, and the world. For each need we say, "Lord, hear our prayer."

◆ All may add their own prayers here.

Let us pray: **Our Father . . . Amen.**

Loving God,
help us to be good Christians,
showing others what it means to follow Jesus.
We ask this in the name of our Risen Lord.

Amen.

✚ All make the Sign of the Cross.

PRAYER FOR THE WEEK

WITH A READING FROM THE GOSPEL FOR **SUNDAY, APRIL 25, 2021**

OPENING

The Fourth Sunday of Easter is often called Good Shepherd Sunday. In the Gospel today, Jesus describes himself as the Good Shepherd. The Good Shepherd knows all of his sheep and protects them from harm. The Good Shepherd unifies his flock and is willing to lay down his life for even one of his flock.

✝ All make the Sign of the Cross.

In the name of the Father, and of the Son, and of the Holy Spirit. Amen.

PSALM

(For a longer psalm, see page xiv.)

Psalm 105:1–2

Let the hearts of those who seek the LORD rejoice.

Let the hearts of those who seek the LORD rejoice.

O give thanks to the LORD, call on his name,
    make known his deeds among the peoples.
Sing to him, sing praises to him;
    tell of all his wonderful works.

Let the hearts of those who seek the LORD rejoice.

◆ All stand and sing **Alleluia.**

GOSPEL

John 10:11–12, 14, 15b–18b

A reading from the holy Gospel according to John.

Jesus said, "I am the good shepherd. The good shepherd lays down his life for the sheep. The hired hand, who is not the shepherd and does not own the sheep, sees the wolf coming and leaves the sheep and runs away—and the wolf snatches them and scatters them. I am the good shepherd. I know my own and my own know me. And I lay down my life for the sheep. I have other sheep that do not belong to this fold. I must bring them also, and they will listen to my voice. So there will be one flock, one shepherd. For this reason the Father loves me, because I lay down my life in order to take it up again. No one takes it from me, but I lay it down of my own accord."

The Gospel of the Lord.

◆ All sit and observe silence.

FOR SILENT REFLECTION

Think about this silently in your heart. How close do you think you must be to Jesus for him to know you and for you to know him?

CLOSING PRAYER

Let us pray to God for our needs and the needs of others: our family, neighborhood, and the world. For each need we say, "Lord, hear our prayer."

◆ All may add their own prayers here.

Let us pray: **Our Father . . . Amen.**

Dear God,
we thank you for giving us our Good Shepherd who loves, cares for, protects, and unites us all. May we always know the sound of his voice and stay close to him.
We ask this through our Risen Lord, Jesus Christ.

Amen.

✝ All make the Sign of the Cross.

OPENING

Yesterday we learned one of the most important names for Jesus: the Good Shepherd. During this fourth week of Easter, we will hear other names for Jesus. Today the prophet Isaiah [ī-ZAY-uh] foretells the birth of a child who shall be called Emmanuel, or "God with us."

✠ All make the Sign of the Cross.

In the name of the Father, and of the Son, and of the Holy Spirit. Amen.

PSALM
(For a longer psalm, see page xiv.)
Psalm 105:1–2

Let the hearts of those who seek the LORD rejoice.

Let the hearts of those who seek the LORD rejoice.

O give thanks to the LORD, call on his name,
    make known his deeds among the peoples.
Sing to him, sing praises to him;
    tell of all his wonderful works.

Let the hearts of those who seek the LORD rejoice.

READING
Isaiah 7:2–3ab, 4ab, 10–11a, 12–14

A reading from the Book of the prophet Isaiah [ī-ZAY-uh].

When the house of David heard that Aram [AYR-uhm] had allied itself with Ephraim [EE-fray-ihm], the heart of Ahaz [AY-haz] and the heart of his people shook as the trees of the forest shake before the wind. Then the LORD said to Isaiah, Go out to meet Ahaz and say to him, Take heed, be quiet, do not fear. Again

the LORD spoke to Ahaz, saying, Ask a sign of the LORD your God. But Ahaz said, I will not ask, and I will not put the LORD to the test. Then Isaiah said: "Hear then, O house of David! Is it too little for you to weary mortals, that you weary my God also? Therefore the Lord himself will give you a sign. Look, the young woman is with child and shall bear a son, and shall name him Immanuel."

The Word of the Lord.

◆ All observe silence.

FOR SILENT REFLECTION

Think about this silently in your heart. What name do you call Jesus?

CLOSING PRAYER

Let us pray to God for our needs and the needs of others: our family, neighborhood, and the world. For each need we say, "Lord, hear our prayer."

◆ All may add their own prayers here.

Let us pray: **Our Father . . . Amen.**

O God with us,
we rejoice and are glad!
We trust in your presence with us always.
May we know, love, and serve you
and our brothers and sisters with all our hearts.
You live and reign with God the Father,
in the unity of the Holy Spirit,
one God, for ever and ever.

Amen.

✠ All make the Sign of the Cross.

PRAYER FOR
TUESDAY, APRIL 27, 2021

OPENING

In today's Gospel, Jesus calls himself the "Light of the World." Light is needed to live. We depend on the sun to nourish us and all the living things on earth. Jesus says he is the Light—the source of what nourishes us and allows us to grow. He is the core of our being and enables us to flourish.

✝ All make the Sign of the Cross.

In the name of the Father, and of the Son, and of the Holy Spirit. Amen.

PSALM

(For a longer psalm, see page xiv.)
Psalm 105:1–2

Let the hearts of those who seek the LORD rejoice.

Let the hearts of those who seek the LORD rejoice.

O give thanks to the LORD, call on his name,
    make known his deeds among the peoples.
Sing to him, sing praises to him;
    tell of all his wonderful works.

Let the hearts of those who seek the LORD rejoice.

◆ All stand and sing **Alleluia.**

GOSPEL

John 8:12–14, 18–19

A reading from the holy Gospel according to John.

Again Jesus spoke to them, saying, "I am the light of the world. Whoever follows me will never walk in darkness but will have the light of life." Then the Pharisees [FAYR-uh-seez] said to him, "You are testifying on your own behalf; your testimony is not valid." Jesus answered, "Even if I testify on my own behalf, my testimony is valid because I know where I have come from and where I am going, but you do not know where I come from or where I am going. I testify on my own behalf, and the Father who sent me testifies on my behalf." Then they said to him, "Where is your Father?" Jesus answered, "You know neither me nor my Father. If you knew me, you would know my Father also."

The Gospel of the Lord.

◆ All sit and observe silence.

FOR SILENT REFLECTION

Think about this silently in your heart. You have the light of Jesus inside you. Do you allow it to shine?

CLOSING PRAYER

Let us pray to God for our needs and the needs of others: our family, neighborhood, and the world. For each need we say, "Lord, hear our prayer."

◆ All may add their own prayers here.

Let us pray: **Our Father . . . Amen.**

God of Light,
you are our Light and life of the world.
May we follow your light always
and bring your light to others.
Through Christ our Risen Lord.

Amen.

✝ All make the Sign of the Cross.

OPENING

Today we remember St. Peter Chanel (1803–1841) and St. Louis Mary Grignion de Montfort (1673–1716). St. Peter was a missionary who worked with the indigenous peoples on the southern Pacific Ocean islands. St. Louis was a priest known for his deep devotion to the Blessed Mother Mary and who preached about God's mercy. In today's reading, the first high priest called by God is Aaron. Jesus, the Son of God, is also called the "high priest."

✚ All make the Sign of the Cross.

In the name of the Father, and of the Son, and of the Holy Spirit. Amen.

PSALM

(For a longer psalm, see page xiv.)
Psalm 105:1–2

Let the hearts of those who seek the LORD rejoice.

Let the hearts of those who seek the LORD rejoice.

O give thanks to the LORD, call on his name,
   make known his deeds among the peoples.
Sing to him, sing praises to him;
   tell of all his wonderful works.

Let the hearts of those who seek the LORD rejoice.

READING

Hebrews 5:1–5

A reading from the Letter to the Hebrews.

Every high priest chosen from among mortals is put in charge of things pertaining to God on their behalf, to offer gifts and sacrifices for sins. He is able to deal gently with the ignorant and wayward, since he himself is subject to weakness; and because of this he must offer sacrifice for his own sins as well as for those of the people. And one does not presume to take this honor, but takes it only when called by God, just as Aaron was. So also Christ did not glorify himself in becoming a high priest, but was appointed by the one who said to him, "You are my Son, today I have begotten you."

The Word of the Lord.

◆ All observe silence.

FOR SILENT REFLECTION

Think about this silently in your heart. Jesus was called by God to be a high priest of all people. How does God call you?

CLOSING PRAYER

Let us pray to God for our needs and the needs of others: our family, neighborhood, and the world. For each need we say, "Lord, hear our prayer."

◆ All may add their own prayers here.

Let us pray: **Our Father . . . Amen.**

Loving God,
thank you for sending us Jesus to teach us how to follow you.
We pray for all the men and women who lead us in your name today.
Through Christ our Risen Lord.

Amen.

✚ All make the Sign of the Cross.

PRAYER FOR
THURSDAY, APRIL 29, 2021

OPENING

Today we honor St. Catherine of Siena, who was an Italian theologian and philosopher (1347–1380). She is one of only four female Doctors of the Church because of her important writings and her leadership. In today's reading, Peter and the Apostles refer to Jesus as their "Leader and Savior."

✦ All make the Sign of the Cross.

In the name of the Father, and of the Son, and of the Holy Spirit. Amen.

PSALM

(For a longer psalm, see page xiv.)
Psalm 105:1–2

Let the hearts of those who seek the LORD rejoice.

Let the hearts of those who seek the LORD rejoice.

O give thanks to the LORD, call on his name,
 make known his deeds among the peoples.
Sing to him, sing praises to him;
 tell of all his wonderful works.

Let the hearts of those who seek the LORD rejoice.

READING

Acts 5:17b, 18, 27b–31

A reading from the Acts of the Apostles.

The high priest and all who were with him arrested the apostles and put them in the public prison. They had them stand before the council. The high priest questioned them, saying, "We gave you strict orders not to teach in Jesus' name, yet here you have filled Jerusalem with your teaching and you are determined to bring this Jesus' blood on us." But Peter and the apostles answered, "We must obey God rather than any human authority. The God of our ancestors raised up Jesus, whom you had killed by hanging him on a tree. God exalted Jesus at his right hand as Leader and Savior that he might give repentance to Israel and forgiveness of sins."

The Word of the Lord.

◆ All observe silence.

FOR SILENT REFLECTION

Think about this silently in your heart. Peter said that they must obey God rather than any human authority. What does that mean?

CLOSING PRAYER

Let us pray to God for our needs and the needs of others: our family, neighborhood, and the world. For each need we say, "Lord, hear our prayer."

◆ All may add their own prayers here.

Let us pray: **Our Father . . . Amen.**

Holy God,
we see your Spirit at work
in the lives of the early Christians.
May we stay strong in our faith,
obeying your commands first.
We pray in the name of our Leader and Savior,
Jesus Christ.

Amen.

✦ All make the Sign of the Cross.

OPENING

Today is the feast of St. Pius V, who led the Church in the 1500s. By the Holy Spirit, this pope ushered in many changes to strengthen and unify the Church, despite many secular challenges. Today we hear a passage from the Book of Revelation. The writer, John, describes a vision he had of Jesus and the end of time. He calls Jesus the "Alpha and the Omega." Alpha and Omega are the first and last characters of the Greek alphabet. They mean the beginning and the end.

✚ All make the Sign of the Cross.

In the name of the Father, and of the Son, and of the Holy Spirit. Amen.

PSALM

(For a longer psalm, see page xiv.)
Psalm 105:1–2

Let the hearts of those who seek the LORD rejoice.

Let the hearts of those who seek the LORD rejoice.

O give thanks to the LORD, call on his name,
    make known his deeds among the peoples.
Sing to him, sing praises to him;
    tell of all his wonderful works.

Let the hearts of those who seek the LORD rejoice.

READING

Revelation 20:11a; 21:1ab, 2abc, 3, 5ab, 6abc

A reading from the Book of Revelation.

Then I saw a great white throne and the one who sat on it. Then I saw a new heaven and a new earth; for the first heaven and the first earth had passed away. And I saw the holy city, the new Jerusalem, coming down out of heaven from God. And I heard a loud voice from the throne saying, "See, the home of God is among mortals. He will dwell with them; they will be his peoples; and God himself will be with them. And the one who was seated on the throne said, "See, I am making all things new." Then he said to me, "It is done! I am the Alpha and the Omega, the beginning and the end."

The Word of the Lord.

◆ All observe silence.

FOR SILENT REFLECTION

Think about this silently in your heart. You have heard many names for Jesus this week. What others do you know?

CLOSING PRAYER

Let us pray to God for our needs and the needs of others: our family, neighborhood, and the world. For each need we say, "Lord, hear our prayer."

◆ All may add their own prayers here.

Let us pray: **Our Father . . . Amen.**

O God,
you are the beginning and the end.
May we be ready for the time when all things are made new
and when Jesus Christ will be all in all.
Through Christ our Lord.

Amen.

✚ All make the Sign of the Cross.

PRAYER SERVICE
TO HONOR MARY IN MAY

Add an image or statue of Mary, flowers, and candles to the sacred space. Prepare six leaders for this service. The third leader will need a Bible for the passages from Luke. Take time to help the lector practice the readings. You may wish to sing "Sing of Mary" as the opening song. If the group will sing, prepare someone to lead it.

FIRST LEADER:

Throughout the month of May, we remember Mary, the Mother of our Lord Jesus. She was a life-giving caregiver for our Savior, and she remains so for us today. She represents the fullness of holiness, for she was conceived without sin and was assumed into heaven because of her special role in our salvation. She serves as an example for all of us to say yes in practical ways to God's Spirit of goodness. Many Catholics turn to this beloved first disciple of Christ for inspiration and for prayer, particularly as the events of Jesus' life unfold in Scripture during the Church year.

SONG LEADER:

◆ Gesture for all to stand, and lead the first few verses of the song.

SECOND LEADER:

✚ All make the Sign of the Cross.

In the name of the Father, and of the Son, and of the Holy Spirit. Amen.

Let us pray:
Almighty Father,
we honor Mary as our Mother
because you chose her to be
the human vessel for
your Son Jesus,
who was both human and divine.

CHILDREN'S DAILY PRAYER 2020–2021, © 2020 Archdiocese of Chicago: Liturgy Training Publications. All rights reserved. Orders: 800-933-1800 or www.LTP.org.

Help us to be open to
the same Spirit
who appeared to Mary,
guiding her throughout her
challenging life with
the Savior of our world.
We ask this through Christ our Lord.

Amen.

◆ Remain standing and sing **Alleluia.**

THIRD LEADER: Luke 1:26–38
A reading from the holy Gospel according
to Luke.

◆ Read the Gospel passage from the Bible.

The Gospel of the Lord.

◆ All sit and observe silence.

FOURTH LEADER:

◆ Gesture for all to stand.

Let us bring our hopes and needs to God as
we respond, "Lord, hear our prayer."
For all mothers
and those who nurture others
throughout life.
May they be open to
God's creative Spirit to bring
new life into the world,

we pray to the Lord . . .

For those facing difficult decisions.
May they look to Mary
for guidance
in following God's plan,

we pray to the Lord . . .

For all married couples.
May they remain devoted
to God, to each other,
and to their Sacrament of Marriage,

we pray to the Lord . . .

For the sick and the abandoned.
For those who have passed
to the other side of life.
May they feel the loving arms
of Mary with Jesus,

we pray to the Lord . . .

FIFTH LEADER:
Let us pray the Hail Mary:

ALL: Hail Mary, full of grace . . .

◆ Pause, and then say:

Let us offer one another a sign of
Christ's peace.

◆ All offer one another a sign of peace.

SIXTH LEADER:
Let us pray Mary's special prayer,
the *Magnificat*:
"My soul magnifies the Lord,
  and my spirit rejoices in God my Savior,
for he has looked with favor on the lowliness
    of his servant.
  Surely, from now on all generations will
    call me blessed;
for the Mighty One has done great things
    for me,
  and holy is his name."

✚ All make the Sign of the Cross.

**In the name of the Father, and of the Son, and
of the Holy Spirit. Amen.**

PRAYER FOR THE WEEK
WITH A READING FROM THE GOSPEL FOR **SUNDAY, MAY 2, 2021**

OPENING

We are still in Easter Time! On this Fifth Sunday of Easter, we hear the Parable of the True Vine. Jesus was talking to his disciples at the Last Supper. Jesus describes his hopes for his disciples. He refers to himself as the true vine, and his followers the branches. Jesus encourages his disciples to "abide," or remain, in him so they will bear much fruit.

✛ All make the Sign of the Cross.

In the name of the Father, and of the Son, and of the Holy Spirit. Amen.

PSALM

(For a longer psalm, see page xv.)
Psalm 118:1–2, 4

The stone that the builders rejected
    has become the chief cornerstone.

**The stone that the builders rejected
    has become the chief cornerstone.**

O give thanks to the LORD, for he is good;
    his steadfast love endures forever!
Let Israel say,
    "His steadfast love endures forever."
Let those who fear the LORD say,
    "His steadfast love endures forever."

**The stone that the builders rejected
has become the chief cornerstone.**

◆ All stand and sing **Alleluia.**

GOSPEL

John 15:1–2a, 4–7

A reading from the holy Gospel according to John.

Jesus said to his disciples, "I am the true vine, and my Father is the vinegrower. He removes every branch in me that bears no fruit. Abide in

276

me as I abide in you. Just as the branch cannot bear fruit by itself unless it abides in the vine, neither can you unless you abide in me. I am the vine, you are the branches. Those who abide in me and I in them bear much fruit, because apart from me you can do nothing. Whoever does not abide in me is thrown away like a branch and withers; such branches are gathered, thrown into the fire, and burned. If you abide in me, and my words abide in you, ask for whatever you wish, and it will be done for you."

The Gospel of the Lord.

◆ All sit and observe silence.

FOR SILENT REFLECTION

Think about this silently in your heart. What fruits are you expected to bear if you remain in Jesus?

CLOSING PRAYER

Let us pray to God for our needs and the needs of others: our family, neighborhood, and the world. For each need we say, "Lord, hear our prayer."

◆ All may add their own prayers here.

Let us pray: **Our Father . . . Amen.**

We continue to rejoice and are glad, O God! as the gardener cares for plants, you care for us.
Help us to bear good fruit by our words and actions.
Through Christ our Lord.

Amen.

✛ All make the Sign of the Cross.

OPENING

In this week's readings, Jesus tries to share much about who he is with his disciples, so that they might understand him and continue following him after he is gone. Today we celebrate the feast day of two of Jesus' Twelve Apostles, St. Philip and St. James.

✛ All make the Sign of the Cross.

In the name of the Father, and of the Son, and of the Holy Spirit. Amen.

PSALM

(For a longer psalm, see page xv.)
Psalm 118:1–2, 4

The stone that the builders rejected
 has become the chief cornerstone.

**The stone that the builders rejected
 has become the chief cornerstone.**

O give thanks to the LORD, for he is good;
 his steadfast love endures forever!
Let Israel say,
 "His steadfast love endures forever."
Let those who fear the LORD say,
 "His steadfast love endures forever."

**The stone that the builders rejected
has become the chief cornerstone.**

◆ All stand and sing **Alleluia.**

GOSPEL

John 10:9–15a

A reading from the holy Gospel according to John.

Jesus said, "I am the gate. Whoever enters by me will be saved, and will come in and go out and find pasture. The thief comes only to steal and kill and destroy. I came that they may have life, and have it abundantly. I am the good shepherd. The good shepherd lays down his life for the sheep. The hired hand, who is not the shepherd and does not own the sheep, sees the wolf coming and leaves the sheep and runs away—and the wolf snatches them and scatters them. The hired hand runs away because a hired hand does not care for the sheep. I am the good shepherd. I know my own and my own know me, just as the Father knows me and I know the Father."

The Gospel of the Lord.

◆ All sit and observe silence.

FOR SILENT REFLECTION

Think about this silently in your heart. Who might be the "hired hand" who is supposed to lead us but does not really care for us? How might we be cautious not to listen to them?

CLOSING PRAYER

Let us pray to God for our needs and the needs of others: our family, neighborhood, and the world. For each need we say, "Lord, hear our prayer."

◆ All may add their own prayers here.

Let us pray: **Our Father . . . Amen.**

Loving God,
thank you for our Good Shepherd.
May we stay close only to him.
Through Christ our Risen Lord.

Amen.

✛ All make the Sign of the Cross.

PRAYER FOR
TUESDAY, MAY 4, 2021

OPENING

Today's reading from Scripture talks about love. The word *love* is mentioned seven times. Jesus tells us to "abide," or remain, in his love. He gives us a new commandment.

✦ All make the Sign of the Cross.

In the name of the Father, and of the Son, and of the Holy Spirit. Amen.

PSALM

(For a longer psalm, see page xv.)
Psalm 118:1–2, 4

The stone that the builders rejected
  has become the chief cornerstone.

**The stone that the builders rejected
  has become the chief cornerstone.**

O give thanks to the LORD, for he is good;
  his steadfast love endures forever!
Let Israel say,
  "His steadfast love endures forever."
Let those who fear the LORD say,
  "His steadfast love endures forever."

**The stone that the builders rejected
has become the chief cornerstone.**

✦ All stand and sing **Alleluia.**

GOSPEL

John 15:9–12

A reading from the holy Gospel according to John.

Jesus said, "As the Father has loved me, so I have loved you; abide in my love. If you keep my commandments, you will abide in my love, just as I have kept my Father's commandments and abide in his love. I have said these things to you so that my joy may be in you, and that your joy may be complete. This is my commandment, that you love one another as I have loved you."

The Gospel of the Lord.

✦ All sit and observe silence.

FOR SILENT REFLECTION

Think about this silently in your heart. How will you show love for another today?

CLOSING PRAYER

Let us pray to God for our needs and the needs of others: our family, neighborhood, and the world. For each need we say, "Lord, hear our prayer."

✦ All may add their own prayers here.

Let us pray: **Our Father . . . Amen.**

God of love,
thank you for your abundant love.
Help us to keep your commandments
and abide in your love.
We ask this in the name of Jesus Christ,
our Risen Lord.

Amen.

✦ All make the Sign of the Cross.

OPENING

In today's Gospel, Jesus is trying to guide his disciples, but they are confused and do not understand. Jesus tells them that, through knowing him, we might also know God. To know God, Jesus tells them that they first have to know him.

✦ All make the Sign of the Cross.

In the name of the Father, and of the Son, and of the Holy Spirit. Amen.

PSALM

(For a longer psalm, see page xv.)
Psalm 118:1–2, 4

The stone that the builders rejected
  has become the chief cornerstone.

**The stone that the builders rejected
  has become the chief cornerstone.**

O give thanks to the LORD, for he is good;
  his steadfast love endures forever!
Let Israel say,
  "His steadfast love endures forever."
Let those who fear the LORD say,
  "His steadfast love endures forever."

**The stone that the builders rejected
has become the chief cornerstone.**

✦ All stand and sing **Alleluia.**

GOSPEL

John 14:6–7a, 8–9b, 10bc, 11

A reading from the holy Gospel according to John.

Jesus said to him, "I am the way, and the truth, and the life. No one comes to the Father except through me. If you know me, you will know my Father also." Philip said to him, "Lord, show us the Father, and we will be satisfied." Jesus said to him, "Have I been with you all this time, Philip, and you still do not know me? Whoever has seen me has seen the Father. The words that I say to you I do not speak on my own; but the Father who dwells in me does his works. Believe me that I am in the Father and the Father is in me; but if you do not, then believe me because of the works themselves."

The Gospel of the Lord.

◆ All sit and observe silence.

FOR SILENT REFLECTION

Think about this silently in your heart. How well do you know Jesus?

CLOSING PRAYER

Let us pray to God for our needs and the needs of others: our family, neighborhood, and the world. For each need we say, "Lord, hear our prayer."

◆ All may add their own prayers here.

Let us pray: **Our Father . . . Amen.**

We continue to praise and thank you, O God,
for the gift of your Son Jesus.
We do not always understand your will,
but we desire to be close to you.
Guide us with your wisdom
so that we might know you more.
Through Christ our Risen Lord.

Amen.

✦ All make the Sign of the Cross.

PRAYER FOR
THURSDAY, MAY 6, 2021

OPENING

Jesus comforts his disciples by telling them that the Holy Spirit, or "Advocate," will be with them after he is gone. The Holy Spirit will continue to teach and guide them as they continue to follow Jesus.

✝ All make the Sign of the Cross.

In the name of the Father, and of the Son, and of the Holy Spirit. Amen.

PSALM

(For a longer psalm, see page xv.)
Psalm 118:1–2, 4

The stone that the builders rejected
  has become the chief cornerstone.

**The stone that the builders rejected
has become the chief cornerstone.**

O give thanks to the LORD, for he is good;
  his steadfast love endures forever!
Let Israel say,
  "His steadfast love endures forever."
Let those who fear the LORD say,
  "His steadfast love endures forever."

**The stone that the builders rejected
has become the chief cornerstone.**

◆ All stand and sing **Alleluia.**

GOSPEL

John 14:23–27

A reading from the holy Gospel according to John.

Jesus said, "Those who love me will keep my word, and my Father will love them, and we will come to them and make our home with them. Whoever does not love me does not keep my words; and the word that you hear is not mine, but is from the Father who sent me. I have said these things to you while I am still with you. But the Advocate, the Holy Spirit, whom the Father will send in my name, will teach you everything, and remind you of all that I have said to you. Peace I leave with you; my peace I give to you. I do not give to you as the world gives. Do not let your hearts be troubled, and do not let them be afraid."

The Gospel of the Lord.

◆ All sit and observe silence.

FOR SILENT REFLECTION

Think about this silently in your heart. An advocate is someone who supports you. How does the Holy Spirit support you?

CLOSING PRAYER

Let us pray to God for our needs and the needs of others: our family, neighborhood, and the world. For each need we say, "Lord, hear our prayer."

◆ All may add their own prayers here.

Let us pray: **Our Father . . . Amen.**

Spirit of God,
be with us when we are in need,
comfort us when we are lonely or afraid,
and guide us to Jesus,
in whose name we pray.

Amen.

✝ All make the Sign of the Cross.

OPENING

Jesus came to us as "light into the world." Light is essential for growth and life—both for us and for all of creation. Jesus tells us that whoever believes in him will not be in darkness. The source of light—and life—is Jesus.

✛ All make the Sign of the Cross.

In the name of the Father, and of the Son, and of the Holy Spirit. Amen.

PSALM

(For a longer psalm, see page xv.)
Psalm 118:1–2, 4

The stone that the builders rejected
  has become the chief cornerstone.

**The stone that the builders rejected
  has become the chief cornerstone.**

O give thanks to the Lord, for he is good;
  his steadfast love endures forever!
Let Israel say,
  "His steadfast love endures forever."
Let those who fear the Lord say,
  "His steadfast love endures forever."

**The stone that the builders rejected
has become the chief cornerstone.**

◆ All stand and sing **Alleluia.**

GOSPEL

John 12:44–46, 49–50

A reading from the holy Gospel according to John.

Then Jesus cried aloud: "Whoever believes in me believes not in me but in him who sent me. And whoever sees me sees him who sent me. I have come as light into the world, so that everyone who believes in me should not remain in the darkness. For I have not spoken on my own, but the Father who sent me has himself given me a commandment about what to say and what to speak. And I know that his commandment is eternal life. What I speak, therefore, I speak just as the Father has told me."

The Gospel of the Lord.

◆ All sit and observe silence.

FOR SILENT REFLECTION

Think about this silently in your heart. In what ways does Jesus cast out the darkness?

CLOSING PRAYER

Let us pray to God for our needs and the needs of others: our family, neighborhood, and the world. For each need we say, "Lord, hear our prayer."

◆ All may add their own prayers here.

Let us pray: **Our Father . . . Amen.**

God of Light,
through your Son Jesus, we can see our
source of life and light.
We give you thanks,
for we celebrate that your Son has cast out
darkness and death
with his rising from the dead.
Alleluia, Alleluia, Alleluia.

Amen.

✛ All make the Sign of the Cross.

PRAYER FOR THE WEEK
WITH A READING FROM THE GOSPEL FOR **SUNDAY, MAY 9, 2021**

OPENING

On this Sixth Sunday of Easter, we hear Jesus calling his disciples his friends. Even if we do not choose Jesus, he has already chosen us. Friends love, care for, and support one another. Jesus calls us to be friends to one another.

✚ All make the Sign of the Cross.

In the name of the Father, and of the Son, and of the Holy Spirit. Amen.

PSALM

(For a longer psalm, see page xv.)
Psalm 118:1–2, 4

The stone that the builders rejected
   has become the chief cornerstone.

**The stone that the builders rejected
   has become the chief cornerstone.**

O give thanks to the LORD, for he is good;
   his steadfast love endures forever!
Let Israel say,
   "His steadfast love endures forever."
Let those who fear the LORD say,
   "His steadfast love endures forever."

**The stone that the builders rejected
has become the chief cornerstone.**

◆ All stand and sing **Alleluia.**

GOSPEL

John 15:9–10, 12–14, 15c–17

A reading from the holy Gospel according to John.

Jesus said, "As the Father has loved me, so I have loved you; abide in my love. If you keep my commandments, you will abide in my love, just as I have kept my Father's commandments and abide in his love. This is my commandment, that you love one another as I have loved you. No one has greater love than this, to lay down one's life for one's friends. You are my friends if you do what I command you. I have called you friends, because I have made known to you everything that I have heard from my Father. You did not choose me but I chose you. And I appointed you to go and bear fruit, fruit that will last, so that the Father will give you whatever you ask him in my name. I am giving you these commands so that you may love one another."

The Gospel of the Lord.

◆ All sit and observe silence.

FOR SILENT REFLECTION

Think about this silently in your heart. How is Jesus your friend?

CLOSING PRAYER

Let us pray to God for our needs and the needs of others: our family, neighborhood, and the world. For each need we say, "Lord, hear our prayer."

◆ All may add their own prayers here.

Let us pray: **Our Father . . . Amen.**

How great is your love, O God,
that you count us as friends.
Help us to understand what that means
for our lives.
We ask this in the name of your Son,
Jesus Christ our Risen Lord.

Amen.

✚ All make the Sign of the Cross.

OPENING

Today is the memorial for St. Damien Joseph de Veuster (1840–1889). St. Damien was a priest from Belgium who worked on the island of Moloka'i in Hawaii. He ministered to the indigenous people who suffered from leprosy, eventually dying from the disease himself. He served the community by treating their disease, attending to their spiritual life, and building homes, schools, hospitals, and churches.

✚ All make the Sign of the Cross.

In the name of the Father, and of the Son, and of the Holy Spirit. Amen.

PSALM

(For a longer psalm, see page xv.)
Psalm 118:1–2, 4

The stone that the builders rejected
    has become the chief cornerstone.

**The stone that the builders rejected
    has become the chief cornerstone.**

O give thanks to the LORD, for he is good;
    his steadfast love endures forever!
Let Israel say,
    "His steadfast love endures forever."
Let those who fear the LORD say,
    "His steadfast love endures forever."

**The stone that the builders rejected
has become the chief cornerstone.**

READING

Acts 6:8ac, 9ac, 10, 13; 7:54, 58–59, 60c; 8:1a

A reading from the Acts of the Apostles.

Stephen did great wonders and signs among the people. Then some of those who belonged to the synagogue of the Freedmen stood up and argued with Stephen. But they could not withstand the wisdom and the Spirit with which he spoke. They set up false witnesses who said, "This man never stops saying things against this holy place and the law." When the Council heard these things, they became enraged and ground their teeth at Stephen. Then they dragged him out of the city and began to stone him; and the witnesses laid their coats at the feet of a young man named Saul. While they were stoning Stephen, he prayed, "Lord Jesus, receive my spirit." When he had said this, he died. And Saul approved of their killing him.

The Word of the Lord.

◆ All observe silence.

FOR SILENT REFLECTION

Think about this silently in your heart. How might you help a community like St. Damien did?

CLOSING PRAYER

Let us pray to God for our needs and the needs of others: our family, neighborhood, and the world. For each need we say, "Lord, hear our prayer."

◆ All may add their own prayers here.

Let us pray: **Our Father . . . Amen.**

Heavenly Father,
help us stay close to you and true to our faith. Through Christ our Lord.

Amen.

✚ All make the Sign of the Cross.

PRAYER FOR
TUESDAY, MAY 11, 2021

OPENING

We continue from yesterday's Scripture of the stoning of St. Stephen and hear about the conversion of St. Paul. Paul was originally named Saul. Saul participated in St. Stephen's death and imprisoned many of the early Christians in Jerusalem for their beliefs.

✤ All make the Sign of the Cross.

In the name of the Father, and of the Son, and of the Holy Spirit. Amen.

PSALM

(For a longer psalm, see page xv.)
Psalm 118:1–2, 4

The stone that the builders rejected
  has become the chief cornerstone.

**The stone that the builders rejected
  has become the chief cornerstone.**

O give thanks to the LORD, for he is good;
  his steadfast love endures forever!
Let Israel say,
  "His steadfast love endures forever."
Let those who fear the LORD say,
  "His steadfast love endures forever."

**The stone that the builders rejected
has become the chief cornerstone.**

READING

Acts 8:1b–8

A reading from the Acts of the Apostles.

That day a severe persecution began against the church in Jerusalem, and all except the apostles were scattered throughout the countryside of Judea [joo-DEE-uh] and Samaria [suh-MAYR-ee-uh]. Devout men buried Stephen and made loud lamentation over him. But Saul was ravaging the church by entering house after house; dragging off both men and women, he committed them to prison. Now those who were scattered went from place to place, proclaiming the word. Philip went down to the city of Samaria and proclaimed the Messiah to them. The crowds with one accord listened eagerly to what was said by Philip, hearing and seeing the signs that he did, for unclean spirits, crying with loud shrieks, came out of many who were possessed; and many others who were paralyzed or lame were cured. So there was great joy in that city.

The Word of the Lord.

◆ All observe silence.

FOR SILENT REFLECTION

Think about this silently in your heart. When you see someone being bullied, how can you stand up for them?.

CLOSING PRAYER

Let us pray to God for our needs and the needs of others: our family, neighborhood, and the world. For each need we say, "Lord, hear our prayer."

◆ All may add their own prayers here.

Let us pray: **Our Father . . . Amen.**

When we make mistakes or go down the wrong path, dearest God, help us to find our way.
We pray in Christ's name.

Amen.

✤ All make the Sign of the Cross.

OPENING

While he was still persecuting Christians, Saul experienced a great light and heard Jesus' voice. Saul was left blind from the vision. The Way is how early followers of Jesus referred to themselves. Today is the feast day of St. Pancras, a young Roman martyr who died at the age of fourteen (c. 289–303). He is the patron saint of children.

✝ All make the Sign of the Cross.

In the name of the Father, and of the Son, and of the Holy Spirit. Amen.

PSALM

(For a longer psalm, see page xv.)
Psalm 118:1–2, 4

The stone that the builders rejected
  has become the chief cornerstone.

**The stone that the builders rejected
  has become the chief cornerstone.**

O give thanks to the LORD, for he is good;
  his steadfast love endures forever!
Let Israel say,
  "His steadfast love endures forever."
Let those who fear the LORD say,
  "His steadfast love endures forever."

**The stone that the builders rejected
has become the chief cornerstone.**

READING

Acts 9:1ac, 2bd, 3–6, 8–9

A reading from the Acts of the Apostles.

Meanwhile Saul went to the high priest so that if he found any who belonged to the Way, he might bring them bound to Jerusalem. Now as he was going along and approaching Damascus [duh-MAS-kuhs], suddenly a light from heaven flashed around him. He fell to the ground and heard a voice saying to him, "Saul, Saul, why do you persecute me?" He asked, "Who are you, Lord?" The reply came, "I am Jesus, whom you are persecuting. But get up and enter the city, and you will be told what you are to do." Saul got up from the ground, and though his eyes were open, he could see nothing; so they led him by the hand and brought him into Damascus. For three days he was without sight, and neither ate nor drank.

The Word of the Lord.

◆ All observe silence.

FOR SILENT REFLECTION

Think about this silently in your heart. Why do you think Saul became blind?

CLOSING PRAYER

Let us pray to God for our needs and the needs of others: our family, neighborhood, and the world. For each need we say, "Lord, hear our prayer."

◆ All may add their own prayers here.

Let us pray: **Our Father . . . Amen.**

Merciful God,
may we see your light every day.
May we share your light with others.
Help us when we stray from your path.
Through Christ our Risen Lord.

Amen.

✝ All make the Sign of the Cross.

PRAYER FOR
THURSDAY, MAY 13, 2021

OPENING

Today is the feast day of Our Lady of Fatima, a title given to the Blessed Virgin Mary after she appeared to three shepherd children in 1917. In today's reading, Jesus sends a disciple named Ananias [a-nuh-NĪ-uhs] to heal Saul's vision and to bring him the Holy Spirit.

✝ All make the Sign of the Cross.

In the name of the Father, and of the Son, and of the Holy Spirit. Amen.

PSALM

(For a longer psalm, see page xv.)
Psalm 118:1–2, 4

The stone that the builders rejected
　has become the chief cornerstone.

**The stone that the builders rejected
　has become the chief cornerstone.**

O give thanks to the LORD, for he is good;
　his steadfast love endures forever!
Let Israel say,
　"His steadfast love endures forever."
Let those who fear the LORD say,
　"His steadfast love endures forever."

**The stone that the builders rejected
has become the chief cornerstone.**

READING

Acts 9:10a, 11–12, 17abce, 18

A reading from the Acts of the Apostles.

Now there was a disciple in Damascus [duh-MAS-kuhs] named Ananias. The Lord said to him, "Get up and go to the street called Straight, and at the house of Judas look for a man of Tarsus named Saul. At this moment he is praying, and he has seen in a vision a man named Ananias come in and lay his hands on him so that he might regain his sight." So Ananias went and entered the house. He laid his hands on Saul and said, "Brother Saul, the Lord Jesus has sent me so that you may regain your sight and be filled with the Holy Spirit." And immediately something like scales fell from his eyes, and his sight was restored. Then he got up and was baptized.

The Word of the Lord.

◆ All observe silence.

FOR SILENT REFLECTION

Think about this silently in your heart. How does God reach out to us and help us "see"?

CLOSING PRAYER

Let us pray to God for our needs and the needs of others: our family, neighborhood, and the world. For each need we say, "Lord, hear our prayer."

◆ All may add their own prayers here.

Let us pray: **Our Father . . . Amen.**

We continue to praise and thank you, O God,
for the gift of your Son Jesus,
who shows us the Way.
May we follow him and help others
know him.
Through Christ our Risen Lord.
Amen.

✝ All make the Sign of the Cross.

OPENING

We come to follow Jesus in various ways. The Holy Spirit works in each of us to know and serve God and our brothers and sisters. Saul's eyes were opened and he became a devoted follower of Jesus. Another of Jesus' Apostles is honored today: St. Matthias was chosen to replace Judas Iscariot.

✚ All make the Sign of the Cross.

In the name of the Father, and of the Son, and of the Holy Spirit. Amen.

PSALM

(For a longer psalm, see page xv.)
Psalm 118:1–2, 4

The stone that the builders rejected
   has become the chief cornerstone.

**The stone that the builders rejected
has become the chief cornerstone.**

O give thanks to the LORD, for he is good;
   his steadfast love endures forever!
Let Israel say,
   "His steadfast love endures forever."
Let those who fear the LORD say,
   "His steadfast love endures forever."

**The stone that the builders rejected
has become the chief cornerstone.**

READING

Acts 9:19–21a, 22–23, 24b–25

A reading from the Acts of the Apostles.

After taking some food, Saul regained his strength. For several days he was with the disciples in Damascus, and immediately he began to proclaim Jesus in the synagogues, saying, "He is the Son of God." All who heard him were amazed and said, "Is not this the man who made havoc in Jerusalem among those who invoked this name?" Saul became increasingly more powerful and confounded the Jews who lived in Damascus by proving that Jesus was the Messiah. After some time had passed, the Jews plotted to kill him. They were watching the gates day and night so that they might kill him; but his disciples took him by night and let him down through an opening in the wall, lowering him in a basket.

The Word of the Lord.

◆ All observe silence.

FOR SILENT REFLECTION

Think about this silently in your heart. Saul had a conversion—a moment in which he was changed forever. Have you ever had a similar experience?

CLOSING PRAYER

Let us pray to God for our needs and the needs of others: our family, neighborhood, and the world. For each need we say, "Lord, hear our prayer."

◆ All may add their own prayers here.

Let us pray: **Our Father . . . Amen.**

Sometimes it is not easy for others to hear your truth, O God.
Send us your Spirit to help open their hearts.
Through Christ our Risen Lord.

Amen.

✚ All make the Sign of the Cross.

PRAYER SERVICE
ASCENSION

Prepare six leaders and a song leader for this service. The second and third leaders will need Bibles to read the Scripture passages and may need help finding and practicing them. You may wish to begin by singing "All Will Be Well" and end with "Sing Out, Earth and Skies." Help the song leader prepare to lead the singing.

SONG LEADER:
Please stand and join in singing our opening song.

FIRST LEADER:
So if you have been raised with Christ, seek the things that are above, where Christ is, seated at the right hand of God.

ALL: Amen.

FIRST LEADER:
Today we celebrate the Solemnity of the Ascension of the Lord. We are joyful on this fortieth day of Easter because Jesus Christ returned to his Father in heaven, and he promised that we could experience his Presence in Spirit forever.

✚ All make the Sign of the Cross.

In the name of the Father, and of the Son, and of the Holy Spirit. Amen.

Let us pray:
Almighty God,
you fulfilled your promise
of sending a Savior
to redeem the world.
Now he sits at your right hand
and your Spirit guides us
with holy Presence.
Help us to listen and act according to
your will

CHILDREN'S DAILY PRAYER 2020–2021, © 2020 Archdiocese of Chicago: Liturgy Training Publications. All rights reserved. Orders: 800-933-1800 or www.LTP.org.

so that we can enter into
your Kingdom too.
We ask this through Christ our Lord.

ALL: Amen.

◆ Gesture for all to sit.

SECOND LEADER: Colossians 3:2–4
A reading from the Letter of Paul to the Colossians.

◆ Read the Scripture passage from the Bible.

The Word of the Lord.

◆ All observe silence.

THIRD LEADER: Acts 1:6–11
A reading from the Acts of the Apostles.

◆ Read the Scripture passage from the Bible.

The Word of the Lord.

◆ All observe silence.

FOURTH LEADER:
Let us stand and bring our hopes and needs to God as we pray, "Lord, hear our prayer."

For our brothers and sisters around the world who do not know Christ.
May they experience
our Risen Lord in eternity,

we pray to the Lord . . .

For our parents and family members
who care for us.
May we remain grateful for their
acts of sacrificial love
that are a reflection of
God's abundant love for us,

we pray to the Lord . . .

For the teachers, school assistants,
and coaches who
guide us in our school activities.
May they continue to
teach us about God
through their
kindness and generosity,

we pray to the Lord . . .

For those who suffer from
illness, hunger, or political strife.
For those who have died,

we pray to the Lord . . .

FIFTH LEADER:
Let us pray the prayer that Jesus taught us:
Our Father . . . Amen.

◆ Pause and then say the following:

Let us offer one another a sign of Christ's peace.

◆ All offer one another a sign of peace.

SIXTH LEADER:
Let us pray:
Lord our God,
your immense love for us
shines for all to see
in the glory of your Resurrection
and in your return to God.
We praise you for your Spirit
of truth and light
and the promise of your
return again.
We ask this through Christ our Lord.

ALL: Amen.

CHILDREN'S DAILY PRAYER 2020–2021, © 2020 Archdiocese of Chicago: Liturgy Training Publications. All rights reserved. Orders: 800-933-1800 or www.LTP.org.

PRAYER FOR THE WEEK
WITH A READING FROM THE GOSPEL FOR **SUNDAY, MAY 16, 2021**

OPENING

Today we celebrate the seventh and final week of Easter Time with the Solemnity of the Ascension of the Lord. Listen closely to what Jesus tells his disciples just before he went up to his Father in heaven.

✛ All make the Sign of the Cross.

In the name of the Father, and of the Son, and of the Holy Spirit. Amen.

PSALM

(For a longer psalm, see page xv.)

Psalm 118:1–2, 4

The stone that the builders rejected
 has become the chief cornerstone.

**The stone that the builders rejected
 has become the chief cornerstone.**

O give thanks to the LORD, for he is good;
 his steadfast love endures forever!
Let Israel say,
 "His steadfast love endures forever."
Let those who fear the LORD say,
 "His steadfast love endures forever."

**The stone that the builders rejected
has become the chief cornerstone.**

◆ All stand and sing **Alleluia.**

GOSPEL

Mark 16:15–20

A reading from the holy Gospel according to Mark.

And Jesus said to the disciples, "Go into all the world and proclaim the good news to the whole creation. The one who believes and is baptized will be saved; but the one who does not believe will be condemned. And these signs will accompany those who believe: by using my name they will cast out demons; they will speak in new tongues; they will pick up snakes in their hands, and if they drink any deadly thing, it will not hurt them; they will lay their hands on the sick, and they will recover." So then the Lord Jesus, after he had spoken to them, was taken up into heaven and sat down at the right hand of God. And they went out and proclaimed the good news everywhere, while the Lord worked with them and confirmed the message by the signs that accompanied it.

The Gospel of the Lord.

◆ All sit and observe silence.

FOR SILENT REFLECTION

Think about this silently in your heart. How do we proclaim the Good News?

CLOSING PRAYER

Let us pray to God for our needs and the needs of others: our family, neighborhood, and the world. For each need we say, "Lord, hear our prayer."

◆ All may add their own prayers here.

Let us pray: **Our Father . . . Amen.**

Although your Son now lives and reigns with you in heaven, glorious God,
Jesus is also with us, until the end of time.
We pray to you in his name.

Amen.

✛ All make the Sign of the Cross.

OPENING

The readings for this week all focus on the events after Christ's Resurrection. According to today's Gospel, the Risen Christ first appears to Mary Magdalene. Although the disciples see the Risen Christ before them, they find it hard to believe.

✣ All make the Sign of the Cross.

In the name of the Father, and of the Son, and of the Holy Spirit. Amen.

PSALM

(For a longer psalm, see page xv.)
Psalm 118:1–2, 4

The stone that the builders rejected
has become the chief cornerstone.

**The stone that the builders rejected
has become the chief cornerstone.**

O give thanks to the LORD, for he is good;
his steadfast love endures forever!
Let Israel say,
"His steadfast love endures forever."
Let those who fear the LORD say,
"His steadfast love endures forever."

**The stone that the builders rejected
has become the chief cornerstone.**

◆ All stand and sing **Alleluia.**

GOSPEL

Mark 16:9–14

A reading from the holy Gospel according to Mark.

Now after Jesus rose early on the first day of the week, he appeared first to Mary Magdalene, from whom he had cast out seven demons. She went out and told those who had been with him, while they were mourning and weeping. But when they heard that he was alive and had been seen by her, they would not believe it. After this he appeared in another form to two of them, as they were walking into the country. And they went back and told the rest, but they did not believe them. Later he appeared to the eleven themselves as they were sitting at the table; and he upbraided them for their lack of faith and stubbornness, because they had not believed those who saw him after he had risen.

The Gospel of the Lord.

◆ All sit and observe silence.

FOR SILENT REFLECTION

Think about this silently in your heart. Why do you think the disciples did not believe Mary Magdalene?

CLOSING PRAYER

Let us pray to God for our needs and the needs of others: our family, neighborhood, and the world. For each need we say, "Lord, hear our prayer."

◆ All may add their own prayers here.

Let us pray: **Our Father . . . Amen.**

O God,
help us see Jesus in the world around us.
Give us the faith and strength to proclaim the Good News.
Through Christ our Risen Lord. Alleluia!

Amen.

✣ All make the Sign of the Cross.

OPENING

In today's Scriptures, Jesus appears to his Apostles. Thomas was not present when Jesus appeared and would not believe the others. Jesus came a second time, when Thomas was present. Listen to what Jesus says to Thomas.

✛ All make the Sign of the Cross.

In the name of the Father, and of the Son, and of the Holy Spirit. Amen.

PSALM

(For a longer psalm, see page xv.)
Psalm 118:1–2, 4

The stone that the builders rejected
  has become the chief cornerstone.

**The stone that the builders rejected
  has become the chief cornerstone.**

O give thanks to the LORD, for he is good;
  his steadfast love endures forever!
Let Israel say,
  "His steadfast love endures forever."
Let those who fear the LORD say,
  "His steadfast love endures forever."

**The stone that the builders rejected
has become the chief cornerstone.**

◆ All stand and sing **Alleluia.**

GOSPEL

John 20:19d, 24acd, 25–27abd, 28–29ac

A reading from the holy Gospel according to John.

Jesus came and stood among the apostles and said, "Peace be with you." But Thomas, one of the twelve, was not with them when Jesus came. So the other disciples told him, "We have seen the Lord." But Thomas said to them,

"Unless I see the mark of the nails in his hands, and put my finger in the mark of the nails and my hand in his side, I will not believe." A week later his disciples were again in the house, and Thomas was with them. Although the doors were shut, Jesus came and stood among them and said, "Peace be with you." Then he said to Thomas, "Put your finger here and see my hands. Do not doubt but believe." Thomas answered him, "My Lord and my God!" Jesus said to him, "Blessed are those who have not seen and yet have come to believe."

The Gospel of the Lord.

◆ All sit and observe silence.

FOR SILENT REFLECTION

Think about this silently in your heart. Do you ever doubt God's presence with you?

CLOSING PRAYER

Let us pray to God for our needs and the needs of others: our family, neighborhood, and the world. For each need we say, "Lord, hear our prayer."

◆ All may add their own prayers here.

Let us pray: **Our Father . . . Amen.**

Loving God,
Jesus said, "Blessed are those who have not seen and yet have come to believe."
Help us to overcome our doubts and fears.
Through Christ our Risen Lord.

Amen.

✛ All make the Sign of the Cross.

OPENING

We hear that Jesus "upbraided" his Apostles for their lack of faith. *To upbraid* is "to scold or to find fault with." Jesus not only appeared to his disciples after his Resurrection but also sent them out to continue his work. That means all followers of Jesus proclaim the Good News to all.

✚ All make the Sign of the Cross.

In the name of the Father, and of the Son, and of the Holy Spirit. Amen.

PSALM

(For a longer psalm, see page xv.)
Psalm 118:1–2, 4

The stone that the builders rejected
   has become the chief cornerstone.

**The stone that the builders rejected
   has become the chief cornerstone.**

O give thanks to the LORD, for he is good;
   his steadfast love endures forever!
Let Israel say,
   "His steadfast love endures forever."
Let those who fear the LORD say,
   "His steadfast love endures forever."

**The stone that the builders rejected
has become the chief cornerstone.**

◆ All stand and sing **Alleluia.**

GOSPEL

Mark 16:14–15, 17, 19ac, 20

A reading from the holy Gospel according to Mark.

Later Jesus appeared to the eleven themselves as they were sitting at the table; and he upbraided them for their lack of faith and stubbornness, because they had not believed those who saw him after he had risen. And he said to them, "Go into all the world and proclaim the good news to the whole creation. And these signs will accompany those who believe: by using my name they will cast out demons; they will speak in new tongues." So then the Lord Jesus, was taken up into heaven and sat down at the right hand of God. And they went out and proclaimed the good news everywhere, while the Lord worked with them and confirmed the message by the signs that accompanied it.

The Gospel of the Lord.

◆ All sit and observe silence.

FOR SILENT REFLECTION

Think about this silently in your heart. How does the Lord work with us today?

CLOSING PRAYER

Let us pray to God for our needs and the needs of others: our family, neighborhood, and the world. For each need we say, "Lord, hear our prayer."

◆ All may add their own prayers here.

Let us pray: **Our Father . . . Amen.**

When we lack faith or are stubborn, help us open our hearts to you, O God.
May we follow Jesus' example.
In his name we pray.

Amen.

✚ All make the Sign of the Cross.

PRAYER FOR
THURSDAY, MAY 20, 2021

OPENING

Today is the memorial of St. Bernardine of Siena (1380–1444). He was an Italian priest who drew the attention of his audience by using themes from the everyday lives of the people. Jesus had the same approach to preaching. In today's reading, St. Paul testifies that Jesus appeared to many of his followers after his Resurrection.

✜ All make the Sign of the Cross.

In the name of the Father, and of the Son, and of the Holy Spirit. Amen.

PSALM

(For a longer psalm, see page xv.)

Psalm 118:1–2, 4

The stone that the builders rejected
  has become the chief cornerstone.

**The stone that the builders rejected
  has become the chief cornerstone.**

O give thanks to the LORD, for he is good;
  his steadfast love endures forever!
Let Israel say,
  "His steadfast love endures forever."
Let those who fear the LORD say,
  "His steadfast love endures forever."

**The stone that the builders rejected
has become the chief cornerstone.**

READING

1 Corinthians 15:1ab, 2a, 3–6ab, 7–8ac

A reading from the First Letter of Paul to the Corinthians.

Now I, Paul, would remind you, brothers and sisters, of the good news that I proclaimed to you, through which also you are being saved.

For I handed on to you as of first importance what I in turn had received: that Christ died for our sins in accordance with the scriptures, and that he was buried, and that he was raised on the third day in accordance with the scriptures, and that he appeared to Cephas [SEE-fuhs], then to the twelve. Then he appeared to more than five hundred brothers and sisters. Then he appeared to James, then to all the apostles. Last of all, he appeared also to me.

The Word of the Lord.

◆ All observe silence.

FOR SILENT REFLECTION

Think about this silently in your heart. Although Jesus doesn't appear to us physically, we know he is with us.

CLOSING PRAYER

Let us pray to God for our needs and the needs of others: our family, neighborhood, and the world. For each need we say, "Lord, hear our prayer."

◆ All may add their own prayers here.

Let us pray: **Our Father . . . Amen.**

Jesus,
thank you for being with us always.
Who live and reign with God the Father,
in the unity of the Holy Spirit,
one God for ever and ever.

Amen.

✜ All make the Sign of the Cross.

OPENING

In today's reading, St. John shares a dream or vision he had while imprisoned for preaching about Jesus. St. Christopher Magallanes (1869–1927), whom we remember today, also did not compromise his faith. He was a priest in Mexico who spread the Good News against the decrees of the Mexican government.

✢ All make the Sign of the Cross.

In the name of the Father, and of the Son, and of the Holy Spirit. Amen.

PSALM

(For a longer psalm, see page xv.)
Psalm 118:1–2, 4

The stone that the builders rejected
   has become the chief cornerstone.

**The stone that the builders rejected
   has become the chief cornerstone.**

O give thanks to the Lord, for he is good;
   his steadfast love endures forever!
Let Israel say,
   "His steadfast love endures forever."
Let those who fear the Lord say,
   "His steadfast love endures forever."

**The stone that the builders rejected
has become the chief cornerstone.**

READING

Revelation 1:9ac, 10b, 12–13, 17–18abc

A reading from the Book of Revelation.

I, John, was on the island called Patmos because of the word of God and the testimony of Jesus. I heard behind me a loud voice like a trumpet. Then I turned to see whose voice it was that spoke to me, and on turning I saw seven golden lampstands, and in the midst of the lampstands, and in the midst of the lampstands I saw one like the Son of Man, clothed with a long robe and with a golden sash across his chest. When I saw him, I fell at his feet as though dead. But he placed his right hand on me, saying, "Do not be afraid; I am the first and the last, and the living one, I was dead and see, I am alive for ever and ever."

The Word of the Lord.

◆ All observe silence.

FOR SILENT REFLECTION

Think about this silently in your heart. What does Jesus mean when he says he is "alive for ever and ever"?

CLOSING PRAYER

Let us pray to God for our needs and the needs of others: our family, neighborhood, and the world. For each need we say, "Lord, hear our prayer."

◆ All may add their own prayers here.

Let us pray: **Our Father . . . Amen.**

You are the beginning and the end,
Lord God,
and you are always with us.
Help us to proclaim your Good News
and to choose you first, as St. Christopher
and his companions did.
Through Christ our Risen Lord.

Amen.

✢ All make the Sign of the Cross.

PRAYER SERVICE
PENTECOST

Prepare a simple environment with a table covered with a red cloth. Leave a Bible and candle off to the side until the entrance procession. If possible, ring wind chimes during the procession. "Come, Holy Ghost," may be sung. Prepare the three leaders, the reader, and the three processors. The processors get in place: chimer, candle bearer, and lector with Bible. As the song begins they move slowly to the table in a solemn manner with chimes ringing gently. At the table the chimer moves to the side, the candle bearer places the candle, and the lector places the Bible. Then the chimes are silenced and the processors move away. When the song ends:

✚ All make the Sign of the Cross.

FIRST LEADER:

> **In the name of the Father and of the Son and of the Holy Spirit. Amen.**

ALL: Amen.

FIRST LEADER:

God came to us in the Person of Jesus
> to let us know
> > how much we are loved and forgiven.

Jesus promised the disciples that when he
> ascended into heaven
> > they would not be left alone.

God the Holy Spirit would be with them
> always.

That promise was for us, too.

Let us pray:
We call on you, Holy Spirit,
> to give us wisdom in everything we do
> and courage to always do the right thing.
> We ask for the gift of wonder and awe
> so we will always know the beauty of
> > God's world.

We ask this through Christ our Lord.

CHILDREN'S DAILY PRAYER 2020–2021, © 2020 Archdiocese of Chicago: Liturgy Training Publications. All rights reserved. Orders: 800-933-1800 or www.LTP.org.

◆ Gesture for all to sit.

LECTOR: Acts 1:8–9; 2:1–4

A reading from the Acts of the Apostles.

◆ Read the passage from the Bible.

The Word of the Lord.

FOR SILENT REFLECTION

FIRST LEADER:

What gifts of the Holy Spirit do we see in
our friends?

◆ All observe silence.

SECOND LEADER:

Let us stand. (pause)

◆ All stand.

We say together, "Come, Holy Spirit, come!"

ALL: Come, Holy Spirit, come!

SECOND LEADER:

Come, Holy Spirit, come!
And from your celestial home
   Shed a ray of light divine!
Come, Father of the poor!
Come, source of all our store!
We say together:

ALL: Come . . .

Heal our wounds, our strength renew;
On our dryness pour your dew;
   Wash the stains of guilt away:
Bend the stubborn heart and will;
Melt the frozen, warm the chill;
   Guide the steps that go astray.

We say together:

ALL: Come . . .
On the faithful, who adore
And confess you, evermore
   In your sevenfold gift descend;
Give them virtue's sure reward;
Give them your salvation, Lord;
   Give them joys that never end. Amen.
We say together:

ALL: Come . . .

THIRD LEADER:

Let us pray:
Holy Spirit, strengthen us with your many
       good gifts.
Help us become more and more
       a part of the Holy Trinity's life of love.
We ask this through Jesus Christ our Lord.

ALL: Amen.

✚ All make the Sign of the Cross.

THIRD LEADER:

     **In the name of the Father and of the
     Son and of the Holy Spirit. Amen.**

Let us offer one another a sign of
Christ's peace.

◆ All exchange a sign of peace.

PRAYER FOR THE WEEK
WITH A READING FROM THE GOSPEL FOR **SUNDAY, MAY 23, 2021**

OPENING

Today we celebrate the solemnity of Pentecost [PEN-tih-kost]. Before Jesus went up to his Father in heaven, he sent the Advocate, or the Holy Spirit, upon the Apostles. On Pentecost we are reminded to pay attention for the ways the Holy Spirit is guiding us, the Church, and all believers.

✛ All make the Sign of the Cross.

In the name of the Father, and of the Son, and of the Holy Spirit. Amen.

PSALM
(For a longer psalm, see page xv.)
Psalm 118:1–2, 4

The stone that the builders rejected
  has become the chief cornerstone.

**The stone that the builders rejected
  has become the chief cornerstone.**

O give thanks to the LORD, for he is good;
  his steadfast love endures forever!
Let Israel say,
  "His steadfast love endures forever."
Let those who fear the LORD say,
  "His steadfast love endures forever."

**The stone that the builders rejected
has become the chief cornerstone.**

◆ All stand and sing **Alleluia.**

GOSPEL
John 15:26abd–27; 16: 12 –15a

A reading from the holy Gospel according to John.

Jesus said to his disciples, "When the Advocate comes, whom I will send to you from the Father, he will testify on my behalf. You also are to testify because you have been with me from the beginning. I still have many things to say to you, but you cannot bear them now. When the Spirit of truth comes, he will guide you into all the truth; for he will not speak on his own, but will speak what he hears, and he will declare to you the things that are to come. He will glorify me, because he will take what is mine and declare it to you. All that the Father has is mine."

The Gospel of the Lord.

◆ All sit and observe silence.

FOR SILENT REFLECTION

Think about this silently in your heart. Pray to the Holy Spirit to guide and lead you.

CLOSING PRAYER

Let us pray to God for our needs and the needs of others: our family, neighborhood, and the world. For each need we say, "Lord, hear our prayer."

◆ All may add their own prayers here.

Let us pray: **Our Father . . . Amen.**

Spirit of God,
you gave the Apostles hope and comfort
and never left them alone.
Enter our hearts and guide us on our mission.
Help us speak the truth of Jesus.
Through Christ our Lord.

Amen.

✛ All make the Sign of the Cross.

ORDINARY TIME SUMMER

MONDAY, MAY 24 — FRIDAY, JUNE 25

SUMMER ORDINARY TIME

THE MEANING OF ORDINARY TIME

We just celebrated the great feasts of Easter and Pentecost and now move back to Ordinary Time—the ordered time when each week has a number. The Prayers for the Week will reflect the Sunday Gospels but during the week we will again "walk through the Bible."

On Pentecost, the Spirit descended upon Jesus' disciples, strengthening them with wisdom and courage. Passages from the Acts of the Apostles and the letters of St. Paul tell stories of the travels of Jesus' disciples to spread his teachings to love God and to love one another.

We will read several stories of Jesus' miracles. Jesus used two languages in his preaching: one was words, particularly the parables, and another was signs, particularly the miracles. Miracles consist of an observable action. But with Jesus' touch or presence something very unusual and unexpected happens: a stormy sea is calmed; hundreds of people are fed from just a few fish and a few loaves of bread; water becomes wine. Like the parables, the miracle stories contain more than what appears to us at first glance. As "signs," they carry a deeper meaning about the Kingdom of God—a time when there will be no suffering, hunger or death. The miracles are an announcement of hope—they are points of light that help us "see" what the Kingdom of God is like.

As we end this school year with the Twelfth Week in Ordinary Time, our focus is mission. The Scripture passages tell us that Jesus told his disciples to go out and proclaim the Kingdom of God and they did. As we prepare for summer vacation, it is a good time to remind ourselves that we are Christ's disciples and our mission is also to proclaim God's love through our words and our actions.

During these weeks of Ordinary Time, we celebrate the Solemnities of the Most Holy Trinity and the Most Sacred Heart of Jesus. A solemnity is a very high celebration in the Church calendar.

PREPARING TO CELEBRATE ORDINARY TIME IN THE CLASSROOM

This will be your last time changing the prayer table-cloth this year. Even if you haven't had a procession each time the cloth changes, try to have one now. As the school year winds down, it is good to bring the students' focus squarely on the prayer life of your classroom community. You may wish to invite the students to choose something to carry in the procession that helped their spiritual growth this year. Clear an area near the prayer table, spread it with a green cloth, and let the children place their objects there. As a final project, ask them to write a short essay or poem about the significance of the object they chose. Suggest that they illustrate their work. Invite them to share their writings aloud during one of your final prayer times together. (Some students might feel uncomfortable sharing private thoughts in front of a group. Don't force them to participate in this aspect of your celebration.) You might even consider collecting all the papers into a booklet, which you can photocopy for each student to keep as a memento of the year.

SACRED SPACE

Bring your potted plant back to the prayer table. You may want to discuss how it might be different from how it looked when you first placed it on the prayer table. Some plants, such as spider plants, send out shoots with new plants on them. If your spider plant is sufficiently mature, you may even have enough "spider babies" to clip and give to each of your students in a paper cup with a little soil in it. Or you may like to keep the table adorned with fresh flowers from a spring garden. Children love to bring flowers from their parents' or grandparents' gardens.

SACRED MUSIC

If you have been singing with your students all year, they will probably be quite comfortable with at least one or two of their favorite hymns. Consider scheduling a visit to one of the other classrooms to offer a small concert or sing-along (an older classroom could visit a younger grade; smaller children could sing for the "big kids"). If your students are particularly confident, you may even suggest that they volunteer to sing for an all-school Mass or end-of-the-year prayer service. If you invite parents to the class for one of your final sessions, don't be shy about including them in your prayer. And by all means, sing for them! Some songs that work well in this season are "Christ for the World We Sing," "Lord, I Want to Be a Christian," and "Spirit of the Living God."

MOVEMENT AND GESTURE

Children love to sing this song by David Haas and add movement.

PRAYER FOR PEACE

"Peace before us, peace behind us, peace under our feet. Peace within us, peace over us, let all around us be peace."

(You can repeat many times, changing out the word "Peace" for "Love," "Light," and "Christ.")

Movement: peace before us (extend arms in front body), peace behind us (extend arms behind body), peace under our feet (bend down and extend arms toward feet), peace within us (stand up and fold hands over heart), peace over us (extend arms over head and open them), let all around us be peace (extend arms in a semicircle in front of body). Repeat movement with each stanza.

PRAYERS FOR ORDINARY TIME

There are only a few precious places in the Gospel where we have the chance to listen to Jesus as he prays to his Father in heaven. In these moments, we can see clearly what it is Jesus wants for the world. The following prayer, taken from the Gospel according to John, shows how much Jesus wants us to abide in his love and to live with each other in the love and peace shared by the Father, Son, and Holy Spirit.

"As you, Father, are in me and I am in you, may my followers also be in us, so that the world may believe that you have sent me. The glory that you have given me I have given them, so that they may be one, as we are one, I in them and you in me, that they may become completely one, so that the world may know that you have sent me and have loved them even as you have loved me" (John 17:21b–23).

A NOTE TO CATECHISTS

You may wish to write the names of your students into your personal calendar during the summer months, so that you will remember to pray for them even when your group is no longer meeting. Prayer is the most useful and effective way we have to be of service to those about whom we care.

GRACE BEFORE MEALS
ORDINARY TIME • SUMMER

LEADER:
O give thanks to the Lord, for he is good;

ALL: for his steadfast love endures forever.

✝ All make the Sign of the Cross.

In the name of the Father, and of the Son, and of the Holy Spirit. Amen.

LEADER:
God of abundance,
your grace fills the hearts of
all those who call you Lord,
and even those who may not
know you yet.
Thank you for the gift of this meal
and the nourishment it will provide.
We are grateful for this time to
share it with each other.
May we work together to fill the plates
of those in our community and around the
world who may experience
extreme hunger or thirst today.
We ask this through Christ our Lord.

ALL: Amen.

✝ All make the Sign of the Cross.

In the name of the Father, and of the Son, and of the Holy Spirit. Amen.

PRAYER AT DAY'S END

ORDINARY TIME • SUMMER

LEADER:

See what love the Father has given us,

ALL: that we should be called children of God.

✝ All make the Sign of the Cross.

In the name of the Father, and of the Son, and of the Holy Spirit. Amen.

LEADER:

Almighty Father,
you created us in your image
of goodness and light.
Grant that we may offer you
all that we are in thanksgiving,
here at the end of our school day,
and this night, when we close our eyes
for restful sleep.
May the peace of Christ remain with us
now and forever.
We ask this in Christ's name.

ALL: Amen.

✝ All make the Sign of the Cross.

In the name of the Father, and of the Son, and of the Holy Spirit. Amen.

PRAYER FOR
MONDAY, MAY 24, 2021

OPENING

Pentecost [PEN-tih-kost] reminds us to pay close attention to how the Holy Spirit is working in our lives, the Church, and the world. The Holy Spirit is always present and empowers us to go out and spread the Gospel.

✝ All make the Sign of the Cross.

In the name of the Father, and of the Son, and of the Holy Spirit. Amen.

PSALM
(For a longer psalm, see page xv.)
Psalm 85:8–9

The LORD speaks of peace to his people.

The LORD speaks of peace to his people.

Let me hear what God the LORD will speak,
   for he will speak peace to his people,
      to his faithful, to those who turn to him in
         their hearts.
Surely his salvation is at hand for those who
         fear him,
   that his glory may dwell in our land.

The LORD speaks of peace to his people.

READING
Acts 2:1–6a, 7–8, 11b–12

A reading from the Acts of the Apostles.

When the day of Pentecost had come, they were all together in one place. And suddenly from heaven there came a sound like the rush of a violent wind, and it filled the entire house where they were sitting. Divided tongues, as of fire, appeared among them, and a tongue rested on each of them. All of them were filled with the Holy Spirit and began to speak in other languages, as the Spirit gave them ability.

Now there were devout Jews from every nation under heaven living in Jerusalem. And at this sound the crowd gathered. Amazed and astonished, they asked, "Are not all these who are speaking Galileans [gal-ih-LEE-uhnz]? And how is it that we hear, each of us, in our own native language? In our own languages we hear them speaking about God's deeds of power." All were amazed and perplexed, saying to one another, "What does this mean?"

The Word of the Lord.

◆ All observe silence.

FOR SILENT REFLECTION

Think about this silently in your heart. How does the Holy Spirit inspire you?

CLOSING PRAYER

Let us pray to God for our needs and the needs of others: our family, neighborhood, and the world. For each need we say, "Lord, hear our prayer."

◆ All may add their own prayers here.

Let us pray: **Our Father . . . Amen.**

O Holy Spirit, fill us with your love
and courage.
Inspire us as you have inspired
generations of disciples.
In Christ's name we pray.

Amen.

✝ All make the Sign of the Cross.

OPENING

Today are the memorials of St. Bede the Venerable (672–735) and St. Mary Magdalene de' Pazzi (1566–1607). St. Bede is credited for writing the Glory Be. By the Holy Spirit, St. Mary Magdalene was gifted with the ability to elevate her spirit in union with God. Today we hear how the Apostles give the gift of healing to a lame man.

✚ All make the Sign of the Cross.

In the name of the Father, and of the Son, and of the Holy Spirit. Amen.

PSALM

(For a longer psalm, see page xv.)
Psalm 85:8–9

The Lord speaks of peace to his people.

The Lord speaks of peace to his people.

Let me hear what God the Lord will speak,
    for he will speak peace to his people,
    to his faithful, to those who turn to him in
        their hearts.
Surely his salvation is at hand for those who
        fear him,
    that his glory may dwell in our land.

The Lord speaks of peace to his people.

READING

Acts 3:1–2a, 3, 6–9, 10b

A reading from the Acts of the Apostles.

One day Peter and John were going up to the temple at the hour of prayer, at three o'clock in the afternoon. And a man lame from birth was being carried in. When he saw Peter and John about to go into the temple, he asked them for alms. But Peter said, "I have no silver or gold, but what I have I give you; in the name of Jesus Christ of Nazareth, stand up and walk." And he took him by the right hand and raised him up; and immediately his feet and ankles were made strong. Jumping up, he stood and began to walk, and he entered the temple with them, walking and leaping and praising God. All the people saw him walking and praising God, and they were filled with wonder and amazement at what had happened to him.

The Word of the Lord.

◆ All observe silence.

FOR SILENT REFLECTION

Think about this silently in your heart. Can you imagine witnessing a miracle?

CLOSING PRAYER

Let us pray to God for our needs and the needs of others: our family, neighborhood, and the world. For each need we say, "Lord, hear our prayer."

◆ All may add their own prayers here.

Let us pray: **Our Father . . . Amen.**

Loving God,
we thank you for the gift of faith
that helps us believe in your many
marvelous deeds.
May we always be open to all your wonders
that surround us.
In Christ's name, we pray.

Amen.

✚ All make the Sign of the Cross.

PRAYER FOR
WEDNESDAY, MAY 26, 2021

OPENING

In today's reading, St. Paul teaches the members of the new Christian communities about the Holy Spirit of God. He is trying to reassure and encourage the early Christians who were being persecuted by the Romans. Today is the feast day of St. Philip Neri (1515–1595). St. Philip was an Italian priest who was well known for his love of music, singing, and humor.

✢ All make the Sign of the Cross.

In the name of the Father, and of the Son, and of the Holy Spirit. Amen.

PSALM

(For a longer psalm, see page xv.)

Psalm 85:8–9

The LORD speaks of peace to his people.

The LORD speaks of peace to his people.

Let me hear what God the LORD will speak,
> for he will speak peace to his people,
> > to his faithful, to those who turn to him in their hearts.
Surely his salvation is at hand for those who fear him,
> that his glory may dwell in our land.

The LORD speaks of peace to his people.

READING

Romans 8:14, 15b–17, 26–27

A reading from the Letter of Paul to the Romans.

For all who are led by the Spirit of God are children of God. You have received a spirit of adoption. When we cry, "Abba! Father!" it is that very Spirit bearing witness with our spirit that we are children of God, and if children, then heirs, heirs of God and joint heirs with Christ—if, in fact, we suffer with him so that we may also be glorified with him. Likewise the Spirit helps us in our weakness; for we do not know how to pray as we ought, but that very Spirit intercedes with sighs too deep for words. And God, who searches the heart, knows what is the mind of the Spirit, because the Spirit intercedes for the saints according to the will of God.

The Word of the Lord.

◆ All observe silence.

FOR SILENT REFLECTION

Think about this silently in your heart. Ask the Holy Spirit for help and guidance when you are in need.

CLOSING PRAYER

Let us pray to God for our needs and the needs of others: our family, neighborhood, and the world. For each need we say, "Lord, hear our prayer."

◆ All may add their own prayers here.

Let us pray: **Our Father . . . Amen.**

Holy Spirit of God,
lead us and help us in our weakness.
Grant us courage and strength when we are in need.
We ask this through Christ our Lord.

Amen.

✢ All make the Sign of the Cross.

OPENING

St. Paul teaches that love—genuine love of our neighbor—is how we follow and fulfill Jesus' work and commandments. Today is the feast day of St. Augustine (c. early sixth century). He was a monk who became the first Archbishop of Canterbury, England.

✛ All make the Sign of the Cross.

> **In the name of the Father, and of the Son, and of the Holy Spirit. Amen.**

PSALM
(For a longer psalm, see page xv.)
Psalm 85:8–9

The Lord speaks of peace to his people.

The Lord speaks of peace to his people.

Let me hear what God the Lord will speak,
   for he will speak peace to his people,
   to his faithful, to those who turn to him in
      their hearts.
Surely his salvation is at hand for those who
      fear him,
   that his glory may dwell in our land.

The Lord speaks of peace to his people.

READING
Romans 12:9–10; 13:8–10

A reading from the Letter of Paul to the Romans.

Let love be genuine; hate what is evil, hold fast to what is good; love one another with mutual affection; outdo one another in showing honor. Owe no one anything, except to love one another; for the one who loves another has fulfilled the law. The commandments, "You shall not commit adultery; You shall not mur-der; You shall not steal; You shall not covet"; and any other commandment, are summed up in this word, "Love your neighbor as yourself." Love does no wrong to a neighbor; therefore, love is the fulfilling of the law.

The Word of the Lord.

◆ All observe silence.

FOR SILENT REFLECTION

Think about this silently in your heart. Why is loving your neighbor as yourself so central to Jesus' message?

CLOSING PRAYER

Let us pray to God for our needs and the needs of others: our family, neighborhood, and the world. For each need we say, "Lord, hear our prayer."

◆ All may add their own prayers here.

Let us pray: **Our Father . . . Amen.**

God of love,
help us to love our neighbors, our enemies,
and strangers as much as ourselves, our
friends, and our family.
Help us to love others as you have loved us.
We pray in the name of Jesus Christ, our Lord.

Amen.

✛ All make the Sign of the Cross.

PRAYER FOR
FRIDAY, MAY 28, 2021

OPENING

Today's reading is from St. Paul to the early Christian communities in Galatia. Paul shares with them the nine fruits, or gifts, of the Holy Spirit and reminds them to let themselves be guided by the Spirit.

✚ All make the Sign of the Cross.

In the name of the Father, and of the Son, and of the Holy Spirit. Amen.

PSALM

(For a longer psalm, see page xv.)
Psalm 85:8–9

The LORD speaks of peace to his people.

The LORD speaks of peace to his people.

Let me hear what God the LORD will speak,
  for he will speak peace to his people,
  to his faithful, to those who turn to him in
    their hearts.
Surely his salvation is at hand for those who
    fear him,
  that his glory may dwell in our land.

The LORD speaks of peace to his people.

READING

Galatians 5:13–14, 22–23b, 25–26

A reading from the Letter of Paul to the Galatians [guh-LAY-shuhnz].

For you were called to freedom, brothers and sisters; only do not use your freedom as an opportunity for self-indulgence, but through love become slaves to one another. For the whole law is summed up in a single commandment, "You shall love your neighbor as yourself." The fruit of the Spirit is love, joy, peace, patience, kindness, generosity, faithfulness, gentleness, and self-control. If we live by the Spirit, let us also be guided by the Spirit. Let us not be conceited, competing against one another, envying one another.

The Word of the Lord.

◆ All observe silence.

FOR SILENT REFLECTION

Think about this silently in your heart. Which fruits of the Holy Spirit do you have? Which fruits do you need?

CLOSING PRAYER

Let us pray to God for our needs and the needs of others: our family, neighborhood, and the world. For each need we say, "Lord, hear our prayer."

◆ All may add their own prayers here.

Let us pray: **Our Father . . . Amen.**

Spirit of God,
fill our hearts with love for our neighbor.
Grant us love, joy, peace, patience, kindness, generosity, faithfulness, gentleness,
and self-control.
We ask this in Christ's name.

Amen.

✚ All make the Sign of the Cross.

PRAYER FOR THE WEEK

OPENING

Today we celebrate the solemnity of the Most Holy Trinity. God is three Persons: the Father, Son, and Holy Spirit. We believe in God, our Creator and Father. Jesus is our Redeemer and Son of God. The Holy Spirit is our Advocate who guides us. In today's Gospel, Jesus tells his disciples to baptize in the names of the Holy Trinity.

✚ All make the Sign of the Cross.

In the name of the Father, and of the Son, and of the Holy Spirit. Amen.

PSALM

(For a longer psalm, see page xv.)
Psalm 85:8–9

The LORD speaks of peace to his people.

The LORD speaks of peace to his people.

Let me hear what God the LORD will speak,
for he will speak peace to his people,
to his faithful, to those who turn to him in
their hearts.
Surely his salvation is at hand for those who
fear him,
that his glory may dwell in our land.

The LORD speaks of peace to his people.

◆ All stand and sing **Alleluia.**

GOSPEL

Matthew 28:16–20

A reading from the holy Gospel according to Matthew.

Now the eleven disciples went to Galilee [GAL-ih-lee], to the mountain to which Jesus had directed them. When they saw him, they worshiped him; but some doubted. And Jesus came and said to them, "All authority in heaven and on earth has been given to me. Go therefore and make disciples of all nations, baptizing them in the name of the Father and of the Son and of the Holy Spirit, and teaching them to obey everything that I have commanded you. And remember, I am with you always, to the end of the age."

The Gospel of the Lord.

◆ All sit and observe silence.

FOR SILENT REFLECTION

Think about this silently in your heart. Jesus tells us that he is with us "always, to the end of the age." How does that make you feel?

CLOSING PRAYER

Let us pray to God for our needs and the needs of others: our family, neighborhood, and the world. For each need we say, "Lord, hear our prayer."

◆ All may add their own prayers here.

Let us pray: **Our Father . . . Amen.**

Everlasting God,
you are loving Father,
Holy Redeemer,
Spirit of Life,
Most Blessed Trinity;
be with us always.
Through Christ our Lord.

Amen.

✚ All make the Sign of the Cross.

OPENING

We celebrate the feast day of the Blessed Virgin Mary. The Visitation occurred when newly pregnant Mary visited her cousin Elizabeth, who was pregnant with her baby John (the Baptist). When Elizabeth met Mary, the baby John leapt with joy within her at the presence of the baby Jesus. Pentecost marked the end of Easter Time. We are now back in Ordinary Time and will hear stories of God's friendship with humankind.

◆ All make the Sign of the Cross.

In the name of the Father, and of the Son, and of the Holy Spirit. Amen.

PSALM
(For a longer psalm, see page xv.)
Psalm 85:8–9

The LORD speaks of peace to his people.

The LORD speaks of peace to his people.

Let me hear what God the LORD will speak,
for he will speak peace to his people,
to his faithful, to those who turn to him in
their hearts.
Surely his salvation is at hand for those who
fear him,
that his glory may dwell in our land.

The LORD speaks of peace to his people.

READING
Exodus 33:7a, 9–11b

A reading from the Book of Exodus.

Now Moses used to take the tent and pitch it outside the camp, far off from the camp; he called it the tent of meeting. When Moses entered the tent, the pillar of cloud would descend and stand at the entrance of the tent, and the LORD would speak with Moses. When all the people saw the pillar of cloud standing at the entrance of the tent, all the people would rise and bow down, all of them, at the entrance of the tent. Thus the LORD used to speak to Moses face to face, as one speaks to a friend.

The Word of the Lord.

◆ All observe silence.

FOR SILENT REFLECTION

Think about this silently in your heart. God talked to Moses face-to-face, as a friend. Do you talk to God as a friend as well?

CLOSING PRAYER

Let us pray to God for our needs and the needs of others: our family, neighborhood, and the world. For each need we say, "Lord, hear our prayer."

◆ All may add their own prayers here.

Let us pray: **Our Father . . . Amen.**

God our friend,
you are patient and kind.
Help us grow in relationship with you,
so that others may come to know you
as a friend too.
We ask this in Christ Jesus' name.

Amen.

✦ All make the Sign of the Cross.

OPENING

Wisdom is the ability to discern what is true, right, or lasting. The spirit of wisdom is not simply knowledge of the world or God but knowing that God is at work in the world. We hear that wisdom is valued above all things. It is the source of all good and godly people. The author personifies wisdom as a woman. St. Justin, whose feast day is today, relied on the spirit of wisdom to become the first Christian philosopher.

✚ All make the Sign of the Cross.

In the name of the Father, and of the Son, and of the Holy Spirit. Amen.

PSALM

(For a longer psalm, see page xv.)
Psalm 85:8–9

The LORD speaks of peace to his people.

The LORD speaks of peace to his people.

Let me hear what God the LORD will speak,
for he will speak peace to his people,
to his faithful, to those who turn to him in
their hearts.
Surely his salvation is at hand for those who
fear him,
that his glory may dwell in our land.

The LORD speaks of peace to his people.

READING
Wisdom 7:7–9b, 10, 27de

A reading from the Book of Wisdom.

Therefore I prayed, and understanding was given me; I called on God, and the spirit of wisdom came to me. I preferred her to scepters and thrones, and I accounted wealth as noth-ing in comparison with her. Neither did I liken to her any priceless gem, because all gold is but a little sand in her sight. I loved her more than health and beauty, and I chose to have her rather than light because her radiance never ceases. She renews all things; in every generation she passes into holy souls and makes them friends of God, and prophets.

The Word of the Lord.

◆ All observe silence.

FOR SILENT REFLECTION

Think about this silently in your heart. How does the spirit of wisdom make you a friend of God?

CLOSING PRAYER

Let us pray to God for our needs and the needs of others: our family, neighborhood, and the world. For each need we say, "Lord, hear our prayer."

◆ All may add their own prayers here.

Let us pray: **Our Father . . . Amen.**

O God,
may the Spirit guide us to the understanding that you are our source of life and love.
Allow us to become better friends with you and with one another.
We ask this in the name of Jesus Christ, your Son, our Lord.

Amen.

✚ All make the Sign of the Cross.

PRAYER FOR
WEDNESDAY, JUNE 2, 2021

OPENING

What is a true friend? By their loyalty, true friends help us become better people. We can share our hopes, happiness, and problems with them, and sometimes we may disagree with them. We can depend on true friends, and if we get sick or in trouble, they are there for us. Even though Jesus is the Son of God and the Messiah, Jesus lived a fully human life. He had friends whom he loved, and he felt both joy and sorrow.

✚ All make the Sign of the Cross.

In the name of the Father, and of the Son, and of the Holy Spirit. Amen.

PSALM

(For a longer psalm, see page xv.)
Psalm 85:8–9

The Lord speaks of peace to his people.

The Lord speaks of peace to his people.

Let me hear what God the Lord will speak,
   for he will speak peace to his people,
   to his faithful, to those who turn to him in
      their hearts.
Surely his salvation is at hand for those who
      fear him,
   that his glory may dwell in our land.

The Lord speaks of peace to his people.

◆ All stand and sing **Alleluia.**

GOSPEL

John 11:1, 3–4b, 11b, 17, 32, 34–36

A reading from the holy Gospel according to John.

Now a certain man was ill, Lazarus of Bethany, the village of Mary and her sister Martha. So the sisters sent a message to Jesus, "Lord, he whom you love is ill." But when Jesus heard it, he said, "This illness does not lead to death. Our friend Lazarus has fallen asleep, but I am going there to awaken him." When Jesus arrived, he found that Lazarus had already been in the tomb for four days. When Mary came where Jesus was and saw him, she knelt at his feet and said to him, "Lord, if you had been here, my brother would not have died." He said, "Where have you laid him?" They said to him, "Lord, come and see." Jesus began to weep. So, the Jews said, "See how he loved him!"

The Gospel of the Lord.

◆ All sit and observe silence.

FOR SILENT REFLECTION

Think about this silently in your heart. What must it feel like to be a friend of Jesus?

CLOSING PRAYER

Let us pray to God for our needs and the needs of others: our family, neighborhood, and the world. For each need we say, "Lord, hear our prayer."

◆ All may add their own prayers here.

Let us pray: **Our Father . . . Amen.**

May we have friends with whom we can share in one another's joys and sorrows, O God.
May we love one another as Jesus has loved us. We ask this in his name.

Amen.

✚ All make the Sign of the Cross.

OPENING

Today is the memorial for St. Charles Lwanga and friends. St. Charles lived in the Kingdom of Buganda, which is in part of Uganda today. He and many other Christian converts were martyred for refusing to give up their new faith. In today's Gospel reading, Jesus shares with his disciples the importance of love and friendship.

✦ All make the Sign of the Cross.

In the name of the Father, and of the Son, and of the Holy Spirit. Amen.

PSALM

(For a longer psalm, see page xv.)
Psalm 85:8–9

The Lord speaks of peace to his people.

The Lord speaks of peace to his people.

Let me hear what God the Lord will speak,
　for he will speak peace to his people,
　to his faithful, to those who turn to him in
　　their hearts.
Surely his salvation is at hand for those who
　　fear him,
　that his glory may dwell in our land.

The Lord speaks of peace to his people.

✦ All stand and sing **Alleluia.**

GOSPEL

John 15:12–15, 17

A reading from the holy Gospel according to John.

Jesus said, "This is my commandment, that you love one another as I have loved you. No one has greater love than this, to lay down one's life for one's friends. You are my friends if you do what I command you. I do not call you servants any longer, because the servant does not know what the master is doing; but I have called you friends, because I have made known to you everything that I have heard from my Father. I am giving you these commands so that you may love one another."

The Gospel of the Lord.

✦ All sit and observe silence.

FOR SILENT REFLECTION

Think about this silently in your heart. How can you be friends with Jesus?

CLOSING PRAYER

Let us pray to God for our needs and the needs of others: our family, neighborhood, and the world. For each need we say, "Lord, hear our prayer."

✦ All may add their own prayers here.

Let us pray: **Our Father . . . Amen.**

O God,
we thank you for the gift of your Son, who loves and cares for us.
May we make friends with those we meet and love them as Jesus would.
As St. Charles and his friends laid down their lives for you,
may we always be faithful to you.
Through Christ our Lord.

Amen.

✦ All make the Sign of the Cross.

PRAYER FOR
FRIDAY, JUNE 4, 2021

OPENING

This week we have heard how Jesus loves us and is our friend. Today we hear how the early Christians were called friends. We are all called to be friends in Jesus.

✢ All make the Sign of the Cross.

In the name of the Father, and of the Son, and of the Holy Spirit. Amen.

PSALM

(For a longer psalm, see page xv.)

Psalm 85:8–9

The LORD speaks of peace to his people.

The LORD speaks of peace to his people.

Let me hear what God the LORD will speak,
　　for he will speak peace to his people,
　　to his faithful, to those who turn to him in
　　　　their hearts.
Surely his salvation is at hand for those who
　　fear him,
　　that his glory may dwell in our land.

The LORD speaks of peace to his people.

READING

3 John 1:1–6a

A reading from the Third Letter of John.

The elder to the beloved Gaius, whom I love in truth. Beloved, I pray that all may go well with you and that you may be in good health, just as it is well with your soul. I was overjoyed when some of the friends arrived and testified to your faithfulness to the truth, namely how you walk in the truth. I have no greater joy than this, to hear that my children are walking in the truth. Beloved, you do faithfully whatever you do for the friends, even though they are strangers to you; they have testified to your love before the church.

The Word of the Lord.

◆ All observe silence.

FOR SILENT REFLECTION

Think about this silently in your heart. How can you share your love for a friend?

CLOSING PRAYER

Let us pray to God for our needs and the needs of others: our family, neighborhood, and the world. For each need we say, "Lord, hear our prayer."

◆ All may add their own prayers here.

Let us pray: **Our Father . . . Amen.**

Holy and loving God,
may we all be sisters and brothers,
neighbors and friends,
through your Son Jesus,
in whose name we pray.

Amen.

✢ All make the Sign of the Cross.

PRAYER FOR THE WEEK
WITH A READING FROM THE GOSPEL FOR **SUNDAY, JUNE 6, 2021**

OPENING

Today is the solemnity of the Body and Blood of Christ. We hear today that Jesus gives us the gift of the Eucharist. During the Passover meal that he shared with his disciples during the Last Supper, Jesus offered his disciples his Body and his Blood. In giving us his Body and Blood, Christ offers us the gift of life. We celebrate that gift at Mass when we receive Holy Communion.

✚ All make the Sign of the Cross.

> **In the name of the Father, and of the Son, and of the Holy Spirit. Amen.**

PSALM

(For a longer psalm, see page xv.)
Psalm 85:8–9

The LORD speaks of peace to his people.

The LORD speaks of peace to his people.

Let me hear what God the LORD will speak,
　for he will speak peace to his people,
　　to his faithful, to those who turn to him in
　　　their hearts.
Surely his salvation is at hand for those who
　　fear him,
　　that his glory may dwell in our land.

The LORD speaks of peace to his people.

◆ All stand and sing **Alleluia.**

GOSPEL

Mark 14:12a, 16c, 22–26

A reading from the holy Gospel according to Mark.

On the first day of Unleavened Bread, when the Passover lamb is sacrificed, Jesus' disciples prepared the Passover meal. While they were eating, he took a loaf of bread, and after blessing it he broke it, gave it to them, and said, "Take; this is my body." Then he took a cup, and after giving thanks he gave it to them, and all of them drank from it. He said to them, "This is my blood of the covenant, which is poured out for many. Truly I tell you, I will never again drink of the fruit of the vine until that day when I drink it new in the kingdom of God." When they had sung the hymn, they went out to the Mount of Olives.

The Gospel of the Lord.

◆ All sit and observe silence.

FOR SILENT REFLECTION

Think about this silently in your heart. Each time we partake of the Body and Blood of Christ, we allow Christ to fill and transform our lives.

CLOSING PRAYER

Let us pray to God for our needs and the needs of others: our family, neighborhood, and the world. For each need we say, "Lord, hear our prayer."

◆ All may add their own prayers here.

Let us pray: **Our Father . . . Amen.**

We pray, O God,
that the gift of the Body and Blood of Christ
will strengthen us to do your will.
We pray in the name of Jesus Christ,
your Son and our Lord.

Amen.

✚ All make the Sign of the Cross.

PRAYER FOR
MONDAY, JUNE 7, 2021

OPENING

This week we will hear stories of miracles in the Bible. Today we will hear miracles from the Old Testament. The Scripture passage today refers to the miraculous way God brought the Hebrew people out of slavery in Egypt.

✚ All make the Sign of the Cross.

In the name of the Father, and of the Son, and of the Holy Spirit. Amen.

PSALM

(For a longer psalm, see page xv.)
Psalm 85:8–9

The LORD speaks of peace to his people.

The LORD speaks of peace to his people.

Let me hear what God the LORD will speak,
  for he will speak peace to his people,
    to his faithful, to those who turn to him in
      their hearts.
Surely his salvation is at hand for those who
    fear him,
  that his glory may dwell in our land.

The LORD speaks of peace to his people.

READING

Deuteronomy 6:1ac,
3a-c, 20–21, 24a, 24cd

A reading from the Book of Deuteronomy.

This is the commandment that the LORD your God charged me to teach you to observe in the land that you are about to cross into and occupy. Hear therefore, O Israel, and observe them diligently, so that it may go well with you, and so that you may multiply greatly in a land flowing with milk and honey. When your children ask you in time to come, "What is the meaning of the decrees and the statutes and the ordinances that the LORD our God has commanded you?" then you shall say to your children, "We were Pharaoh's [FAYR-oh] slaves in Egypt, but the LORD brought us out of Egypt with a mighty hand. Then the LORD commanded us to observe all these statutes for our lasting good, so as to keep us alive, as is now the case."

The Word of the Lord.

◆ All observe silence.

FOR SILENT REFLECTION

Think about this silently in your heart. How would you know if something was a miracle from God?

CLOSING PRAYER

Let us pray to God for our needs and the needs of others: our family, neighborhood, and the world. For each need we say, "Lord, hear our prayer."

◆ All may add their own prayers here.

Let us pray: **Our Father . . . Amen.**

Almighty God,
throughout history, you have brought freedom to your people.
By our faith in you, let us be free from the slavery of sin.
May we observe your commandments faithfully.
We ask this through Christ our Lord.

Amen.

✚ All make the Sign of the Cross.

OPENING

In today's Gospel, we hear of a great storm that arises while Jesus and his disciples were in a boat. The disciples were afraid. Listen carefully to what Jesus tells the wind and what he asks his disciples.

✦ All make the Sign of the Cross.

In the name of the Father, and of the Son, and of the Holy Spirit. Amen.

PSALM

(For a longer psalm, see page xv.)
Psalm 85:8–9

The LORD speaks of peace to his people.

The LORD speaks of peace to his people.

Let me hear what God the LORD will speak,
for he will speak peace to his people,
to his faithful, to those who turn to him in their hearts.
Surely his salvation is at hand for those who fear him,
that his glory may dwell in our land.

The LORD speaks of peace to his people.

✦ All stand and sing **Alleluia.**

GOSPEL

Mark 4:35b–36a, 37–41

A reading from the holy Gospel according to Mark.

When evening had come, Jesus said to them, "Let us go across to the other side." And leaving the crowd behind, they took him with them in the boat. A great windstorm arose, and the waves beat into the boat, so that the boat was already being swamped. But Jesus was in the stern, asleep on the cushion; and they woke him up and said to him, "Teacher, do you not care that we are perishing?" He woke up and rebuked the wind, and said to the sea, "Peace! Be still!" Then the wind ceased, and there was a dead calm. He said to them, "Why are you afraid? Have you still no faith?" And they were filled with great awe and said to one another, "Who then is this, that even the wind and the sea obey him?"

The Gospel of the Lord.

◆ All sit and observe silence.

FOR SILENT REFLECTION

Think about this silently in your heart. Why did Jesus use this moment to perform a miracle?

CLOSING PRAYER

Let us pray to God for our needs and the needs of others: our family, neighborhood, and the world. For each need we say, "Lord, hear our prayer."

◆ All may add their own prayers here.

Let us pray: **Our Father . . . Amen.**

Christ our Lord,
sometimes we feel small and afraid.
You are our comfort and our refuge.
Grant us peace.
You live and reign with God the Father,
in the unity of the Holy Spirit,
one God, for ever and ever.

Amen.

✦ All make the Sign of the Cross.

PRAYER FOR
WEDNESDAY, JUNE 9, 2021

OPENING

In today's Gospel, Jesus walks on water. He reassures the disciples not to be afraid.

✦ All make the Sign of the Cross.

In the name of the Father, and of the Son, and of the Holy Spirit. Amen.

PSALM

(For a longer psalm, see page xv.)
Psalm 85:8–9

The Lord speaks of peace to his people.

The Lord speaks of peace to his people.

Let me hear what God the Lord will speak,
  for he will speak peace to his people,
    to his faithful, to those who turn to him in
      their hearts.
Surely his salvation is at hand for those who
    fear him,
  that his glory may dwell in our land.

The Lord speaks of peace to his people.

◆ All stand and sing **Alleluia.**

GOSPEL

Mark 6:45–51

A reading from the holy Gospel according to Mark.

Jesus made his disciples get into the boat and go on ahead to the other side, to Bethsaida [beth-SAY-uh-duh], while he dismissed the crowd. After saying farewell to them, he went up on the mountain to pray. When evening came, the boat was out on the sea, and he was alone on the land. When he saw that they were straining at the oars against an adverse wind, he came towards them early in the morning, walking on the sea. He intended to pass them by. But when they saw him walking on the sea, they thought it was a ghost and cried out; for they all saw him and were terrified. But immediately he spoke to them and said, "Take heart, it is I; do not be afraid." Then he got into the boat with them and the wind ceased. And they were utterly astounded.

The Gospel of the Lord.

◆ All sit and observe silence.

FOR SILENT REFLECTION

Think about this silently in your heart. Imagine Jesus telling you "Take heart, it is I; do not be afraid."

CLOSING PRAYER

Let us pray to God for our needs and the needs of others: our family, neighborhood, and the world. For each need we say, "Lord, hear our prayer."

◆ All may add their own prayers here.

Let us pray: **Our Father . . . Amen.**

Almighty God,
help us to trust and have faith in you,
so that we may have the courage to face
any storm.
Grant us peace.
Through Christ our Lord.

Amen.

✦ All make the Sign of the Cross.

OPENING

Jesus gave his disciples the gift of the Holy Spirit at Pentecost to help them as they proclaimed the Good News to many lands. Jesus gave them the authority to perform miracles and to cast out unclean spirits. Philip was one of the Apostles who spread Jesus' teachings.

✦ All make the Sign of the Cross.

> **In the name of the Father, and of the Son, and of the Holy Spirit. Amen.**

PSALM

(For a longer psalm, see page xv.)
Psalm 85:8–9

The LORD speaks of peace to his people.

The LORD speaks of peace to his people.

Let me hear what God the LORD will speak,
    for he will speak peace to his people,
      to his faithful, to those who turn to him in
        their hearts.
Surely his salvation is at hand for those who
      fear him,
    that his glory may dwell in our land.

The LORD speaks of peace to his people.

READING

Acts 8:5–6, 9, 12–13

A reading from the Acts of the Apostles.

Philip went down to the city of Samaria [suh-MAYR-ee-uh] and proclaimed the Messiah [meh-SĪ-uh] to them. The crowds with one accord listened eagerly to what was said by Philip, hearing and seeing the signs that he did. Now a certain man named Simon had previously practiced magic in the city and amazed the people of Samaria, saying that he was someone great. But when they believed Philip, who was proclaiming the good news about the kingdom of God and the name of Jesus Christ, they were baptized, both men and women. Even Simon himself believed. After being baptized, he stayed constantly with Philip and was amazed when he saw the signs and great miracles that took place.

The Word of the Lord.

✦ All observe silence.

FOR SILENT REFLECTION

Think about this silently in your heart. Although you may be young, your presence and friendship can be healing for others.

CLOSING PRAYER

Let us pray to God for our needs and the needs of others: our family, neighborhood, and the world. For each need we say, "Lord, hear our prayer."

✦ All may add their own prayers here.

Let us pray: **Our Father . . . Amen.**

Dear God,
we know you have many disciples who
spread your teachings to the world.
Help us be like those disciples and
to be compassionate to those that we meet.
We ask this in Christ Jesus' name.

Amen.

✦ All make the Sign of the Cross.

OPENING

Jesus cures a boy from unclean spirits. The disciples were confused as to why they could not cure him. Listen closely to what Jesus says. Today is also the feast day of St. Barnabas, who worked alongside St. Paul to proclaim the Good News to the Gentiles, or non-Jewish people.

✛ All make the Sign of the Cross.

In the name of the Father, and of the Son, and of the Holy Spirit. Amen.

PSALM

(For a longer psalm, see page xv.)
Psalm 85:8–9

The Lord speaks of peace to his people.

The Lord speaks of peace to his people.

Let me hear what God the Lord will speak,
   for he will speak peace to his people,
   to his faithful, to those who turn to him in
      their hearts.
Surely his salvation is at hand for those who
      fear him,
   that his glory may dwell in our land.

The Lord speaks of peace to his people.

◆ All stand and sing **Alleluia.**

GOSPEL

Matthew 17:14–16, 17c–21

A reading from the holy Gospel according to Matthew.

When they came to the crowd, a man came to him, knelt before him, and said, "Lord, have mercy on my son, for he is an epileptic and he suffers terribly; he often falls into the fire and often into the water. And I brought him to your disciples, but they could not cure him." Jesus answered, "Bring him here to me." And Jesus rebuked the demon, and it came out of him, and the boy was cured instantly. Then the disciples came to Jesus privately and said, "Why could we not cast it out?" He said to them, "Because of your little faith. For truly I tell you, if you have faith the size of a mustard seed, you will say to this mountain, 'Move from here to there', and it will move; and nothing will be impossible for you."

The Gospel of the Lord.

◆ All sit and observe silence.

FOR SILENT REFLECTION

Think about this silently in your heart. Today is the also feast day of the Sacred Heart of Jesus, whose heart overflows with tender, compassionate love. Reflect on Jesus' love for all of creation,

CLOSING PRAYER

Let us pray to God for our needs and the needs of others: our family, neighborhood, and the world. For each need we say, "Lord, hear our prayer."

◆ All may add their own prayers here.

Let us pray: **Our Father . . . Amen.**

May we have enough faith, O God,
to build your Kingdom here on earth.
Through Christ our Lord.

Amen.

✛ All make the Sign of the Cross.

PRAYER FOR THE WEEK

WITH A READING FROM THE GOSPEL FOR **SUNDAY, JUNE 13, 2021**

OPENING

Jesus often used imagery from everyday life to teach about the Kingdom of God. Many of his followers were farmers and could understand how the smallest of seeds could grow into a magnificent creation.

✛ All make the Sign of the Cross.

In the name of the Father, and of the Son, and of the Holy Spirit. Amen.

PSALM

(For a longer psalm, see page xv.)
Psalm 85:8–9

The LORD speaks of peace to his people.

The LORD speaks of peace to his people.

Let me hear what God the LORD will speak,
for he will speak peace to his people,
to his faithful, to those who turn to him in their hearts.
Surely his salvation is at hand for those who fear him,
that his glory may dwell in our land.

The LORD speaks of peace to his people.

◆ All stand and sing **Alleluia.**

GOSPEL

Mark 4:26–32

A reading from the holy Gospel according to Mark.

Jesus said, "The kingdom of God is as if someone would scatter seed on the ground, and would sleep and rise night and day, and the seed would sprout and grow, he does not know how. The earth produces of itself, first the stalk, then the head, then the full grain in the head. But when the grain is ripe, at once he goes in with his sickle, because the harvest has come."

He also said, "With what can we compare the kingdom of God, or what parable will we use for it? It is like a mustard seed, which, when sown upon the ground, is the smallest of all the seeds on earth; yet when it is sown it grows up and becomes the greatest of all shrubs, and puts forth large branches, so that the birds of the air can make nests in its shade."

The Gospel of the Lord.

◆ All sit and observe silence.

FOR SILENT REFLECTION

Think about this silently in your heart. What helps a small amount of faith grow into a lifetime of service to God?

CLOSING PRAYER

Let us pray to God for our needs and the needs of others: our family, neighborhood, and the world. For each need we say, "Lord, hear our prayer."

◆ All may add their own prayers here.

Let us pray: **Our Father . . . Amen.**

Creator God,
thank you for the mystery of life.
You are our source of being and of love.
May we continue to grow in love and faith.
Through Christ our Lord.

Amen.

✛ All make the Sign of the Cross.

PRAYER FOR
MONDAY, JUNE 14, 2021

OPENING

This week's theme is our call to go forth to proclaim the Good News. In today's Gospel, Jesus gives his disciples special instructions on how to go out and serve the people. Listen closely to his words.

✝ All make the Sign of the Cross.

In the name of the Father, and of the Son, and of the Holy Spirit. Amen.

PSALM

(For a longer psalm, see page xv.)
Psalm 85:8–9

The LORD speaks of peace to his people.

The LORD speaks of peace to his people.

Let me hear what God the LORD will speak,
for he will speak peace to his people,
to his faithful, to those who turn to him in
their hearts.
Surely his salvation is at hand for those who
fear him,
that his glory may dwell in our land.

The LORD speaks of peace to his people.

◆ All stand and sing **Alleluia.**

GOSPEL

Mark 6:7–13

A reading from the holy Gospel according to Mark.

Jesus called the twelve and began to send them out two by two, and gave them authority over the unclean spirits. He ordered them to take nothing for their journey except a staff; no bread, no bag, no money in their belts; but to wear sandals and not to put on two tunics. He said to them, "Wherever you enter a house, stay there until you leave the place. If any place will not welcome you and they refuse to hear you, as you leave, shake off the dust that is on your feet as a testimony against them." So they went out and proclaimed that all should repent. They cast out many demons, and anointed with oil many who were sick and cured them.

The Gospel of the Lord.

◆ All sit and observe silence.

FOR SILENT REFLECTION

Think about this silently in your heart. What do you tell others about your faith?

CLOSING PRAYER

Let us pray to God for our needs and the needs of others: our family, neighborhood, and the world. For each need we say, "Lord, hear our prayer."

◆ All may add their own prayers here.

Let us pray: **Our Father . . . Amen.**

Dear God,
may we be messengers of your Good News
to all we meet.
May we continue the work of the Twelve so
that others will know of your saving love.
We ask this through Christ our Lord.

Amen.

✝ All make the Sign of the Cross.

OPENING

Today we hear that before Jesus ascended into heaven, he gave his Apostles directions on what to do when he was gone. The word *Gospel* means "the good news." It is the story of Jesus' life, his teachings of forgiveness and love, his death and Resurrection, and his ascension into heaven.

✚ All make the Sign of the Cross.

In the name of the Father, and of the Son, and of the Holy Spirit. Amen.

PSALM

(For a longer psalm, see page xv.)
Psalm 85:8–9

The Lord speaks of peace to his people.

The Lord speaks of peace to his people.

Let me hear what God the Lord will speak,
for he will speak peace to his people,
to his faithful, to those who turn to him in
their hearts.
Surely his salvation is at hand for those who
fear him,
that his glory may dwell in our land.

The Lord speaks of peace to his people.

◆ All stand and sing **Alleluia.**

GOSPEL

Mark 16:12–16a, 19–20a

A reading from the holy Gospel according to Mark.

Jesus appeared in another form to two of them, as they were walking into the country. And they went back and told the rest, but they did not believe them. Later he appeared to the eleven themselves as they were sitting at the table; and he upbraided them for their lack of faith and stubbornness, because they had not believed those who saw him after he had risen. And he said to them, "Go into all the world and proclaim the good news to the whole creation. The one who believes and is baptized will be saved." So then the Lord Jesus, after he had spoken to them, was taken up into heaven and sat down at the right hand of God. And they went out and proclaimed the good news everywhere.

The Gospel of the Lord.

◆ All sit and observe silence.

FOR SILENT REFLECTION

Think about this silently in your heart. How do you share the Good News?

CLOSING PRAYER

Let us pray to God for our needs and the needs of others: our family, neighborhood, and the world. For each need we say, "Lord, hear our prayer."

◆ All may add their own prayers here.

Let us pray: **Our Father . . . Amen.**

May we be messengers of your
Good News, O God.
May we continue the work of the Twelve so
that others will know of your saving love.
We ask this through Christ our Lord.

Amen.

✚ All make the Sign of the Cross.

OPENING

Last week we observed the feast of St. Barnabas, who preached to the Gentiles, or people or nations that were not Jewish. We will hear why in today's Gospel. Sts. Paul and Barnabas try to preach the Good News to the Jews, but they did not want to listen to them.

✦ All make the Sign of the Cross.

In the name of the Father, and of the Son, and of the Holy Spirit. Amen.

PSALM

(For a longer psalm, see page xv.)
Psalm 85:8–9

The LORD speaks of peace to his people.

The LORD speaks of peace to his people.

Let me hear what God the LORD will speak,
   for he will speak peace to his people,
     to his faithful, to those who turn to him in
      their hearts.
Surely his salvation is at hand for those who
     fear him,
   that his glory may dwell in our land.

The LORD speaks of peace to his people.

READING

Acts 13:43b–47

A reading from the Acts of the Apostles.

Many Jews and devout converts to Judaism followed Paul and Barnabas, who spoke to them and urged them to continue in the grace of God. The next sabbath almost the whole city gathered to hear the word of the Lord. But when the Jews saw the crowds, they were filled with jealousy; and blaspheming, they contradicted what was spoken by Paul. Then both Paul and Barnabas spoke out boldly, saying, "It was necessary that the word of God should be spoken first to you. Since you reject it and judge yourselves to be unworthy of eternal life, we are now turning to the Gentiles. For so the Lord has commanded us, saying, 'I have set you to be a light for the Gentiles, so that you may bring salvation to the ends of the earth.'"

The Word of the Lord.

◆ All observe silence.

FOR SILENT REFLECTION

Think about this silently in your heart. Jesus came for all people and for all nations.

CLOSING PRAYER

Let us pray to God for our needs and the needs of others: our family, neighborhood, and the world. For each need we say, "Lord, hear our prayer."

◆ All may add their own prayers here.

Let us pray: **Our Father . . . Amen.**

Lord God,
you came to the world for all people.
Thank you for the generations of disciples
who have built your Kingdom on earth.
May we follow in their footsteps
and continue to show others how much you
love all of your creation.
Through Christ our Lord.

Amen.

✦ All make the Sign of the Cross.

OPENING

Sts. Paul and Barnabas traveled extensively to proclaim the Good News. In each place, they appointed leaders to continue their ministry after they had left. In this way, Paul established a network of churches and followers of Jesus throughout many lands.

✛ All make the Sign of the Cross.

In the name of the Father, and of the Son, and of the Holy Spirit. Amen.

PSALM

(For a longer psalm, see page xv.)
Psalm 85:8–9

The LORD speaks of peace to his people.

The LORD speaks of peace to his people.

Let me hear what God the LORD will speak,
    for he will speak peace to his people,
  to his faithful, to those who turn to him in
      their hearts.
Surely his salvation is at hand for those who
      fear him,
  that his glory may dwell in our land.

The LORD speaks of peace to his people.

READING

Acts 14:21–22a, 23–25, 26a, 27

A reading from the Acts of the Apostles.

After Paul and Barnabas had proclaimed the good news to that city and had made many disciples, they returned to Lystra [LIS-truh], then on to Iconium [ī-KOH-nee-uhm] and Antioch [AN-tee-ahk]. There they strengthened the souls of the disciples and encouraged them to continue in the faith. And after they had appointed elders for them in each church, with prayer and fasting they entrusted them to the Lord in whom they had come to believe. Then they passed through Pisidia [pih-SID-ee-uh] and came to Pamphylia [pam-FIL-ee-uh]. When they had spoken the word in Perga [PER-guh], they went down to Attalia [at-uh-LĪ-uh]. From there they sailed back to Antioch [AN-tee-ahk]. When they arrived, they called the church together and related all that God had done with them, and how he had opened a door of faith for the Gentiles [JEN-tīls].

The Word of the Lord.

◆ All observe silence.

FOR SILENT REFLECTION

Think about this silently in your heart. Thank God for all the people who work to keep your Church community strong.

CLOSING PRAYER

Let us pray to God for our needs and the needs of others: our family, neighborhood, and the world. For each need we say, "Lord, hear our prayer."

◆ All may add their own prayers here.

Let us pray: **Our Father . . . Amen.**

May we be encouraging to others in their own faith journey, O God,
so that we all grow together in prayer and love.
We pray in Christ's name.

Amen.

✛ All make the Sign of the Cross.

PRAYER FOR
FRIDAY, JUNE 18, 2021

OPENING

In today's reading, St. Paul writes to the new Christian churches in Corinth [KOHR-ihnth], and observes that following Jesus Christ is like having a new life. Paul describes himself as an ambassador, or representative, of Christ. He encourages all to this new life in Christ.

✚ All make the Sign of the Cross.

In the name of the Father, and of the Son, and of the Holy Spirit. Amen.

PSALM

(For a longer psalm, see page xv.)
Psalm 85:8–9

The Lord speaks of peace to his people.

The Lord speaks of peace to his people.

Let me hear what God the Lord will speak,
   for he will speak peace to his people,
     to his faithful, to those who turn to him in
      their hearts.
Surely his salvation is at hand for those who
     fear him,
     that his glory may dwell in our land.

The Lord speaks of peace to his people.

READING

2 Corinthians 1:1b–2; 5:17, 20; 6:1–2

A reading from the Second Letter of Paul to the Corinthians [kohr-IN-thee-uhnz].

To the church of God that is in Corinth [KOHR-ihnth], including all the saints throughout Achaia [uh-KAY-yuh]: Grace to you and peace from God our Father and the Lord Jesus Christ. So if anyone is in Christ, there is a new creation: everything old has passed away; see, everything has become new!

So we are ambassadors for Christ, since God is making his appeal through us; we entreat you on behalf of Christ, be reconciled to God. As we work together with him, we urge you also not to accept the grace of God in vain. For he says, "At an acceptable time I have listened to you, and on a day of salvation I have helped you." See, now is the acceptable time; see, now is the day of salvation!

The Word of the Lord.

◆ All observe silence.

FOR SILENT REFLECTION

Think about this silently in your heart. How can you be an ambassador for Christ?

CLOSING PRAYER

Let us pray to God for our needs and the needs of others: our family, neighborhood, and the world. For each need we say, "Lord, hear our prayer."

◆ All may add their own prayers here.

Let us pray: **Our Father . . . Amen.**

Dear God,
help us to be leaders in our faith,
supporting one another
and spreading Jesus' love, forgiveness,
and grace with others.
We ask this through Christ our Lord.

Amen.

✚ All make the Sign of the Cross.

PRAYER FOR THE WEEK

WITH A READING FROM THE GOSPEL FOR **SUNDAY, JUNE 20, 2021**

OPENING

When Jesus greets his disciples, he often says, "Peace be with you." In today's Gospel, we hear that Jesus greets even a stormy sea with "peace." Despite the disciples' fear, and despite nature's wildness, Jesus is calm, quiet, and peaceful.

✚ All make the Sign of the Cross.

In the name of the Father, and of the Son, and of the Holy Spirit. Amen.

PSALM

(For a longer psalm, see page xv.)
Psalm 85:8–9

The LORD speaks of peace to his people.

The LORD speaks of peace to his people.

Let me hear what God the LORD will speak,
 for he will speak peace to his people,
  to his faithful, to those who turn to him in
   their hearts.
Surely his salvation is at hand for those who
  fear him,
 that his glory may dwell in our land.

The LORD speaks of peace to his people.

◆ All stand and sing **Alleluia.**

GOSPEL

Mark 4:35–36a, 37–41

A reading from the holy Gospel according to Mark.

On that day, when evening had come, Jesus said to them, "Let us go across to the other side." And leaving the crowd behind, they took him with them in the boat, just as he was. A great windstorm arose, and the waves beat into the boat, so that the boat was already being swamped. But he was in the stern, asleep on the cushion; and they woke him up and said to him, "Teacher, do you not care that we are perishing?" He woke up and rebuked the wind, and said to the sea, "Peace! Be still!" Then the wind ceased, and there was a dead calm. He said to them, "Why are you afraid? Have you still no faith?" And they were filled with great awe and said to one another, "Who then is this, that even the wind and the sea obey him?"

The Gospel of the Lord.

◆ All sit and observe silence.

FOR SILENT REFLECTION

Think about this silently in your heart. Jesus is also known as the Prince of Peace. Calm your mind, hearts, and bodies to the peace of Jesus.

CLOSING PRAYER

Let us pray to God for our needs and the needs of others: our family, neighborhood, and the world. For each need we say, "Lord, hear our prayer."

◆ All may add their own prayers here.

Let us pray: **Our Father . . . Amen.**

O Father,
may we rest in your arms
and give ourselves to your calming ways.
Bring us peace in our hearts.
Through Christ our Lord, who is the
Prince of Peace.

Amen.

✚ All make the Sign of the Cross.

OPENING

Today is the memorial for St. Aloysius Gonzaga [al-oh-WISH-uhs guhn-ZAHG-uh] (1568–1591). Although St. Aloysius was born into a wealthy family in Italy, he decided to become a missionary with the Jesuit order. He died at twenty-three years old, caring for victims of the plague. He is the patron of young people,

✚ All make the Sign of the Cross.

In the name of the Father, and of the Son, and of the Holy Spirit. Amen.

PSALM

(For a longer psalm, see page xv.)
Psalm 85:8–9

The Lord speaks of peace to his people.

The Lord speaks of peace to his people.

Let me hear what God the Lord will speak,
   for he will speak peace to his people,
   to his faithful, to those who turn to him in
      their hearts.
Surely his salvation is at hand for those who
      fear him,
   that his glory may dwell in our land.

The Lord speaks of peace to his people.

◆ All stand and sing **Alleluia.**

GOSPEL

Mark 3:13a, 14, 19b–20, 31–35

A reading from the holy Gospel according to Mark.

Jesus went up the mountain and called to him those whom he wanted. And he appointed twelve, whom he also named apostles, to be with him, and to be sent out to proclaim the message. Then he went home; and the crowd came together again, so that they could not even eat. Then his mother and his brothers came; and standing outside, they sent to him and called him. A crowd was sitting around him; and they said to him, "Your mother and your brothers and sisters are outside, asking for you." And he replied, "Who are my mother and my brothers?" And looking at those who sat around him, he said, "Here are my mother and my brothers! Whoever does the will of God is my brother and sister and mother."

The Gospel of the Lord.

◆ All sit and observe silence.

FOR SILENT REFLECTION

Think about this silently in your heart. We are all part of Jesus' family.

CLOSING PRAYER

Let us pray to God for our needs and the needs of others: our family, neighborhood, and the world. For each need we say, "Lord, hear our prayer."

◆ All may add their own prayers here.

Let us pray: **Our Father . . . Amen.**

May we work with our brothers and sisters to proclaim your Good News, O God!
In Christ's name we pray.

Amen.

✚ All make the Sign of the Cross.

OPENING

Today we remember three saints, two of whom were bishops and the other an intensely spiritual man. Sts. Paulinus of Nola (354–431) and John Fisher (1469–1535) were bishops who were devoted to Christ. They and St. Thomas More (1478–1535) upheld the teachings of the Church. Today's reading tells us of early Christians who lived according to what Jesus taught.

✦ All make the Sign of the Cross.

In the name of the Father, and of the Son, and of the Holy Spirit. Amen.

PSALM

(For a longer psalm, see page xv.)
Psalm 85:8–9

The LORD speaks of peace to his people.

The LORD speaks of peace to his people.

Let me hear what God the LORD will speak,
   for he will speak peace to his people,
     to his faithful, to those who turn to him in
      their hearts.
Surely his salvation is at hand for those who
     fear him,
   that his glory may dwell in our land.

The LORD speaks of peace to his people.

READING

Acts 2:38, 43–47

A reading from the Acts of the Apostles.

Peter said to them, "Repent, and be baptized every one of you in the name of Jesus Christ so that your sins may be forgiven; and you will receive the gift of the Holy Spirit." Awe came upon everyone, because many wonders and signs were being done by the apostles. All who believed were together and had all things in common; they would sell their possessions and goods and distribute the proceeds to all, as any had need. Day by day, as they spent much time together in the temple, they broke bread at home and ate their food with glad and generous hearts, praising God and having the goodwill of all the people. And day by day the Lord added to their number those who were being saved.

The Word of the Lord.

◆ All observe silence.

FOR SILENT REFLECTION

Think about this silently in your heart. How do you uphold the teachings of the Church?

CLOSING PRAYER

Let us pray to God for our needs and the needs of others: our family, neighborhood, and the world. For each need we say, "Lord, hear our prayer."

◆ All may add their own prayers here.

Let us pray: **Our Father . . . Amen.**

Loving God,
help us find joy and gladness in
following you.
Grant us happy hearts to bring others to
know you.
We pray in Christ's name.

Amen.

✦ All make the Sign of the Cross.

OPENING

The remaining readings this week are reminders from St. Paul to the early Christian communities. He said that followers of Jesus should love each other, speak the truth, put aside anger, forgive readily, and rejoice in Jesus Christ. Today St. Paul reminds the Roman community of the Great Commandment: to love your neighbor as yourself.

✢ All make the Sign of the Cross.

In the name of the Father, and of the Son, and of the Holy Spirit. Amen.

PSALM

(For a longer psalm, see page xv.)
Psalm 85:8–9

The LORD speaks of peace to his people.

The LORD speaks of peace to his people.

Let me hear what God the LORD will speak,
for he will speak peace to his people,
to his faithful, to those who turn to him in
their hearts.
Surely his salvation is at hand for those who
fear him,
that his glory may dwell in our land.

The LORD speaks of peace to his people.

READING

Romans 12:1a–c, 9–10; 13:8–10

A reading from the Letter of Paul to the Romans.

I appeal to you therefore, brothers and sisters, by the mercies of God, to present your bodies as a living sacrifice, holy and acceptable to God. Let love be genuine; hate what is evil, hold fast to what is good; love one another with mutual affection; outdo one another in showing honor. Owe no one anything, except to love one another; for the one who loves another has fulfilled the law. The commandments, "You shall not commit adultery; You shall not murder; You shall not steal; You shall not covet"; and any other commandment, are summed up in this word, "Love your neighbor as yourself." Love does no wrong to a neighbor; therefore, love is the fulfilling of the law.

The Word of the Lord.

◆ All observe silence.

FOR SILENT REFLECTION

Think about this silently in your heart. How does your Church community serve God?

CLOSING PRAYER

Let us pray to God for our needs and the needs of others: our family, neighborhood, and the world. For each need we say, "Lord, hear our prayer."

◆ All may add their own prayers here.

Let us pray: **Our Father . . . Amen.**

God of love,
thank you for your holy Word.
Remind us that we are not too young
or too small to help bring about
your Kingdom.
We ask this in the name of Jesus Christ,
our Lord.

Amen.

✢ All make the Sign of the Cross.

OPENING

Today is the feast the Nativity (birth) of John the Baptist. The angel Gabriel appeared to Zechariah [zek-uh-RĪ-uh], John's father, and told him that he and his wife Elizabeth would have a child in their old age. When Mary, the mother of Jesus, approached Elizabeth, who was pregnant with John, John leapt with joy inside his mother's womb. John the Baptist spent his life preparing the way for Jesus. Today we hear more from St. Paul.

✚ All make the Sign of the Cross.

In the name of the Father, and of the Son, and of the Holy Spirit. Amen.

PSALM

(For a longer psalm, see page xv.)
Psalm 85:8–9

The LORD speaks of peace to his people.

The LORD speaks of peace to his people.

Let me hear what God the LORD will speak,
  for he will speak peace to his people,
    to his faithful, to those who turn to him in
      their hearts.
Surely his salvation is at hand for those who
      fear him,
    that his glory may dwell in our land.

The LORD speaks of peace to his people.

READING

Ephesians 4:25–27, 29–32

A reading from the Letter of Paul to the Ephesians [ee-FEE-zhuhnz].

So then, putting away falsehood, let all of us speak the truth to our neighbors, for we are members of one another. Be angry but do not sin; do not let the sun go down on your anger, and do not make room for the devil. Let no evil talk come out of your mouths, but only what is useful for building up, as there is need, so that your words may give grace to those who hear. And do not grieve the Holy Spirit of God, with which you were marked with a seal for the day of redemption. Put away from you all bitterness and wrath and anger and wrangling and slander, together with all malice, and be kind to one another, tenderhearted, forgiving one another, as God in Christ has forgiven you.

The Word of the Lord.

◆ All observe silence.

FOR SILENT REFLECTION

Think about this silently in your heart. Which words of St. Paul's do you need to act upon?

CLOSING PRAYER

Let us pray to God for our needs and the needs of others: our family, neighborhood, and the world. For each need we say, "Lord, hear our prayer."

◆ All may add their own prayers here.

Let us pray: **Our Father . . . Amen.**

Glory to you, O God,
for the great gift of John the Baptist, who helped the world welcome the Son of God. May we continue to live as Jesus taught us. We ask this through Christ our Lord.

Amen.

✚ All make the Sign of the Cross.

OPENING

St. Paul reminds the Philippians [fih-LIP-ee-uhnz] to stand firm in their faith and rejoice in the Lord always. St. Paul encourages us to "Keep on doing the things that you have learned and received and heard and seen." As the school year ends, continue to pray and grow in your faith.

✦ All make the Sign of the Cross.

In the name of the Father, and of the Son, and of the Holy Spirit. Amen.

PSALM

(For a longer psalm, see page xv.)
Psalm 85:8–9

The LORD speaks of peace to his people.

The LORD speaks of peace to his people.

Let me hear what God the LORD will speak,
  for he will speak peace to his people,
  to his faithful, to those who turn to him in
    their hearts.
Surely his salvation is at hand for those who
    fear him,
  that his glory may dwell in our land.

The LORD speaks of peace to his people.

READING

Philippians 4:1, 4–5a, 7–9

A reading from the Letter of Paul to the Philippians [fih-LIP-ee-uhnz].

Therefore, my brothers and sisters, whom I love and long for, my joy and crown, stand firm in the Lord in this way, my beloved. Rejoice in the Lord always; again I will say, Rejoice. Let your gentleness be known to everyone. And the peace of God, which surpasses all understand-ing, will guard your hearts and your minds in Christ Jesus. Finally, beloved, whatever is true, whatever is honorable, whatever is just, whatever is pure, whatever is pleasing, whatever is commendable, if there is any excellence and if there is anything worthy of praise, think about these things. Keep on doing the things that you have learned and received and heard and seen in me, and the God of peace will be with you.

The Word of the Lord.

◆ All observe silence.

FOR SILENT REFLECTION

Think about this silently in your heart. Remember that the God of peace is always with you.

CLOSING PRAYER

Let us pray to God for our needs and the needs of others: our family, neighborhood, and the world. For each need we say, "Lord, hear our prayer."

◆ All may add their own prayers here.

Let us pray: **Our Father . . . Amen.**

God of love and peace,
we rejoice in you!
Thank you for all you have given and taught us this year.
Watch over us during these summer months, and may we continue our journey of faith.
Through Christ our Lord.

Amen.

✦ All make the Sign of the Cross.

✤ All make the Sign of the Cross.

ALL: In the name of the Father, and of the Son, and of the Holy Spirit. Amen.

LEADER:
Loving God,
you created all the people of the world,
and you know each of us by name.
We thank you for N., who today
 celebrates his/her birthday.
Bless him/her with your love and friendship
that he/she may grow in wisdom, knowledge,
 and grace.
May he/she love his/her family always
and be faithful to his/her friends.

Grant this through Christ our Lord.

ALL: Amen.

LEADER:
Let us bow our heads and pray for N.

 ◆ All observe silence.

LEADER:
May God, in whose presence our ancestors walked, bless you.

ALL: Amen.

LEADER:
May God, who has been your shepherd from birth until now, keep you.

ALL: Amen.

LEADER:
May God, who saves you from all harm, give you peace.

ALL: Amen.

 ✤ All make the Sign of the Cross.

 In the name of the Father, and of the Son, and of the Holy Spirit. Amen.

PRAYER SERVICE
LAST DAY OF SCHOOL

Prepare eight leaders for this service. The fourth leader will need a Bible for the Scripture passage and may need help practicing the reading. You may wish to begin by singing "In the Lord I'll Be Ever Thankful" and end with "Send Forth Your Spirit, O Lord." If the group will sing, prepare a song leader.

FIRST LEADER:

Our school year is drawing to a close, and we can see in ourselves so much growth! With each passing day, God worked through each person to make a new creation. Together, let us thank our Creator for the many blessed memories we've shared in our time together.

SECOND LEADER:

✛ All make the sign of the Cross.

In the name of the Father, and of the Son, and of the Holy Spirit. Amen.

Let us pray:
God of all creation,
we are blessed to be with one another
in this time and place.
We are excited to start our break,
yet we may feel sad as we
think about friends
we may not see for a while.
In these times of change,
help us to stay
connected with you, Lord,
for you desire happiness and peace
for all your brothers and sisters.
We ask this through Jesus Christ our Lord.

ALL: Amen.

THIRD LEADER: Psalm 119:1–3, 10–11, 41–42, 89–90, 105

Let us repeat the psalm response: Your word is a lamp to my feet and a light to my path.

ALL: Your word is a lamp to my feet and a light to my path.

Happy are those whose way is blameless,
  who walk in the law of the LORD.
Happy are those who keep his decrees,
  who seek him with their whole heart,
who also do no wrong,
  but walk in his ways.

ALL: Your word is a lamp to my feet and a light to my path.

With my whole heart I seek you;
  do not let me stray from your
    commandments.
I treasure your word in my heart,
  so that I may not sin against you.

ALL: Your word is a lamp to my feet and a light to my path.

Let your steadfast love come to me, O LORD,
  your salvation according to your promise.
Then I shall have an answer for those who
    taunt me,
  for I trust in your word.

ALL: Your word is a lamp to my feet and a light to my path.

The LORD exists forever;
  your word is firmly fixed in heaven.
Your faithfulness endures to all generations;
  you have established the earth, and it
    stands fast.

ALL: Your word is a lamp to my feet and a light to my path.

CHILDREN'S DAILY PRAYER 2020–2021, © 2020 Archdiocese of Chicago: Liturgy Training Publications. All rights reserved. Orders: 800-933-1800 or www.LTP.org.

FOURTH LEADER: Romans 12:9–18

A reading from the Letter of Paul to the Romans.

✛ Read the Scripture passage from the Bible.

The Word of the Lord.

✛ All observe silence.

FIFTH LEADER:

Let us bring our hopes and needs to God as we
pray, "Lord, hear our prayer."
For our teachers, administrators,
volunteers, coaches, and school staff
who worked hard to produce our
quality learning time together,

we pray to the Lord . . .

For our parents, grandparents,
and family members who helped us
with homework and other tasks
throughout the year,

we pray to the Lord . . .

For the friends we've made
and those on the horizon,
may they reflect the warmth and compassion
that Jesus feels for us,

we pray to the Lord . . .

For those who are dealing with sickness,
job loss, or other difficulties in life,
for those who have gone before us
to the other side of life,
may they experience the peace of Christ,

we pray to the Lord . . .

SIXTH LEADER:

Lord Jesus,
your gentle Spirit has
nudged and guided us
these past several months.
May we continue to seek your wisdom
as we daily pray to you,
ever mindful of
how much you care for us.
We ask this in your name.

Amen.

SEVENTH LEADER:

Let us offer to one another a sign of
Christ's peace:

✛ All offer one another a sign of peace.

EIGHTH LEADER:

Let us pray:
Creator God,
you are Lord of all things,
and you are always with us.
May we embrace
all our new experiences
in our break from school.
Help us to listen to you,
source of all truth,
and go forth to
new adventures,
cherishing the love that
we've shared this year.

ALL: Amen.

✛ All make the Sign of the Cross.

PRAYER SERVICE
FOR SAD DAYS

The following prayer can be used when there is a sad or tragic event in the school community. This may be an illness or death of a student, faculty, or staff member, or a parent of a student. It may also be used at a time of a local or national crisis when the school gathers to pray. For this prayer, an adult should take the part of the leader as it is important to offer a few words that describe the particular need or concern.

✝ All make the Sign of the Cross.

ALL: In the name of the Father, and of the Son, and of the Holy Spirit. Amen.

LEADER:
We gather today to pray for [name the person or concern].
We trust, O God, that you hear us.
We trust that you understand the suffering and pain of your people.
We trust that you are with all those in need.
Let us listen to the Word of God.

READER: Matthew 11:28–30
A reading from the holy Gospel according to Matthew.

"Come to me, all you that are weary and are carrying heavy burdens, and I will give you rest. Take my yoke upon you, and learn from me; for I am gentle and humble in heart, and you will find rest for your souls. For my yoke is easy, and my burden is light."

LEADER:
Let us take a few moments to pray in our hearts for [name the person or concern].

LEADER:
Let us pray:
God of all,
help us to remember that your son Jesus suffered, died, and rose so that we might know of your great love.

He invites us to bring our cares and concerns to you in prayer, and so we ask you to be with [name the persons]. Give them courage and peace.

We ask you also to be with us during this time of difficulty. Help us to trust that you are always with us.

◆ [If appropriate, invite spontaneous prayers from those gathered.]

LEADER:
Assured of your great love, we pray:
Our Father . . . Amen.

◆ Pause and say:

As we conclude our prayer, let us offer one another the sign of Christ's peace.

◆ All offer one another a sign of peace.

LEADER:
May God the Creator bless us:

✝ All make the Sign of the Cross.

In the name of the Father, and of the Son, and of the Holy Spirit. Amen.

CHILDREN'S DAILY PRAYER 2020–2021, © 2020 Archdiocese of Chicago: Liturgy Training Publications. All rights reserved. Orders: 800-933-1800 or www.LTP.org.

PSALMS AND CANTICLES

PSALM 23

This psalm is appropriate during all liturgical seasons. It may be prayed in times of difficulty or stress, when comfort is needed, or to meditate on Christ's presence in the sacraments.

The LORD is my shepherd, I shall not want.
  He makes me lie down in green pastures;
he leads me beside still waters;
  he restores my soul.
He leads me in right paths
  for his name's sake.

Even though I walk through the darkest valley,
  I fear no evil;
for you are with me;
  your rod and your staff—
  they comfort me.

You prepare a table before me
  in the presence of my enemies;
you anoint my head with oil;
  my cup overflows.
Surely goodness and mercy shall follow me
  all the days of my life,
and I shall dwell in the house of the LORD
  my whole life long.

PSALM 27

Psalm 27:1, 4–5, 7–9, 13–14

Use this psalm during times of darkness, anxiety, or uncertainty. This psalm is also an affirmation of God's goodness at any moment in life.

The LORD is my light and my salvation;
   whom shall I fear?
The LORD is the stronghold of my life;
   of whom shall I be afraid?

One thing I asked of the LORD,
   that will I seek after:
to live in the house of the LORD
   all the days of my life,
to behold the beauty of the LORD,
   and to inquire in his temple.

For he will hide me in his shelter
   in the day of trouble;
he will conceal me under the cover of his tent;
   he will set me high on a rock.

Hear, O LORD, when I cry aloud,
   be gracious to me and answer me!
"Come," my heart says, "seek his face!"
   Your face, LORD do I seek.
   Do not hide your face from me.

I believe that I shall see the goodness of the LORD
   in the land of the living.
Wait for the LORD;
   be strong, and let your heart take courage;
   wait for the LORD!

PSALM 34

Psalm 34:1–8

This psalm of trust in God's power may be prayed by anyone seeking to wonder and rejoice in Christ's presence in the Eucharist. It is especially appropriate for those preparing to celebrate first Holy Communion.

I will bless the LORD at all times;
   his praise shall continually be in my mouth.
My soul makes its boast in the LORD;
   let the humble hear and be glad.
O magnify the LORD with me,
   and let us exalt his name together.

I sought the LORD, and he answered me,
   and delivered me from all my fears.
Look to him, and be radiant;
   so your faces shall never be ashamed.
This poor soul cried, and was heard by the LORD,
   and was saved from every trouble.
The angel of the LORD encamps
   around those who fear him, and delivers them.
O taste and see that the LORD is good;
   happy are those who take refuge in him.

PSALM 46

Psalm 46:1–5

*This psalm may be used during times of suffering, confusion,
or fear. Its offer of comfort and renewal will give cause for hope
in any extremity.*

God is our refuge and strength,
   a very present help in trouble.
Therefore we will not fear, though the earth should change,
   though the mountains shake in the heart of the sea;
though its waters roar and foam,
   though the mountains tremble with its tumult.

There is a river whose streams make glad the city of God,
   the holy habitation of the Most High.
God is in the midst of the city; it shall not be moved;
   God will help it when the morning dawns.

PSALM 51

Psalm 51:1–2, 6, 10, 12, 15

*This is a penitential psalm that is especially appropriate during
a communal celebration of the Sacrament of Reconciliation.
It can also be incorporated into any Lenten prayer service.*

Have mercy on me, O God,
   according to your steadfast love;
according to your abundant mercy
   blot out my transgressions.
Wash me thoroughly from my iniquity,
   and cleanse me from my sin.

You desire truth in the inward being;
   therefore teach me wisdom in my secret heart.

Create in me a clean heart, O God,
   and put a new and right spirit within me.
Restore to me the joy of your salvation,
   and sustain in me a willing spirit.

O Lord, open my lips,
   and my mouth will declare your praise.

PSALM 84

Psalm 84:1–2, 10–12

This is a good psalm to pray when preparing to enter a church. It helps to foster a great love for God's dwelling place.

How lovely is your dwelling place,
    O LORD of hosts!
My soul longs, indeed it faints
    for the courts of the LORD;
my heart and my flesh sing for joy
    to the living God.
For a day in your courts is better
    than a thousand elsewhere.
I would rather be a doorkeeper in the house of my God
    than live in the tents of wickedness.
For the LORD God is a sun and shield;
    he bestows favor and honor.
No good thing does the LORD withhold
    from those who walk uprightly.
O LORD of hosts,
    happy is everyone who trusts in you.

PSALMS

PSALM 100

This is a joyful psalm of thanksgiving that helps orient the heart to God.

Make a joyful noise to the LORD, all the earth.
   Worship the LORD with gladness;
   come into his presence with singing.
Know that the LORD is God.
   It is he that made us, and we are his;
   we are his people, and the sheep of his pasture.
Enter his gates with thanksgiving,
   and his courts with praise.
   Give thanks to him, bless his name.
For the LORD is good;
   his steadfast love endures forever,
   and his faithfulness to all generations.

PSALM 103

Psalm 103:1–5, 19–22

This is a deeply meditative psalm of grateful acknowledgment of God's gifts and mercy.

Bless the LORD, O my soul,
and all that is within me,
bless his holy name.
Bless the LORD, O my soul,
and do not forget all his benefits—
who forgives all your iniquity,
who heals all your diseases,
who redeems your life from the Pit,
who crowns you with steadfast love and mercy,
who satisfies you with good as long as you live
so that your youth is renewed like the eagle's.

The LORD has established his throne in the heavens,
and his kingdom rules over all.
Bless the LORD, O you his angels,
you mighty ones who do his bidding,
obedient to his spoken word.
Bless the LORD, all his works,
in all places of his dominion.
Bless the LORD, O my soul.

PSALMS

PSALM 139

Psalm 139:1–6, 13–16

This psalm expresses the wonder and awe of our mysterious relationship to the God who knows us intimately and loves us completely.

O LORD, you have searched me and known me.
You know when I sit down and when I rise up;
   you discern my thoughts from far away.
You search out my path and my lying down,
   and are acquainted with all my ways.
Even before a word is on my tongue,
   O LORD, you know it completely.
You hem me in, behind and before,
   and lay your hand upon me.
Such knowledge is too wonderful for me;
   it is so high that I cannot attain it.

For it was you who formed my inward parts;
   you knit me together in my mother's womb.
I praise you, for I am fearfully and wonderfully made.
   Wonderful are your works;
that I know very well.
   My frame was not hidden from you,
when I was being made in secret,
   intricately woven in the depths of the earth.
Your eyes beheld my unformed substance.
In your book were written
all the days that were formed for me,
   when none of them as yet existed.

THE *MAGNIFICAT* OF MARY

Luke 1:46–55

Mary prayed with these words when she visited her relative, Elizabeth, after Elizabeth declared, "Blessed are you among women and blessed is the fruit of your womb!" For centuries, this beautiful song of praise and trust has been the Church's evening prayer.

And Mary said,
"My soul magnifies the Lord,
   and my spirit rejoices in God my savior,
for he has looked with favor on the lowliness of his servant.
   Surely, from now on all generations will call me blessed;
for the Mighty One has done great things for me,
   and holy is his name.
His mercy is for those who fear him
   from generation to generation.
He has shown strength with his arm;
   he has scattered the proud in the thoughts of their hearts.
He has brought down the powerful from their thrones,
   and lifted up the lowly;
he has filled the hungry with good things,
   and sent the rich away empty.
He has helped his servant Israel,
   in remembrance of his mercy,
according to the promise he made to our ancestors,
   to Abraham and to his descendants forever."

CANTICLES

THE *BENEDICTUS* OF ZECHARIAH

Luke 1:68–79

Zechariah had been struck mute during the pregnancy of his wife, Elizabeth. After their baby was born, on the day when they gave him his name, Zechariah's voice was restored and he spoke these prophetic words over his child, John the Baptist. His prophecy is part of the Church's traditional morning prayer.

"Blessed be the Lord God of Israel,
    for he has looked favorably on his people and redeemed them.
He has raised up a mighty savior for us
    in the house of his servant David,
as he spoke through the mouth of his holy prophets from of old,
        that we would be saved from our enemies and from the hand
            of all who hate us.
Thus he has shown the mercy promised to our ancestors,
    and has remembered his holy covenant,
the oath that he swore to our ancestor Abraham,
    to grant us that we, being rescued from the hands
        of our enemies,
might serve him without fear, in holiness and righteousness,
    before him all our days.
And you, child, will be called the prophet of the Most High;
    for you will go before the Lord to prepare his ways,
to give knowledge of salvation to his people
    by the forgiveness of their sins.
By the tender mercy of our God,
    the dawn from on high will break upon us,
to give light to those who sit in darkness and in the shadow
        of death,
    to guide our feet into the way of peace."

RESOURCES FOR PRAYING WITH CHILDREN

In addition to *Children's Daily Prayer*, teachers, principals, and catechists may find these LTP resources to be helpful in their work of developing prayer services and preparing children for Mass and reception of the sacraments.

PREPARING MASSES WITH CHILDREN: 15 EASY STEPS

A resource to assist teachers and catechists in preparing children to participate fully in the Mass.

FROM MASS TO MISSION

A small guide that explains the significance of the Mass for living a Christian life. There is a guide for children and a guide for teens; each has a leader's guide to accompany the book.

THE YEAR OF GRACE LITURGICAL CALENDAR

This annual circular calendar displays the liturgical year. It highlights the color for each liturgical season and provides a visual guide to the major feasts and saints' days throughout the year. Each year, the calendar has beautiful art to illustrate a particular theme or liturgical focus.

CHILDREN'S LITURGY OF THE WORD

An annual publication that offers a guide to help prepare a Liturgy of the Word for children on Sundays and Holydays of Obligation.

BLESSINGS AND PRAYERS THROUGH THE YEAR: A RESOURCE FOR SCHOOL AND PARISH

This is an illustrated collection of prayers and blessings and prayer services, which includes two CD-ROMS of music with vocal instruction and musical accompaniment to facilitate singing.

COMPANION TO THE CALENDAR: A GUIDE TO THE SAINTS, SEASONS, AND HOLIDAYS OF THE YEAR.

An invaluable resource for learning more about the particular saint or feast of the day. This book could be used to help children learn more about their patron saint or saints of special interest.

SCHOOL YEAR, CHURCH YEAR: CUSTOMS AND DECORATIONS FOR THE CLASSROOM

Teachers and catechists who wish to create an environment in the classroom that reflects the liturgical season will find many creative and doable ideas in this book.